EVOLVING PARADIGMS IN TOURISM AND HOSPITALITY IN DEVELOPING COUNTRIES

A Case Study of India

Advances in Hospitality and Tourism

EVOLVING PARADIGMS IN TOURISM AND HOSPITALITY IN DEVELOPING COUNTRIES

A Case Study of India

Edited by

Bindi Varghese

Apple Academic Press Inc.	Apple Academic Press Inc.
3333 Mistwell Crescent	9 Spinnaker Way
Oakville, ON L6L 0A2 Canada	Waretown, NJ 08758 USA

© 2019 by Apple Academic Press, Inc.

First issued in paperback 2021

Exclusive worldwide distribution by CRC Press, a member of Taylor & Francis Group
No claim to original U.S. Government works

ISBN 13: 978-1-77-463069-3 (pbk)
ISBN 13: 978-1-77-188630-7 (hbk)

Library and Archives Canada Cataloguing in Publication

Evolving paradigms in tourism and hospitality in developing countries : a case study of India / edited by Bindi Varghese.

(Advances in hospitality and tourism book series)
Includes bibliographical references and index.
Issued in print and electronic formats.
ISBN 978-1-77188-630-7 (hardcover).--ISBN 978-1-315-10304-4 (PDF)

1. Tourism--India--Case studies. 2. Hospitality industry--
India--Case studies. I. Varghese, Bindi, editor II. Series: Advances
in hospitality and tourism book series

| G155.I4E96 2018 | 338.4'7910954 | C2018-900514-9 | C2018-900515-7 |

Library of Congress Cataloging-in-Publication Data

Names: Varghese, Bindi, editor.

Title: Evolving paradigms in tourism and hospitality in developing countries : a case study of india / editor, Bindi Varghese.

Description: Oakville, ON ; Waretown, NJ : Apple Academic Press, 2018. | Includes bibliographical references and index.

Identifiers: LCCN 2018002172 (print) | LCCN 2018006979 (ebook) | ISBN 9781315103044 (ebook) | ISBN 9781771886307 (hardcover : alk. paper)

Subjects: LCSH: Tourism--India. | Tourism--Social aspects--India. | Hospitality industry--India. | Hospitality industry--Social aspects--India.

Classification: LCC G155.I4 (ebook) | LCC G155.I4 E86 2018 (print) | DDC 338.4/79154--dc23

LC record available at https://lccn.loc.gov/2018002172

Apple Academic Press also publishes its books in a variety of electronic formats. Some content that appears in print may not be available in electronic format. For information about Apple Academic Press products, visit our website at **www.appleacademicpress.com** and the CRC Press website at **www.crcpress.com**

ADVANCES IN HOSPITALITY AND TOURISM BOOK SERIES BY APPLE ACADEMIC PRESS, INC.

Editor-in-Chief:
Mahmood A. Khan, PhD
Professor, Department of Hospitality and Tourism Management,
Pamplin College of Business, Virginia Polytechnic Institute and
State University, Falls Church, Virginia, USA
Email: mahmood@vt.edu

This series reports on research developments and advances in the rapidly growing area of hospitality and tourism. Each volume in this series present s state-of-the-art information on a specialized topic of current interest. These one-of-a-kind publications are valuable resources for academia as well as for professionals in the industrial sector.

Books in the Series:
Food Safety: Researching the Hazard in Hazardous Foods
Editors: Barbara Almanza, PhD, RD, and Richard Ghiselli, PhD

Strategic Winery Tourism and Management: Building Competitive Winery Tourism and Winery Management Strategy
Editor: Kyuho Lee, PhD

Sustainability, Social Responsibility and Innovations in the Hospitality Industry
Editor: H. G. Parsa, PhD
Consulting Editor: Vivaja "Vi" Narapareddy, PhD
Associate Editors: SooCheong (Shawn) Jang, PhD,
Marival Segarra-Oña, PhD, and Rachel J. C. Chen, PhD, CHE

Managing Sustainability in the Hospitality and Tourism Industry: Paradigms and Directions for the Future
Editor: Vinnie Jauhari, PhD

Management Science in Hospitality and Tourism: Theory, Practice, and Applications
Editors: Muzaffer Uysal, PhD, Zvi Schwartz, PhD,
and Ercan Sirakaya-Turk, PhD

Tourism in Central Asia: Issues and Challenges
Editors: Kemal Kantarci, PhD, Muzaffer Uysal, PhD,
and Vincent Magnini, PhD

**Poverty Alleviation through Tourism Development:
A Comprehensive and Integrated Approach**
Robertico Croes, PhD, and Manuel Rivera, PhD

Chinese Outbound Tourism 2.0
Editor: Xiang (Robert) Li, PhD

**Hospitality Marketing and Consumer Behavior:
Creating Memorable Experiences**
Editor: Vinnie Jauhari, PhD

Women and Travel: Historical and Contemporary Perspectives
Editors: Catheryn Khoo-Lattimore, PhD, and Erica Wilson, PhD

Wilderness of Wildlife Tourism
Editor: Johra Kayeser Fatima, PhD

Medical Tourism and Wellness: Hospitality Bridging Healthcare (H2H)©
Editor: Frederick J. DeMicco, PhD, RD

Sustainable Viticulture: The Vines and Wines of Burgundy
Claude Chapuis

The Indian Hospitality Industry: Dynamics and Future Trends
Editors: Sandeep Munjal and Sudhanshu Bhushan

**Tourism Development and Destination Branding through Content
Marketing Strategies and Social Media**
Editor: Anukrati Sharma, PhD

**Evolving Paradigms in Tourism and Hospitality in Developing
Countries: A Case Study of India**
Editor: Bindi Varghese, PhD

**The Hospitality and Tourism Industry in China: New Growth,
Trends, and Developments**
Editor: Jinlin Zhao, PhD

**Labor in Tourism and Hospitality Industry: Skills, Ethics, Issues,
and Rights**
Abdallah M. Elshaer, PhD, and Asmaa M. Marzouk, PhD

ABOUT THE SERIES EDITOR

Mahmood A. Khan, PhD, is a Professor in the Department of Hospitality and Tourism Management, Pamplin College of Business at Virginia Tech's National Capital Region campus. He has served in teaching, research, and administrative positions for the past 35 years, working at major U.S. universities. Dr. Khan is the author of seven books and has traveled extensively for teaching and consulting on management issues and franchising. He has been invited by national and international corporations to serve as a speaker, keynote speaker, and seminar presenter on different topics related to franchising and services management.

Dr. Khan has received the Steven Fletcher Award for his outstanding contribution to hospitality education and research. He is also a recipient of the John Wiley & Sons Award for lifetime contribution to outstanding research and scholarship; the Donald K. Tressler Award for scholarship; and the Cesar Ritz Award for scholarly contribution. He also received the Outstanding Doctoral Faculty Award from Pamplin College of Business.

He has served on the Board of Governors of the Educational Foundation of the International Franchise Association, on the Board of Directors of the Virginia Hospitality and Tourism Association, as a Trustee of the International College of Hospitality Management, and as a Trustee on the Foundation of the Hospitality Sales and Marketing Association's International Association. He is also a member of several professional associations.

CONTENTS

ABOUT THE EDITOR

Dr. Bindi Varghese holds a doctorate in commerce, specializing in tourism. As an academician and tourism professional, she has over sixteen years of academic and industrial experience. Currently, she is affiliated with Christ (Deemed to be University) as an associate professor and Research Coordinator at School of Business Studies and Social Sciences, Bannerghatta Road Campus. She has served many educational institutions in South India and has served as a national and international expert for a decade among the educational institutions of India. Currently, she is actively associated with the Indian Tourism Congress (ITC) and the Kerala Development Society (KDS), New Delhi.

With a passion for research, she has guided MPhil and PhD scholars. The active research undertaken include: impact assessment studies, medical tourism, DMOs, and ecological studies.

Dr. Bindi completed a major research project on "Strategic Intervention of Destination Management Organizations to Enhance Competitiveness of Tourism Destinations—A Model for Karnataka, India," funded by Christ (Deemed to be University). The study has been presented to the Karnataka Government, India, as an annexure. This action research proposes a strategic model to the Government of Karnataka to improve the quality of tourism in the State. This completed study was funded by Christ (Deemed to be University), Center for Research (2013–2016).

Along with her academic expertise, she is also an issue editor for *ATNA—Journal of Tourism Studies*, published by Christ (Deemed to be University), Bangalore. She has extensively written for national and international peer-reviewed journals and is very well recognized in the academic circle in India. She has authored a book on medical tourism in

India and has also contributed chapters to edited books and has published several articles in areas of destination management, governance, medical tourism, e-tourism, and so forth.

As an educationist, with her experience and expertise, she is frequently invited to address students from other institutions and at various industry summits. Apart from the academic journal, Dr. Bindi also writes for leading newspapers and travel magazines in tourism and hospitality.

CONTRIBUTORS

Anu Ajayagosh is an academic consultant in Toronto, Canada. She has worked as a coordinator for business commerce vocational courses with NMKRV College for Women, Bangalore, India. Anu has completed her MPhil and Master's degree in Tourism from Christ (Deemed to be University), Bangalore. She holds IATA-UFTAA certification from SATM, Kochi. Being an enthusiastic researcher she has presented and published various research papers in national and international conferences and seminars. Her research interest includes cultural studies and sustainability.

Shamima Akhtar works with TriCounty OIC—an organization dedicated to training and education in Pennsylvania, USA. Prior to relocating to the USA, Shamima worked with Kashmir University, India, as a lecturer in the Tourism Studies Department. In addition to the work as an academician, she also has experienced travel and tourism corporate life while working for different organizations. She has had affiliations with Colorado State University, USA, for her academic growth. Her research interests lie in sustainable tourism practices and destination marketing. Fortifying her research, she has immensely contributed to national and international journals.

K. J. Anson is an assistant professor at the Department of Commerce, Christ (Deemed to be University), Bangalore, India. He has completed an MPhil, and with his academic expertise he has widely written in peer-reviewed journals and is a regular invitee among the scholarly talks and discussion forums. He is currently pursuing his PhD in behavioral finance. He has a keen interest in interdisciplinary research and has presented papers widely in tourism and hospitality by applying newer methodologies of research into areas of contemporary concern.

Jose K. Antony is an assistant professor in the discipline of tourism studies, Christ (Deemed to be University), Bangalore, India. Having completed his Master's in Tourism Administration from Bangalore University and Master's in Philosophy (Tourism) from Christ (Deemed to be University), he also holds wide experience in working with the airline and travel industry. His interests in research lie in talent management and organizational and travel behavior.

Arjun B. S. is an assistant professor of accounts and finance in the School of Business Studies and Social Studies, Christ (Deemed to be University), Bangalore, India. He has widely published in the topmost Indian and international journals, and his specific research interest include behavioral finance, econometrics, and corporate finance. Currently, he is pursuing his PhD and has completed a minor funded research project in the domain of socially responsible investment.

Dr. Githa U. Badikillaya is the Founder Director, Destination Heritage, and is a folklorist, Indologist, independent researcher and freelance writer. She has a PhD in Jaina folklore and a postgraduate diploma in Indology and in journalism. She has contributed articles extensively for leading newspapers and journals. As a researcher she has documented the sociocultural happenings at four Kumbha Melas and has widely presented and published her work in topmost academic journals. She was a board member for Child Labour, Ministry of Labour, Government of India, and her passion for India's cultural heritage culminated in her forming an organization for its promotion and understanding known as Destination Heritage, which conducts heritage walks and monthly talks.

Dr. Anu Chandran R. C. is currently working as assistant professor in the Department of Tourism Studies, Pondicherry Central University, India. Along with his academic expertise, he has worked as Divisional Tourism Officer in Andhra Pradesh Tourism, India. Dr. Anu has a PhD in management studies from the University of Kerala, India. He has published four books and has also published several papers in international and national journals. He holds academic and cocurricular positions such as associate editor of the journal *Bharatha Patrika*; and editor of *Yatra*, Annual Souvenir Publication of Tourism Studies, Pondicherry University.

Venan Bonaventure Dias is the founder of Antonios Services, Goa, India and provides services such as career counseling and guidance. He has around 19 years of corporate experience in India and abroad, and has such roles as human resource manager, training and development administrator and was also associated with premier institutes such as Christ (Deemed to be University), IASMS, and Symbiosis in Bangalore and Fr. Agnel College of Arts and Science in Goa. He has also extensively researched in different arena of tourism and largely published in peer-reviewed journals.

Professor Cheryl Poornima Smith e Venan Dias is the Head of the Department of (MA Tourism and Heritage Management) at S.S. Dempo College of Commerce and Economics, Altinho, Panaji, Goa, India. With 16 years of corporate and academic experience, she has written widely on tourism and has also presented and published papers in peer-reviewed journals. Her research interest is in the domain of strategic human resource management.

Nagarjuna G. is a lecturer at the Department of Travel and Tourism, Mount Carmel College, Bangalore, India. He pursued his MPhil in tourism from Christ (Deemed to be University) and later joined Christ (Deemed to be University) as a research assistant for a major research project. He has presented immensely at seminars and conferences at national and international levels. He has published articles in acclaimed journals and also participated in research workshops. Currently, he is pursuing his PhD from Christ (Deemed to be University), Bangalore. His research interest is in the domain of education tourism and sustainable tourism.

Dr. B. George is an Associate Professor and Head, Department of Tourism Management, Madurai Kamaraj University College, Madurai, India. He was awarded his doctorate from Madurai Kamaraj University and has been serving the cause of tourism education for 21 years. He has written eight books that are course materials for tourism for eight universities in Tamil Nadu and Pondicherry, India. He has widely published on tourism and is a member of the Board of Studies on Curriculum and Research at many universities in the South Indian States and also a member of Tamil Nadu Public Service Commission (TNPSC) Board and UGC Board on Tourism.

Dr. Ginu George is a senior research executive at Arya Systems, Hyderabad, India, who undertakes studies about the market on building information modeling and generating leads covering the Middle East, Singapore, and Malaysia regions. Her expertise is in marketing, and she has academic experience handling the graduate and postgraduate courses. Her research interest is employee engagement. Along with teaching experience, she has published and presented papers in international refereed journals.

Sandhya H. completed her Masters in Tourism Administration (MTA) from Christ (Deemed to be University), Bangalore, India by securing the first rank. Currently she is working as an Assistant Professor at St. Micheals College, Cherthala, Kerala. She is an enthusiastic researcher and is currently pursuing a Masters of Philosophy (Tourism) program. Her research interests include tourism marketing, destination management, and destination branding. She has worked as a Research Associate on a major research project on destination management organizations. She also has industry experience working with one of the leading multinational tour operations company, Kuoni SOTC, Bangalore.

Pinky Jacob is a product support specialist at TravelClick, Melbourne, Australia, which is a leading provider of hospitality industry revenue-generating solutions. She completed her Master's in Philosophy (Tourism) from Christ (Deemed to be University), Bangalore, India and cleared UGC/NET-Tourism (2012). She worked with NMKRV Institute as a program coordinator, and with her experience in the tourism industry, she has widely written and presented papers at international and national conferences. Her interest in research involves topics related to destination management and social and responsible tourism.

Megha Jacob is an economist with KDS-Delhi, India. She has received a BA in Economics (Hons) from the University of Delhi and MSc in Economics from Madras School of Economics. She has participated in socioeconomic studies for several Ministries of Government of India and has published work in the field of development economics.

Dr. Jacob John has a PhD in economics and an MBA in finance with over 30 years of experience in managing projects in such fields as education, employment, health, and local governance. He is the President of KDS–Delhi, a socioeconomic research organization in New Delhi, India. He has served the United Nation Industrial Development Organisation (UNIDO) in India and Italy as a national and international expert for a decade. He has published several books and articles in the areas of decentralized governance, local government economics, and development economics.

Dr. Suja John is an associate professor with Christ (Deemed to be University), Bangalore, India, and has an academic experience of 16 years. She has completed a funded minor research program on wine tourism and has published widely written in peer-reviewed journals and is a frequent invitee among the scholarly talks and discussion forums at various international conferences in the United States. Her research interest is in the area of sustainable tourism and environmental studies.

Rosma Mary Jolly is an assistant professor from the faculty of BBA (Finance) at St. Mary's College, Thrissur, Kerala, India. She has pursued her MPhil in Marketing and holds MCom. and BEd. Her expertise is in marketing and she has academic experience handling graduate and postgraduate courses. Rosma has presented papers at various international and national conferences, and her specific research interest in the HR and marketing domains.

Emilda K. Joseph is an assistant professor at the Department of Tourism Studies, Christ College at the Mahatma University of Kerala, India. She received her Master's in Philosophy (Tourism) from Christ (Deemed to be University), Bangalore, India and has to her credit an array of paper presentations at various international and national forums. Her research interest is in sustainable tourism. She has presented papers at various international and national conferences and is currently pursuing her Doctor of Philosophy in tourism from Christ (Deemed to be University), Bangalore.

Dr. Tomy K. Kallarakal is a professor and associate dean of commerce, Christ (Deemed to be University), Bangalore, India. He has over 30 years of academic experience and has widely published papers in reputed refereed journals and has contributed chapters to edited volumes. He was appointed by the university as associate director of TQMS since 2007. Dr. Tomy has handled several prestigious roles in the university as a part of his academic career. His research interests are in the area of human resource development and organizational behavior.

Dr. Anupama S. Kotur (Kaddi) Project Head - Trips Academy and Visiting Faculty - Symbiosis Center for Management Studies, Pune, India, She holds a PhD in Tourism and Hospitality, IGNOU, New Delhi, and currently she is an assistant professor, Department of Travel and Tourism, St. Joseph's College of Commerce, Bangalore, India. She is a gold medalist in Master of Tourism Administration, Bangalore, and has over one decade in industry and academics. Dr. Anupama has taught both undergraduate and postgraduate courses in cultural tourism and destination management. Her research interest is in wine tourism, and special interest tourism and she has widely published in those areas in journals and has made several chapter contributions. Dr. Anupama is also an associate member of the Indian Tourism and Hospitality Congress.

Professor Selva Kumar holds a Master is of Philosophy in Tourism and Hotel Management Science with over 18 years of academic and corporate experience. He is currently working with the Army Institute of Hotel Management and Catering Technology Bangalore, India. He has worked as an Assistant Dean Academics, Munnar Catering College, Kerala and has also served as head of the department (HOD) in Mohamed Sathak College of Arts and Science Chennai. He is a passionate researcher, and his research areas include heritage and cultural tourism, culinary historiography, and also other multidisciplinary areas related to hospitality and tourism studies.

Sneha N. is an Assistant Professor and Research Scholar at the Department of Travel and Tourism, Mount Carmel College (Autonomous), Bengaluru, India. She worked with leading corporate companies in Bengaluru in the travel domain and later started her academic journey. With her academic and industrial experience in tourism, she has widely published in the domain of social media, customer relationship management and tourism marketing. Currently, she is pursuing her Ph.D programme from Madurai Kamaraj University, Madurai, India.

Suraj Nair is the co-founder of Travel Spends. With over two decade of industrial experience, he has immensely contributed to leading industry forums and international conferences. He has won widespread professional endorsements from fellow colleagues across service delivery, change management, people leadership, business development, travel technology, planning, and strategy formulation. Suraj was the Co-Head of the Corporate Travel Business at Thomas Cook and is credited with the launch of the first India-centric whitepaper on "Corporate Travel—Trends, Opportunity and Outlook 2011" and "Convergence of Travel and Technology" in 2012. He conceived and conceptualized Travel MindSpeak in 2013, a knowledge-sharing platform among corporate buyers and travel management professionals for sharing best practices and fostering discussions and collaboration.

Dr. N. Chaitanya Pradeep is currently associated with the School of Business Studies and Social Sciences, Christ (Deemed to be University), Bangalore, India. He served as a Senior Research Associate at the Centre for Human Rights, University of Hyderabad, and is a past Research Fellow of the Bureau of Police Research and Development (BPRD, Union Ministry of Home Affairs, New Delhi). He holds a PhD and MPhil from the

University of Hyderabad. He also is associated with the Centre for Public Policy and Governance, Administrative Staff College of India (ASCI, 2005–2009). He has published widely in the field of police reforms with a particular interest in morale and motivation and has delivered lectures on police, integrity, democratizing the police, and human rights.

Nikhil Raj works as an assistant professor in the Department of Tourism Management Jyothi Nivas College Autonomous, India. He has over 12 years of academic and industrial experience. He holds an MPhil in Tourism, India and IATA certification from Christ (Deemed to be University). He has widely published and presented research papers and won an award for the best research article from FKCCI Bangalore. His current research interest is based on new expanses of tourism and hospitality, and his articles appear in both national and international journals.

Gowri Shankar R. is an assistant professor of accounts and finance in the School of Business Studies and Social Studies, Christ (Deemed to be University), Bangalore, India. He has published many research papers in Indian and international journals. His specific research interest includes behavioral finance, corporate finance, and brand valuation. He has also completed a minor funded research project in the domain of SRI.

Avin Thaliath is currently an assistant professor, Department of Hotel Management, Christ (Deemed to be University), Bangalore, India. He is a bronze medalist of Bangalore University in 2004 for the Bachelor of Hotel Management degree, fortifying his education in his field of interest. He took up an advanced level program in Chocolaterie and Sugar at Feves the Choco Creation of Pastry Fine Arts, Malaysia. He is a Golden Certificate Awardee of the Vatel Scholarship, Nimes, France. Chef Avin is a member of several professional bodies and has authored a number of academic journals, books, and monographs. With a profile as strong as his, Chef Avin has also been featured on television talk shows. He is currently pursuing his PhD.

Dr. Joby Thomas, with over 18 years of industry and academic experience, has done his doctoral study from Mangalore University, India. He has also completed a major research project titled "An Evaluation of Eco and Sustainable Practices of Selected Resorts in Karnataka," funded by Christ (Deemed to be University). Dr. Joby Thomas is also the Executive Editor of *ATNA—Journal of Tourism Studies*, published by Christ (Deemed to be

University), Bangalore. Currently, he serves as an associate professor in tourism and academic coordinator, School of Business Studies and Social Sciences, at Christ (Deemed to be University), Bangalore, India.

PREFACE

The tourism industry is multifaceted in nature, and its resourcefulness caters to fascinate diverse domains. This comprehensive book adopts an integrated and interdisciplinary approach to elucidate the evolving paradigms in tourism and hospitality segment. The prelude of the book sturdily describes immense value creation that demonstrates a wide array of concepts and concurrent research domains appealing to the global segment.

This volume is indispensable in portraying the current global tourism and travel trends and is divided into three parts: tourism and destination management, operational and managerial perspectives in service sector, and emerging areas in tourism. The indicated sections cover every aspect involved in travel business and are of high use for the student community pursuing wide-ranging research interests.

This compilation is a synergy of various active and in-depth research, where the contributors have explored diverse topics and conducted exploratory investigation to frame their theories and outcomes to determine the philosophies of the research.

In addition, this compilation also deals with experiential aspects contributed by the travel professionals and practitioners to academia. The dynamics of tourism, however, is much more intriguing beyond a naïve representation. This book was envisioned keeping in mind the dearth of active research in concurrent areas, which is essential for academic learning and scientific explorations. Contemporaneous areas are well investigated at the global front, but it is imperative to embrace the outcomes of exploratory studies that will be necessary for building an extensive and broader understanding.

The strength of this book is particularly apparent where the considerations deliberate on a travel and tourism business. This book makes a valuable contribution to the collection and presentation of such an organized body of knowledge on the different aspects of tourism that I hope will stimulate discussions and debate on the travel and tourism arena among the business schools and by professional advisors.

The **learning objectives** are focused toward enhancing better theoretical and conceptual clarity in the most recent emerging areas that are researched and explored by the academicians and the representatives of the trade. The rich content in this book is a result of either a doctoral thesis or action research undertaken by the domain specialist and, hence, can help students better understand the researched arena and process the information presented. There are a number of pedagogical features integrated into this textbook.

The **scope of this book** is extensive and widespread, gauging different spheres of the travel fraternity and is based on the foregoing discussion by the academia and commerce internationally, as tourism takes strong roots that will support an ever-strengthening travel sector. As students, academicians and practitioners associated with services in general, and hospitality services in particular, the thrive is to lift and popularize understanding of what tourism research is to be and delve deep into its complexities, nuances, and logic. In particular, it is important to look at the associated dominant rhetoric of success.

The **objective** of the book is to draw together a comprehensive and consolidated collection of streams of knowledge relative to travel, tourism, and hospitality services into a package that rate high on "readability." An intense effort has taken to compile rich content and varied learning approaches. The book is organized into three parts. Part One provides a rich exploration of theoretical frameworks and debates with their application to hospitality services through reconnoitering tourism and destination management. It covers an array of themes, including the theory of the destination management; the historical development of culture and art forms; the failure of literature adequately to test out the success with safety concerns and so forth. Part Two focuses on some of the fundamental issues associated with the structuring and outlaying of operational and managerial perspectives in service sector. At this sub-sector level, our understanding of travel trade has progressed, as various interpretations on the arena of tourism indicate the similarities and disparities emerging. Part Three culminates with the emerging areas of tourism and the chapters are dedicated to the newly emerged arenas which serve to elucidate and consolidate the range of key issues that emerge from the travel business. This book will alert and stimulate the reader to the emerging paradigm of travel trade, while taking into account, managing and monitoring the resources drawing varied perceptions if success is to be achieved.

The first chapter describes the need for an effective destination manage-ment model for global competency. *Bindi Varghese* provides insight into the intervention of destination management organization (DMO), and this exploratory study applies a thematic analysis network, which ventured into several aspects and functionalities of destination management. The economic importance of the tourism business and travel market segment tends to be underestimated when destination management is ignored. This research adopts an integrated approach with a framework connecting scientific traditions of destination management and competitiveness with a case study of Karnataka's (India) destinations. Being that Karnataka can be consided "Mini Incredible India," this chapter describes how versatile the state is in terms of its tourism potentiality. The collective investiga-tion of the development of tourism in the state and the recent narrative of regional planning directs towards conclusions regarding the role of DMOs in tourism with contemporary development, which has resulted in the creation of a competency model and the role of a methodical plan-ning approach. DMOs are necessary for the long-term sustainability of the destination and, therefore, the success of the destination depends on the success of the DMOs. Security issues play a predominant role in devel-oping tourism industry of any country.

In the second chapter, *N. Chaitanya Pradeep* sheds light on this market segment using up-to-date issues, with a particular focus on the challenges and opportunities of the Tourist Police System in India. Pradeep explores the law enforcement agency in the discourse of tourism studies in India. Examining various policing styles specific to tourist areas and analyzing the suitability and applicability of the same in the Indian context is the crux of the subject.

Anu Chandran offers a perspective on visitor management and commu-nity participation in an ecotourism destination by outlining the corner-stones of a comprehensive eco-travel management strategy. This chapter deals with the challenges currently faced by the Kanha Tiger Reserve, Madhya Pradesh. This chapter brings to light the challenges pertaining to sustainable ecotourism and also analyses the impact of tourism, such as an unregulated influx of tourists. Anu details the onset of the prospects and potentials of wildlife tourism, which is examined with the imperatives and implications of visitor management and concludes by commenting on the adaptation measures taken by the Kanha Tiger Reserve.

Jacob John and *Megha Jacob* investigate the empowerment of marginalized communities and tourism, which plays a central role in the cultural tourism domain. Promotion of Dalit art forms in tourism can contribute to the social and economic progression of marginalized communities and contemporary tourism is an ideal pedagogic measure to reduce the existing inequalities and discriminations. The authors discuss critically to what extent special interventions are required for the progression and welfare of Theyyam dancers through various government initiatives. An action plan is presented for promoting Theyyam as a religious and cultural event within the framework of tourism promotion programs in India, which rounds off the article.

Tourists have to make numerous decisions and they are normally considered to be rational decision makers who always try to maximize their utilities. *Jose K. Antony* and *Joby Thomas* start by giving a detailed analysis of the causes and effects of perceived risk, which is widely engaged in the study of consumer behavior in marketing research as consumer behaviors are instances of risk taking. They then discuss the effects of fluctuating risks on travelers' mobility. Historic highs in travel purchase behavior showed a significant impact on the structure of the global travel and tourism industry. The chapter concludes with a description of the key challenges for the global travel and tourism industry, and varied dimensions of perceived risks were identified and were engaged in order to identify characters of heterogeneity among tourist groups, based on their risk perception patterns.

Emilda K. Joseph envisages the community-based waste management strategies for sustainable tourism in backwater regions. Waste disposal is a serious problem in the areas where tourist arrivals and tourist activities are very high. She goes on to describe the implications of improper waste disposal that would bring serious negative impacts on host communities and destination. Local communities are being threatened due to improper waste management. She sketches the basic outlines for a sustainable mobility future. The chapter depicts the relationship between tourism and waste management and then describes the functional principle of "waste management."

For destination to emerge successfully, it not only has to promise quality services to the tourists but also deploy the right manpower with the right attitude and skill set to ensure the overall customer satisfaction. *Sandhya Hariprasad* and *Bindi Varghese* analyze civil disturbances on the tourism sector with an impact study on Kerala tourism, India. They describe the challenges faced by the travel trade due to civil instability and political disturbances. The chapter emphasizes the political alliances in the state that have been strengthened in such a manner that Kerala, India, is subjected to hartals almost every fortnight. They outline how flexible strategies could be devised that would make global travel more tourist friendly and offer advice to travel operators on how to organize their marketing efforts in order to be able to reach their target audience efficiently and effectively, now and in the future. Decision makers from the political and economic spheres show the various aspects of the multifaceted concept of civil disturbances and make recommendations for planning schemes and initiatives for the tourism industry.

Modern perspectives look at the city as more than a mere focus on people and think it as a hub of trade, culture, information, and industry. *K. Selvakumar* describes the history of the development of the heritage and history of Kumbakonam, (Tamil Nadu, India) for effective historical tourism. The role played by Darasuram in Kumbakonam, Tamil Nadu, is a concrete example of successful heritage tourism. With increasing urbanization, cities play ever more important roles in their country's economic development and may perform a vital function in global or regional networks. This chapter establishes that heritage tourism is a "need to have," not just a "nice to have."

The second section of the book is a comprehensive outlook on the operational and managerial perspectives in the tourism sector. Chapters in this section take an audacious look beyond the "horizon of tourism" and consider best practices, with a completive edge to deal with the complexities of travel trade; conscious effort, undertaken through some seminal works with managerial and enterprising aspects in the travel segment.

Human behavior scientists over the years have conducted various studies and have established that the performance of employees in any organization is determined largely by their motivational behavior. *Tomy Kallarakal* establishes the association between motivational behavior and organizational culture of tourism employees and has analyzed whether differences in demographic variables would account for significant differences in motivational behavior. This chapter unleashes a need for a thorough revamping of the prevailing practices in tourism organizations to nurture the motivational behavior of the manpower and thereby help these organizations deliver quality service.

Ginu George illustrates the importance of employee engagement as a critical factor in recent years because organizations with engaged employees are inclined to out-perform. The chapter offers a transformed perspective on employee performance by outlining the cornerstones of a comprehensive business travel management strategy by a higher level of determination to stay. This chapter advocates looking beyond the "horizon of tourism" and considering employee engagement as a best practice and illustrates an innovative mechanism to reinforce manpower management. The outcomes indicated that psychological climate has a substantial and affirmative relationship on employee engagement.

Gauging the current context, monetary currency becomes an important medium of exchange, unlike historical times. *Anson K. J.* and *Avin Thaliath* delve deeper into a speculative and a rational question whether there is an influence of foreign exchange volatility on foreign tourist arrivals. Therefore, the chapter substantiates and quantifies that there is a significant relationship between exchange rates and economic development. This also impacts the sectoral contribution. Introspecting from the perspective of the Indian context, it is envisaged that areas with exchange rate that are more stable or less flexible tend to attract more tourists and offer "barrier-free" tourism. The authors use up-to-date figures relevant to this frequently underestimated market segment. Concrete examples show how "social inclusion" can be practiced.

Chapter 13 in this section deals with issues in tourism product and communication policies. As in other industries, effective marketing strategies are of great importance for the competitiveness of the global tourism industry. *Rosma Mary Jolly* reconnoiters on changing values in modern societies: they are changing from hedonic fun societies to meaningful societies. Understanding this change, it is necessary in order to be able to continue to offer marketable tourism products. Celebrity endorsement is one of the major forms of advertising in which a business organization makes use of famous individuals or well-known organizations in order to boost consumer interest. The chapter also investigates the various motivating factors of the endorsers taken into consideration to visit the advertised destination. The superlative practice examples can serve as a guide for other tourist destinations.

In the wake of economic and tourism booms, this chapter describes the status quo in the tourism and travel industry. *Cheryl Poornima Smith e Venan Dias* and *Venan Bonaventure Dias* describe that in the hospitality industry talent development generally associates with an availability of open source talent, which is accessible in the form of graduates who possess a certain level of inbuilt talent. This chapter attempts to address research questions associated with the important constituents of talent development, external influxes, and facilitators associated with talent development and to position talent development internationally. It also looks at interventions taken up by the Indian government toward talent development.

Education is one of the resilient foundations that enable the individual to develop his competency and skills. *Nagarjuna G.* describes the tourism industry expectation on competencies. This chapter outlines a conceptual framework suggesting that tourism education incorporate necessary skills and abilities in curriculum and extracurriculum that will meet the necessary competency requirements of the industry.

Gowri Shankar R. and *Arjun B. S.* look at a new paradigm in tourism and hospitality sector. A specially conducted socially responsible investment (SRI) empirical study deals with the following questions: How important is SRI when considering a person's conventional investment orientation. This chapter deals with principal variances between SRI and conventional investing; where the former considers monetary returns alongside social, ethical, and environmental practices, the latter considers only monetary returns. This is gaining importance both among practitioners and academicians.

Cultural heritage can be conserved, and existential glitches of indigenous people can be resolved with the help of tourism. Culture as a tourist attraction, in a specially conducted empirical study, deals with the following questions: What is the relevance of culture when considering a destination choice? What is the significance for cultural attractions and potential demand organized cultural travel? *Pinky Jacob*, in this chapter, has carried out empirical investigation on the sociocultural impacts of the Namdapha Eco-Cultural Festival on the local residents of Miao. This seminal work has revealed a remarkable transformation into a modern economic structure with a diverse cultural range.

The third section of the book is an all-inclusive proposition on the emerging areas in the tourism sector. It gauges diverse perspectives to look beyond the interdisciplinarity of tourism and bears in mind divergent concepts as a result of exploratory, empirical, and conceptual frameworks corresponding to different thematic aspects as per the philosophies of research. This segment is voluminous and is cognizant towards multi-variate aspects under the travel and tourism domain.

Cultural acclimatization and hybridity in art and architecture is a fragmentary process that is falling due to trade and missionary activities from the historic times. This cultural assimilation developed into new artistic trends with heterogeneous rudiments bearing the facades of two or more cultures. *Githa U. Badikillaya* narrates the Indian hybridity in its cultural expression, giving a better understanding of one's cultural heritage. The cultural heritage must be preserved and not just in order to use it in the future for its tourist attraction potential. It is now widely recognized that tourism can play an important role.

Medical tourism is multifaceted in nature as its versatility deals with many variants to different segments that come from diverse backgrounds. There is vast potential for the Indian healthcare system to reach out with its services at an international level. Using examples from Canada, the United States, Bali, and the South Pacific, *Bindi Varghese* demonstrates how medical tourism could be enhanced and the existential problems could be resolved by portraying competitive Indian healthcare destinations that could outlay its identity with an effective economic system with a high degree, dependent on tourism that could succeed.

Culture does not endure in any precincts, and it extends in diverse ways in one's life. Understanding the cultural context, the temples of Kerala, India, have always acted as a center for arts and as an upbringing ground for the artists. *Anu Ajayagosh* narrates on the commercialization of art forms with a detailed outlook from a Kerala, India, tourism perspective. This chapter provides a deep insight on the contributions of government and other stakeholders for sustaining these art forms for future generations. It appears that less significance and low remunerations are the rationales behind declined popularity of the art forms in Kerala, India.

Today's society faces, like no generation before, certain complex threats at pilgrim destinations, first, to guarantee well planned and exotic destinations, and second, to reduce and abolish environmental damage caused by overcrowding and overwhelming responses to religiously driven destinations. *Nikhil Raj* in his seminal work, inspects the problems faced by Hindu pilgrim centers in Kerala, India, and the crisis management initiative undertaken by the authorities. Examining the interest of the pilgrims and the locals are safeguarded, and some environmental threats faced by

Hindu pilgrim centers in Kerala, India, are also detrimental and at par with the increasing population of pilgrims.

History of the development of sustainable tourism and the role played by the United Nations in promoting sustainable tourism are some concrete examples of successful sustainable tourism. *Shamima Akhtar* outlines some of the historic highs with sustainable tourism indicators, substantiating with the concepts, frameworks, and applications. While looking into the sustainability aspects, this chapter describes the logic behind the use and creation of assessment tools with an overview of sustainable tourism development.

The modern media world is essential for an effective communication policy for companies. *Sneha N.* and *B. George* provide deep insights into the functional mechanisms of classic and digital media. Digital information and telecommunication technology will remain driving forces behind processes of change in the tourism industry. This chapter shows how social media and metasearch will change travel processes.

There are 25 chapters in all, written by leading personalities from the hospitality services sector, and drawn from the worlds of both academia and commerce. These contributors have reviewed the current state of knowledge, presented real-world examples, and established innovative perspectives on tourism and hospitality services. The result is content that is academically challenging and determined to motivate, enable contextualization, and facilitate the linkage of theory to practice.

This work could not have been accomplished without the extraordinary dedication on behalf of the contributors, who for the most part have taken time for contributing to the knowledge of travel and tourism industry. I would like to acknowledge the academic and technical support rendered by Christ (Deemed to be University) in drafting this book. From the bottom of my heart, I want to thank all of the contributors who have helped to make this idea a reality.

My sincere thanks to Dr. Jyothi Kumar, Associate Dean, School of Business Studies and Social Sciences, and Dr. Tomy K. Kallarakal for their cordial support and guidance.

My colleagues from the Department of Tourism and School of Business Studies and Social Sciences have been instrumental in rendering support and encouragement and having confidence in me. Finally, above all, I would again like to express my gratitude to my family for all their help and encouragement throughout, and once again my book is dedicated to them.

Please enjoy the book and share it with others.

INTRODUCTION

Introspecting on the nature of tourism and its fragmented nature, this book explores how tourism typically works with newer dimensions in contemporary research. Complexities in tourism indicate its challenge in unifying it with a common ideology towards tourism. Tourism offers opportunities for economic, social and ecological development, but only if the newer perspective is well researched and are not overlooked. Contemporary research indicates varied risks add to the complexity of the travel segment, but the massive volumes of tourist traffic and a large share of land and resource consumption connected to travel are indeed signifant risks. Sensitive ecosystems and broader touristic ideologies and concepts are also the areas that are particularly interesting for tourism. The progression towards planning and impact assessment is iterative, and thereby the significance should be a high level of interface between the integral aspects involved in tourism in a sequential order. The various steps in these processes are integral and are compiled in this volume with a comprehensive level of understanding.

However, the philosophy toward tourism is an integrated approach to the fragmented tourism industry by propagating unity to the idea of tourism. This process can boost destination image, credibility of services, and largely, political and social acceptance. This volume briefly indicates explores several newer researched areas that invite stakeholder engagement. These initiatives could deploy quality trade of tourism, which is essential and is vital in heading towards competitiveness. The multifaceted nature of tourism is particularly evident as business leaders interpret tourism within the scope of their industry, as government officials interpret tourism according to their departmental responsibilities, and as various interest groups pursue an interpretation that serves their particular purposes. Seldom are the interests of tourism with its most expansive form incorporating social, cultural, environmental, economic, technological, trade, psychological, political, and many other dimensions. There is general concurrence that the pursuit of planning is seldom as successful.

The analogy in hospitality and tourism management is classically connected with the management of tourism services. Tourism is a composition of activities, services and industries that work together with a massive synergy in collating the travel experience. Service providers are very enterprising engage with emergence and dynamism to meet the new tourist or future tourist requisites. This longitudinal compilation is extensive and widespread, gauging different spheres of the travel fraternity and is based on the foregoing discussion by academia and commerce internationally, as tourism takes strong roots that will support an ever-strengthening travel sector. As students, academicians, and practitioners associated with services in general, and hospitality services in particular, the thrive is to lift and popularize understanding of what tourism research is to be and delve deep into its complexities, nuances, and logic. In particular, it is important to look behind the associated dominant rhetoric of success. The volume is an enticement of a comprehensive and consolidated collection of streams of knowledge relative to travel, tourism and hospitality services into a package that rates high on "readability." An intense effort has taken to compile rich content and varied learning approaches.

The dimensions covered examine an integrated approach to explain the evolving paradigms in the multifaceted tourism and hospitality sector. It portrays current global tourism and travel trends and is divided into three parts: tourism and destination management; operational and managerial perspectives in the service sector; and emerging areas in tourism. This compilation highlights the concurrent and live research works by renowned professionals and scientists from academia and the travel industry.

PART I

Tourism and Destination Management

CHAPTER 1

DESTINATION MANAGEMENT AND COMPETITIVENESS: INTERVENTION OF DESTINATION MANAGEMENT ORGANIZATIONS FOR GLOBAL COMPETENCY FROM AN INDIAN PERSPECTIVE

BINDI VARGHESE

Christ (Deemed to be University), Bangalore, Karnataka, India

CONTENTS

ABSTRACT

Tourism is a strategic economic activity in Karnataka, India, but the uniqueness of the governing bodies accentuates the integrated planning pioneering with several distinguishing features. The urban and territorial changes occurring due to tourism are well-introspected areas in contemporary scientific literature. This chapter adopts an integrative approach with a framework connecting scientific traditions of tourism and its evolving paradigms. Destination management and competitiveness describe how a country can revitalize its resources in terms of its tourism potentiality. The collective investigation of the development of tourism and the recent narration of regional planning directs toward conclusions regarding the role of destination management organizations (DMO) in tourism with contemporary development. This process has resulted in the creation of a competency model and the role of a methodical planning approach. This study emphasizes on the role of DMOs, responding to the need for a destination management. For this purpose, the various functionalities, activities, and roles of DMOs are evaluated through literature reviews. This chapter delves into a qualitative exploratory research design and corroborates with in-depth executive interviews from the public-sector and private-sector domains. The data is analyzed with computer-assisted qualitative data analysis method (NVivo). This exploratory study applied a thematic analysis network that ventured into several aspects and functionalities of destination management such as destination governance, funding, stakeholder relationships, competitiveness, and performance. This organization plays an important role in one way or another as it contributes in a large way toward development within a destination.

1.1   INTRODUCTION

The tourism industry is a young and rapidly growing industry. It creates abundant opportunities and benefits to the society if managed in a systematic manner. It is widely sought after due to the positive impacts it has on the destination. A unique feature of tourism is its "multiplier effect" that creates employment generation and various business opportunities and they trickle down to the different levels of the society (Pestana et al., 2011). For effective and efficient tourism, there should be proper coordination and cooperation among the various participants. A collaborative effort by the government bodies, local community, nongovernmental organizations and other stakeholders results in tourism success, thereby leading to the success of the destination (Žužić, 2012). Tourism, being one of the largest economic sectors, plays a very important role in regional development. To emerge successfully as a competent destination, the tourism sector should be backed by the strong network of policies and laws and calculated decision-making capabilities. This calls for systematic planning and research before making giant leaps in the market. The fragmented nature of tourism industry requires utmost coordination and collaboration among its players.

1.1.1 TOURISM IN INDIA

Tourism in India is being promoted globally with the tagline "Incredible India." This unique campaign was started in 2002 by V Sunil, the creative director and Amitabh Kant, the then joint secretary (Competitiveness of tourism, 2002). This venture aimed at promoting Indian tourism globally by giving an insight into the wide variety of products it can offer. According to the Ministry of Tourism reports, the campaign has increased tourism up to 16% in the first year itself. The campaign was a tie-up between the Ministry and the advertising and marketing firm Ogilvy & Mather (O&M) with the main objective to promote the tourist inflow to the country. The campaign portrayed the unique cultures and traditions of the country and also its scenic beauty. Attractive pictures and creative captions helped in capturing the attention of tourists from various parts of the world (The Government of India Ministry of Tourism, 2003). In short, a firm growth-oriented tourism destination like India is accepted as a total package destination in its entirety (Report on Incredible India, Govt. of India, p. 34). Invariably, it is one land with many distinct cultures, offering a mix of travel experiences to its benefactors.

1.1.2 TOURISM POLICIES OF INDIA

In India, the Tourism Ministry handles the tourism-related activities of the nation with the support of the National Tourism Organization (NTO) alongside with State Tourism Organization (STO). As Harril (2012) states, "a National Tourism Office (NTO) is an entity with overall responsibility for marketing a country as a tourist destination." The "Results-framework document," The Ministry of Tourism (2012) states the vision for India as, "Promoting India as a major tourist destination so as to achieve a superior quality of life for People of India through tourism, which would provide a unique opportunity for physical invigoration, mental rejuvenation, cultural enrichment and spiritual elevation" (p. 2). Therefore, tourism in India is been widely promoted by collaborative efforts by the Ministry of Tourism as well as the private members and key stakeholders of the tourism system of the country. With effective advertising and marketing campaigns, the country is coming up with new and innovative ideas to attract and draw the attention of the potential tourists while encouraging them to visit the country.

1.1.3   NEED FOR DESTINATION MANAGEMENT

For a destination to be successful and attract tourist inflow, it needs to develop a full-fledged destination management organization (DMO) that functions as an apex organization to manage the resources and at the same time ensures all the facilities and activities that satisfy the needs of the tourists. The success of tourist destinations calls for a balanced tourism development and integrates understanding on research and a cooperative effort to sustain the sought tourism initiatives for retaining competitiveness. Destination management ensures optimum allocation and utilization of resources for the best possible use and in the most sustainable manner. It provides a plinth for the marketing and promotional activities at the destination and ensures a smooth conduct of the tourism industry. Destination management essentially includes activities such as visitor management and resource management. Magas (2010) discusses the tourism trends and new challenges such as sociocultural aspects, consumption changes, and technological aspects, along with the integral planning of tourism product toward the tourism experience. DMO can, therefore, be a strategic leader and a destination developer which will simplify partnership and cooperation in accordance with the common vision of the destination. For ensuring the quality of services and facilities at the destination, it is highly essential to develop a DMO that can monitor the quality aspects of the resources at the destination.

Due to the high growth and development of the tourism industry, controlling the impacts on the destinations is a necessity. The economic gain and the impacts on the environment have to be balanced. Here,

DMOs play a crucial role in instigating appropriate measures and practices to maintain and stabilize the growth of tourism and control its negative impacts. Furthermore, Presenza et al. (2006) contemplates on the managerial concerns of a destination, stakeholder coordination, and destination audit. The primary functions of DMO include marketing and managing a destination in the most effective and systematic way. DMOs also contribute toward the framing of the destination's vision, goals, and objectives. While introspecting on the functions and activities of a DMO, Buhalis (2000) discusses the strategic marketing and management of destinations as a prime function of DMOs. Literature substantiates that marketing a destination should balance the strategic objectives of all stakeholders as well as maintain the sustainability of local resources. A destination is categorized by a combination of brands (products, services, and experiences provided locally) and a political and legal framework. This complexity of destinations extends to the multifaceted relationships of stakeholders; thus, destinations are one of the most difficult entities to market. Hence, DMOs are essential so as to plan and market a region as well as have the power and resources to undertake action toward achieving its strategic objectives.

1.1.4 FIVE A'S OF TOURISM AND DESTINATION MANAGEMENT ORGANIZATIONS

The need for DMOs substantiates the basic "A"s of tourism (Ritchie and Crouch, 2003). The infrastructure of a destination is a mix of all the inbuilt facilities at the destination provided and maintained for the benefit of the visitors. Inadequate infrastructure can affect the competitiveness of a destination. Therefore, DMOs and other industry associations play a major role in this regard.

Accessibility is a prime factor that plays a major role in deciding on which destination to visit. A potential tourist evaluates the major possibilities and difficulties, if any, involved in getting to the destination while deciding on their holiday. Accessibility is highly influenced by the geographic location of a destination, the rules and regulations governing the entry to a destination as well as the formalities and barriers in obtaining the permission to enter in a destination (Ritchie and Crouch, 2003).

Managing the resources at the destination is yet another factor that enhances the destination's appeal. Resources at a destination can be physical, cultural, historical, human, or financial resources. There exist complex components in a destination, which are the human resources of the destination. A DMO has very limited or less control over the human resources as they tend to be either overlooked or underestimated in most of the cases (Županović, 2010). For a destination to be competitive and successful, it should ensure that they deliver the most unique, memorable, and unforgettable holiday to the visitors (Meriläinen and Lemmetyinen, 2011). The tourism industry, being a service-oriented industry, is highly intangible. Therefore, the suppliers and businesses face a major challenge when it comes to satisfying the needs of the tourists as there might be a considerable gap between their expectations and the actual delivery of the service (p. 67). A tourism product is, therefore, a mix of the attractions, accessibility, accommodation facilities, other amenities and facilities available to the tourist at the destination, the hospitality, and attitude of the service providers and so forth.

Therefore, a tourist destination area has the following characteristics: recognition, definable appeal to traveler, coherence in its geography and amongst its tourist-related features, and political integrity, so that effective communications take place leading to viable decision-making (Blank, 1989, as cited by Harill in destination management: new challenges, new needs, p. 448). A DMO, as discussed earlier, functions as a nerve center of the destination and ensures that the tourism system in the destination is well-managed and well-structured ensuring proper and systematic flow of information through various levels. Optimum utilization of resources, conservation and preservation of the resources at the destination, proper infrastructure management, maintaining sustainability, and stakeholder cooperation are pivotal (Wagenseil, 2010).

Many countries are realizing the need for standardizing their tourism activities and hence have sensed the importance of establishing a DMO to effectively manage the tourism business (Gretzel, 2008). There are different types and forms of DMOs that exist today. They take different forms and shapes in different countries, but the core function of DMO remains the same. Through the literature reviews, the destinations that have an established DMO were identified. It is also evident that few countries follow a mixed approach to destination management. For instance, Australia is promoted by combining the efforts of a destination marketing organization, Regional Tourism Organization (RTO), STO and Convention and Visitor Bureaus (Ford and Peeper, 2012). Other examples of countries that follow such a collaborative system are Croatia,

Dubai, certain parts of the United States and the United Kingdom, and so forth (p. 438). Therefore, DMOs play a crucial role in a destination, not only in marketing but also in bringing about sustainable development, coordinating stakeholder interests, and sustenance of the competitiveness within the destination so as to properly manage the destination. Though marketing may be the primary function, there could be various issues a DMO has to tackle such as the challenges that may arise in future marketing of destination product (Fyall and Leask, 2006). Therefore, tourism destination analyzes two main functions: destination management and destination marketing functions.

1.2 THE MARKETING PERSPECTIVE OF DESTINATION MANAGEMENT ORGANIZATIONS

The main task or one of the most important functions of DMOs is effective marketing of the tourist destination. It is essential to explore into promotion studies and recognize the importance of marketing as being the primary managerial function of DMOs (Dore and Crouch, 2003). Wang and Fesenmaier (2007) articulate that the tourism industry being fragmented seeks for coordination and collaboration between the various players in destination marketing. Similarly, D'Angella and Go (2009) focus on collaborative tourism marketing practice, in particular, the relationship between the DMO and tourism firms. Successful marketing of a destination requires an effective and healthy management mechanism (Zhang and Murphy, 2009). A DMO can also be consortia (Žužić, 2012) seen in the Istrian model of destination management where a consortium is built by identifying destinations with special features to offer to specified tourists target groups. Another study conducted by Atorough and Martin (2012) in Scotland explores the need of developing a single regional DMO. The creation of a DMO would bring about a coordinated approach to destination marketing by bringing all the stakeholders together, funding, and pooling the resources. Thus, the DMO would have the private and public sector stakeholders would have their own political structure. Moreover, by coordinating and collaborating with various organizations, it can bring in new business to the area. So, it can be gathered that one of the basic necessities of a successful DMO is a strong collaborative relationship between all the stakeholders of the destination.

1.2.1 THE MANAGEMENT PERSPECTIVE OF DESTINATION MANAGEMENT ORGANIZATIONS

With the increasing tourism destination competitiveness, the limitations of the traditional approaches need to be overcome by new approaches and propose the systems approach for tourism destination planning and management, debates Carlsen (1999). As the tourism sector is decentralized, it creates a major setback to competition. Therefore, so as to bring about enhanced competitiveness, coordination, good communication, and effective management of all the supply providers are the key requirements for successful destination management.

Destination management has gained prominence over the recent decade and its importance is emphasized by its ability to enhance destination competitiveness. Destination management is viewed as an intraorganizational phenomenon though it functions independently (Meriläinen and Lemmetyinen, 2011). The debate often arises regarding the management perspective that is viewed as an isolated unit. Mostly, management of destinations stops before ascertaining destination competitiveness and does not investigate further into managing destination as a network. Hence, destination management is an important criterion for minimizing the negative impacts that tourism might have on the destination, as Carlsen (1999) states that "uncontrolled tourism will have negative impacts and … it is important to comprehend the tourism system so as to negate rise of issues." Laesser and Beritelli (2013) describe the domain of tourism destination management, "tourism destination management comprises the following domains of activity: planning (within tourism-related domains); lobbying (on behalf of all tourism stakeholders); marketing (in a comprehensive way—that is, product and pricing, at least to some extent promotion and distribution); and service coordination (aimed at creating a seamless customer experience)" (p. 47).

The tourism system is an open system as it reciprocates to changes in the environment, primarily due to the causal aspect of tourism development, and its interdependency with the natural environment as the tourism system shares a symbiotic relationship. This trait of the tourism systems creates major implications for tourism planners and destination managers. Therefore, it is imperative of DMOs to understand the destination management requirements pertaining to each destination.

1.2.2 DESTINATION MANAGEMENT ORGANIZATIONS FOR GLOBAL COMPETENCY

Tourism being the major product of tourism-dependent regions, it is important to sustain the destination—this is supported by Bošković et al. (2012) as they explore the increased need of finding out destination competitive disadvantages so as to sustain the destination in the long run. The competitiveness of a destination is vital as it can make or break the destination as Gruescu et al. (2009) state that the destination is the very root of a tourism system, with it being composed of several products and services, which makes it very complex to manage and market.

To understand the concept of competitiveness to a destination and its relevance to DMOs, it is important to delve into gathering an understanding of primary and secondary tourism supply, which is an aspect that can prove to be advantageous, as primary tourism supply cannot be reproduced effectively such as natural beauty, climate, and so forth. Secondary tourism supplies such as tourist infrastructure, quality of management, skill of workforce, and so forth are produced and improved, which would prove to be a competitive advantage (Vodeb, 2012). Comparative advantage comprises resources available to the destination whereas destination competitiveness is its ability to use these resources effectively. It could happen that the comparative advantage is lost due to the noncompetitive secondary tourism supply, so the competitiveness of a destination can be judged upon its ability to deliver goods and services that perform better than any other destinations. It is the task of understanding the fundamental duty of tourism management—that is, tourist destination competitiveness, this an important factor as it influences the growth of market share (Omerzel, 2006).

1.2.3 DESTINATION MANAGEMENT: A MAJOR PARAMETER IN TOURISM POLICY

A tourism policy has macro and microelements that include planning, development and destination management practices as described by Ritchie and Crouch (2003) who define a tourism policy as "a set of regulations, guidelines, directives and development/promotion objectives and strategies that provide a framework within which the collective and individual decisions directly affecting tourism development and the daily activities within a destination are taken" (p. 148). Therefore, a tourism policy gives direction to regions' tourism efforts and identifies areas that need attention in terms of development or management.

There are several factors that are to be taken into consideration while crafting a destinations' policy. The most important factors to be observed are the competitiveness and sustainability of the destination (p. 145). Competitiveness of a destination is the capability of the destination to stand as profitable in the tourism market, in other words, to attract visitors and maintain the well-being of the destination. Ritchie and Crouch (2003) indicate areas that a tourism policy must broadly address to achieve overall destination management and ensure the long-term success of the destination. The indicators are system definition, philosophy or values at the destination, vision, positioning, and branding of the destination, development, competitive, and collaborative analysis, monitoring and evaluation, and destination audit (p. 63). Unless there are effective destination management practices within a destination, it will deteriorate in the future or rather in the long run. The elements of a successful "total tourism destination management" require both the aspects of business management as well as environment management to be satisfied so as to achieve that fine balance within the destination.

1.3   OPERATIONAL PERSPECTIVES OF DESTINATION MANAGEMENT ORGANIZATIONS

DMOs are basically a firm or a unit focusing on increasing tourism at a destination, as well as improving its public image. They are mainly concerned with marketing as they bring buyers and sellers together, thereby contributing to the effective satisfaction of the customers. They also generate the demand for a place so that they can emerge competent in the market.

According to Ritchie and Crouch (2003), DMOs follow three major levels of operation. They are as follows:

1. **National level:** At the national level, they are referred to as NTOs or Authorities (NTAs) responsible for management and marketing

at a national level. British Tourism Authority and Australian Tourism Commission are examples.

2. **State/regional/provincial level:** At the state/regional/provincial level, they are often referred to as RTOs, STOs or the Provincial Department of Tourism. They undertake the activities of destination management at a regional or state level.

3. **Urban/municipal/city–state level:** At this level, the organization is mainly responsible for management/marketing in a small geographic area. The organization structure is frequently as a Convention and Visitor Bureau.

Therefore, a DMO is a body to instigate a standard process of marketing and managing a destination to attract visitors and improve the tourist flow to the destination and to synergize the activities on the destinations. The DMO can be structured differently in different countries at the discretion of the tourism governing body and its principal stakeholders. Researchers have various standpoints such as DMO, destination marketing organization, STOs, convention visitor bureaus, Regional Tourist Board, visitor tourist information centers, destination marketing information system, destination management system, Tourism Development Action Programs, Destination Management Company, Consortia, and so on. These are all forms of DMOs but their nature and functions will vary according to their levels and geographic areas.

Thus, a destination comprises several organizations, all functioning in unison; in brief, it is the governing bodies that administer the region, the business that is managed therein, and the community that resides there. The uniqueness of the tourism industry is that there needs to be harmony in the destination; most importantly, the destination should join hands in welcoming a tourist to the destination as the tourist expects a unique and memorable experience. To provide a wholesome experience for the tourist, all stakeholders of the destination must impart value to the tourist. A minor setback in the total experience offered to the tourist can create a totally negative impression of the destination, which in turn leads to bad publicity and a slack in the chance of revisitation. The role of stakeholders is essential in a destination as acknowledged by Ruhanen (2012) that academics and nongovernmental organizations have stressed the importance of including the stakeholders' perspective in the planning process; however, this has been ignored in practice, so the ill effects of unplanned tourism development hit the resident community. The strategic visioning is a means to address the stakeholder's interest and achieve sustainable tourism objectives by adopting a participatory model to engage the community with the various stakeholders and government bodies. In the long run, a destination must handle and manage the coordination between all the stakeholders at a destination so as to ensure its long-term competitiveness.

1.3.1 TYPES OF DESTINATION MANAGEMENT ORGANIZATIONS

While evaluating DMOs from a global perspective, scientific research reviews corroborated on the existence of DMOs among 47 countries and 28 countries that have active functional DMOs. The archetype and structure of the DMOs in practice have been identified and presented in Table 1.1.

TABLE 1.1   Types of DMOs in the Global Context.

Researcher(s)	Type of DMO	Country/region
Ford and Peeper (2012)	Convention Visitor Bureaus (CVBs)	The United States of America
Pike (2004)	National Tourism Office (NTO): China National Tourism Administration (CNTA) and Mexico Government Tourism Office	China
Choi et al. (2007)	Destination marketing organizations	Macau
Palmer and Bejou (1995)	Tourism Development Action Programs (TDAPs)	United Kingdom
Palmer and Bejou (1995)	Visitor and Convention Bureaus (VCBs)	The United States of America
(Žužić, 2012)	City Level Consortium: Verona Tuttintorno	Italy
Tian et al. (2011)	DMO: Beijing Tourism Development Committee (BTDC)	China

The DMOs deals with several categories to bring to the highlight: destinations' overall management, competency of a destination, governance, quality control, stakeholder management, infrastructural development, and marketing, and eventually leading to setting a benchmark that states a standard of quality services and products that is offered to the tourists and thereby achieve overall satisfaction of consumers. DMOs bring in a body of control that oversees the destination and at the same time, achieves visitor satisfaction. It brings about a total management system and helps in coordinating and controlling the flow of tourists, tackles present trends and challenges and be that platform for all stakeholders to come in contact with the potential tourists. Harril (2012) states that successful DMOs have established partnerships and collaborative networks, the best suggested means of collaboration are to employ a strategy of collaboration with stakeholders to institutionalize the collaboration with strategic stakeholders by ensuring they are represented by the board of directors.

1.3.2 ROLE OF DESTINATION MANAGEMENT ORGANIZATION

DMO will be a dominant and most influential body to manage a destination, evolving into a "total destination management system." It can become the ultimate source of strategic intelligence and grow as a communication center for a destination. Therefore, globally DMOs are predominantly considered as nongovernmental bodies, which are voluntary in nature and are probably supported by the host government. It is to initiate a standardized procedure to market a destination by attracting the right volume of tourists and to synergize tourist activities at the destinations (Vajcnerova and Ryglova, 2010). Visitor-centered approach to the economic and cultural development of a destination will balance and integrate the interests of visitors, service providers, and the community. Core DMO function is to market the destination as attractive to visitors (i.e., generating prospects) through marketing and promotional activities such as branding, advertising, media production, and so forth. Providing suppliers with market intelligence and cost-effective access to distribution channels (tour wholesalers, travel media, and online channel) are other functions. The interest also will be on providing some level of support to the visitor at the destination (information leaflets and visitor centers) (p. 73) (Fig. 1.1).

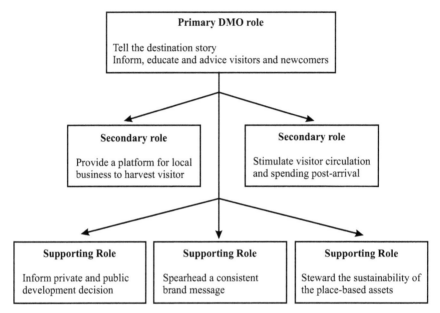

FIGURE 1.1   Role of destination management organization.

1.4 CORE FUNCTIONS OF DESTINATION MANAGEMENT ORGANIZATIONS

Presenza et al. (2005) proposed a model that describes the activities or functions undertaken by DMOs. The activities of DMOs as under two broad heads: the external destination marketing (EDM) function and the internal destination development (IDD) function. EDM function covers the marketing and promotional campaigns and activities undertaken by the DMO to attract more tourists to the destination whereas the IDD focuses on activities relating to the development of the destination, funding for development, deployment of resources, maintaining sustainability, and so forth. The core functionalities of DMOs are also on marketing and branding.

Many arguments and differences of opinions have been raised in this context recently. There have been varied studies and researches conducted on the marketing concept of DMO but little or few have been done on the management perspective. But to what extent do DMOs actually undertake effective marketing and utilize the various means of promoting a destination is the concern. Several authors question the terminology of DMO as did Pike (2013) who looks into the contentious issue regarding the tendency of authors in referring to destination marketing organizations as DMOs. Both these terms differ on several grounds mainly that destination marketing organizations rarely practice destination management. Moreover, an analysis is required on the grounds of conducting more academic research regarding the complexities of destination management.

Therefore, a DMO can be understood as a collaborative effort of the principal stakeholders of the destination, which includes government, private parties, nongovernmental organizations, and the community in effective marketing and promoting a destination. It is presumed to undertake the resource management and allocation at the destination and plan the tourism sector to avoid wastage and depletion of natural resources. It also performs the key functions such as branding the destination and benchmarking the services, ensuring the right investment schemes, timely and proper implantation of policies and plans, and the overall management and marketing of the destination. Practicing and conducting tourism activities in the most sustainable manner and at the same time maintaining its competitiveness is a key challenge faced by destinations. Future of DMOs and how they might evolve in response to the changing needs of the tourism system and external change drivers (Pollock, 2008).

1.4.1 METHODOLOGICAL PATH ASSESSMENT

Qualitative data analysis (QDA) process confirms the procedures engaged in structuring and analyzing the data. A "typical" QDA process involves a series of interviews or focus groups from which information is recorded and transcribed and then "coded" into various categories. The field notes, recorded as linear text, are also added to the repository of data and coded. To unleash the intricacies involved in the research, an analytic hierarchy was employed. Cataloging the raw data enabled a better understanding and with content abstraction, the primary analytical task involved in the qualitative aspect of research is appropriately refined (Fig. 1.2).

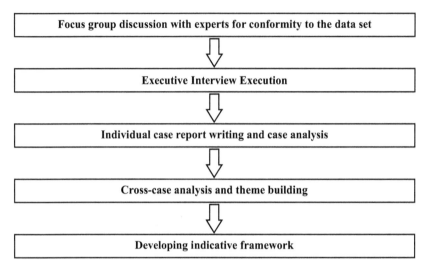

FIGURE 1.2   Methodological path assessment.

From the interviews and discussions conducted with eminent repre-sentatives from the tourism industry, a significant misconception was observed in the perception of the private stakeholders toward the concept of DMOs. The definition of DMOs as perceived by the industry partici-pants are the organizations that undertake the ground handling services at the destination, are well-informed and aware of the destination, and are a "one-stop shop" for availing all the services at the destination ranging from accommodation to arranging guides and entry passes for various events and sightseeing at the destination. These ground-handling compa-nies may be the tourism suppliers for the travel companies that purchase these services in bulk from the suppliers and compile them to develop an all-inclusive package that is offered to the customers.

As DMOs are not very popular in India, the industry participants are also unaware of the concept of DMOs and their implications and func-tions. Though they have cognizance on the functioning of DMOs through observation and knowledge from scholarly works and articles, they lack in experience as such an idea has not been successfully implemented and practiced in the country. Many examples of DMOs were quoted by the respondents during the interview, which includes destinations such as Switzerland, Australia, Singapore, and the Western countries, which are preferred destinations for the Indian market.

Wang and Fesenmaier (2007) say that the tourism industry being fragmented seeks for coordination and collaboration between the various players in destination marketing. Henderson described alignment as a working partnership that reflects a long-term commitment, a sense of mutual cooperation, shared risks and benefits, and other qualities consistent with the concept and theories of participatory decision-making (as cited by Singh and Hu, 2008, p. 931). Therefore, collaborative marketing efforts will lead the path to effective destination marketing. Collaborative marketing practices with the Department of Tourism, Government of India was limited as the majority of the respondents belonged to travel companies undertaking the outbound tourism needs of the tourists (Fig. 1.3).

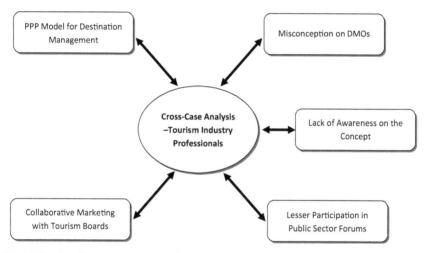

FIGURE 1.3 Cross-case analysis of representatives from the travel trade.

The public-sector views on destination management emphasized on bringing about a sustainable outlook in tourism for the long-term success of the destination. The public-sector leaders envisaged the need for empowering the destinations and the local authorities who participate in tourism at the destination. This contributes to increased local community involvement in tourism, optimum representation of stakeholders in the tourism sector, and thereby better coordination and cooperation throughout the sector. Benchmarking and standardizing the destination and its services is another predominant segment. The eventual aim of DMOs is to set a benchmark to the destination to allow the destination to stand out and attract potentials tourists from all over the globe. As Martin and Tomáš (2012) say that, like every other industry, even tourism faces constant competition and that it is the role of regional government and destination management institutions to utilize quality strategies and planning to achieve competitiveness in their respective destinations. The core emphasis is stressed on strategic planning as it is the key to work along changing trends, markets, and competition as it is this which provides a competitive edge to a destination (Fig. 1.4).

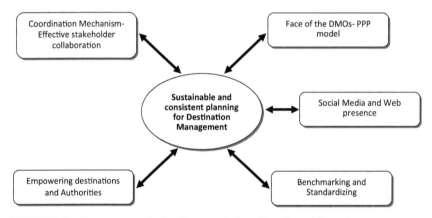

FIGURE 1.4   Cross-case analysis of representatives from the public sector.

1.4.2   *IMPLICATIONS FOR DESTINATION MANAGEMENT ORGANIZATIONS*

The interface between DMOs and industry partnership with organizational strategies can create an organizational setting to obtain more benefits. DMOs have been identified as destination managers, critical for the success of the development of services for tourists and stakeholders. Several implications from this chapter can be drawn to guide destination managers' decisions as follows:

- **Long-term partnerships:** A long-term perspective on interorganizational partnership through establishing DMOs will standardize the procedures for destination development. Facilitating partner involvement can amalgamate setting up benchmarks for destination branding. Thus, although DMOs need to first identify potential partners with long-lasting relationships that are critical for DMOs, it is often one or several partners that ultimately provide competent service.

- **DMOs for collaboration:** DMOs to actively search for partners and integrate them into the DMO partner network. In contrast, DMOs often develop new services without any assistance of partners.
- **DMOs, with M for management:** DMOs are innovative and they develop new services for destination visitors and destination stakeholders. The development of new services identified DMOs as destination developers.

1.5   CONCLUSION

Effective planning and development within the destination and leading the destination toward destination development with long-term sustainability of the destination is imperative. Conscious and holistic application of Destination Management measures may help to manage visitor demand proactively and ensure that the resource remains for future generations. Thus, a DMO can be a nongovernmental/technical body or voluntary in nature. It needs to be effectively supported by the host government and the other participants of the tourism network. In the long run, a destination must handle and coordinate with its principal stakeholders so as to ensure productivity and competitiveness over a long period of time. This chapter concludes on the note that DMOs are necessary for the long-term sustainability of the destination and therefore, the success of the destination depends on the success of the DMOs.

KEYWORDS

- tourism
- destination management
- integrated planning
- destination management organizations (DMOs)
- destination management
- destination marketing
- competitive advantage
- destination governance
- stakeholder relationships
- destination competitiveness

REFERENCES

Atorough, P.; Martin, A. The Politics of Destination Marketing: Assessing Stakeholder Interaction Choice Orientations Toward a DMO Formation, Using The Thomas-Kilmann Conflict Mode Instrument. *J. Place Manage. Dev.* **2012**, *5*(1), 35–55. DOI: 10.1108/17538331211209031.

Blank, U. *The Community Tourism Imperative: The Necessity, The Opportunities, Its Potential State Colege,* VenturePublishing Inc.: PA, 1989.

Bošković, et. al. Business Tourism Destination Competitiveness: A Case of Vojvodina Province (Serbia). *Ekonomska istraživanja.* **2012**, *25*(2), 311–322. Sveučilište jurja dobrile u puli, odjel za ekonomiju i turizam'dr. mijo mirković' Publisher.

Buhalis, D. Marketing the Competitive Destination of the Future. *Tourism Manage.* **2000**, *21*(1), 97–116.

Carlsen, J. A Systems Approach to Island Tourism Destination Management. *Syst. Res. Behav. Sci.* **1999**, *16*(4), 321–327.

D'Angella, F.; Go, F. M. Tale of Two Cities' Collaborative Tourism Marketing: Towards a Theory of Destination Stakeholder Assessment. *Tourism Manage.* **2009**, *30*, 429–440. DOI: 10.1016/j.tourman.2008.07.012.

Dore, L.; Crouch, G. I. Promoting Destinations: An Exploratory Study of Publicity Programmes used by National Tourism Organizations. *J. Vacation Mark.* **2003**, *9*(2), 137–149.

Ford, R.; Peeper, W. Eds. *Ann. Tourism Res.* **2008**, *35*, 1083–1093. DOI:10.1016/j. annals.2008.06.

Fyall, A.; Leask, A. Destination Marketing: Future Issues-Strategic Challenges. *Tourism and Hospitality Res.* **2006**, *7*(1), 50–60.

Gretzel, U. Managing Destination Marketing Organizations: The Task, Role, and Responsibilities of Convention and Visitor Bureau Executive, Ford, R., Peeper, W., Eds.; *Ann. Tourism Res.* **2008**, *35*, 1083–1093. DOI:10.1016/j.annals.2008.06.

Gruescu, R.; Nanu, R.; Pirvu, G. Destination Competitiveness: A Framework for Future Research. Zagreb. *Int. Rev. Econ. Bus.* **2009**, *12*(1), 83–96.

Harril, R. Destination Management: New Challenges, New Needs. In *The Sage Handbook of Tourism Studies*; Jamal, T., Robinson, M., Eds.; MPG Books Group: Great Britain, 2012, pp 432–447.

Laesser, C.; Beritelli, P. St. Gallen Consensus on Destination Management. *J. Destination Mark. Manage.* **2013**, *2*, 46–49. DOI: 10.1016/j.jdmm.2012.11.003.

Magas, D. *Why the Destination Management Organization?* In *Tourism and Hospitality Management 2010, Conference Proceedings* 2010; pp 1041–1047.

Martin, L.; Tomáš, K. Tourism Destination Benchmarking: Evaluation and Selection of the Benchmarking Partners. *J. Competitiveness,* **2012**, *4*(1), 99–166. DOI: 10.7441/joc.2012.01.08.

Meriläinen, K.; Lemmetyinen, A. Destination Network Management: A Conceptual Analysis. *Tourism Rev.* **2011**, *66*(3), 25–31. DOI: 10.1108/16605371111175302.

Ministry of Tourism Government of India. *Competitiveness of Tourism Sector in India with Selected other Countries of the World.* 2002. http://tourism.gov.in/writereaddata/CMSPagePicture/file/marketresearch/studyreports/IndiaTourismGlobal.pdf

Omerzel, D. G. Competitiveness of Slovenia as a Tourist Destination. *Managing Global Trans.* **2006,** *4*(2), 167–189.

Palmer, A.; Bejou, D. Tourism Destination Marketing Alliances. *Ann. Tourism Res.* **1995,** *22*(3), 616–629.

Pestana, B.; Laurent, B.; Nicolas, P.; Elisabeth, R.; Bernardin, S.; Assaf, A. Performance of French Destinations: Tourism Attraction Perspectives. *Tourism Manage.* **2011,** *32*(1), 141–146.

Pike, S. Destination Marketing and Management: Theories and Applications. *Tourism Manage.* **2013,** *34*, 247–253.

Pollock, A. Speculation on the Future of Destination Marketing Organizations (DMOs): A Conceptual Discussion Paper. *DestiCorp.* 2008. http://dmopro.com/LinkClick.aspx?file ticket=aQCuHD5of9Y=&tabid=63.

Presenza, A.; Sheehan, L.; Ritchie, J. R. B. *Towards a Model of the Roles and Activities of Destination Management Organizations,* 2005. Unpublished manuscript. http://www.academia.edu/1009194/Towards_a_model_of_the_roles_and_activities_of_destination_management_organizations.

Presenza, A.; Sheehan, L.; Ritchie, J. R. B. *Towards a Model of the Roles and Activities of Destination Management Organizations.* 2006. http://www.academia.edu/1009194/Towards_a_model_of_the_roles_and_activities_of_destination_management_organizations.

Ritchie, J.; Crouch, G. *The Competitive Destination,* 1st ed.; CABI Pub.: Oxon, UK, 2003.

Ruhanen, L. Strategic Visioning: Integrating Sustainable Development Principles in Tourism Destination Planning. *Acta Turistica.* **2012,** *24*(2), 149–176.

Singh, N.; Hu, C. Understanding Strategic Alignment for Destination Marketing and the 2004 Athens Olympic Games: Implications from Extracted Tacit Knowledge. *Tourism Manage.* **2008,** *29,* 929–939. DOI: 10.1016/j.tourman.2007.11.005.

The Government of India Ministry of Tourism and Culture Department of Tourism Market Research Division. *20-Year Perspective Plan for the Development of Sustainable Tourism in Karnataka,* 2003. http://tourism.gov.in/CMSPagePicture/file/marketresearch/statewise20-yrsplan/karnataka.

The Ministry of Tourism. *Results-Framework Document (RFD) for Ministry of Tourism—(2012–2013).* 2012. http://tourism.gov.in/writereaddata/Uploaded/RFD/050220121004071.pdf.

Tian, X.; Huang, R.; Busby, G. An Investigation of DMOs in China: With Particular Reference to Beijing Tourism Development Committee (BTDC). *Acta Turistica* **2011,** *23,* 105–238.

Vajcnerova, I.; Ryglova, K. The Application of Quality Management Principles into the Management of the Destination. *Bus. Rev. Cambridge* **2010,** *16*(1), 306–311.

Vodeb, K. Competitiveness of Frontier Region and Tourism Destination Management. *Managing Global Trans.* **2012,** *10*(1), 51–68.

Wagenseil, U. (2010) Destination and DMO and, Boundaries, Timisoara and Fagaras, *Unit for Sustainable Development of Tourism.* Turism Durabil.ro.

Wang, Y.; Fesenmaier, D. R. Collaborative Destination Marketing: A Case Study of Elkhart County, Indiana. *Tourism Manage.* **2007,** *28*, 863–875. DOI:10.1016/j.tourman.2006.02.007.

Zhang, Y.; Murphy, P. Supply-Chain Considerations in Marketing Underdeveloped Regional Destinations: A Case Study of Chinese Tourism to the Goldfields Region of Victoria. *Tourism Manage.* **2009,** *30,* 278–287. DOI: 10.1016/j.tourman.2008.07.004.

Županović, I. *New Postulates in Strategic Management of Integrated Tourist Destination Product in Montenegro.* Tourism & Hospitality Management, 2010.

Žužić, K. *Destination Management Systems: Examples of Italian Models and the Proposal of an Istrian Model.* Tourism & Hospitality Management, 2012.

CHAPTER 2

POLICING TOURISM: CHALLENGES AND OPPORTUNITIES OF TOURIST POLICE SYSTEM IN INDIA

N. CHAITANYA PRADEEP

School of Business Studies and Social Sciences, Christ (Deemed to be University), Bangalore, India

CONTENTS

ABSTRACT

Security issues play a predominant role in developing tourism industry of any country. Though creating a conducive environment in terms of peace and a sense of security among the foreign tourists is a prime requisite for the tourism industry, there are hardly few studies carried out to explore the position of law enforcement agency in the discourse of tourism studies in India. In fact, the security status of foreign tourists cannot be seen with a narrowest perspective, that is, law and order, but it has multiple effects on brand image, external affairs, and, of course, the economy of the country. Realizing this, law enforcement agencies of few developed countries have advanced their training techniques and tuned approaches and methods of policing as per the unique growing security challenges of tourist places. "Tourist-oriented policing" is one of the outcomes of the new innovations in policing. But, in Third World countries, the role of policing in shaping the brand image of destination places is yet to be realized. In India, security of foreign tourists has become a subject of frequent criticism for its inefficiency and ineffectiveness. Furthermore, the sexual violence against women tourists along with drug trafficking in tourist areas apparently made policing more complex. This clearly indicates that Indian police is yet to gear up its methods in proportion to the challenges thrown by the tourism industry. In this context, the paper explores the emerging challenges of policing in tourist areas and institutional inadequacies in the Indian police system. The study completely relies on secondary data including the earlier studies on best practices of tourism policing in select countries, reports of National Crime Records Bureau, Ministry of Tourism, newspaper, and media. The literature substantiates unique security problems relating to crimes against tourists that may call for separate approaches and analyses in the domain of security studies. The existing literature also indicates that studies on the role and significance of law enforcement agency in developing Indian tourism industry are relatively less explored. In addition, the study found that police reforms initiated by the successive governments at center as well as state governments had a cynical approach in addressing the security challenges of the tourism industry. The chapter examines various policing styles specific to tourist areas and analyzes the suitability and applicability of the same in the Indian context. The paper also suggests thrust areas of tourist policing reforms and offers feasible solutions.

2.1 INTRODUCTION

Safety and security is increasingly relevant in choosing to visit a destination, and it has become a critical key. Crimes against tourists can impede tourism by significantly damaging a location's image. Therefore, the most important prerequisite for a successful tourist industry is a reputation for having crime under control and guaranteeing tourists' safety (Ferreira and Harmse, 2000). In addition, tourism has become a major source in the economic, social, and cultural life of many countries in the world. Tourism, directly and indirectly, supports 204 million jobs and is responsible for more than 10% of global domestic products (Brunt and Hambly, 1999). In historical terms, tourism activity is a relatively new development, and it is only recently that academics have considered it worthy of study. The economic and security significance of tourism and its supposed positive role in the national and regional development were, perhaps, the first areas to be explored.

2.2 CONCEPTUAL UNDERSTANDING

According to Halloway (1998, p. 36), "tourism" is defined as follows: Tourism related to the movement of people and their stay away from their homes for more than 24 h, whereas according to George and Rivett-Carnac (2005, p. 2), the World Tourism Organization has devised a broader definition of tourism—tourism as the activities of persons traveling to and staying in places outside their usual environment for not more than one consecutive year for leisure, business, and other purposes. It is when people travel away from where they live and work for at least 24 h, but not for longer than 1 year, and it also refers to the activities people take part in while they are away. Weaver and Lawton (2006) view tourism as the sum of the processes, activities, and outcomes arising from the interactions among tourists, tourism suppliers, host governments, host communities, and origin governments that are involved in the attracting and hosting of visitors. Modern tourism is one of those terms that most people understand, yet few people define well. There seems to be no definitive definition of "tourism." Tourism is defined as: "the practice of traveling for recreation; the guidance or management of tourists; the promotion and encouragement of touring; the accommodation of tourists" (Merriam-Webster's Collegiate Dictionary, 1993, p. 1248).

Other scholars and tourism scientists present alternative definitions. For example, in the preface to The Tourism System, David Pattison (1985), then head of the Scottish Tourism Board, writes: "From an image viewpoint, tourism is presently thought of in ambiguous terms. No definitions of tourism are universally accepted. There is a link between tourism, travel, recreation, and leisure, yet the link is fuzzy..." (Pattison, 1985, p. xvi). On the other hand, Choy et al. (1989) in the work The Travel Industry define tourism by stating: "the travel industry will be defined as "the composite of organizations, both public and private, that are involved in the development, production, and marketing of products and services to serve the needs of travelers" (pp. 4–5).

According to Cage (2002), a "tourist" is defined as a person who travels away from his or her home for whatever reason, be it for a holiday, to do business, to represent his country in sport, and to attend a religious function or to attend a conference. According to Siegel (2005), crime is a violation of societal rules of behavior as interpreted and expressed by the criminal law, which reflects public opinion, traditional values, and the viewpoint of people currently holding social and political power. Individuals who violate these rules are subject to sanctions by the state authority and result in social stigma and the loss of status. Crime is a term that seems to defy precise definition. Criminal behavior can be seen as behavior in violation of the law. The criminal law, in turn, is defined conventionally as a body of specific rules regarding human conduct that have been promulgated by political authority and which apply uniformly to all members of the classes to which are enforced by punishment and administered by the state. It is a freedom from danger or risks and you feel you are safe around that area. In this regard, the Encyclopedia Americana Volume 24 (1986) describes the concept "safety" as the condition of being free from the danger of harm. As a legal concept, it implies a state of relative security from accidental injury or death due to measures designed to guard against accidents, laws that encourage the maintenance of safety standards are often called safety. Goeldner and Ritchie (2006, p. 3) define tourism policy as a set of regulations, rules, guidelines, directives, and development or promotion of objectives and strategies that provide a framework within which the collective and individual decisions directly affecting long-term tourism development and the daily activities within a destination are taken. It is the way in which tourism must be done. Tourism policy is a strategy for the development of the tourism sector, which establishes objectives and guidelines as a basis for what needs to be done.

Alternative perspective captures tourism policy as a guideline that provides a framework for tourism stakeholders to do their work efficiently. It is aimed at developing management to perform well in the tourism industry. A review of the literature demonstrates that there is no one definition of the term "tourism," or any one single word to describe the industry. In the United States, travel or "travel and tourism" is the preferred colloquial; whereas, in many other countries, the term "tourism" tends to dominate. Moreover, there is no set definition for the term "tourist" or how this phrase differs from others, such as visitor or even day-tripper. For example, is a person who leaves his or her town to shop in a town nearby a tourist or a visitor? What if the same person stays in a taxable place of lodging? Are day-trippers tourists, visitors, or neither? What about cruise passengers who spend just a few hours in a port of call? What are they to be called?

2.3   TOURISM SECURITY

Considering how imprecise the terms "tourism" and "travel and tourism" are, it should not be surprising that in a composite industry such as tourism, the expression "tourism security" also suffers from the absence of a precise definition. This lack of precision with the terminology does not imply that tourism security practitioners are unaware of their major responsibility, which is to ensure both safety and security. What it does mean is that there are often questions as to who does what, as well as determining the boundaries of different roles. Just as in the case of law enforcement, police officers know that their job is fluid; they must always be prepared for the unexpected. Many police officers will state that their main responsibilities are to serve and protect anyone in their zone of duty, no matter where the person is originally from or how long he or she will stay in the area.

2.3.1   TOURISM SECURITY AND THE CRIMINAL BEHAVIOR

To complicate matters further, tourism security deals with much more than just criminal behavior. Tourism professionals must continually fight against criminals who would seek to develop either a parasitic relationship with tourism or seek to take advantage of tourists and visitors.

Visitors are often victims of acts that may not be illegal but are immoral and destroy a locale's reputation. For example, shop owners may bother (harass) visitors, without technically breaking the law, to the point where the visitors no longer feel comfortable. Furthermore, local mores and customs mean that what is acceptable behavior in one culture may not be acceptable in another. Often, these cultural clashes are likely to occur in places where multiple cultures, and diverse economic statuses, are placed within the same geographic locale or forced to intermix with each other. To add to the difficulties, there is a general confusion between issues of security, safety, and, in this book, what we call "tourism surety." In a number of European languages such as French, Portuguese, and Spanish, the same word is used for both security and safety. Security and safety experts do not always agree where one concept ends and another begins. For example, we speak of food safety, but if a person intentionally alters food so as to sicken someone else, then this act is no longer a food-safety issue but becomes a food-security issue. In the same manner, tourism specialists must worry about a traveler who deliberately carries a communicative disease from one locale to another for the purpose of harming others. Is such an act one of biological terrorism, a security matter, or an issue of safety? Furthermore, studies are required to address these fundamental questions. However, fundamentally it can be understood that tourism security is beyond the criminal behavior.

2.4 THEORETICAL UNDERSTANDING: CRIME AND TOURISM

There are several perspectives relating to tourism and crime. Among them, psychosociological theories are considered to be more relevant to the policing perspective. Current literature suggests that a range of socio-psychological theories, mainly social disorganization theory, hot-spot theory, and routine activity theory have been applied to examine the issues relating to the victimization of tourists.

2.4.1 SOCIAL DISORGANIZATION THEORY

Social disorganization is a theoretical perspective that explains ecological differences in levels of crime based on structural and cultural factors shaping the nature of the social order across communities (Shaw and McKay, 1942). Mainly, the theory focuses on how the covariates of urban growth impact the criminal behavior of the particular society. Social disorganization theory argues that trends in criminal behavior are subject to the active role of self-regulatory mechanisms that determined social integration of neighborhoods, which in turn impacts social interactions or the presence of delinquent subcultures. Three factors are found to be responsible in growth in crime rate in tourist destinations (Blau and Blau, 1982). They include attractiveness of the destination, opportunity, and accessibility. The mass tourism model initiated from the 1980s onward brought social, cultural, and economic changes to many tourist destinations, which boosted the growth of crime against tourists. Based on the earlier studies relating to crime in tourist destinations, authors framed hypotheses to explore the correlation between the vulnerability of mass tourists compared with local people; then, possibility of frequent types of crime among tourists and residents in terms of property crime and violent crimes, the correlation between the number of victims of crime and levels of tourist density or urban growth in the tourist destination in a particular period. The studies have also used social disorganization theory, consisting of the indexes of residential instability, population heterogeneity, and socioeconomic deprivation to estimate the effects on the two violent crime measures of a baseline model (Martínez et al., 2009). The drug overdose measure was added to the baseline model to evaluate the impact of drug activity on assault and robbery rates, controlling for the baseline indicators. Studies have established that tourist destinations with disorganized societies and ethnic heterogeneity and the societies that are part of urban transformation are more prone to criminal activities (Blau and Blau, 1982). It was also found by the studies that socially disorganized societies will have a lower capacity for social control and disallows tourists to engage in sociocultural activities, which may potentially lead to increased violence against tourists.

2.4.2   HOT-SPOT THEORY

One of the widely applied theories to examine the relationship between tourism growth and crime is hot-spot theory. The theory offers a framework to identify the crime-prone areas geographically. It argues that there are places (geographic areas) where tourism activities converge (restaurants, bars, discotheques, attractions, transport hubs, and hotels) and which are particularly prone to incidents of tourist victimization. In addition, the theory helps to understand why certain locations in tourist destinations seem to expose tourists to incidences of victimization. Places where tourists are at the greatest risk of becoming victimized have been shown to cluster in specific types of places or hot spots (Crotts, 1996). These hot spots provide a place of opportunity at which predatory crimes can occur. These areas were also called "criminogenic" locations, where tourists become vulnerable to risk due to insecurity (Ryan and Kinder, 1996). The study found that understaffed police was the common cause in the most reported crimes. In the case of Dade County, the most important area of tourist attractions in Miami, around 29% of property crimes and 37% of violent crimes against tourists were reported. This hot-spot theory broadly argues that a series of conditions are generally unified to make tourists an easy target for crime. The conditions include the "accidental tourist" (being in the wrong place at the wrong time); the tourist industry "provides" victims (due to lack of information about criminogenic locations), but this can be avoided by doing proper inquiry about the security status of the tourist sport. The tourist is seen as a specific target because of the ease of carrying out the crime and the low probability that an official report will be made, but this can be controlled by increasing visible policing. The tourist is considered by the criminal to be a legitimate target because tourists are seen as symbols of global capitalism, thereby making it justifiable to commit crimes against them. But it is not rational to call all tourists as capitalists. Therefore, by bringing awareness to reduce hate crime, the aforesaid conditions can be controlled.

2.4.3   ROUTINE ACTIVITY THEORY

Ecological perspective to the crime has been developed by some thinkers in the field of criminology. In this regard, human ecology has been identified as a platform to examine the trends in crime and argued that better understanding of the relationship between routine activities theory and hot-spot theory can help the researchers to correlate crime and tourism (Schiebler et al., 1996). According to routine activity theory, criminal acts as a routine activity for those persons pursuing a criminal lifestyle. This kind of predatory crime requires three basic elements: a suitable victim or target, a motivated offender (usually someone who has adopted a criminal lifestyle), and a relative absence of "capable guardians" (such as law enforcement officers or security guards) to police tourist areas.

The hot-spot theory argues that a break in the individual's routine influences the subsequent degree of exposure to crime, namely by a decrease in one's level of alertness and an increase in one's sense of security. Further, this theory identifies three elements that are associated with the time and space of crime, a target, an offender, and security. If these elements do not simultaneously converge, the probability of occurring crime will be lower or even zero. This "crime triangle" is based on a suitable target (less vigilant tourists, with more money, who are less compliant with safety norms and frequent places where they are unaware of the potential danger), a likely offender, and the ineffectiveness of security measures to prevent criminal acts (Mawby, 2000, p. 109). This theory supports the hypothesis that the increase of tourists in an area makes tourists potential victims of crime when the level of security is reduced or ineffective. This theory supports the existence of four elements that enhance the risk of criminal acts against tourists: values (visible and quantity), inertia (lack of response from police or law enforcement officers), visibility (exposure of the tourist-target), and access (proximity and access to the tourist-target).

2.5   APPROACHES TOWARD CRIME AND TOURISM

The tourism-crime relationship is becoming increasingly researched in the field of tourism. The existing literature suggests that crime and tourism can also be explained from the tourist's perspective. This perspective broadly categorizes the crime relating to tourists from the victim and accused point of view that is the tourism as victimization of tourists and *Tourists as Victims of Crime*. As indicated by many researchers in the past, tourism is becoming a growing industry sector for many countries, contributing to the standard of living of the host's society and the locals' quality of life as the income resulting from tourism expenditure increases (Foster, 1985). Tourism contribution is noticeable in the development and innovation of the host's infrastructure with the expansion of construction projects such as new roads, buildings, and airports for better receipt of tourism impacts and exploitation of cultural exchange between tourists (Inskeep, 1991).

Moreover, as shown by several studies (Allen et al., 1988; Davis et al., 1988), many opportunities are generated from tourism referring to entertainment, leisure, shopping, and consumption activities. For these reasons, many countries spend millions on promoting their tourism product and attracting as many tourists as possible and at the same time the amount of money earned. In 2014, the Cyprus Tourism Organisation's budget allocated to promotion and publicity was € 27 million (Cyprus Gazette, 2015). Research into tourism and crime (Perry and Potgieter, 2013; Kokkinos and Kapardis, 2012) has focused on a number of topics, namely: tourists as both offenders as well as victims, higher level of offending in tourist areas, the impact of tourism on a region's crime level, tourism and terrorism, tourism as instrumental for deviance or offending, and, finally, how the authorities respond to the issue of tourism and crime, especially as far as crime prevention measures are concerned. Let us next consider the evidence for tourists as offenders before examining the evidence for the criminal victimization of tourists, especially in comparison with local residents, a distinction emphasized by Albuquerque and McElroy (1999).

Tourism management and tourism academics have reported more studies of tourists as offenders than as victims and have paid even less attention to tourists' experience of and fear of crime. Mention was made above that tourists are particularly vulnerable to criminal victimization. This is surprising given that "crime has significant impacts on the tourism industry" (Perry and Potgieter, 2013, p. 104). Comparing tourists and local residents as victims of crime, it needs to be acknowledged that tourists are, of course, more vulnerable for a number of reasons, such as they frequent specific high-risk locations such as nightclubs; generally speaking, are not familiar with the area they are holidaying in; often do not speak the local language; carry such valuables that are sought after criminals such as cameras and cash. They are often overcharged or swindled or defrauded, and, finally, recent years have seen international terrorists attacking tourists resorts to kill citizens of particular countries (e.g., Israel) holidaying there and/or to damage the economy of a country. Not surprisingly, perhaps, when Albuquerque and McElroy (1999) analyzed crime data for Barbados for 1989–1993 and reported that tourists had a greater crime victimization rate than local residents and, also, tourists' victimization involved property crime and robbery whereas locals experienced violent crime.

It should be noted in this context that when comparing victimization of tourists with locals, one should also consider possible differences in reportability of different offenses and as a function of the whether the victim and/or the offender is a local or a tourist. As far as crime victimization of tourists is concerned, Mawby et al. (2000) and Brunt et al. (1999) carried out a postal victim survey of a national sample ($N=514$) of British people focusing on their last holiday and found that (a) those surveyed experienced higher victimization rates than they would have done at home, and (b) while criminological research indicates that fear of crime normally exceeds one's actual risk of crime victimization, for the sample surveyed, risk exceeded their fear. Significantly, although many of the respondents said they had taken how they perceived safety into account when choosing where to go on holidays, only a small number of them considered crime a problem while on holiday. Biagi et al. (2012) examined whether crime in Italy is affected by tourist arrivals. By using data for the period 1985–2003, they found that there was a positive correlation between tourism and crime tourist destinations. However, when they controlled for the difference between tourists and local residents to be victimized, no significant differences were found.

The discussion of the literature on tourists and criminal offenders shows a link between tourism and property-related offenses. The present paper reports findings from an examination of the relationship between tourism and crime, taking into account the money spent by a tourist. Assuming that most tourists who are victims of crime report it to the local police, who, in turn, record the offenses reported to them, it would not be unreasonable for one to hypothesize that tourism increases crime in tourist destinations because it creates opportunities for local criminals to address certain tourists' demands for drugs and/or sex; among the tourists, there are persons who routinely commit crime, including football hooligans and drug "mules." Tourists are vulnerable for being victimized (see below) and local criminals are presented with additional opportunities to offend. Of course, it is not uncommon for certain tourists, especially those with a criminal record for property offenses in their own country and who travel on low budgets to commit property offenses or sell drugs or prostitute themselves to meet the cost of their holidays. Low-cost air travel has vastly increased the opportunities for such persons, too, to holiday overseas.

Ochrym (1990) examined the mean crime rates in three tourist areas (including Atlantic City where casino gaming was legalized in 1976) and two urban centers in New Jersey and found that tourist destinations had mean crime rates significantly higher from urban centers. As criminologists are not tired of reminding us, crime is, generally speaking, an urban problem. The early study by Jud (1975) of a cross-section of 32 Mexican cities for the year 1970 examined the relationship between tourism and crime controlling for urbanization and found that the volume of officially recorded crime and property-related crime (theft, fraud, and robbery) are closely related to crime in a positive way. A weak relationship between tourism and crime that was reported for a cross-section of 50 US states by Pizam (1982) found that total crime and property-related offenses such as theft, fraud, and robbery were positively correlated with tourism but offenses against the person (assault, abduction, kidnapping, rape, and murder) were not. Kokkinos and Kapardis (2014) found in their study of the impact of tourism on crime in Cyprus during 2009–2012 that, contrary to popular belief, tourist offenders in Cyprus did not significantly contribute directly to increases in the total volume of crime by offense type. A positive relationship between tourism and economic-related offenses was reported by McPheters and Stronge (1974) in Miami, Florida, who, used time series analysis and found (like Fuji and Mak, 1980—cited by Biagia et al., 2012) a significant seasonality to tourism and increases in theft, burglary, and robbery. In support of earlier studies, Campaniello (2011) found that when Italy hosted the Football World Cup, there was a significant increase in property offenses. Further evidence that tourism is associated with economics-related crimes was reported by Biagi and Detotto (2014) for a cross-section of Italian provinces. Regarding the impact of tourism on crime in different countries, in their study of 46 European countries, Van Tran and Bridges (2009—cited by Biagi et al., 2013) reported that as the rate of tourists arriving in a country increased, crimes against the person were reduced.

As Biagi et al. (2012) reminded their readers, a mere correlation between tourism and crime does not tell us whether the victims of the crimes attributable to tourism are other tourists or local residents. Biagi et al. tested whether total crime in Italy was affected by tourism during the period 1985–2003. Controlling for the propensity of tourists and residents to be victimized, the likelihood was quite similar for the two groups and concluded that it was urbanization that appeared to provide the main explanation for the effect of tourism on crime.

We see that the weight of the evidence, taking the quality of methodology into account, with the notable exception of Van Tran and Bridges (2009), points to a positive relationship between tourism and crime when controlling for urbanization.

2.6   CONTEXTUALIZING "CRIME AND TOURISM"

Brunt et al. (2000, p. 417) and George (2010, p. 807) identify several broad areas of interest/themes in the literature focusing on tourism and crime: tourist areas as areas of high crime, tourists as victims, tourists as offenders, tourism generating higher levels of deviant or illegal activity/tourism impacting on crime levels, terrorism and tourism, local and tourists' perceptions of crime, and policy responses to tourism and crime/tourism-crime prevention measures. Nkosi (2010) states that tourism is a human activity that is sensitive and reacts rapidly to crime. Furthermore, Boakye (2011) argues that providing security has become an imperative and any destination that ignores this responsibility stands to lose out on the keen competition for the tourist dollar. Linking crime to tourism is an emerging field in both criminology (Steyn et al., 2009) and tourism studies. Tourism studies itself has a well-established interdisciplinary tradition and certainly, crime research requires multifaceted and interdisciplinary theoretical and methodological approaches given the complexity of issues as well as the range of stakeholders involved. There is hardly any extensive studies carried in the Indian context. However, in South Africa, few studies exist that examine the relationships between crime and tourism specifically (see, e.g., Bloom, 1996; Donaldson and Ferreira, 2008; Ferreira and Harmse, 2000; George, 2003, 2010; Ntuli and Potgieter, 2001). These studies indicate that the negative perceptions of personal safety and high levels of crime in South Africa is a threat to the tourism industry and economic development more generally. Furthermore, as personal experience and word-of-mouth remain key factors in influencing visitation (both first-time and repeat) in South Africa, it is imperative that tourists do not become victims of crime or feel threatened. Although earlier studies warn about the increase in crime levels and the decrease in tourism arrivals (e.g., Ferreira and Harmse, 2000), more recent studies show that crime rates have stabilized (albeit at a high level) and in some instances are decreasing (South African Police Service, 2010a, 2010b), and both domestic and international tourism is increasing (South African Tourism (SAT), 2010).

This trend is dissimilar to other patterns in the world and requires further research to examine why South Africa continues to be a key tourism destination despite being viewed as the crime capital of the world. In part, this apparent contradiction could be attributed to the trend that foreign tourists visit established tourist areas such as ecotourism sites and selected locations in a few cities such as Cape Town. These are often high-end attractions with good infrastructure and safety and security measures, which include strict access control.

2.7   CRIME VICTIMIZATION AND TOURISM

In relation to crime specifically, most studies focus on victim surveys focusing on resident experiences. To the best of the author's knowledge, there are no studies that specifically focus on tourists who are victims. However, as indicated earlier, crime has significant impacts on the tourism industry. Furthermore, as Jones (2008) states, people on holiday are not only more likely to be victimized but are also routinely let down by the criminal justice system. Furthermore, she illustrates that the tourist can often be an offender (a particularly neglected aspect of crime and tourism research in South Africa given the almost exclusive focus on tourists as potential victims). She makes particular reference to the impact of alcohol on visitors, football hooligans, drug "mules," gamblers, and sex tourists. Thus, crime often exists to serve the demands of specific types of tourists. Nkosi's (2010) study on the impact of crime on tourism in Umhlathuze, KwaZulu-Natal focuses on ensuring the safety and security of tourists. The study neglects to consider that the tourists themselves could be offenders. The focus on crimes committed against tourists fails to unpack the range of issues linked to crime and tourism. Earlier studies show clear differences in crime, victimization for tourists and residents. Boakye (2011) illustrates that tourists are more vulnerable and are particularly prone to crime. Bernasco and Luykx (2003) illustrate that attractiveness, opportunity, and accessibility are key factors influencing crimes against property. Tourists, in particular, are vulnerable as they tend to frequent specific locations, are conspicuous and easily noticeable, are unfamiliar with the environment, may not know the local language and customs, and usually carry valuables such as cameras and cash. Steyn et al. (2009) specifically argue that there is the widespread acceptance of the fact that tourists run a higher than average risk of being victimized, and that there is an increase in terrorism directed specifically at tourists and resort areas. George (2003) indicates that three main types of crime are experienced by tourists: physical (such as property crimes, bodily harm, and sexual abuse), economic (such as arbitrary price increases, swindling, and fraud), or psychological (such as harassment and instilling fear). Swart et al. (2010) state that crime restricts and limits people's movement, options, and participation in activities and opportunities. In the South African context, George (2003, p. 583) states, "As research suggests, tourists have every reason to fear crime, as they are more susceptible to crime victimization than local residents in areas that have high crime rates." SAT (2007) indicates that fear of crime as well as safety feature of South Africa as a tourist destination in all international source markets (North America and Western Europe, in particular). The fear of crime significantly informs images of destinations and influences decisions potential tourists make.

2.8 CRIME AGAINST FOREIGNERS IN INDIA

A total of 7,679,099 foreigners (including 3,399,272 foreigners on tourist visa) visited India during 2014 as compared with 6,967,601 in 2013, showing an increase of 10.21%. Last 5 years' figures, as published in "Immigration Control and Measures in India—2014" by Central Foreigners Bureau, Bureau of Immigration, Ministry of Home Affairs, clearly indicate the rising trends in arrival of foreigners. Thus, it is imperative to study the safety and security of visiting foreigners. In this context, the Bureau has made an effort to analyze patterns of crime against foreigners, inter alia, and foreign tourists. The Bureau has started collecting data on crimes committed on forcigners including foreign tourists since 2014 under the revised performance of "Crime in India."

A total of 486 cases of crimes against foreigners were reported in the country of which 384 cases were under crime against foreign tourists during 2014, constituting 79.0% of total crime against foreigners. Among 486 cases of crime against foreigners, majority of cases were reported in Delhi (164 cases) followed by Goa (73 cases), Uttar Pradesh (66 cases), Maharashtra (59 cases), Rajasthan (36 cases), Karnataka (14 cases), and Bihar (13 cases); these eight states together accounted for 87.4% of total such cases reported in the country (425 out of 486 cases). Delhi has reported highest incidents of crime against foreign tourists accounting for 35.2% (135 out of 384 cases) followed by Goa (66 cases), Uttar Pradesh (64 cases), Rajasthan (31 cases), Maharashtra (25 cases), Bihar (13 cases), and Karnataka (11 cases), and these states accounted for 17.2, 16.7, 8.1, 6.5, 3.4, and 2.8% of such crimes, respectively during 2014. Among 486 cases of crime against foreigners, maximum cases were reported under thefts accounting for 53.5% (260 cases) followed by assault on foreign women with intent to outrage their modesty (39 cases), rape, robbery and cheating (22 cases each), and forgery (21 cases) during 2014. A total of 45 and 34 cases were of unclassified category "other Indian Penal Code (IPC) and other Special and Local Law (SLL) crimes," respectively. Most of the cases of theft (116 out of 260 cases), assault on women with intent to outrage her modesty (10 out of 39 cases), rape (8 out of 22 cases), and cheating (9 out of 22 cases) were reported in Delhi alone accounting for 44.6, 25.6, 36.4, and 40.9%, respectively of total such crimes reported in the country during 2014.

Under crime against foreign tourists, more than half of total cases were reported under theft (223 cases), which accounted for 58.1% followed by assault on foreign tourists women with intent to outrage her modesty (33 cases), robbery (21 cases), and rape, and cheating (17 cases each). A total of 28 and 26 cases were of unclassified category of other IPC and other SLL crimes, respectively. Out of 223 theft cases, maximum theft cases under crime against foreign tourists were reported in Delhi (97 cases), which accounted for 43.5% of total such crimes reported in the country followed by Goa (36 cases) and Uttar Pradesh (29 cases) during 2014. Maximum cases of assault on foreign tourists (women) with intent to outrage their modesty were reported in Delhi (nine cases) followed by Uttar Pradesh (six cases) and Kerala, and Goa (four cases each); these five states together accounted for 69.7% of total such cases reported in the country during 2014. Out of 17 rape cases against foreign tourists in the country, six cases in Delhi, three cases in Karnataka, two each cases Goa, Rajasthan, Tamil Nadu, and West Bengal were reported during 2014. Four cases of murder and three cases of insult to modesty of women under crime against foreign tourists were also reported during 2014. Three each cases of forgery in respect of foreign tourists were reported in Rajasthan and Delhi during 2014. Out of 21 cases of robbery of foreign tourists, eight and four cases of robbery were reported in Uttar Pradesh and Maharashtra, respectively during 2014.

2.9 VISITOR PERCEPTIONS IN RELATION TO CRIME AND SAFETY IN INDIA

Third World nations have generally been considered more dangerous than developed nations as travel destinations. However, a recent trend has emerged in which developed nations are listed among the places where travelers run a high risk of becoming criminally victimized. Theatrically, the experiences of visiting India, the ways of travel, the purposes of travel, times of going abroad, and days of staying, and so on, all affected tourists' familiarity and understanding toward India, and then affected the risk awareness as well (George, 2003). The survey (Lin et al., 2010) discovered that only the purpose of travel had the significant relation with perception of victim possibility. This study classified travel crime into violence crime, property crime, sexual crime, right violated crime, and harassment. According to the perception of international tourists, it is quite possible to be harassed, defrauded, and robbed in India. It also showed that international tourists have more experiences of being harassed, defrauded, and robbed. On the other hand, the victim's experiences of violence crime and sexual crime are comparatively less, and so is the perception of risk estimation. In fact, there are not many serious victim cases while traveling. Tourists' perception of all kinds of crime victims extremely matches their true victim experiences.

This study showed that two-thirds of tourists have experienced harassment in India. Half of them have been defrauded. The issues of harassment and fraud that happened to international tourists, not only affect the tour quality, but also threaten the image of the city, and even more, the prosperity of the whole tourism. Hence, the authority should take them seriously and seek out better solutions. As to the practical implications, harassment and unfaithful business dealings are continuing problems without easy solutions. In cooperation with associations of vendors, training programs can be instigated to encourage friendly behavior and to eliminate tourist's complaints. It was also discovered that tourists who have more interests in India would revisit in spite of high possibility of being crime victims. Meanwhile, they would not advise others not to visit even though there are safety problems in India. It is perceived that tourists' belief and attitudes are less affected by risk. For developing the tourist market, multiple art and abundant cultural heritage should be greatly focused on. Accordingly, the risk international tourists consider might be possibly left behind so as to give a boost to the tourism.

2.10 RELATIONSHIP BETWEEN TOURISM AND CRIME: AN ANALYSIS

The perspective of examining the relationship between tourism and crime can be traced back to the pioneering work of Jud (1975) and Pizam (1982).

The study conducted by Jude examined the relationship crime and tourism in 34 Mexican states and found that property-related offenses were more strongly related to tourism, whereas violent offenses were only marginally associated with it (Jude, 1975, p. 328). In fact, violence offenses were mostly connected to natives. Conversely, a nationwide survey conducted in the United States disproves the link between tourism and crime (Pizam, 1982). However, a cross-cultural study revealed that tourism was perceived to lead to an increase in organized crime (Pizam and Telisman-Kosuta 1989). A study conducted in Hawaii found that an increased number of tourists is directly proportional to increased levels of burglary and rape (Fujii and Mak, 1980). A similar kind of study was conducted in America, which has established a strong relationship between increases in tourist arrivals and expenditures in the Virgin Islands and property crime. According to this study, the growing tourism market itself is the reason for the growing victimization of the tourists turning to the Caribbean (De Albuquerque, 1981). Another study that has focused on the relative contribution of various modernizing influences, including tourism, on the increased incidence of crime. The findings were mixed but did suggest that crime rate against tourists is seasonal. It means the study found some increase in property-related offenses (including robbery) during the peak tourist season and declines in the off-season (McElroy, 1982; De Albuquerque, 1983).

However, broadly there exist two schools of thoughts on the relationship between crime and tourism. Some studies have established a direct link between the increase in number of crimes and the increase in tourists in the destination; the second considers that an increase in crime can be directly linked to the type of tourists found in the destination, as this typology is important in the categorization of tourist experience and security aspects. Studies have also tried to correlate the results with human ecology and sociology of the respective countries or states. Further, rapid growth, in other words, mass tourism itself is another factor that contributed the growth of victimization of tourists. There are also other important factors in the victimization of tourists, such as ethnicity, the choice of accommodation type, age, whether one is traveling alone or with others, gender, nationality, among others. It should also be noted that studies of the relationship between crime and tourism seasonality have concluded that crimes such as thefts, robberies, kidnappings, and murders increase dramatically during "high season" periods when compared with other times of the year.

Tourists were mostly victimized by two types of crimes, namely, organized or planned crimes (e.g., terrorism), opportunistic crimes, with or without violence and impersonal, against an unknown tourist. But it can be economic, psychological, or sexual intention. Tourism provides an interactive platform among different elements that include tourists, the place, local residents, and services in general. It can be understood from the literature that the increased incidents in victimization of tourists are in proportion to growth in tourism industry. But the opportunity for crime is not only concentrated especially in economic crimes (e.g., theft and fraud) but also crimes involving physical or sexual assault. This is mainly due to drastic cultural dissimilarities, ethnicity, the choice of accommodation type, age, whether one is traveling alone or with others, gender, and nationality.

2.11 CRIME PREVENTION STRATEGIES IN RELATION TO TOURISM

There are several theories and strategies developed to prevent and control the crime against tourists, but few strategies were operational in achieving the success. Some studies focus on examining situational crime prevention measures that build on Newman's theory of defensible space and Crime Prevention Through Environmental Design (CPTED). The concept of "defensible space" was first explicated by Oscar Newman in a 1972 book by the same title. The concept, which contains elements of a theory of crime as well as a set of urban design principles, became popular in the 1970s as urban crime problems continued to rise. Defensible space is a principle of crime prevention that has become embodied in current public policy through "Secured by Design," a scheme operated by the police providing advice to housing developers. Through enclavization, for instance, cul-de-sac layouts, the intention is to create exclusive living environments, which will precipitate territoriality and a sense of community in residents, resulting in collective action against crime (Steventon, 2010). The implication is that these reactions are invoked by design factors alone. This theory observes that locations can be "defended" and risks reduced by physical infrastructure as well as surveillance technology and measures (including visible policing). The other strategy CPTED coined by C. Ray Jeffery defined it as a multidisciplinary approach to deterring criminal behavior through environmental design. CPTED strategies rely upon the ability to influence offender decisions that precede criminal acts by affecting the built, social, and administrative environment (Essential feature of safer places Booklet, 2007). That is why this CPTED is viewed as an extended version of defensible space. Later, it was more extensively applied and consequently expanded the scope of the theory. The environment never influences behavior directly, but only through the brain. Any model of crime prevention must include both the brain and the physical environment. Because the approach contained in Jeffery's CPTED model is today based on many fields, including scientific knowledge of modern brain sciences, a focus on only external environmental crime prevention is inadequate as it ignores another entire dimension of Crime Prevention Through Environment (CPTE) …, that is, the internal environment (Robinson, 1996). By and large, this perspective has proved to be a successful approach in keeping major tourist destinations safe. The most successful example is the sense of safety experienced by the tourists during South Africa's hosting of the 2010 FIFA World Cup, the largest sports event to take place in the country and on the African continent. Although crime and safety issues were the key concerns in relation to South Africa's ability to host the World Cup and in terms of influencing tourist arrivals, these fears did not materialize. During the World Cup, security measures were increased significantly through visible policing and major event locations (stadium precincts, public viewing areas such as fan parks, transport hubs, and key tourist destinations) were manually kept under strict surveillance with controlled access. The success of the safety and security strategies implemented with the strategies adopted from CPTE during the World Cup played a major role in influencing the widespread positive media coverage that South Africa received during the World Cup.

2.12   WAY-OUT: THE CONCEPT OF RESPONSIBLE TOURISM

Effective policing is an essential platform to control crime in tourist places. In this context, responsible tourism has become a way-out for so many governments. The concept of responsible tourism was extensively discussed and defined in Cape Town in 2002 alongside the World Summit on Sustainable Development. The definition, proposed at the Cape Town Declaration, is now widely accepted and has been adopted by the World Travel Market in 2007 for celebrating World Responsible Tourism Day. Responsible Tourism is about "making better places for people to live in and better places for people to visit." Responsible Tourism obligates that operators, hoteliers, governments, local people, and tourists take responsibility, take action to make tourism more sustainable. This concept complies with the principles of *social and economic justice* and exerts full respect toward the *environment and its cultures.* It recognizes the *centrality of the local host community* and its right to act as a protagonist in developing a sustainable and responsible tourism. Responsible tourism actuates to foster a *positive interaction between* the tourist industry, the local communities, and the travelers (Italian Association for Responsible Tourism (aitr.org, 2005)). There are important stakeholders and factors involved in the process of achieving responsible tourism. The below given figure explains the working process of the concept (Figure 2.1).

FIGURE 2.1   Major stakeholders and factors in responsible tourism.
Source: AITR, 2005.

Key stakeholders and factors responsible for achieving the responsible tourism are environment, society, culture, and economy. First, it is very important for the local government to minimize that impact of tourists on the local social environment. The impact can be in terms of culture, self-respect, and identity. Adequate space needs to be given to the local people to play a central role in the touristic development in their respective territories. The involvement of the local community through a participatory democracy and in the decision-making process is essential for a sustainable touristic development. In this concept, local self-governments can play a predominant role. The other major concern would be culture. It is crucial to bring awareness to the tourists to respect the local culture by including its essence in the overall touristic development. Focusing on and creating an awareness of the local culture, its traditions, the lifestyle, the local gastronomy, the handcrafts, and so forth ensures mutual respect to each other through proper interaction between the tourist and local community. Socialist perspective may really help when it comes to economic spear. It is the responsibility of the state government to frame a proper policy to ensure equal distribution of economic benefits for the local population and its hosting territory.

2.13   EXPERIENCES OF VISIBLE POLICING

The idea of dedicated tourist police is not new. It has been experienced by different countries especially where the tourism industry was well-developed. Dedicated tourist police are specially trained to interact with the tourists, assist with directions, and are knowledgeable about the tourism products in a specific location. Many countries with a critical mass of tourism, especially in the developing world where the average person may not speak any English, often have separate "tourist police" forces. In every country we had been in, prior to Egypt, the essential functions of tourist police have been to act as English-speaking policemen for whatever visitors may need, to police tourist areas for additional security and peace of mind, to prevent tourists from interacting with "regular" police, who may not speak English or might be incompetent or corrupt, and so forth. Egyptian government has initiated this provision of establishing dedicated police services. The tourism and antiquities police covering every single spot tourist could go to like sites, museums, and hotels. In South Africa, police are also trained to interact with tourists in a positive manner.

Studies were also conducted to examine the impact of the working of dedicated police. Significantly, a study conducted in Ghana reveals that the presence of uniformed security made the majority of the tourists to feel uncomfortable and more fearful (Boakye, 2009). Therefore, it is important to ensure that police presence does not constantly remind tourists of crime. Moreover, training to be offered to police personnel needs be categorized into two. On one hand, police have to be trained on how to handle crimes against tourists and on the other hand, crimes committed by tourists. The latter one is relatively more challenging because it requires constant surveillance on the movement of tourist. Police services, infrastructure, and judicial processes need to be developed to deal with transient populations in line with policing in industrialized areas. Furthermore, it is also observed that a cyclic process of iterative innovation in which government seeks to solve narrowly circumscribed crime problems, and then leverages each success to generate wider hope and confidence in the criminal justice system (Stone, 2006). Furthermore, the merging of secure and safe environments with sports, leisure, and tourism spaces will provide a foundation in which both hard infrastructure (tourism support facilities) and softer issues (safety, security, and perceptions of crime) are important parts of the planning and developments (Donaldson and Ferreira, 2008). A key criterion in terms of rating destinations and establishments is the level of safety. Tourism certification is attracting significant interest within the industry because it has emerged as a mechanism for marketing and profiling, especially to the rapidly growing clientele base who are interested in supporting responsible tourism. Therefore, it provides potentially an effective mechanism for higher safety standards from the tourism industry (Spenceley, 2004).

The literature on crime and tourism tells that crime and violence can have a potential impact on development process because it is linked largely to high levels of poverty and distrust within society (Nkosi, 2010; Pillay, 2008; Stone, 2006). This implies that a long-term strategy cannot focus on tourism per se but must tackle the development challenges that countries face. This needs to be supported by effective policing and a criminal justice system that works. Economic factors, in terms of fair distribution of profit in tourism business between locals and entertainment business stakeholders, are critical issue to address. From the crime point-of-view, the growing problem of organized crime and corruption, which requires a different approach to that of poverty-related crimes needs to be controlled on a long-term basis. It is also important to have an international strategy as a significant number of key tourism-related criminal activities such as drug trafficking have cross-border partners in line with the concept of Interpol. These types of crime require international collaboration and resources. In this regard, political commitment at international plat for becomes significant. In addition, activities such as providing the necessary information for both tourists and residents to make informed decisions will work as preventive measures. This implies collecting and providing statistics on crime. Even countries such as India have begun to collect statistics relating to crime against tourists and crime committed by tourists. This requires more detailed research and a critical examination of existing data. Media and governments can play a predominant role in publicizing relevant safety and security information (including what to avoid, what to do if attacked, contact numbers, and information services, etc.).

2.14   TOPPS: A MODEL OF POLICING TOURIST CRIME

At present, numerous communities have established special police units to ensure the safety of tourists as part of strengthening the tourism industry. The widely debated police model is "TOPPs," which is an acronym standing for tourism-oriented policing or protection services. In Spanish, the word is often translated as "Seguridadturı́stica" or "politur" (a composite word of the two Spanish words policı́a and turismo). TOPPs units differentiate themselves from typical law enforcement by how they judge success. Classical police departments judge success by the number of crimes solved. The presence of TOPPS exists not only in the United States but also in much of the English-speaking countries. The tourism industry did practically nothing to change that fact. For example, prior to and for a time after 9/11, US police departments' involvement with tourism was minimal (Tarlow, 2001a). It was not uncommon for police departments to state that they took pride in the fact that they treated tourists just like anyone else. This preferential treatment is based on the argument that taxpaying citizens deserve relatively more security than anyone else. In some communities, there are special TOPPs units, whereas in other communities, the police department has embraced the TOPPs philosophy and has integrated this philosophy into its everyday policing. TOPPs radically challenge the standard paradigm of law enforcement. Below is a listing of some of the major TOPPs philosophical concepts that TOPPs uses to challenge the existing paradigm. Tourism security is part of the entire tourism system, and a failure in security can cause system shut down or collapse. This principle is a fundamental concept of TOPPs. In addition, the TOPPs ideal challenges the notion that security is a "needed headache" that must be kept to a minimum. Another principle, that is, customer service and good security are part of the same tourism system and without them, tourism often withers. Tourism security encompasses a far greater role than classical law enforcement.

Performance measurements were also radically different from the traditional policing in which emphasis is not on the number of crimes solved but rather on the number of crimes prevented. In this way, the philosophy is more proactive rather than reactive. This philosophy seriously questions statistical orientation of traditional policing. The approach of TOPPs' draws a line between tourism safety and tourism crime. That means a tourism safety unit is far superior to a tourism crime unit. The former name implies a proactive policy of crime prevention whereas the latter indicated the seeking to solve crimes that have occurred. The management of TOPPs evaluates the performance by measuring police personnel's successes in "nonevents" rather than events. Sometimes, the terms may vary from country to country. In India, the same terms are called as sovereign and nonsovereign tasks. Government and tourism officials and many police officials look at the concept of security with a traditional approach, that is, security as an unwanted but necessary expense (Tarlow, 2001b). This approach is very much similar to the approach of liberals toward the concept of democracy which they call as a necessary evil. The prevailing opinion was that "security added nothing to the bottom line." The TOPPs philosophy reverses this assumption and sees security as an important post 9/11 marketing tool. Those who embrace the TOPPs philosophy argue that if used properly, security (TOPPs) adds to a community or an attraction's bottom line.

At the same time, there exists criticism on the approach of the TOPPs. For example, the differences of perspective of criminals cannot be tackled in an unformed way. Terrorists may see tourism areas as an ideal opportunity to create economic instability by creating terror among the business class. On the contrary, terrorists and criminals often do not wish to destroy a tourism locale; instead, they view that locale as an ideal "fishing" ground to harvest an abundance of riches. A philosophical question, yet to be resolved is, do law enforcement agents and tourism security professionals have a special role in protecting the economic viability of a locale so as to provide tourism with extra levels of protection? Reputation protection is a prime requisite for the tourism industry. It is an undeniable fact that crimes and acts of terrorism against tourism entities receive a great deal of media attention. For example, the Natalie Holloway case in Aruba in 2005 cost the island not only millions of dollars in lost tourism revenue but also prestige and reputation. The security lapse in tourism industry effects on long-term basis. Thus, the philosophy of TOPPs needs to be tuned according to the socio, economic, and ecological requirements of the respective tourist places.

2.15 CONCLUSION

The apprehension over the nexus between tourism and crime has emerged as a global issue, gaining prominence in the media and political debates. But, it is yet to be realized in Third World including India. Exploring the issues pertaining to crime and tourism is important as effective crime prevention and changing negative perceptions can contribute significantly to economic growth by promoting investments and tourism. Discussing as part of the literature on operation meaning and concepts on policing and different models relating to the security of tourist areas, it is apparent that there is no commonly acceptable standard terminology available to describe the policing in tourism. However, the usage of terms was broadly determined by the approaches adopted by various police systems across the countries. Positive policing, entertainment policing, and tourism-oriented policing can be referred as few examples. Sometimes, terms were chosen due to the place where the act of policing is being done. Therefore, it is called as entertainment policing or tourist policing. In the Indian context, the government needs to adopt the concept of responsible tourism.

In this regard, TOPPs can be the right choice to curtail the growing violence against foreign tourists as it helps the police to identify the tourist-specific security problems and train the police staff to handle challenges accordingly. Further, techniques of problem-oriented policing become more relevant to identify the problems but to address them, community-oriented policing needs to be adopted as a philosophy of policing. In addition, the government of India needs to ensure that the cultural identity of the foreigners is preserved during their visit. This approach of preserving the identity of foreigners enhances their sense of safety and security. The comments by the Union Cultural Minister of India on suggesting dress code for female tourists send wrong signals to the foreign visitors in general and female tourists in specific. This, in fact, creates insecurity among female tourists. Instead, the government needs to initiate a national policy on tourist security and establish dedicated police personnel to face the tourist-specific challenges. But materializing this idea is subject to state governments' cooperation. However, significantly, some state governments have already introduced a dedicated police staff to take care of tourist-specific challenges. This clearly indicates that there is a growing need for center–state collaboration. But in India, the successive governments and academics treated law and order and security-related issues as unproductive. This perception is the root cause of the underdevelopment status of security studies in the development discourse in general and tourism studies in specific. Hence, it is high time to establish that policing is the platform for economic development and productivity. Further, studies have to explore the correlation between the economic and security significance of tourism and its supposed positive role in the national and regional development were, perhaps, the first areas to be explored. This may result in identifying new avenues in security and tourism studies.

KEYWORDS

- **tourist-oriented policing**
- **crime**
- **safety**
- **security**
- **India**

REFERENCES

Albuquerque, K.; McElroy, J. Tourism and Crime in the Caribbean. *Ann. Tourism Res.* **1999,** *26*(4), 966–984.

Allen, L. R.; Long, P. T.; Perdue, R. R.; Kieselbach, S. The Impact of Tourism Development on Residents' Perceptions of Community Life. *J. Travel Res.* **1988,** *27*(1), 16–21.

Bernasco, W.; Luykx, F. Effects of Attractiveness, Opportunity and Accessibility to Burglars on Residential Burglary Rates of Urban Neighbourhoods. *Criminology* **2003,** *41,* 981–1001.

Biagi, B.; Detotto, C. Crime as Tourism Externality. *Reg. Stud.* **2014,** *48*(4), 693–709.

Biagi, B.; Giovanna, M.; Detotto, C. The Effect of Tourism on Crime in Italy: A Dynamic Panel Approach. *Economics* **2012,** 26. [Open Access Journal].

Biagi, E.; Candela, M.; Turroni, S.; Garagnani, P.; Franceschi, C.; Brigidi, P. Ageing and Gut Microbes: Perspectives for Health Maintenance and Longevity. *Pharmacol. Res.* **2013,** *69,* 11–20.

Blau, J. R.; Blau, P. M. The Cost of Inequality: Metropolitan Structure and Violent Crime. *Am. Sociol. Rev.* **1982a,** *47,* 45–62.

Blau, J. R.; Blau, P. M. The Cost of Inequality: Metropolitan Structure and Violent Crime. *Am. Sociol. Rev.* **1982b,** 47(1), 114–129.

Bloom, J. A South African Perspective of the Effects of Crime and Violence on the Tourism Industry. In *Tourism, Crime, and International Security Issues;* Pizam, A., Mansfield, Y., Eds.; John Wiley and Sons: Chichester, 1996; pp 91–102.

Boakye, K. A. Tourists' Views on Safety and Vulnerability: A Study of Some Selected Towns in Ghana. *Tourism Manage.* **2011** [as Cited in Edwin C. Perry and Cheryl Potgieter. Crime and Tourism in South Africa. *J. Hum. Ecol.* **2013,** *43*(1), 101–111].

Brunt, P.; Hambly, Z. Tourism and Crime: A Research Agenda. *Crime Prev. Community Saf. Int. J.* **1999,** *1*(2), 25–36.

Brunt, P.; Mawby, R.; Hambly, A. Tourist Victimization and the Fear of Crime on Holiday. *Tourism Manage.* **1999,** *21*(4), pp 417–424.

Brunt, P.; Mawby, R.; Hambly, Z. Tourist Victimization and the Fear of Crime on Holiday. *Tourism Manage.* **2000,** *21,* 417–424.

Cage, K. *Focus on Tourism;* Maskew-Miller Longman Publishers: Cape Town, 2002.

Campaniello, N. Mega Events in Sports and Crime: Evidence from the 1990 Football World Cup. *J. Sport Econo.* 2011. http://www.academia.edu/394292/ Mega_Events_in_Sports_and_Crime_Evidence_from_the_1990_Football_World_Cup.

Choy, D.; Gee, C.; Makens, J. *The Travel Industry;* 2nd ed.; Van Nostrand-Reinhold: New York, NY, 1989.

Crotts, J. C. Theoretical Perspectives on Tourist Criminal Victimisation. *J. Tourism Stud.* **1996,** *7,* 1–8.

Cyprus Gazette. *Cyprus Official Government Gazette, Issue 4278, App. 1, Part II;* Cyprus Government Printing Office: Nicosia, 2015.

Davis, D.; Allen, J.; Consenza, R. M. Segmenting Local Residents by Their Attitudes, Interests and Opinions Toward Tourism. *J. Travel Res.* **1988,** *27*(2), 2–8.

De Albuquerque, K. *Tourism and Crime in the Caribbean: Some Lessons from the United States Virgin Islands.* Paper presented at the Third Annual Meeting of the Association of Caribbean Studies, Port-au-Prince, Haiti, 1981.

De Albuquerque, K. *Tourism and Crime in the Caribbean: Some Lessons from the United States Virgin Islands.* Paper presented at the Third Annual Meeting of the Association of Caribbean Studies, Port-au-Prince, Haiti, 1983.

Donaldson, R.; Ferreira, S. Perceptions of International Visitors to South Africa on Safety and Security: Implications for the 2010 FIFA World Cup. Report Prepared for Cape Town Routes Unlimited, Cape Town, 2008.

Ferreira, S.; Harmse, A. Crime and Tourism in South Africa: International Tourists' Perception and Risk. *S. Afr. Geogr. J.* **2000,** *82*(2), 80–85.

Foster, D. *Travel and Tourism Management;* MacMillan: London, 1985.

Fujii, E. T.; Mak, J. Tourism and Crime: Implications for Regional Development Policy. Reg. Stud. **1980,** *14,* pp 27–36.

George, R. Tourist's Perceptions of Safety and Security While Visiting Cape Town. *Tourism Manage.* 2003, *24,* 575–585.

George, R Visitor Perceptions of Crime-Safety and Attitudes Towards Risk: The Case of Table Mountain National Park, Cape Town. *Tourism Manage.* **2010,** *31,* 806–815.

George, R.; Rivett-Carnac, K. *Oxford Successful Tourism.* Oxford University Press Southern Africa: Cape Town, 2005.

Goeldner, C. R.; Brent Ritchie, J. R. *Tourism: Principles, Practices. Philosophies;* John Wiley & Sons: New Jersey, 2006.

Halloway, J. *The Business of Tourism;* 5th ed.; Longman: Harlow UK. 1998; p 36.

Inskeep, E. *Tourism Planning an Integrated and Sustainable Development Approach;* Van Nostrand Reinhold: London, 1991

Jones, C. *Tourism and Crime, Whose Problem? A Cornish Perspective.* Ph.D. Thesis, Unpublished. Plymouth: University of Plymouth, 2008.

Jud, D. G. Tourism and Crime in Mexico. *Soc. Sci. Q.* **1975,** *56*(2), 324–330.

Kokkinos, M.; Kapardis, A. Disaggregating Tourists in Cyprus by Money Spent and Criminal Offending. *J. Tourism Res.* **2012,** *11,* 61–70. http://jotr.eu/index.php/tourism-management (accessed June 22, 2016).

Lin, R.-J.; Chen, R.-H.; Chiu, K. K.-S. Customer Relationship Management and Innovation Capability: An Empirical Study. *Ind. Manage. Data Syst.* **2010,** *110*(1), 111–133.

Martínez, R.; Jr, Rosenfeld, R.; Mares, D. Social Disorganization, Drug Market Activity, and Neighborhood Violent Crime. *Urban Aff. Rev. Thousand Oaks, Calif* **2008,** *43*(6), 846–874.

Mawby, R. I. Tourists' Perceptions of Security: The Risk-Fear Paradox. *Tourism Econ.* **2000,** *6*(2), 109–121.

Mawby, R. I.; Brunt, P.; Hambly, Z. Fear of Crime Among British Holidaymakers. *Br. J. Criminol.* **2000,** *40*(3), 468–479.

McElroy, J. C. Attribution Theory: A Leadership Theory for Leaders. *Leadership Organ. Dev. J.* **1982,** *3*(4), 27–30.

McPheters, L. R.; Stronge, W. B. Crime as an Environmental Externality of Tourism: Miami, Florida. *Land Econ.* **1974,** *50,* 288–292.

Merriam-Webster's Collegiate Dictionary. Merriam-Webster Publishers, 1993; p 1248.

Nkosi, G. S. The Impact of Crime on Tourism in the City of u Mhlathuze, KwaZulu-Natal. *South Asian J. Tourism and Heritage Stud.* **2010,** *3*(2), 76–81.

Ntuli, T. G.; Potgieter, P. J. Exploring the Impact of Crime on Tourism in St Lucia. *Acta Criminol.* **2001,** *14*(1), 60–70.

Ochrym, R. G. Street Crime, Tourism and Casinos: An Empirical Evaluation. *J. Gambling Stud.* **1990,** *6*(2), 127–138.

Pattison, D. Preface. In *The Tourism System: An Introductory Text;* Mill, R. C., Morrison, A., Eds.; Prentice Hall: Upper Saddle River, NJ, 1985; p xvi.

Perry, E. C.; Potgieter, C. Crime and Tourism in South Africa? *J. Hum. Ecol.* **2013,** *43*(1), 101–111.

Pillay, S Crime, Community and the Governance of Violence in Post-Apartheid South Africa. *Politikon* **2008,** *35*(2), 141–158.

Pizam, A. Tourism and Crime: Is There a Relationship? *J. Travel Res.* **1982,** *20*, 7–10.

Pizam, A.; Telisman-Kosuta, N. Tourism as a Factor of Change: Results and Analysis. In *Tourism as a Factor of Change: A Socio-Cultural Study;* Bytstrzanowski, J., Ed.; Vienna Centre: Vienna, 1989; pp 60–63.

Robinson, S. L. Trust and Breach of the Psychological Contract. *Administrative Sci. Q.* **1996,** *41*(4), 574–599

Ryan, C.; Kinde, R. The Deviant Tourist and the Crimogenic Place—The Case of the Tourist and the New Zealand Prostitute. In *Tourism, Crime and International Security Issues;* Pizam, A., Mansfield, Y., Eds.; Wiley: New York, 1996; pp 23–36.

Schiebler, S. A.; Crotts, J. C.; Hollings, R. Florida Tourists' Vulnerability to Crime. In *Tourism, Crime and International Security Issues;* Pizam, A., Mansfield, Y., Eds.; Wiley: New York, 1996; pp 37–49.

Shaw, C. R.; McKay, H. D. *Juvenile Delinquency and Urban Areas;* The University of Chicago Press: Chicago, 1942.

Siegel, L. J. *Criminology the Core,* 2nd ed; Thomson: Boston, USA, 2005.

South African Tourism. State of Tourism Report, Department of Tourism, Republic of South Africa, 2010, pp 1–39.

South African Police Service. *Annual Crime Statistics for 2009/10.* Commission of South African Police Services: Pretoria, 2010a.

South African Police Service. State of Security for the FIFA World Cup. Address by the National Commissioner of the SAPS General Bheki Cele to the National Press Club on the Sheraton Hotel-Pretoria, 2010b.

Spenceley, A. *Tourism Certification in Africa: Marketing, Incentives and Monitoring;* A Report to the International Eco-Tourism Society. Transboundary Protected Areas Research Initiative: Witwatersrand, 2004.

Steventon, G. Defensible Space: A Critical Review of the Theory and Practice of a Crime Prevention Strategy. *Urban Des. Int.* **2010,** *1*(3), 235–245.

Steyn, J.; De Beer, M.; Fouché, H. In Anticipation of the 2010 Soccer World Cup in South Africa: Occurrence of Street Robberies on Durban's 'Golden Mile'. *Acta Criminol.* **2009,** *22*(3), 98–117.

Stone, C. Crime, Justice, and Growth in South Africa: Toward a Plausible Contribution from Criminal Justice to Economic Growth. Centre for International Development at Harvard University. Harvard University: Boston, 2006; Working Paper No.131.

Swart, R. J.; Biesbroek, G. R.; Carter, T. R.; Cowan, C.; Henrichs, T.; Mela, H.; Morecroft, M. D.; Rey, D. Europe Adapts to Climate Change: Comparing National Adaptation Strategies. *Global Environ. Change* **2010,** *20*(3), 440–450.

Tarlow, P. E. Tourism Safety and Security. In *The SAGE Handbook of Tourism Studies;* Jamal, T., Robinson, M., Eds.; Sage: Los Angeles, CA, 2001a; p 466.

Tarlow, P. E. Tourism Oriented Policing and the Tourism Industry. *Int. J. Event Manage. Res.* Special Edition: Risk Management, **2001b,** *VIII*(1), 1–18.

Van Tran, X.; Bridges, F. S. Tourism and Crime in European nations. *e-Rev. Tourism Res. (eRTR).* **2009,** *7*(3).

Weaver, D.; Lawton, L. *Sustainable Tourism: Theory and Practice,* 3rd ed.; John Wiley & Sons: New York, 2006.

Working Paper No. 131. Boston: Harvard University.

CHAPTER 3

VISITOR MANAGEMENT AND COMMUNITY PARTICIPATION IN AN ECOTOURISM DESTINATION: THE CASE OF KANHA TIGER RESERVE, MADHYA PRADESH, INDIA

ANU CHANDRAN

Department of Tourism Studies, Pondicherry University, Pondicherry, India

CONTENTS

ABSTRACT

Ecotourism has emerged as an ideal and alternative option to protect wildlife sanctuaries and national parks. In the modern day, ecotourism offerings focus on providing exciting wilderness experiences to nature enthusiasts, bird watchers, wildlife photographers, ecotourists, and so on. The fruitful implementation of ecotourism projects and propositions depends on a great deal on the conservation of forests and wildlife in the protected areas. Madhya Pradesh, a renowned tourism haven acclaimed as *The Heart of Incredible India,* is a forefront runner in the setting up of ecotourism projects with the profound involvement of Ecodevelopment Committees. With ecologically sound and conservation-oriented initiatives, Madhya Pradesh aims to conserve the natural resources through ecotourism practices and achieve sustainable forest management. The management of Kanha Tiger Reserve (KTR) has recognized ecotourism as a significant means for the generation of revenue and also job creation for the local communities. It has been realized that ecotourism is immensely contributing to the socio-economic development of the areas. In this backdrop, this work attempts to study two important constructs, *visitor management* and *community participation*, for sustainable ecotourism. This chapter is driven by visitors as an integral part of ecotourism projects and their presence and productive involvement can make the projects more sustainable. Furthermore, community empowerment and initiatives in KTR shall reinforce sustainable ecotourism in the protected area. Although visitor management by the park managers will lead to maintenance of carrying capacity, community participation is bound to result in both resource protection and promotion of wildlife tourism. This chapter brings to light the challenges pertaining to sustainable ecotourism and also analyzes the impact of tourism that is an unregulated influx of tourists. The prospects and potentials of wildlife tourism in KTR were also examined with the imperatives and implications of visitor management.

3.1 INTRODUCTION

Globally, low-impact ecotourism has become central to all tourism ventures in botanical gardens, biological parks, bird sanctuaries, hills, beaches, national parks, and wildlife sanctuaries. The adverse impacts and ill effects of mass tourism activities are mitigated by judicious implementation of ecotourism projects. Ecotourism has set the paradigm for conserving the ecology and environment through the proactive participation of local communities. The signature aspect of ecotourism is that it motivates tourists to help protect the nature and culture of destinations. Some of the famous ecotourism destinations of the world are Brazil, Rwanda, Australia, Costa Rica, Bolivia, Galapagos Islands, and South Africa. The Oslo Declaration of Ecotourism has made the efforts through public and private organizations at the international and national levels to reinforce the commitments toward implementing the principles and following religiously the practices of sustainable tourism at the ecotourism sites. Ecotourism is a responsible form of tourism which helps tourists to be in sync with nature. It holds the key to sustainable development of destination ecology. Wildlife tourism is a stark offshoot of ecotourism which enables tourists to observe, view, and have exciting encounters with faunal species in a natural setting. Wildlife tourism has set the ball rolling for lots of conservation projects and volunteerism programs. The imperatives of wildlife tourism mound its offerings as part of soft tourism that entails a reduced impact on the environment. Wildlife tourism is not only highly purposeful but also eco-friendly and sustainable in character. The Kanha Tiger Reserve (KTR) in Madhya Pradesh is home to some fabulous tourist spots and hence warrants a community-driven, low-impact ecotourism, which will be an add-on to maintain the integrity of its fragile resources. Madhya Pradesh (MP) Tourism Department underscores the importance of furthering the positive impacts of ecotourism to synergize conservation, communities, and sustainable development programs. It goes without saying that ecotourism in premier tourism centers such as KTR, possessing invaluable flora and fauna can maintain the pristine and endearing ambiance and vibes by adopting ecotourism practices, which also fosters a great deal to build environmental awareness among the tourists, local communities, and other stakeholders. MP Tourism Department and Madhya Pradesh Tourism Development Corporation have mapped the progress the sector brings to host communities by providing direct financial benefits.

Ecotourism initiatives in KTR support human rights and eliminate poaching, hunting, deforestation, construction works, and other adverse impacts. Ecotourism in KTR has in the past decade or so enhanced the standards of living of the local population. "Real" ecotourists who respect the integrity of the vulnerable eco-resources and who do not compromise on the ethical responsibilities are of late visiting KTR. Yet, innovative approaches are much desired with regard to ecotourism marketing. The target markets need to configure educated, environmentally conscious tourists explorative on flora and fauna, preferring interaction and cultural learning, seeking mental and physical challenges, and evincing interest in intimate involvement with the lifestyles, customs, and practices of the traditional communities and indigenous folks in the centers of their visits.

Attempts must be made to clarify the nature of ecotourism in KTR for the products and activities to gain an advantageous position in the minds of prospective tourists. The main concern for the destination designers and park managers will be charting the ways and means of providing ecologically sound and friendly tourism with the ideal management of landscapes and sites in which it has taken off. It is an unvarnished fact that ecotourism can act as a powerful and meaningful tool in ecological and environmental conservation and experiential tourism in KTR if the four goals of tourism planning, namely, enhanced visitor satisfaction, better business models, sustainable eco-cultural resource use, and community integration are attained. This study reiterates the significance of sensible tourism in an ecologically fragile protected area such as KTR by distinguishing the wider and deeper implications of visitor management strategies and multidimensional perspectives of community participation. Albeit, the proliferation of ecotourism propositions should not eventually turn up to be causative factors for environmental and social stress amongst host population.

3.2 OBJECTIVES OF THE STUDY

This work has been undertaken with the broad objective of unraveling the mechanisms by which KTR attains the goal of better visitor management and ascertain how the communities can play vital roles in employing a conservation ethic to the natural resources and ecosystems in the protected area. This chapter addresses the certain specific objectives. One of them is to highlight the prospects and attributes of ecotourism in KTR and thereby to analyze the approaches and measures with regard to visitor management in the park. It is crucial also to examine the forms and extent of community involvement in both resource protection and ecotourism practices.

3.3 SCOPE OF THE STUDY

The scope of this work envelops the ecotourism projects in one of the beaming national parks of the country—the KTR, located in a top-notch tourism destination—Madhya Pradesh, focusing on the visitor management agenda devised by the park managers in mitigating the negative impacts of tourism as well as the dynamics of community involvement in resource protection. This study moots some enlightening perspectives of visitor management and community participation, which can control the deterioration of the environment and natural resources in KTR due to unplanned and uncontrolled activities. The current work also sounds the alarm bell for the Government machinery and public sector undertakings to strengthen their political willpower and induces them to enact measures through good governance toward the ethical advancement of sociocultural and environmental dimensions of KTR.

3.4 REVIEW OF LITERATURE

Contemplating through the literature, there are four integral thematic reflections on the ecotourism paradigms, namely: visitor satisfaction, community participation, responsible tourism (RT), and community empowerment.

3.4.1 VISITOR SATISFACTION

The term *visitor* means a person visiting someone or somewhere socially or as a tourist. *Satisfaction* is defined as fulfillment of one's wishes, expectations, or needs or the pleasure derived from this. The visitor is also defined as any person traveling to a place other than of his/her usual environment for less than 12 following months and whose main purpose of travel is not to work for pay in the place visited. Visitor satisfaction is one of the most frequently examined topics in the hospitality and tourism field as it plays an important role in the survival and future of any tourism products and services (Gursoy, et al., 2007). According to Backman, et al. (2000), nature-based tourism attraction satisfaction is measured using dimensions such as programmatic, responsiveness, tangible, empathy, assurance, and reliability. Ballantyne et al. (2011) studied on visitor memories at one of the four marine-based wildlife tourism venues at Southeast Queensland. Visitor memories of wildlife tourism are classified into four levels of visitor response with regard to wildlife experience (Kozak and Rimmington, 2000). Finally, the level of satisfaction attained by an individual may influence their future intentions, in terms of revisiting a destination and/or recommending it to other people.

3.4.2 COMMUNITY PARTICIPATION

According to Godfrey and Clarke (2000), "communities form a basic element in modern tourism as they are ... the focal point for the supply of accommodation, catering, information, transport facilities, and services. Their local natural environment, buildings and institutions, their people, culture and history, all constitute core elements of what the tourists come to see; whether as towns, villages or cities, every community has tourism at one level or the other and are affected by the growth and development of the industry (p. 3)."

On the other hand, Scherl and Edwards (2007) describe local communities as "... groups of people with a common identity and who may be involved in an array of related aspects of livelihoods. They further note that local communities often have customary rights related to the area and its natural resources and a strong relationship with the area culturally, socially, economically and spiritually."

3.4.3 RESPONSIBLE TOURISM

RT emerged in the 1980s and in terms of interpretation and application in tourism is well-conveyed by the following: "Responsible tourism is not a tourism product or brand. It represents a way of doing tourism planning, policy and development to ensure that benefits are optimally distributed among impacted populations, governments, tourists, and investors" (Husbands and Harrison, 1996, p. 1; cited in Scheyvens, 2002, p. 186). The concept of RT was developed as a result of evaluating some of the potential problems connected with tourism such as the environmental, economic, and social impact it has on destinations (Nash, 2001; Pieroni, 2003; Barretto, 2007; Goodwin, 2009; Rivera-Mateos and Rodriguez-Garcia,

2012; Leslie, 2012). RT is about providing better holiday experience for the guest and good business opportunities to enjoy a better quality of life through increased socioeconomic benefits and improved natural resource management (Spenceley et al., 2002). Among the core values of RT found in the Cape Town Declaration are commitments to mutual respect, diversity, transparency, sustainability, and quality (Cape Town Declaration, 2002). These values need to be evidenced in any RT-reporting process for progress to continue and for the approach to be valued in making "better places for people to live in and better place for people to visit." Since the United Nations adopted the Millennium Development Goals in 2000, tourism has been recognized as one of the key factors toward poverty alleviation, gender equality, environmental sustainability, and the empowerment of marginalized communities with particular emphasis on building and strengthening human capital through tourism education and training (Moscardo, 2008; Novelli and Hellwig, 2011; Saarinen et al., 2011; Spenceley, 2008; Sofield, 2003; UNWTO, 2006).

3.4.4   COMMUNITY EMPOWERMENT

Community empowerment refers to the process of enabling communities to increase control over their lives. "Communities" are groups of people that may or may not be spatially connected, but who share common interests, concerns, or identities. There are basically four types of empowerment; they are economic empowerment, psychological empowerment, social empowerment, and political empowerment.

3.5   RESEARCH DESIGN

3.5.1   DATA COLLECTION

Both primary and secondary data were gathered to derive inferences on the four themes framed for the operational convenience of the study and also for arriving at lucid and comprehensive outputs, that are "visitor management," "community participation," "ecotourism," and "sustainable development paradigm" in the KTR. Primary data were collected through personal interviews with park managers and forest officials and focus group interviews with the local communities. Secondary data were collected from dossiers and reports of consultants, tourism promotional literature, indigenous manuscripts and materials, and notes of visitors, tourists' blogs, and travelogues.

3.5.2   DATA ANALYSIS

The data have been codified under the four themes mentioned above as part of the thematic and content analysis and described in detail under various headings. A conceptual model has also been formulated on the basis of the structuring of insights obtained from the fieldwork.

3.6   KANHA TIGER RESERVE (KTR)—A KALEIDOSCOPIC VIEW

One of the biggest and enamoring national parks and tiger reserves in India, Kanha is spread over Mandla and Balaghat districts of Madhya Pradesh. A paradise for wildlife enthusiasts and nature lovers, the faunal species have fascinating dwellings in a natural habitat at the KTR. Kanha is reputed worldwide for its anthropological and natural attributes. Kanha possesses a distinct image as a serene and dotting sanctuary for exotic flora and fauna that are well maintained. The lush sal, beaming bamboo forests, gorgeous grassy meadows, and riveting ravines of Kanha inspired the noted author Rudyard Kipling to pen his famous novel *Jungle Book*. KTR dots a significant position among the ecotourism sites of Madhya Pradesh owing to its exquisite natural and cultural attractions. The idyllic and majestic topography encompasses plateaus, meadows, and valleys. Sulkum, Nila, Banjar, and Hallon are the roaring rivers of Kanha that water the sparkling floral species on the banks. Regarded as a meticulously managed national park in Asia, scores of tourists throng Kanha throughout the year though the peak season to visit is during the months from October to March. Kanha is divided into six ranges for appropriate maintenance, namely, Kisli, Kanha, Sarhi, and Mukki in the western block and Bhaisanghat and Supkhar in the eastern sector. The Reserve's total area is 1945 km² which consists of a core area of 940 km². Surrounded by the buffer zone of 1005 km², there are about 155 villages in the buffer zone and about 255 villages within the radius of 10 km. The entire core zone is a reserved forest with three subdivisions and six forest ranges. Kanha receives an average annual rainfall of approximately 1600 mm. The forest lands of Kanha are inhabited by two aboriginal tribes—the Gonds and the Baigas. The Kanha National Park has bagged several prestigious awards instituted by Department of Tourism, Govt. of India. In 2000, Kanha was awarded as the best tourism-friendly national park. In the 1990s, several initiatives commenced with a view to enhancing the features of the KTR including the park's biodiversity and expansion of tourist infrastructure.

The buoyant tiger is the keystone species of Kanha. Other notable species in the park comprise swamp deer, wildcat, fox, jackal, and leopards. Many species of turtles are also spotted in and around the park.

3.7 THE FACETS OF ECOTOURISM IN KTR

KTR is abundantly blessed by nature and therefore it is not a wonder that Kanha has emerged as a reputed ecotourism site in India. The park is managed efficiently, and the carrying capacity is maintained diligently. The rates and timings are well chalked out. The number of vehicles allowed to enter the national park in each shift is regulated. The safari activities are also well planned without disturbing the faunal species. The Field Director is entrusted with the responsibility of planning ecotourism programs in the park. This is performed in consultation with the field staff and officers of the core and buffer divisions and the proposals are submitted to the Principal Chief Conservator of Forests and Member Secretary, National Tiger Conservation Authority (NTCA), New Delhi through the Principal Chief Conservator of Forests, Bhopal. There is also an office of the Deputy Director (Buffer) under the management of KTR. Ecotourism is conducted in 20% of the total area under four zones, namely, Kanha, Kisli, Mukki, and Sarhi zones. To enter the Kanha zone, safari tourists have to pay extra fees as it is a sensitive area in the middle of the core area. The roads of KTR are opened and closed as per the park management policy and requirements. During mating seasons and other crucial times, the entry is restricted. Numerous checks are in place to offset the negative impacts on the fragile ecosystem and biodiversity of KTR. A Local Advisory Committee has been constituted for the KTR to discharge functions pertaining to ecotourism in tandem with the Madhya Pradesh Tiger Foundation Society. The authorities have determined the physical, real, effective, and permissible levels of carrying capacity. As per the NTCA guidelines, the park management has started ecotourism activities in the buffer zone. As part of the activities, the traditional knowledge and ethnographic attributes of the local communities are tapped effectively. The zoning system enables the park managers to maintain low-impact tourism throughout the season. Vehicles plying for safaris are advised to maintain a certain distance from animals. Luring or feeding wild animals is prohibited. The presence of authorized guides inside the safari vehicles is mandatory. There are well-equipped visitor facility centers in the ecotourism zones. The reserve management is engaging mobile forest guards selected from local communities. The Ecologically sensitive areas are properly monitored. Self-guided nature trails are offered in the park. Signages are required for proper visitor management. A nature museum will definitely entice the visitors. The *machans* offer a panoramic view of the exotic wildness to the tourists. In Khatia and Khapa ranges, jungle trails are arranged avoiding vehicles.

3.7.1 PERSPECTIVES OF VISITOR MANAGEMENT— INFERENCES AND RECOMMENDATIONS

It has been observed during the field visits to KTR that experiential ecotourism has become a major trend in the park. Ecotourism has built an influential market base in KTR due to the commendable efforts of the stakeholders, and it woos visitors committed to a green economy. Special interest ecotours are offered to tourists.

Smart growth strategies are proposed in the ecotourism zones of KTR to arrest uncontrolled growth. Park managers can dish out a permit system to control the visitors' numbers. Live history interpretation of the ecological aspects in indigenous zones by qualified people will be much appreciated by the visitors. Based on the extent of the fragility of the ecosystem in KTR, the areas can be delineated and earmarked for tourism as minor or controlled access, greater visitor use, planned use (camping, trails, etc.), intensive use areas, and others. Supplementary accommodation such as ecolodges would enhance tourists' experiences. They use renewable energy, reduce waste, grow organic gardens, and avoid destruction of native vegetation. Tour companies can initiate CSR programs such as the adoption of tourist spots, fauna, and so on. Such efforts will stabilize resource protection. Mechanisms for visitor management strategies by assessing and examining the scientific knowledge of visitor impact ensure sound development of ecotourism in KTR. Without proper evaluation and monitoring of ecotourism ventures, there will not be sustainable and equitable development. KTR should not expose its ecotourism sites to excessive tourists' footfalls. Overconsumption will deteriorate the quality of the destination in the long run. It is detrimental to the progress of ecotourism.

Now, there are positive checks in place to regulate visitor traffic inside the park which is, of course, a good practice. Visitor movement inside the park is also supervised. Trampling which flattens the vital vegetative covers has been avoided. Special ecomuseums, bullock cart rides, home stays, herbal gardens, ethnic cultural shows, souvenir outlets, ethnic bio food outlets, night safari, elephant kraals, and so on can be incepted in the park for better visitor experience. The opening of wild safari at Khatia will go a long way in managing tourists pressure, especially during the peak season/rush hours.

3.7.2 PERSPECTIVES OF COMMUNITY MANAGEMENT— INFERENCES AND RECOMMENDATIONS

The local communities are being part of solid waste management, sewage treatment, and pollution control mechanisms, which can be improved a lot by the progression of their ecological awareness through ecotourism capacity building programs. The human assets crunch issue can be effectively addressed by training local people instead of migrants. Such efforts can also avoid putting extra strain on local infrastructures. What traditional communities and indigenous groups do to preserve their places arouse the interests of tourists? It can be promoted as part of the cultural ecology.

The native dwellers must be made aware of the need to live in harmony with nature. Ecotourism in KTR must enhance respect for the cultural sensitivities of the local population through some serious soul-searching. The development of linkages into the local economy and local sourcing of goods and services would do much to cut down leakages from the local economy and to maximize the benefits of tourism to the natural areas of KTR. Therefore, there is a significant potential role for local communities in developing and selling complementary products to tourists. These complementary products configure local crafts, local cuisine, storytelling, guided visits, ethnic performances, and so on. Local communities must also have to be consulted for any development project in the park. Eco Development Committees can arrange jungle walks in the Khatia and Khapa ranges and bullock cart rides at Khatia and Mukki. In Sarhi and Mukki, homestays can be arranged by the local communities (Fig. 3.1).

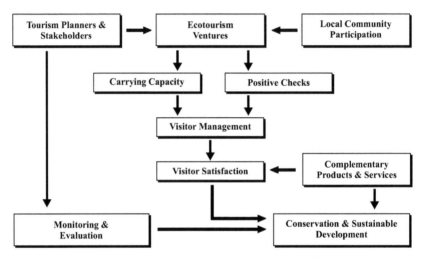

FIGURE 3.1   Model for holistic development of ecotourism in KTR.

3.8   CONCLUSION

KTR is relishing on its repute as a well-managed park and reserve. Ecotourism is a dynamic incentive for conservation of its flora and fauna. Though many sites are opened for tourism, there is a definitive regulation for tourists' activities in the park. Yet, consistent and continuous efforts are required to evaluate the impacts of tourism and to monitor the quality of experiences of tourists. Also, visitor movement inside the park needs to be thoroughly checked. Concrete policy initiatives are required to empower the local communities to actively take part in the affairs of tourism. Lots of indigenous potentials are left untapped. Cultural ecology is a prime aspect that can make the world of good to catapult the interests and ideals of ecotourism.

KEYWORDS

- **ecotourism in protected areas**
- **community participation**
- **visitor management**
- **empowerment**
- **conservation**
- **sustainable development**

REFERENCES

Backman, K.; Backman, S; Malinovsky, J. An Assessment of Service Quality in a Nature-Based Tourism Setting. *J. Qual. Assur. Hosp. Tourism* **2000**, *1*(2), 9–29.

Ballantyne, R.; Packer, J.; Sutherland, L. A. Visitor's Memories of Wildlife Tourism: Implications for the Design of Powerful Interpretive Experience. *Tourism Manage.* **2011**, *32*(4), 770–779.

Barretto, M. *Turismoy Cultura, Pasos,* edita,1. ACAy PASOS: ElSauzal, 2007.

Goodwin, H. Taking Responsible for Tourism, ICRT Occasional Paper, 2009.

Husbands, W.; Harrison, L. C. *Practicing Responsible Tourism: Understanding Tourism Today to Prepare for Tomorrow. Practicing Responsible Tourism: International Case Studies in Tourism Planning, Policy, and Development.* Harrison, L. C., Husbands, W., Eds.; John Wiley: New York, 1996.

Kozak, M.; Rimmington, M. Tourist Satisfaction with Mallorca, Spain, as of Season Holiday Destination. *J. Travel Res.* **2000**, *38*, 260–269.

Leslie, D. *Responsible Tourism*; CABI: Wallingford, 2012.

Madhya Pradesh Ecotourism Development Board. http://mfp.mpforest.org/eco/.

Moscardo, G. *Building Community Capacity for Tourism Development*; CABI: Wallingford, 2008.

Nash, D. *Anthropology of Tourism*; Elsevier: Oxford, 2001.

Novelli, M.; Hellwig, A. The UN Millennium Development chels, Tourism, and Development: The Tour Operator Perspective. *Curr. Issues Tourism* **2011**, *14*(3), 205–220.

Pieroni, O. Le Contraddizioni Dellecoturismmo. In *Viaggiare, conoscere e rispettarenlambiente*. Pieroni, O, Romita, T, Eds.; Soveria Mannelli: Rubbettino, 2003.

Rivera-Mateos, M.; Rodriguez-Garcia, L., Eds. *Turismo Responsible Sostenibilidaad y Desarollo Local Comunitario*. Universidad de Cordoba: Cordoba, 2012.

Saarinen, J.; Rogerson, C.; Manwa, H. Tourism and Millennium Development Goals: Tourism for Global Development? *Curr. Issues Tourism* **2011**, *14*(3), 201–203.

Scherl, L. M; Edwards, S. Tourism, Indigenous and Local Communities and Protected Areas in Developing Nations. In *Tourism and Protected Areas: Benefits beyond Boundaries;* Bushell, R.; Eagles, P. F. J. Eds.; CABI: Wallingford, 2007.

Sofield, T. H. B. *Empowerment for Sustainable Tourism Development;* Elsevier Science Ltd.: Oxford, 2003.

Spenceley, A. *Responsible Tourism: Current Issues for Conservation and Development*; Earth Scan: London, 2008.

Spenceley, A.; Relly, P.; Keyser, H.; Warmeant, P.; Mckenzie, M.; Metaboge, A.; et al. Responsible Tourism Manual for South Africa. Department of Environmental Affairs and Tourism, 2002.

The International Ecotourism Society. *Introduction & Concepts of Ecotourism.* http://www.ecotourism.org/.

CHAPTER 4

EMPOWERMENT OF MARGINALIZED COMMUNITIES AND TOURISM: A CASE STUDY OF *THEYYAM* DANCE, AN INDIAN PERSPECTIVE

JACOB JOHN[1] and MEGHA JACOB[2]

[1]*KDS, Delhi, India*

[2]*Jesus and Mary College, University of Delhi, Delhi, India*

CONTENTS

ABSTRACT

Promotion of Dalit art forms under tourism can contribute to the social and economic empowerment of these marginalized communities, and modern tourism is a strong instrument to reduce the existing power inequalities and discriminations. This chapter discusses the potentials of promoting the artistic or cultural performance of marginalized communities within the framework of tourism promotion as a tool to empower the scheduled castes/scheduled tribe socially and economically in Indian society. Apart from various sociocultural aspects of *Theyyam*, it covers the potential of *Theyyam* dancers in the context of employment creation and income generation. *Theyyam* can be promoted within the framework of religious tourism, which in turn can lead to the development of northern part of Kerala, India. Special interventions are required for the upliftment and welfare of *Theyyam* dancers through various government programs, an action plan is presented for promoting *Theyyam* as a religious and cultural event within the framework of tourism promotion programs in India.

4.1   INTRODUCTION

The tourism sector in India is yet to recognize the contribution of Dalits[1] and Adivasis or indigenous people in respect of culture, arts, and handicrafts. From an economic perspective, tourism has the potential for the development of Dalits in India, and it is significant to encourage business and public organization to involve in the promotion of *Theyyam* dance from this angle. Culture and art forms have become a powerful and liberating communication tool for Dalits in India. Their art forms have been counter-hegemonic discourse in several cases and have started to enter the popular media and attracted by various segments of the society, especially the middle class. There is a quest among the Dalits to give a new dimension to their cultural art forms such as Parayattam, Kaniyattam, and *Theyyam*, affirming their liberation. Their singing, drumming, strumming, and dancing redefines Dalits' perspective (George, 2005). *Theyyam* dance in Kerala, India is an effective tool and weapon to resist and fight back against an unjust social system. Several scholars have indicated a strong relationship between tourism and Dalit arts. Simpson and Ladle (2007) have emphasized the need for developing economically viable enterprises that give livelihood support to local communities by promoting indigenous cultures. Promotion of Dalit art forms under tourism can contribute to the social and economic empowerment of these marginalized communities.

---

[1] Dalit, means "divided" or "oppressed." It is the political name of castes in India that are "untouchable." Though the name Dalit has been in existence since the nineteenth century, the economist and reformer B. R. Ambedkar (1891–1956) popularized the term.

Modern tourism is a strong instrument to reduce the existing power inequalities and discriminations. There are several such Dalit arts in India today in which Dalits express their feeling in line with their struggles for rights in relation to caste, class, gender, livelihood, rights, and so forth. The chapter discusses the potentials of promoting the artistic or cultural performance of marginalized communities within the framework of tourism promotion as a tool to empower the scheduled castes (SC)/scheduled tribe (ST) socially and economically in Indian society. It discusses various sociocultural aspects of *Theyyam*, a dance system, which has a close relationship with the social systems and caste structure. The chapter analyzes the potential of *Theyyam* dancers in the context of employment creation and income generation. The current chapter is based on a household survey conducted in Kannur and Kasargode districts of Kerala, India to analyze cultural and religious dimensions of *Theyyam* dance and to study health, social, and economic problems of *Theyyam* dancers. It enlists the special interventions required for the upliftment and welfare of *Theyyam* dancers through various government programs and brings out an action plan for promoting *Theyyam* as a religious and cultural event within the framework of tourism promotion programs in India.

4.2 *THEYYAM* DANCE: A DALIT CULTURAL ART FORM

4.2.1 FEATURES OF THEYYAM DANCE

It is a dance performance of a section of the indigenous community that combines instruments and vocals. It is a unique art form that blends religious beliefs, art, dance, and music. *Theyyam*, a 40-min dance performance, is completely devotional both in its ethos and rendition. Artists perform with necessary fasting and preparation as the whole dance program is a dedication to God. *Theyyam* is not just a dance but a practice with twin elements of art and religious devotion. Though it is exclusive to male artists, younger girls below the age of 10 or women above 40 are performers in exceptional cases. Different rituals associated with the dance with different practices such as worship of spirit, ancestors, heroes, trees, animals, serpents, goddesses of the disease, and the village deity.

The performer invokes the deity and dances while the singer or artist also recites poems in praise of the deity or narrate the story relevant to the deity. The performance ends with the distribution of "adayaalam" or "kuri" (usually rice with turmeric) to the devotees and blessings on them. The assembled devotees, in turn, offer money to the shrine. The dancers need to undergo rigorous training on characteristic traits of the deity they play. It is important for dancers to approach physically and spiritually the divine trance in which the *Theyyam* is performed. The artist is trained by the Chieftain[2] on all the nuances of the performance—such as the makeup and songs. *Theyyams* play an important role in the general life of people in north Kerala, India as they used to pray to *Theyyam* God to solve their family problems, health issues, social problems, and so forth. The performance takes place in the "Kavu"[3] or in the courtyards of the *Tharavadu*.[4] The worship places are decorated with sculptures made of wood. These places are quite different in nature when compared with the other Indian Hindu temples. God may be represented by a sword, carved stones, a stool, and a piece of wood or mask. The performers wear exotic dresses, colorful costumes, and elaborate headgear. The performer wears a skirt or waist dress made of bamboo splices or coconut fronds covered with red cloth, the face and body are carefully painted with natural and colorful dyes. The painting of the body is varied according to the deity who is being invoked. The headdress or muti is also different for each *Theyyam* while some of them are 50–60-ft high. These are made of areca nut tree or drumstick tree wood or bamboo splices and decorated elaborately with colored cloths, coconut leaves, flowers, and so forth. Ornaments such as wristlets, anklets, and necklaces are used.

A *Theyyam* dance performance is a team effort and three sets of people associated with *Theyyam* are the dance performer, makeup artist, and prop makers. Each team consists of 12–15 persons comprising the sacred dance performer, the costume decorator, the face painter, the craft maker, lamp carrier, makeup man, singer, assistants, and instrumentalists. It is quite interesting to understand that all the members of the dance team are experienced with all the activities. They are not separate classes but are mutually exclusive. The same person can act as the dancer, makeup man, or the costume decorator as the case may be. The functional distribution of activities is allocated as per requirements. Prop makers make a wide range

---

[2] Chieftain is an experienced *Theyyam* dancer who is above 50 years and is not fit for the performance.
[3] Kavu is a *sacred grove* of trees of special religious importance to Hindu culture.
[4] *Tharavadu* is a Malayalam word which means ancestral home. A person's *Tharavadu* is used to show her/his root and identity him/her even after living in a different place.

of dance materials such as a skirt or waist dress made of bamboo splices or coconut fronds covered with red cloth. The dance performer has to acquire several skills such as singing, material making, playing the drums, and effective presentation. The presence of mind and ability to take extempore decisions, and also effectively communicate such decisions to help settle disputes that are brought before the *Theyyam* and diplomacy in handling representatives from different communities and positions are required in the dance performance.

4.2.2 CASTES AND THEYYAM RIGHTS

The dance system has a close relationship with the social systems and caste structure. The *Theyyam* performer called *Kolakkaran* or *Koladhari*, in Malayalam, belongs to SC/ST. The exclusive right to perform dance is given to SC or ST who are from the lower strata of the society, and people outside prescribed castes are not allowed to perform the dance. *Theyyam* performers are mainly from Malayan, Vannan, Mavilan, Vettuvan, Pulayan, and Kopalan. Velan, Malayan, and Vannan are the predominant communities that have traditionally performed *Theyyams*. The principal deity in *Theyyam* is Sree Muthappan, whereas there are over 450 varieties of forms of dances depicting various deities. Sree Muthappan *Theyyam* is performed around the year whereas the other *Theyyams* are performed seasonally. In some Kavus, the Perum Kaliyattam *Theyyam* festival is conducted at intervals of 12 or more years.

4.2.3 THEME OF THEYYAM DANCE AND CASTE DIMENSIONS

The *Theyyam* dances are performed mainly as religious offerings of four major categories of the people. The main and prominent category is the local community. Second, a joint family called *Tharavadu* (ancestral home) also offers *Theyyam* dances. The third category is a single family. Apart from these categories of offerings in Kerala, India nonresident Keralites offer *Theyyams* in other parts of India and even abroad. The results of our field survey clearly show that about 95% of offerings of dance were made by the local community during 2013–2014. *Tharavadu* (a Malayalam word that means ancestral home) had offered just 2.5% dance performances. About 2% dance offerings were made by single families. A nonresident outside Kerala, India had also made offerings.

In an upper caste-dominated society, *Theyyam* came as a platform for some positive relationships, interactions, and cooperation between upper castes and SC/ST. It is a custom of worship that dates back several thousand years. The words of SC/ST dancers during the *Theyyam* performance are venerated by the people belonging to upper caste as the Divine Will. Individuals or families belonging to upper caste sponsor or offer the dance. When the performance ends, the dancers resume their ordinary roles in the lowermost strata of society with no special distinction or recognition. In the past, *Theyyam* dances were tools and weapons to resist and fight back against an unjust social system as a religious revelation. The result of our field survey clearly shows that the dance influences a section of upper castes (21%) in their positive attitudes toward lower castes. Although there are upper caste people who refuse to mix with or eat with the lower caste, several others (52%) have started to interact with the dancers in their day-to-day life. It may be noted that, over the last 20–30 years, *Theyyam* artists have used it to inspire self-confidence among the members of SC/ST. According to 58% respondents covered under the survey, members of SC/ST see the upper castes bowing down to the deities who have entered SC/ST as a positive and inspiring action. Some of the new generation dancers consider this response from upper castes as an encouraging action. Recently, a section of new generation dancers started showing interest in the performance as *Theyyam* has made a positive impact on their self-esteem as a *Theyyam* artist. The policy change of Communist Party of India (Marxist).[CPI (M)], the dominant political party in Kannur and Kasargode districts, has also played a significant role in enhancing the level of interest in *Theyyam*. During the 1980s and 1990s, CPI (M) and Kerala, India Shastra Sahitya Parishat, two atheist organizations had discouraged their members and supporters from performing or sponsoring *Theyyam* dance performances. As a result, the participation of new generation had declined. But the situation has undergone a sea change now as both the organizations have found it as a good art form for the new generation. Even the members and supporters of Communist Party perform *Theyyam* dances as they view it as an art form. Recently, there is a revival as this art form is introduced in many universities. Now there is an increased acceptance of this dance form as people wanted to identify themselves as an artist. A segment of multinational companies has started to sponsor the *Theyyam* dance as a traditional form of art. These factors have resulted in the enhanced social acceptance of the *Theyyam* dance. Multiple factors have influenced people in the selection of the *Theyyam* dance as a livelihood: family traditions along with religious belief, family traditions without religious belief, livelihood, and love for art (Table 4.1).

TABLE 4.1 Dance Performers: Reasons for Selecting *Theyyam* Dance. (*Source:* Field Survey.)

Main reasons	Responses	
	Number	**%**
Family Traditions with religious belief	111	55.5
Family Traditions without religious belief	70	35
Livelihood	18	9
Love for art	1	0.5
Total	200	100

Religious believers and nonbelievers take up *Theyyam* dance as part of their family tradition.

4.3 CHALLENGES OF *THEYYAM* DANCERS

In this section, a wide range of problems of *Theyyam* dancers are discussed in a comparative perspective. *Theyyam* dance performances have several serious occupational hazards that adversely affect the health of the performers. The health of a significant number of dance performers has deteriorated after their long involvement in the dance performance. By and large, health deterioration is directly related to the rituals followed by the dancers and their livelihood issues. A dance performer is required to follow certain strict rituals. Although some rituals are common to all varieties of *Theyyam*, a few varieties have special rituals that have serious health implications on dance performers. Certain *Theyyam* performances involve dangerous activities. In the case of *Theechamundi*, dancers need to fall into the fire early in the morning. Some *Theyyams* are performed with fire bowls around the body of the performer. *Ottakolam Theyyam* performer needs to enter fire heaps 100 times or so. *Puthia Bhagavathy* and *Kandakarnan Theyyam* dancers act with the fire bowls around their body. In *Puthiya Bhagavathy*, the dancer is required to walk on hot coals repeatedly; whereas, in *Thottunkara Bhagavathy Theyyam*, the dancer has to accept and consume animal blood from the sacrifices conducted.

The *Theyyam* dancer's preparation takes a long duration of time, between 11 and 36 h, to create each costume with bamboo textile and silver decorations, and so on. The face painting and preparations on the performance day need a long time in the range of 4–5 h. The headgears are of different types—some are more than 22-ft high. Rituals start in the previous evening and a rigorous fasting is required. A *Theyyam* can last more than 12 or even 24 h during which he may not be able to take food or drink water, putting a strain on his body. During the season, he works continuously day and night for weeks together, leading to a lot of pressure on him. Hypertension is a common phenomenon in *Theyyam* artists. The eye makeup affects the eyes of the performer. Many performers take alcohol after the dance performances to overcome the strain, but which again has a detrimental effect on his health. As discussed earlier, consumption of alcohol is a prerequisite for a particular variety of *Theyyam* dance. Blood circulation gets affected due to the *Theyyam* frame being tied to different parts of the body. Arthritis is another common illness found in performers. The *Theyyam* performances are a day and night activity. A *Theyyam* performer leads a secluded life by observing extreme purity of mind and body. On the *Theyyam* day and the days before, he takes simple vegetarian foods such as simple grains, fruits, and tender coconut water to keep his body steady for performing the sacred dances. The major occupational hazards reported by *Theyyam* dancers during the field survey are reported in Table 4.2. Most of the dance performers (95%) have indicated long working hours without proper food and sleep as a serious health problem. According to 62% dance performers, income from the dance is quite inadequate, and they are engaged in part-time jobs to supplement their income to support the family. This has required overtime work and day and night activities resulting in several types of health problems. Prevalence of hypertension is reported by over 42% dance performers. It is significant to understand that eye makeup has caused eye sickness for about 32% of the dance performers. Alcoholic addictions (22%) and rheumatic problems (28%) are reported by dancers.

TABLE 4.2 *Theyyam* Dancers: Major Occupational Hazards and Health Problems. (*Source:* Field Survey.)

Occupational hazards	%
Working hours for dance performance:12–24 h without any break, proper food, and sleep	95
Along with dance performance and additional livelihood, activity to support the family resulting in health problems	62
Hypertension	42
Eye makeup affects the eyes of the performer adversely resulting in eye sickness	32
Rheumatism	28
Arthritis	33
Dance performers drink alcohol on regular basis to overcome the strain: alcoholic addiction	22

It is found that about 22% dance performers, who had consumed alcohol on regular basis to overcome the strain, became alcoholic addicts. About 33% have reported arthritis as a common illness found in performers. It may be noted that blood circulation gets affected due to the *Theyyam* frame being tied to different parts of the body It is quite clear that several factors take a toll on the performers' health. Although there is no clear evidence of low life expectancy, the working age of *Theyyam* dancers has reduced significantly as they stop working at the age of 45–50 years.

Performers do not have a group or individual health insurance protections. As a result, many of them do not get timely treatment for diseases. Chronic ill health cases such as rheumatic disorders are reported by a large number of *Theyyam* dancers. *Theyyam* dancers have been undergoing a struggle for livelihood and fighting for their survival with acute poverty and poor health. While the earning from *Theyyam* activities remains abysmally low, they cannot afford to have a minimum standard of living. They are compelled to engage in other activities to supplement their meager income from *Theyyam*. Some of these dancers, after spending the whole night in a dance performance continue to work in other fields during the daytime. A few *Theyyam* dancers work as private bus assistants on a daily wage basis. They do not get time to take any rest. About 89% dancers are the single source of income for their respective families, and they need to engage in other part-time jobs during daytime and off-season. A serious concern for *Theyyam* dancers is the lack of coverage of any social security system, especially health insurance. The results of the analysis of health problems of *Theyyam* dancers in comparison with SC/ST nondancers and with upper castes are presented in Table 4.3. About 32% *Theyyam* dancers covered under the survey have reported eye sickness against 2% SC/ST nondancers and 3.5% upper castes. About 42% *Theyyam* dancers covered under the survey have reported hypertension against 10% SC/ST nondancers and 12% upper castes. In the case of other health problems such as alcohol addiction, rheumatic problems, and overtime work for livelihood, *Theyyam* dancers covered under the survey have reported a much higher level of prevalence compared with the other two categories. It is quite evident that the health problems reported by *Theyyam* dancers are not prevalent among other sections covered under the survey. The physical exertion of the performer, the engagement with harmful substances, such as alcohol and fire cause stress on the mental health of the dancers. Social discrimination also causes some level of mental agony. Low self-esteem of the dancer is a prospective risk factor for depression. It is also found that a small section of dancers' children has a low level of self-esteem. The performance of *Theyyam* dance has affected the health status of *Theyyam* dancers adversely.

TABLE 4.3   Problems of *Theyyam* dancers in a Comparative Perspective (%). (*Source:* Field Survey.)

Health problems	SC/ST *Theyyam* dancers	SC/ST non-*Theyyam* dancers	Upper castes
Eye sickness	32	2	3.5
Hypertension	42	10	12
Alcoholic addiction	12	2	4.5
Rheumatism	28	7	6
Overtime work for livelihood	62	6	3

4.4   PROMOTION OF *THEYYAM,* A DALIT ART FORM: AN ACTION PLAN

In view of its uniqueness as a Dalit art form and various cultural dimensions, there is a good scope for promoting *Theyyam* dance in India. However, special interventions are required for the promotion of the art form and the upliftment and welfare of *Theyyam* dancers.

4.4.1   MINISTRY OF TOURISM AND MINISTRY OF CULTURE

The prevailing health, social, and economic problems of *Theyyam* dancers compel their children to engage in more economically viable and less strenuous livelihood and career. As a result, the new generation is not enthusiastic in taking *Theyyam* as a livelihood. This leads to a diminished number of artists and ultimately the loss of a unique cultural phenomenon that is a part of the heritage of SC/ST as well as India. *Theyyam* is not in the professional art list though it has several unique features. The new generation should be encouraged to learn and perform the art. The cultural dimensions of the *Theyyam* dance should get adequate significance and there is a need for promoting *Theyyam* dance as a traditional dance. In this context, it is important to provide necessary support to the Ministry of Culture to promote *Theyyam* dance as a cultural program. There is a good scope for promoting *Theyyam* under the category of sponsored tourism. It can be promoted under the category of religious tourism also. It needs a special focus as an art to be promoted as an item for seasonal tourism. Ministry of Tourism, Government of India, and Department of Tourism, Government of Kerala, India should take appropriate measures to promote *Theyyam* dance.

4.4.2   EMPOWERMENT OF A WEAKER COMMUNITY THROUGH IDENTIFICATION AND PROMOTION OF CULTURAL HERITAGE IN INDIA

A medium of artistic or cultural performance can be effectively used as a tool to reduce or remove the suppression of SC/ST in a society. *Theyyam* dance performance is the mixture of playfulness and seriousness, and the worship of a *Theyyam* deity results in unifying society rather than dividing it. For example, in "Pottan Theyyam," the performer abuses, reviles, and even physically mistreats the highest authority with unusual anger. *Theyyam* performer, in trance, speaks out the frustration and resentment of his community. Sometimes, the performer cracks jokes that would make the devotees laugh and try to make people laugh even when playing with fire. At the same time, he will make serious criticism. In a certain stage of the dance, he enacts the collective wish of the community he represents. In all forms of *Theyyam* dance, the words of SC/ST dancers during the performance are venerated by the upper castes as the Divine Will. Through the medium of trance, the dancer who represents deity of the respective *Theyyam* acquired a voice and is able to speak directly to the upper castes against social injustices. It is quite evident that *Theyyam* dance has become a strong medium for spreading the message of social equity and social harmony in Kerala, India. *Theyyam* has become a platform for some positive relationships, interactions, and cooperation between upper castes and SC/ST. A section of new generation dancers has started to show interest in the performance as *Theyyam* has made a positive impact on their self-esteem as a *Theyyam* artist. *Theyyam* dances are now effective tools and weapons to resist and fight back against an unjust social system as a religious revelation during a particular dance performance influences a considerable section of upper castes in their positive attitudes toward lower castes. State governments with the support of local government institutions and civil society organizations can identify traditional art forms or cultural heritage of SC/ST. In every state, there may be similar artistic or cultural performance of SC/ST that may be identified and promoted in an effective way.

4.4.3 THE POPULARIZATION OF ART AND HONORING THEYYAM ARTISTS

There is no written document for training new artists, and currently the training is dependent mainly on the knowledge that is transferred from generations to the head of the families. Documentation of the rituals and customs of the training methodology is very important. Various aspects of dances, especially the songs and stories, have to be recorded in a form that enables the dancers to share it with the new generations. The proper orientation needs to be provided to dancers to reduce their work pressure and exhaustion. Steps may be taken to organize programs for interested people on different dimensions of *Theyyam* dance. This will help them in acquiring the skill and enable them to become dance professionals. At present, conflict of interest exists between the new and the old generation dancers as there is a divide between the old school of thoughts and new school of thoughts. There are new developments in this art form such as the introduction of Mudras for more acceptances, which has influenced a fraction of the dancers. Modernization and commercialization of art forms have started among the newly educated artists. The new generation is educated and they have a view that the art form should be taken out from the currently confined enactment to a wide panorama as it will create more opportunity for the artists and popularize the art. But this view is opposed by the orthodox people who are in the age group of 60 and above, as they do not want to move away from the traditional setup. Appropriate promotional activities, with the support of relevant ministries and departments, can address these issues. Promotional activities especially measures such as honoring *Theyyam* artists like any other art forms can attract a new generation of the *Theyyam* families.

4.4.4   INSURANCE, PENSION, AND OTHER WELFARE SCHEMES

At present, *Theyyam* dancers are quite vulnerable to various uncertainties and no support system is available for the ailing *Theyyam* artists during the fag end of their career. They do not get the benefit of any social security system. It is important to provide them the benefit of a regular pension scheme. Currently, a meager amount of Rs. 800 is being given by the state government of Kerala, India as financial support to *Theyyam* dancers. The present financial help should be converted into a regular pension scheme. A minimum of Rs. 3000 should be given as a monthly pension to all the *Theyyam* dancers when they reach the age of 50 years irrespective of their financial status. Most of the *Theyyam* dance format is very risky and involves tremendous physical exertion and hard work. Considering the high risk, a proper insurance coverage, risk allowance, and medical insurance scheme should be made available to *Theyyam* dancers. *Theyyam* dancers need special attention especially in respect of the education of the children. A number of students' scholarships and lump sum grant to the students should be revised periodically. A scheme for providing financial help for the marriage of daughters of *Theyyam* dancers may be set up. A contributory welfare fund may be devised for *Theyyam* artists. Appropriate steps may be taken to create a welfare fund for *Theyyam* dancers. Accordingly, temples can set aside a specific amount of money for a welfare fund, to which the artists can also contribute to each performance. This can be used to help artists when they are forced to retire due to ill health or old age. A welfare fund can help many artists to address their financial and health problems. As *Theyyam* dancing is quite a seasonal activity, most of the artists depend on 5–6 months' earnings for the expenditure in the entire year. An attractive scheme may be devised to provide a livelihood support. The scheme should encompass interest-free loans, training programs, marketing support, and others. The livelihood projects can include setting up of craft centers for making jewelry and other ornaments, fabric-making units for costumes, for makeup artists, and so on.

4.5 CONCLUSION

The experiences of *Theyyam* dance, a popular Dalit art in the northern part of Kerala, India, deserve to be shared with the other Indian states by promoting *Theyyam* as a religious and cultural event within the framework of tourism promotion activities in India. *Theyyam* dance, a mixture of ancient and modern cultures, can be promoted within the framework of religious tourism, which in turn can lead to the development of northern part of Kerala, India. This will bring a significant improvement and positive changes in the economy of northern Kerala, India as a result of the inflow of a large number of religious tourists. This will further encourage local people to preserve the *Theyyam* dance as a religious festival and cultural event. It will provide several opportunities for tourism marketers to concentrate on this destination to market their tourism services. There will be a substantial impact on the local economy and local community. Apart from employment generation, the cultural values can be embedded. As there is a close link between religion and culture in India, the motivation of national and international tourists may be varied. A concrete strategy needs to be formulated to overcome the seasonality of *Theyyam* dance and other logistic issues. Concrete measures with the active involvement of Ministry of Culture and Ministry of Tourism,

Government of India, and Department of Tourism, Government of Kerala, India is required for the promotion of the art form and the upliftment and welfare of *Theyyam* dancers.

KEYWORDS

- **religious tourism**
- **sponsor tourism**
- **seasonal tourism**
- **Dalit art forms**

REFERENCES

Bhattacharya, A. Community Empowerment through Creative Industries and Tourism. 2015. www.banglanatak.com (accessed Oct 5, 2015).

George, G. M. *Cultural History and Emergent Dalit Alternatives*, 3 June, 2005. www. kdsonline.org. (accessed Sept 4, 2015).

John, J. Socio-Economic and Health Problems of Theyyam Dancers belonging to Scheduled Castes of Kerala. Kerala Development Society, New Delhi, March, 2015. KDS working Paper series 3–15. www.kdsonline.org.

Kannan, Y. V. *Theyyangalum Anushtanangalum Oru Pattanam (Malayalam);* Kerala Basha Institute: Thiruvananthapuram, 2011.

Kerala Sangeeta Nataka Academy. Theyyam, Thrissur, 2000.

Nagarajan, S. Close Encounter with Theyyams, Hindu daily dated 4 August 2012. http://www.thehindu.com.

Simpson, M. C.; Ladle, R. Implementing Sustainable Tourism Indicators for Destinations Using a Quantifiable Tourism Sustainability Index. *J. Sustainable Tourism* 2007.

CHAPTER 5

INFLUENCE OF PERCEIVED RISKS ON THE DESTINATION CHOICE PROCESS: AN INDIAN PERSPECTIVE

JOSE K. ANTONY[1] and JOBY THOMAS[2]

[1]*School of Business Studies and Social Sciences, Christ (Deemed to be University), Bangalore, India*

[2]*School of Business Studies and Social Sciences, Christ (Deemed to be University), Bangalore, India*

CONTENTS

ABSTRACT

Tourists have to make numerous decisions and they are normally considered to be rational decision makers who always try to maximize their utilities. They do this by assessing costs and benefits of their actions before committing themselves to any purchase. But making travel decisions is never a simple task; tourism purchase decisions are quite often risky, require extensive problem solving, and advance planning. Every potential tourist will face a certain level of risk while traveling as the travel experience relies heavily on intangible services. Tourists make travel choices with no expectation of any kind of economic or material return, rather they expect intangible results such as pleasure and satisfaction. Perceived risk has been widely employed in the study of consumer behavior in marketing research as consumer behaviors are instances of risk-taking. Actions of consumers will regularly yield consequences that they may not be able to anticipate with any approximating degree of certainty, and some of these at least are likely to turn unpleasant. Today, consumers are rarely in a state of mind to anticipate the exact probabilities associated with their purchases.

Research on perceived risk related to tourism has most often been neglected, and in-depth studies on the same have not been extensively undertaken, especially on the South Indian tourists. In this context, the study investigated the risk perception of tourists traveling from South India and determined the influence that the perceived risks would have on the choice of tourist destinations.

The study is conceptual in nature as it is mainly based on reviews of various literature on tourist risk perceptions. Numerous dimensions of perceived risks were identified and were engaged to identify characters of heterogeneity among tourist groups, based on their risk perception patterns. The findings would thereby enable travel organizations to market tourist destinations accordingly to them.

5.1   INTRODUCTION

Travel is an exciting phenomenon in the world today (Cohen, 1995) and the Tourism 2020 Vision by the World Tourism Organization (WTO, 2003) forecasts that international tourist arrivals will reach more than 1.56 billion by the year 2020. This will be more than twice the number in 2000. According to Goeldner, Ritchie, and McIntosh in 2000 and Plog in 1991, the planning and anticipation exercises leading up to a trip can be an exciting as well as an enjoyable experience. International tourism has become one of the essential phenomena in the 20th century, and it may be referred to as the travel undertaken by a large number of people across borders of countries, either for pleasure and leisure purposes or for business purposes for a small period of time. On the other hand, according to the WTO (1995), the residents of a particular region traveling only within that region refers to domestic tourism. A study by Nicolau and Mas in 2005 identified and studied this difference between individuals who chose domestic travel and those who chose international vacations. It also studied the destination preference of travelers who had children below the age of 16. The study found that individuals with a higher education and those who were more interested in gathering information and knowledge about cultures had a greater propensity to travel to international destinations. The results from the study strongly implied that different forms of the tourists' demographic and socio-psychographic characteristics influenced their need to choose international or noninternational travel.

However, making travel decisions, be it to an international or national destination, is never an easy task as a tourist has to take many decisions concerning time, finance, transportation, alternative destinations, and activities involved. More importantly, every traveler will face some amount of risk while traveling, mainly because the experience during travel relies heavily on numerous kinds of intangible services that need to be consumed simultaneously as they are produced (Zeithaml, 1981). It is not easy to test services such as goods when they are being bought (Guseman, 1981) and this most often confuses consumers when they select services, as services vary in their quality. Therefore, there is a very high element of risk associated with services, a major factor being that it is very difficult to evaluate services before the experience. Furthermore, even after an experience, there is no tangible element to prove a good experience. Although perceived risk has been widely employed as a major factor in the fields pertaining to the studies on Consumer Behavior, and its influence on marketing and market research, researchers in the areas revolving around perceived risk in international travel and tourism have been most often neglected (Yavas, 1987; Verhage et al., 1990; Lepp and Gibson, 2003). Thus, studying the factors influencing perceived risk from the tourism context will be beneficial to both the tourists and the marketers. This chapter investigates the risk perception of tourists traveling from South India and to determine the influence that the perceived risks could have in the choice of tourism destinations. Through intense literature reviews, numerous dimensions of perceived risk were identified, of which five dimensions were proposed for this study, namely, Health Risk, Financial Risk, Time Risk, Safety and Security Risk, and Information and Communication Risk.

Through Information Technology, it is now possible to obtain 'virtually enhanced experiences' of the destinations and its attractions. This helps one to a great extent in reducing the perceived risks of travelers (Cho, 2002). Cho investigated the effects of the virtual experiences and he understood that virtual tours on a destination offered the visitors a more positive image of the destination. On the practical side, Hampton Inn, a major hotel chain in the United States of America, offers its guests a 100% satisfaction guarantee program, wherein the guests need not have to pay for the room and its facilities if they are not satisfied during their stay. This type of a technique for promotion can attract the guests as it will help to reduce the perceived financial risk associated with their stay in a hotel, but it may still not be able to offer 100% satisfaction. In case the guest remained unsatisfied, it was also noted that the unsatisfactory experience the guest experienced in the hotel could not be changed or erased from his or her mind. The world has not forgotten the catastrophic events that unfolded in the United States on September 11, 2001, wherein many foreign tourists became victims of the tragic terrorist attacks. It took more than 10 years for the tourist arrivals in the United States to recover to the normal figures before those attacks (TIA, 2003).

Not to forget similar events that unfolded in the Asian continent after the severe acute respiratory syndrome outbreak and the Gulf War. This was again followed by the tragic tsunami that struck Southeast Asia and the Asian subcontinent in 2005 (WTO, 2005), more recently the massive earthquake in the foothills of the Himalayas in Nepal. All these incidents added into negatively affecting the risk perception of tourists on international travel. Such incidents can result in undue stress in travelers and can also lead to serious economic losses and ramifications for the stakeholders in the travel industry. Investigating and studying these stress-leading factors can, therefore, be beneficial and helpful to the travelers as well as to the marketers. Thus, this chapter examines factors that can influence leisure and pleasure travel purchase decisions during travel. The main focus of the research study was the role of perceived risks while making travel decisions. Many factors including the knowledge of destinations were examined to find out if they could influence an individual's choice of a destination.

5.2 NEED FOR THE STUDY

The study concentrated on perceived risks as dominant and major factors affecting decisions of tourists from South India on travel. For example, one of the major risks that can influence destination choice is Information and Communication Risk. Communication Risk is mainly caused due to language barriers. Language barriers can have an impact on any stage of travel (Cohen and Cooper, 2004). Destination marketers and travel service providers always have to provide accurate information to travelers, the absence of which leads to Information Risk. Some tourists may turn out to be more attractive to the Hospitality and Travel industry at times of crisis, as they could be less sensitive to external risks.

Therefore, a very clear understanding of perceived risk will enable destination marketers and travel professionals to identify tourist groups based on risk perceptions and help market tourist destinations accordingly to them.

5.3 OBJECTIVES OF THE STUDY

The basic objective of the study was to understand the influence of demographic variables on the risk perception of tourists and to ascertain the most prominent dimensions of perceived risks among tourists. During the study, efforts were also made to distinguish tourists on the basis of the heterogeneity in their risk perception patterns and to determine the influence of perceived risks in the choice of tourist destinations.

5.4   REVIEW OF LITERATURE

From the time risk was introduced as a concept, especially in the subject of Economics, somewhere around the 1920s (Knight, 1948), the concept has been successfully employed in studying consumer decision-making and its theories not only in the field of Economics but also in Finance and Decision Sciences, as found by Dowling and Staelin (1994). The Expected Utility Theory proposed by Von Neumann and Morgenstern (1947) to analyze the process of decision-making under the influence of risk factors had been accepted as a normative model of rational choice for a long time till the Prospect Theory was proposed as an alternative model by Kahneman and Tversky (1979). Another theory, the Skew-Symmetric Bilinear (SSB) Utility Theory, was proposed by Fishburn (1982). The Expected Utility Theory was successful to a large extent in establishing a set of prominent factors that formed the fundamental for analyzing substitute decisions, and these factors were later cut down to three basic ones through research, namely, transitivity, independence, and choices. The Prospect Theory further violated the axioms of the Expected Utility Theory through predictions made in behavior by Currim and Sarin (1989). The SSB Utility Theory used a number of factors that were weak to accommodate the seen behavior but powerful enough to have a more influential appeal, as studied by Bell and Farquhar (1986). In the field of marketing research, Bauer (1960) was the first to propose an observation on consumer buying behavior as an incidence of enduring risk. This was because consumer buying behavior involved numerous actions of the buyer that could result in situations, which the buyer could not foresee with any approximate degree of certainty, and some of them were at least likely to turn uncomfortable.

The author also mentioned that an individual could respond to and cope with risk only as they subjectively perceived it, and it was this subjective perception of perceived risk that ultimately influenced consumer decisions. According to the Merriam-Webster Dictionary, 'Risk' is defined as any possibility of loss or injury. Knight's definition of 'risk' is the known possibility that is normally attributed to the outcomes of many decisions. 'Uncertainty' exists whenever there is a lack of concrete knowledge and information on a possibility. Both, Bauer's argument about perceived risk and Knight's definition of risk, indicated the presence of a similar concept, which excluded the unknown probability that existed with risk. Cox (1967) commented that buyers are never completely in a situation to identify the aftereffects associated with their direct purchases. Marketers, however, have always used both these concepts over the other as identified by Mitchell (1994). Many researchers have also employed Hofstede's (1984) Uncertainty Avoidance Model, which is used as a measure of intolerance to risk. This model was used to investigate the purchase behavior of international tourists, especially in the studies conducted by Money and Crotts (2003). Hofstede through the model had clearly stated that "uncertainty avoidance" was not the same as "risk avoidance" but many subsequent researches wrongly interpreted "uncertainty avoidance" as "risk avoidance."

5.5 DIMENSIONS OF PERCEIVED RISKS

'Risk' is often expressed as the chance that an event may occur, whereas 'uncertainty' is normally a circumstance during which something can happen, which the individual will have absolutely no idea about. The definition of risk still remained nonstandardized, and a study by Schiffman and Kanuk (2000) even suggested another definition of perceived risk. It stated perceived risk as a level of uncertainty that consumers could face when they were not able to foresee the aftereffects of their purchase decisions. This definition also highlighted relevant dimensions of perceived risk, namely, the dimensions of uncertainty and outcome. Later, Yates and Stone (1992) offered three different views on the confusion revolving around the explanations on risk, namely, the risk construct is made up of several individual risk elements, the risk may involve several different and distinct elements, and risks may unfold in many different ways during different situations and events.

Since the time of Bauer, many research studies on buyer behavior have also evaluated various elements of the risk perception construct. Brooker (1984), Kaplan et al. (1972, 1974), Laroche et al. (2004), Greatorex and Mitchell (1990), Ryan and Peter (1976), and Gronhaug and Stone (1993) were instrumental in studying about perceived risk as one of the most prominent and powerful factors in explaining consumer behavior. Jacoby and Kaplan (1972) were the first to operationalize the construct of perceived risk. Through their study, they identified five important dimensions of risk, namely, financial, psychological, performance, physical, and social risks. Their study identified that of all the dimensions, performance risk had the highest degree of correlation between all the perception factors of risk followed by financial risk.

Financial risk was more prominent when it came to dealing with tangible products. Performance risk was also found to be more predictive out of all the factors that influenced the overall perception of risk. Another study by Roselius (1971) had earlier examined the four types of loss, namely, loss resulting from ego, danger, time, and money, related to risk perception. The study found loyalty and image of the brand to be the two strongest relievers of risk. Peter and Ryan (1976) studied the relationship between loyalty toward the brand and perceived risk. Perceived risk was identified to be a strong forecaster of brand preference for those buyers who considered the brand preference to be as important.

Brooker (1984) further examined the six types of perceived risks that had been adopted from these two earlier studies by Jacoby and Kaplan (1972) and by Roselius (1971). According to Brooker's results, the strongest dimensions of risk were performance risk and financial risk, whereas the two least related risk dimensions were a physical risk and social risk. Stone and Gronhaug (1993) further developed the multiple indicators that were used for measuring the six dimensions influencing risk, which were identified in earlier studies by Jacoby and Kaplan and by Roselius. Psychological and financial risks were identified by them to be the most significant factors that could impact the overall perception of risk in the consumer buying behavior.

The presence of perceived risk in four countries spanning across Asia and Europe, namely, Turkey, Saudi Arabia, Thailand, and the Netherlands was examined by Verhage et al. (1990). Perceived risk related to the buying of products for daily use was observed in all the countries, but no relationship was being able to be identified the risks perceived and brand loyalty. The degree of risk perception was also found to vary between the countries. Although buyers in Turkey experienced a considerably lower level of risk while buying products than the buyers from other countries, the study also found that the construct of perceiving risk remained convincing in all the countries. Techniques to reduce risk had to be developed for each individual country.

The study by Mitchell and Greatorex (1990) examined the difference in perceived risk between the consumers from the United States and consumers from other countries. The study found the risk perception to be very high among the nonnationals, and both the groups also exhibited a significant difference in the psychological loss. In contrast to other earlier studies, the study also pinpointed that loyalty toward the brand was the most noteworthy reliever to risk. The impact of intangibility on risk perception with the help of six generic products that represented varying degrees of intangibility was investigated by Laroche et al. (2004).

Three dimensions of intangibility were identified, namely, physical, mental, and general. Of these, physical intangibility was observed to be strongly related to the risk elements associated with physical goods, whereas mental intangibility was found to be strongly related to the risk elements associated with services. Therefore, it was further inferred that the influence of tangibility on the risk perception was different for services and physical goods. Gursoy (2001) suggested that risk can always be viewed with an element of involvement that will directly affect the search for information. Gursoy and Gavcar (2003) further identified that the involvement of international tourists with a holiday destination involves a three-dimensional relation, namely, risk probability, risk importance, and pleasure or interest. However, Chaudhuri in the year 2000 verified four significantly very different models to analyze the impact of perceived risk while searching for information and knowledge. They were the risk as a moderator, as an involvement, as an antecedent, and risk as a consequence. The study results revealed that risk could be categorized under the constructs of function and emotion. Moutinho (2000) was the first researcher to provide a comprehensive analysis of risk perceived in relation to tourist character. His simple take on perceived risk, to be a combination of consequences and uncertainty, was found to be more generalized than the other definitions that were already studied and discussed. Uncertainties about the product, the place, and the modes of purchase, uncertainties arising out of financial and psychosocial consequences, and the subjective uncertainties encountered by the tourists were the four views that were proposed through his study.

Moutinho also examined the relationship between the risk perception elements to more clearly understand the tourist's perception of risk involved in purchase decisions. The destination image is another significant focal area in tourism research that involves the perception of risk, as studied by many, most notably Baloglu (1996), Baloglu along with McCleary (1999), and Beerli and Martin (2004). The studies on destination image included several indicators, most importantly perception on personal safety among the various cognitive components of the image. Relationships between leisure activities involved in international travel and travel decisions have also been investigated in many studies. The study by Cheron and Ritchie (1982) found that there existed very distinct differences between the kind and form of risk experienced while using tangible goods and undertaking leisure activities. The psychological element of the risk perceived was found to be strongly related to the risk perception revolving around leisure activities, as for tangible goods, performance risk was found to be more strongly influential (Kaplan and Jacoby, 1972).

The relationship between risk perception and decision-making in international travel was first examined by Yavas (1987). Four reasons that perception of risk could be the primary influence in decision-making during international travel were identified by him, namely, the anxiety resulting because of the inability to anticipate expected benefits from a holiday, high-involvement situations accompanying decision-making during international travel, risk perception of first-time international travelers, and cultural differences during travel.

In his study, Yavas stressed on five dimensions of risk that could be perceived during foreign travel, namely, risks associated with money, time, health, social, and ego. Health risk was found to be more strongly influential in the study, followed by the risk of time. To investigate the perception of risk associated with pleasure travel, seven dimensions of perceived risks were employed by Roehl and Fesenmaier (1992). They identified three perceived risk groups, namely, Risk Neutral group, Functional Risk group, and Place Risk group. These groups differed on the basis of the trips undertaken more recently and the benefits they wished from their travel. Seven perceived risk components, namely, physical risk, financial risk, social risk, time risk, equipment risk, satisfaction risk, and psychological risk were used as independent variables for the study. The physical risk was the possibility of attracting physical danger, injury, or sickness while traveling, financial risk was the likelihood that the travel may not be able to provide value for the money spent, and the social risk was the possibility that a trip may affect others' opinion of the tourist and the destination.

Time risk involved the likelihood that a trip may take too much time or it can be a waste of time, equipment risk was the possibility that mechanical or equipment failures can occur during a trip, satisfaction risk was the likelihood that a trip may not be able to provide personal satisfaction, and psychological risk was the possibility that a trip may not reflect an individual's personality or self-image. Mitchell and Vassos (1997) studied the difference between perceived risk and risk reduction among undergraduate students from Great Britain and Cyprus while undertaking package holidays. They found that the statement, "your hotel will not be as nice as it appears in the brochure picture," in their questionnaire had the highest risk factor. The two statements in the questionnaire, namely, "reading independent travel reviews" and "purchasing some kind of travel insurance" were most useful in helping to reduce the risk strategies. Sonmez and Graefe identified through their study in 1998 that some destinations were avoided because of the perceptions of risk and feelings of safety during travel to those destinations. Relationships between the behavior of travelers and risk perception were also found to be precise to situations.

This suggested that it may not always be appropriate to simplify the buying behavior of goods to the travel decisions. Martinez (2000) used the Expected Value Model to experiment the traveler's perception of risk. The study mainly revolved around the US tourist's subjective assignment of risk perception of victimization of criminals on the US side of the United States–Mexico Border. The results from the study exhibited an objective measure of risk at the United States–Mexico Border. Lepp and Gibson, more recently in 2003, studied the interrelationship between the perception of risk and the preference for familiarity or novelty associated with international travel.

5.6   PERSONAL FACTORS OF TRAVELERS

Sociodemographic and psychological factors are more commonly referred to as the personal factors that can affect the perception of risk of travelers. These factors include the gender, age, education level, motivation levels, personality, and values of the respondents, to name a few. The factors were mainly identified from the perspective of the subject of Consumer Behavior (Beerli and Martin, 2004). Language ability was also included among the factors as language is mainly polished and obtained through education. Reviews of previous studies organized on psychographics and language ability were also undertaken for the study.

5.7   PSYCHOGRAPHIC CHARACTERISTICS OF TRAVELERS

Travel, tourism, and hospitality research have always relied upon psychographic characteristics (Chandler and Costello, 2002). Venturesomeness was first developed as an important dimension by Plog (1994). It was used as one of the best measures of the travelers' psychographic characteristics, and other than this, there was no standard category or technique of defining behavior. It was Demby (1994) who first claimed to develop the concept of psychographics. According to Demby, psychographics was stated as "the use of psychological, sociological, and anthropological factors, such as the benefits desired from the behavior being studied, self-concept and lifestyle, to determine how the market can be segmented by the propensity of consumer groups within the market, and their reasons to take decisions about products, persons, ideologies or hold an attitude or use a medium."

Chandler and Costello, more recently in 2002, studied that personal values, lifestyle, and activity–level preferences that included personal attitudes, interests, opinions, own personality, and several other individual characteristics and traits were hugely influenced by psychographic characteristics. Psychographic characteristics were able to provide a deep understanding of the ways of living of the consumers (Schewe and Calantone, 1977). Their study measured the concepts of activities, interests, opinions, and other characteristics revolving around the life cycle stages, income, and education levels, among many others. They also stated that demographic variables were more descriptive in nature whereas psychographic characteristics were more useful in understanding the psychological attitudes of the buyers. The study also concluded that psychographic characteristics became more effective when they were studied along with the demographic information. It was observed that many past studies in tourism and hospitality research did not clearly indicate the term 'psychographic characteristics,' although most of the studies used some form of psychographic constructs.

Through their studies, Sonmez (1994) and Yavas (1987) explored the needs to study more into the relationships between psychographic and demographic characteristics, and the decisions involving risks of travelers, respectively. Many instruments, such as Plog's Concept, Role of Tourists, the Tourist Role Preference Questionnaire (TRPQ), the International Tourist Role (ITR) Scale, and Novelty Seeking Measures, have been developed over the years to measure the psychographic characteristics of tourists.

Plog employed a widely used psychographic approach, in which the relationship between the type of personality and choice of destinations were undertaken. Plog (2002) identified a form of personality wherein he could easily differentiate between flyers and nonflyers. He termed flyers as allocentric and tourists who do not like to fly as psychocentric. Later, these terms were modified into venturers and dependables, respectively. Another important development was that Plog (1990) criticized the study of Smith (1990) by pointing out numerous mistakes. Smith reported that no support could be provided to the theory of psychographics. Smith failed to substantiate the 21-item measurement scale that he used in the study. This scale was quite different from that developed by Plog. Plog's scale was found to be more original—it was a four-point scale, which included very important, somewhat important, not very important, and not at all important. These scales were used to set scores for all the 21 items in Plog's questionnaire.

The scales were further condensed into three points so as to relate to the classification of allocentric, psychocentric, and mid-centric tourists. Although Plog used a nationwide sample to develop the study, Smith identified a smaller sample of long-haul travelers, whom he grouped as allocentric in nature. Another study (Nickerson and Ellis, 1991) further identified Plog's Model to be using the Activation Theory as proposed by Fiske and Maddi (1961). The findings of Plog (1990) were compared with different types of personalities and personal values with the support of a group of domestic US tourists (Madrigal, 1995). In the research that was undertaken by Madrigal, the personal values scale named as the List of Values demonstrated itself as an efficient tool to predict the differences in traveler groups by using Plog's lifestyle and activity-based preferences.

Chandler and Costello (2002) further developed a chart exhibiting the profiles of heritage destination visitors. Visitors, in their study, were categorized into six groups, namely, active venturers, active centrics, active dependables, mellow venturers, mellow centrics, and mellow dependables. However, one of the major drawbacks of this study was that more than 83% of the respondents fell into the categories of either active or mellow centrics. Based on the need for novelty or familiarity, it was Cohen (1972) who proposed another typology of tourists. This typology categorized tourists into four categories, namely, the organized mass tourist (less chance to buy a packaged tour even though they were least adventurous); the individual mass tourist (more chance to buy a package tour but wanted some amount of control over the time and the itinerary); the explorer (searches for reliable transportation and comfortable accommodation even though they arrange the trip); and the drifter (wants to venture out farther away from the accustomed way of life, but without the help of any timetable or itinerary).

Based on Cohen's (1974) classification of tourists, a more elaborate 15 tourist-related roles were proposed by Pearce (1982), which included the tourist, traveler, holidaymaker, jet-setter, conservationist, explorer, missionary, businessmen, migrant, anthropologist, hippie, religious pilgrim, international athlete, overseas student, and overseas journalist. The vacation market in Alaska was segmented in a study by Snepenger (1987) with the help of Cohen's typology. The results from his study that had number of female travelers showed that the average age of the organized mass tourists was mostly in the 50s; the individual mass tourists, having equal number of males and females, were in the age group of the late 40s and early 50s; and the explorers, consisting of more number of male travelers, were between the ages of late 30s and early 40s.

A study by Lepp and Gibson (2003) also found that health risk was perceived to be higher in the organized mass tourist and independent mass tourist groups. The level of this form of risk was perceived much lower among the explorers and drifters. Moreover, the concern for risks related to terrorism and food were perceived to be higher among the organized mass tourists.

Yiannakis and Gibson (1992) created a questionnaire with 13 pairs of tourist role-measuring statements. The TRPQ as it was called displayed dimensions on three poles, namely, the relation between stimulation and tranquility on the Y-axis, the relation between familiarity and strangeness on the X-axis, and the relation between independence and structure on the Z-axis. The three poles required the respondents to mark their actual behaviors while traveling on vacations based on different roles that were provided. It was better to measure past travel experience using the TRPQ. Mo, Howard, and Havitz (1993) developed the ITR scale as a measurement instrument to study more in-depth about Cohen's (1972) typology of international tourists. The 20-item questionnaire designed by Cohen was further redesigned with the support of the original 62 items. In the study, the ITR scale displayed three dimensions, namely, the individual's need for familiarity and novelty when choosing to travel to international destinations, that was called the destination-oriented dimension; the individual's preference to travel internationally with or without the support of organized travel services, that was denoted as the travel services dimension; and the preference of the individual to maintain wide-reaching social exchange with the local people when traveling to global destinations, that was termed as the social contact dimension. Significantly, the three dimensions noted above appeared to be very similar and close to the factors revealed in the TRPQ scale (Yiannakis and Gibson, 1992).

Mo et al. (1994) also specified that the ITR scale was found to be a better tool in measuring the tourists' preferences of both experienced travelers as well as the nonexperienced travelers, rather than measuring the tourists' behaviors. According to Basala and Klenosky (2001), both the past and the future travel behavior and preferences could be successfully measured using the TRPQ scale and this was indirectly helpful in analyzing past experiences of tourists. The ITR scale based on various preferences on types of vacations that included the language, cotravelers, and accommodation facilities, examined the differences that arose among the average travelers, novelty-seeking travelers, and familiarity-seeking travelers.

The results showed that while novelty-seeking travelers preferred locally owned accommodation facilities, the average travelers and the familiarity seeking travelers preferred international hotel chains. All the three categories of travelers displayed the minimum preference when it came to traveling alone and all opinioned that they were more than willing to visit a place where they were more comfortable with the native language. Jiang et al. (2000) further validated the ITR scale through their studies. Their study changed the wordings and rearranged the order of a few questions. They rewrote the actual 21 items and scaled them down into 16 items using exploratory and confirmatory factor analysis.

The novelty factor in the tourism context was further studied by Lee and Crompton (1992) and they developed a questionnaire with 21 items. Novelty in their study was defined "as a multidimensional construct consisting of six dimensions," namely, elements associated with thrill, adventure, surprise, escape, avoidance of boredom, and change from the normal routine, that overlapped each other. During the process of pretest and analysis, two of the dimensions, namely, adventure and escape, were omitted and only the remaining four dimensions were included into the final version of the scale. Among the psychographic measurements, the search for novelty was selected the most appropriate for the study.

5.8   SIGNIFICANCE OF LANGUAGE

Language and its significance in travel and tourism have remained the least studied topic. Cohen and Cooper (1986) were the first to focus their studies on the importance of language in tourism. Mathieson and Geoffrey (1982) through their research found that language could be a very useful indicator to study the social impacts of tourism. The language was also reflective of the sociocultural changes that might influence international travel.

The tourists' behavior to a large extent could be influenced by language. Barriers to communication are the major challenges encountered in transcultural travel, and it could also influence decisions and choices of destinations during travel. Pinhey and Iverson (1994) investigated the concerns for safety among Japanese visitors to Guam. The study revealed a positive and very strong correlation between security and safety perception and confidence in communication.

Yavas (1987) identified through his study that travelers in the Middle East with high-risk perception preferred other similar Arab countries due to the same religion, heritage, and most importantly, a common language. A study on exchange visitors who traveled to the United States and China, between 1985 and 1987, reported problems in communication that included language and lack of information (Wei et al., 1989). Tapachai and Waryszak (2000) performed a research on the image of a tourist destination, and they inferred that language played a pivotal role in creating an attractive destination image.

This 'no barrier on language' was one main reason that Australians preferred to travel to the United States. More recently, Basala and Klenosky (2001) studied the influence of language on destination choices. From their study, it was inferred that the familiarity-seeking travelers laid a lot of emphasis on the language spoken. The study showed great influence of language on individuals who were classified as familiarity seekers during travel. It was more important for this group of travelers that the language spoken in the destination was the same as their local language. Therefore, it was concluded that when there was a barrier in communication, it elevated the perceived risk. It became more important to communicate with the consumers when the consumers perceived higher risk (Basala and Klenosky, 2001).

5.9 FAMILIARITY WITH THE DESTINATION

Earlier, it was always thought that the construct of prior knowledge had two very different viewpoints, that of being familiar with the destination and being an expert with the destination (Alba and Hutchinson, 1987). Another viewpoint was also studied and added on to the construct by Cho (2002), namely, past experience along with expertise and familiarity. His study showed a strong correlation between expertise and familiarity, and therefore the study concluded that familiarity and expertise formed two-dimensional viewpoints of prior knowledge along with past experience. Having been to a destination before can, to a great extent, impact the expertise on a destination, familiarity with a destination, and more involvement in information search behavior about the destination (Gursoy, 2001). The study ended up testing only the relationship between expertise and familiarity with information search behavior. As the study did not verify the variables of previous visits, the result showed only a positive direct relationship between expertise and familiarity. The study ended up having only two dimensions, that of familiarity or expertise and prior experience, as was identified by Cho (2002).

Both, past experience and familiarity, were observed to be negatively associated with risk perception (Cheron and Ritchie, 1982; Lepp and Gibson, 2003). Lepp and Gibson (2003) explored the relationship between travel decision and familiarity and between familiarity and knowledge search (Hales and Shams, 1990; Millman and Pizam, 1995). Different views have been conceptualized on familiarity with the tourist destination. Srull (1983) described the construct of familiarity as being a level of awareness about the product or service.

This may not importantly emerge out of actual experience. The frequency of previous visits was used as a measure of familiarity in a study conducted by Millman and Pizam (1983), and they found that the interest and likelihood of visiting a destination had an effect on the familiarity with a destination. With the support of informational and experiential dimensions, a familiarity index was developed by Baloglu (1995). Gursoy (2001) developed familiarity as a one-dimensional concept, and he inferred that familiarity of a destination would influence external information search behavior. A study on the selection of holiday destinations in Europe by Arab travelers found that majority of the respondents were willing to travel abroad to the European countries only if they were familiar with the destination (Hales and Shams, 1990). A study on the behavior of vacation travelers found that perception of risk had a very strong negative association with novelty or familiarity (Cheron and Ritchie, 1982). The study proved that the more familiar travelers were with leisure activities, the lesser were the risks perceived.

5.10   PRIOR EXPERIENCE AT THE DESTINATION

Prior experience at the destination (Vogt and Andereck, 2003) is another important element that can influence the tourist decision-making process. Bettman and Park (1980) found through their study that travelers who were inexperienced spend more time studying about the destination by evaluating the various levels of attributes. They tried hard to develop choice criteria very similar to the consumers who possessed knowledge and experience. Many researchers in the past investigated the relationship between prior experience and travel purchase decisions (Mazursky, 1989), the image of the destination (Millman and Pizam, 1995; Baloglu and McCleary, 1999; Vogt and Andereck, 2003), and search for information (Cho, 2002). The personal travel experience could affect the perceptions of risk and safety (Sonmez and Graefe, 1998). This affected the chances of confirming or eliminating the perceptions. The experiences enabled the travelers to lower their perception of risk.

The study found that prior travel experience to destinations not only enhanced their need and willingness to travel there again, but they were also ready to explore other new and unexplored places in the destinations, which were otherwise measured to be risky (Sonmez and Graefe, 1998). Moutinho (1987) in his study found that the experience during the vacation was inversely proportional to the perceived level of risk during vacation purchase. Research also proved that perception of risks related to health, food, and terrorism are lesser when travelers have more experience in the destination (Lepp and Gibson, 2003). Jeng (2000) observed the step-by-step process of travel planning and inferred that travel planning involved decision behavior in multiple stages. Tourists normally have to make a number of decisions, in addition to the actual decision on choosing the travel destination before embarking on the trip. Some of the decisions included the number and profile of members in the travel group, the date of travel, the length of travel, the modes of transportation to be used, the routing of travel, the available budget, the destinations to be involved, and the touristic interests (Fesenmaier and Jeng, 2000; Moutinho, 1987).

Most research on touristic decisions has focused on choices of destinations and other influencing factors on destination choices (Dellaert et al., 1998; Shin, 1998; Um and Crompton, 1990; Crouch and Louviere, 2000). All the studies found that during the travel planning process, travelers usually consider only few travel destinations (Woodside and Sherrell, 1977). The Evoked Set Concept was used to create the model for choosing a travel destination (Howard, 1963). A general model was later developed on leisure travel destination awareness and choice by Woodside and Lysonski (1989), and the model described that awareness about a destination involved four categories of sets, namely, the consideration set, insert set, unavailable and aware set, and inept set. Further study to identify the traveler's potential awareness and evoked sets was undertaken by Um and Crompton (1990). In leisure travel, the influence of attitude on the destination choice process was also studied. The study revealed different dimensions of attitude, satisfaction of need, motivations for traveling, the challenges involved, newness of relaxation, learning outcomes, sense of curiosity, social acceptance, the tourists' need to act according to the opinions of their social groups, the ability to travel, and the individual's ability in terms of money, time, skill, and health.

5.11 FACTORS INFLUENCING MOTIVATION

The push and pull factors of motivation were another set of major factors that influenced travel decisions, and these factors were studied by a number of researchers (Klenosky, 2002; Lee et al., 2002). Klenosky (2002) related the push motivational elements to the needs, wants, and desires of the traveler. These included the traveler's need to escape, interactions with other members of the society, desire for rest and relaxation, to name a few. The pull factors were related to the destination, its features, and attributes. Some examples of the pull factors included the presence of attractions in the destination such as the sun, sand, and surf, for example. A study on the five standard push factors and the seven standard pull factors showed that individual travelers mainly moved in search of similar needs such as the novelty, and this similar reason influenced the choice of travel destinations that were very different (Yuan and McDonald, 1990). The push motivation factors were employed in a study on Japanese overseas travelers (Cha et al., 1995). The research grouped together the Japanese travelers into three very different groups, namely, the novelty seekers, the sports seekers, and the family or relaxation seekers. In another study conducted on pleasure travelers from Germany to Canada, United States of America, and Asia, the construct on environment and safety was measured by three factors, the safety of the traveler when traveling alone, hygiene and cleanliness, and quality of air, water, and soil (Lee et al., 2002). The results from the study revealed that motivational factors played a key role in influencing destination choice.

The traditional processes involved in decision-making incorporated rules that used several alternative choices to identify the best alternative (Crompton, 1992; Crompton and Ankomah, 1993; Van Raaij and Crotts, 1994; Ankomah et al., 1996). A set of propositions were developed by Crompton and Ankomah (1993) that were based on the consideration set and the final choice decisions. Researchers also proposed many more forms of sets. But contrary to many studies that focused purely on choice sets, Lindh (1998) found through his study that Swedish household travelers considered only one destination for a trip without the support of any alternative destinations. This proved that they do not make any strong and elaborate plans for their trips. Hence, in the absence of any alternative choice destinations, the three important decision stages, namely, whether to travel or not, the destination to which to travel to, and how to travel to the destination were not processed sequentially in the tourists' mind. They were often chosen individually. This result implied that factors such as risk perception, prior experience, and personal attributes could influence every stage of the decision-making process during travel.

As there is intangibility in the return on large travel purchase decisions over a long period of time, decision-making during travel purchase is a highly unique process (Moutinho, 1987). Four exquisite forms of travel purchase decisions were presented in the study by Mathieson and Wall (1982). They were the experiential characteristics of the tourism product that did not provide any form of tangible returns, substantial expenses incurred on the tourism product, careful planning before the actual travel purchase and actual visitation to the site of production, which is the destination, unlike other tangible products. One of the major attributes, that defined the difference while decision-making between purchasing the tangible goods and services like travel, was the concept of intangibility (Hudson and Gilbert, 2000). The first model that emphasized on the challenges, valuation of risk perception, and their influence on decision-making was proposed by Schmoll (1977).

Substantiated with an extensive description of the travel buying process by offering a model consisting of four specifications, namely, the stimuli to travel, the external influencing factors, the personal and social factors that could influence travel behavior, and finally the features of the tourist destination. The model could successfully illustrate all the factors involved in the travel purchase decision process. The difficulty in quantifying the relevancy of the variables and testing the interrelationships between the variables turned out to be one of the important drawbacks of the model. The September 11, 2001, terrorist attacks resulted in complete chaos in the international travel and tourism market. It caused the loss of almost 10 million jobs in the highly sensitive industry and many international, national, and regional airlines ran into bankruptcy (Plog, 2004). But the study also revealed that post 9/11, Americans continued to travel. The major effect was that travelers preferred to move by road rather than fly and most of the travelers preferred visiting destinations closer by. This form of behavior was also observed during the Gulf War among the travelers from the United Kingdom. Though there was a significant decline in air travel to all foreign locations, there was a big up to sea travel from the United Kingdom to neighboring France (Coshall, 2003). The studies proved that during such challenging situations, the travelers instead of canceling their entire trip, preferred to change their modes of travel (Plog, 2004).

Studying the correlation between perception of risk and travel purchase decisions, Yavas (1987) ascertained three major causes for foreign travel decisions to be influenced by risk perception as the primary force. These included services and products with the fundamental difference of intangibility, this difference in intangibility that resulted in the inability to correctly infer the benefits from the travel that could result in anxiety, the high involvement situations arising from undertaking travel to foreign destinations, and the risk perception that could influence the travelers' decisions, especially when adopting something totally new. The influence of perceived risks also had the power to affect and alter the nature of travel purchase decisions (Sonmez and Graefe, 1998). Two forms of travel purchase decisions are studied further, namely, the likelihood of travel and style of travel.

5.12   LIKELIHOOD OF TRAVEL

Norman (1995) studied the correlation between the risk perception constraints and the general travel purchase decisions to travel or not. This model was more general in nature and was purely based on the assumption that would-be-travelers first decided whether they wanted to travel or not, and then only would they decide on the destination to which they wanted to travel. Zimmer et al. (1995) investigated the sociodemographic factors of senior nationals in Canada and how they influenced the travel purchase decisions. Age was found to be the most reliable predictor to differentiate the travelers from the nontravelers. Two other variables that showed high correlation with the ability to travel were education and the number of mobility problems. Other variables that were included in the study were self-assessed health status of the travelers, their income level, and their ability to handle money, chronic health conditions, and their interest in spending money on recreation. Sonmez and Graefe (1998) also found that individuals were more likely to not travel to certain destinations where they perceived a higher level of risk. The researchers examined the likelihood of visiting and avoiding particular regions.

5.13   STYLE OF TRAVEL

The literature on travel style provides various diverse categories of classification and there seems to be no absolute consent on travel styles established as yet. Taylor (1998) identified three travel philosophies from the data collected from respondents of 13 different countries between 1986 and 1990. He labeled them as planned travel or package travel, 37.5%; independent travel or travelers making their own travel arrangements, 33.5%; and reluctant travel or individuals who do not like traveling, 29%. The proportions given represented the average for respondents of all the 13 countries. Even though there were considerable differences in proportions across the countries, the three travel philosophy segments were identified in all of the countries. Taylor (1998) suggested that travel style information contributed to a better understanding of international tourism as a growth or a decline in either independent or planned travel required different marketing strategies. It was essential to understand the factors that influenced travelers to select a travel style. Plog (2004) also classified four types of travel style, the independent travel, the escorted tour, the inclusive package, and the partial package. Madrigal (1995) examined personality type and personal values in his study to predict travel type, group, and independent travel with the support of a sample of US domestic travelers. The results that were derived from the discriminant analysis showed that personal values strongly discriminated group travelers from independent travelers.

Group travelers always value being well-respected by others they meet and always share noble relationships with others. Independent travelers were mainly inclined to value self-fulfillment and accomplishment. A study of mainland American visitors to the Hawaii Islands revealed that elderly visitor parties always wanted to visit many destinations in the company of very few people in the party. They intended to make brief visits, and those who were on their first trip to Hawaii were more likely to purchase package tours than travel independently (Sheldon and Mak, 1987). Unlike few other studies that suggested that novelty seekers preferred traveling alone and were less likely to buy an organized group tour, Basala and Klenosky (2001) identified that novelty seekers preferred traveling with friends the most and traveling alone the least. They felt the results of their study were based in part on the travel scenario they used, which described the destination as having a strong history of instability and terrorism activities (Basala and Klenosky, 2001).

Quiroga (1990) studied and found that personal safety was the most important reason to participate in package tour activities for travelers above the age of 65 years, whereas it was the least important for respondents under 26 years of age in a sample of Latin American tourists on a guided tour to Europe. A detailed advantage of organized tours opted by travelers in the order of importance comprised the comprehensive way of traveling, economic reasons, personal safety, lack of worry, and to make new friends (Quiroga, 1990). Safety was found to be not only an important factor for seniors but also for travelers in all age categories. Money and Crotts (2003) suggested that consumers with a medial level of uncertainty avoidance would purchase fewer prepackaged trips and would stay longer at a destination. They would visit more destinations compared with high uncertainty avoidance consumers. The researchers found that high-risk aversion individuals were more likely to travel in bigger groups of people and visit fewer destinations with shorter average lengths of stay. On the other hand, the independent travelers were willing to undertake more risks in selecting vacations when levels of risk were perceived to be really low or irrelevant (Hyde and Lawson, 2003).

5.14   RESEARCH GAP

Through the in-depth reviews of literature carried out, it is evident that a number of important studies have already been completed on the impact of perceived risk on travelers and on the destination choice process. But the number of research studies performed on the risk perception of tourists from South India has been limited. The present study aimed to evaluate the risk perception of tourists from South India and its impact on their destination choice process. The study will also try to identify heterogeneity among the tourists based on their risk perception patterns. The secondary data gathered through the literature were supplemented with the primary data that were collected from the population and the sample group under the area of investigation through a survey involving a scheduled questionnaire. Based on the nature of the data collected, data analysis techniques were employed to identify a character of heterogeneity among tourist groups based on risk perception. The findings would thereby enable travel organizations to market tourist destinations accordingly to them.

5.15   FINDINGS FROM THE STUDY

The study found that there was a significant relationship between anxiety about safety and security as a perceived risk factor and gender of the tourists from South India. Based on the gender, the tourists felt the need to always try to experience cultures and customs very different from their own. The study also found that there was a significant relationship between the tourists' age groups and starting a holiday without medicines and first aid. Tourists from South India showed interest in reading and studying about the culture of the destinations that they planned to visit. Employment status also impacted the use of telecommunication devices during a holiday. Irrespective of the perceived risks, the choice between the package and nonpackage tours also influenced the choice of the holiday destination as there was a significant relationship between the choice of the package tour and the tourists experiencing something totally new from what they have already experienced before.

These findings are further explained as follows: Safety of belongings was the most important perceived risk during travel. South Indian tourists always preferred carrying heavy luggage during travel and they were always afraid of losing or misplacing their belongings during travel. Tourists were also very careful about their health during travel. They were always afraid of falling sick from having the local food and water during travel and therefore they never left for a holiday without carrying their medicines and first aid, they also preferred the most comfortable mode of transportation during a holiday. Tourists seek to experience something totally new during a holiday. Their ideal holiday involved experiencing things that were totally new from what they had already experienced before. For that very purpose, tourists did not plan their holidays in detail as it took away some of the unexpectedness in the destinations. They liked holidays that were educational as the same routine work bored them. Tourists looked forward to exploring new things during travel. During a holiday, they always tried to experience cultures and customs very different from their own, and they always tried to explore new things in the holiday destination that they visited. During the holiday, tourists from South India always looked forward to a change in the environment very different from their own. Perceived risk about comfort and well-being in the destination was another factor that influenced destination choice. Tourists always made sure that they were comfortable with the holiday destinations that they chose and they always looked forward to enhancing their feeling of well-being during a holiday. They did not travel to a destination unless they were confident about the safety of the destination. Influence of family and friends did have an impact on the choice of a holiday destination.

Tourists in certain age group categories feared that family and friends could disapprove of their choice of a holiday destination. Most of the tourists felt safe traveling to a destination because everyone else went there and they also wanted to travel to a holiday destination to enhance their self-image among their family and friends. Majority of the tourists were afraid that they might spend a lot of money during the holiday and they also thought that more time spent on a holiday would make it more pleasurable and enjoyable. The majority of the tourists from South India look forward to a thrilling experience during a holiday. The tourists, especially those belonging to the younger age group, felt good being a little scared during a holiday. They liked to do frightening, thrilling, and daring activities during a holiday. They enjoyed experiencing surprises during the holiday and looked forward to seeking adventure during the holiday trip.

Some of the tourists look forward to learning and involvement in the holiday destination. They were interested in interacting with the local community during the holiday. Majority of the tourists spend time reading and studying about the culture of the destination that they plan to visit to reduce their perceived risk about the destination. They always want a sense of discovery to be part of their holiday, and they like to take a holiday from time to time as it helps them to unwind. The majority of the tourists relied on the internet for gathering information on the destinations that they planned to visit. Magazines, television advertisements, and travel programs are also depended upon for gathering information on the destinations. Information from friends and relatives were also used in making travel plans, but it was found that very few tourists relied on travel agents for information about the destinations they planned to visit. Safety and security of the tourists did not influence the choice of a destination. Some of the tourists felt that anxiety about safety and security prevented them from taking risks during travel. Local news about a destination did influence their holiday there. Civil unrest usually demotivates them from traveling to a destination, but the tourists did not mind traveling to a destination that was politically unstable. They do not like to travel alone for fear of safety and security. Confidence in communicating in the destination was not a major factor that influenced the choice of a destination. Majority of the tourists are assured of communicating confidently with anyone during a holiday. Most of the tourists felt it important to use telecommunication devices during a holiday and they preferred to always carry and use their smartphones during a holiday. Majority of the tourists felt that their knowledge of English language was enough to help them in communicating with different cultures as they did not know any foreign language.

There is a significant relationship between the gender and anxiety about safety and security as a perceived risk factor. Female tourists felt that anxiety about safety and security always prevented them from taking risks during travel, whereas their male counterparts were not averse to taking risks during travel for fear of their safety and security. Many of the tourists agree that they always read and study the culture of the destination that they plan to visit. There exists a significant relationship between choice of package tour and tourists experiencing something totally new from what they have already experienced before. The majority of the tourists preferred to travel on a fully packaged tour. They agreed that fully packaged tours could offer them experiences that were totally new from what they had already experienced before.

The amount of risk involved in choosing a partially packaged tour was highest as it offered the highest risk in offering experiences that were totally new from what they had already experienced before. Mapping the risk perceptions, majority of the tourists took a neutral stand that they may or may not focus on their comfort with the holiday destination that is chosen. Irrespective of their annual income, they wished for more comfort in the holiday destinations they chose to visit. The investigation found that as the income of the tourists increased, so did their need for more comfort with the holiday destination they chose.

5.16   SUGGESTIVE IMPLICATIONS

Every individual, irrespective of the nature of their employment, takes a holiday from time to time as it helps them to unwind. Therefore, the travel professional should be ready to cater to the needs of all categories of tourists and provide them a relaxing and different environment. Comfort and well-being of the tourists are to be ensured in all destinations. Safety of belongings is the foremost perceived risk that majority of tourists traveling from South India have. Travel professionals are to advise the tourists to make sure that their valuables are safe with them at all times. Tourists are to be cautious when they display valuables, and it is always best to dress conservatively so that they may not be identified as tourists. Tourists should be advised to exercise caution while consuming local food and drinks. Travel professionals can instruct all tourists, irrespective of their age, to carry the necessary medicines and first aid with them, should they get hurt or fall ill. Travel professionals need to understand the travel needs completely and arrange the most comfortable mode of transportation for the tourists during a holiday. Travel professionals should be careful when handling tourists of a younger age group from South India as these tourists have very less risk perception about getting hurt during a holiday.

These tourists have to be oriented on the isolated, unfamiliar, and unsafe places at the destinations and should be cautioned on the control they should implement on the intake of alcohol and drugs. Travel professionals should ensure that the tourists do not end up paying a lot of money at the destination, and they should orient the tourists on responsible spending at the destination. The time spent at the holiday destination should make the holiday more pleasurable and enjoyable. There will be tourists who will want to enjoy surprises during the holiday and will be looking forward to seeking adventure at the destination. This has to be coupled with elements of learning and involvement in the holiday destination. Tourists should be oriented to spend a large amount of time reading and studying about the cultures of the destinations that they plan to visit. Communication and differences in language can be a major factor in choosing a holiday destination. Body language and hand gestures, that are nonverbal communication cues, may be considered harmless but may turn out to be offensive in the destinations of choice.

This list of gestures that are considered rude in other places may grow beyond the obvious. Travel professionals understand the importance for tourists of using telecommunication devices at the destination; therefore, they should be able to orient the tourists about the use of mobile phones, availability of the internet, and use of other forms of communication applications at the destinations. Travel professionals should never send tourists to destinations that are politically unstable or destinations that can experience civil unrest as they can be a threat to the tourists' safety and security. Male tourists are normally less concerned about their safety and security, and this might stimulate them from taking such risks during travel.

5.17   CONCLUSION

This chapter envisages developing an understanding of the dimensions of perceived risk and its impact on the destination choice process of tourists from South India. Numerous factors of perceived risk were identified and addressed through the study. The perceived risks varied according to the nature of the destination. For example, tourists who wanted new and different experiences while traveling perceived very fewer risks, whereas tourists who have visited a destination before also perceived lesser risk while traveling. It was such types of overall perceptions of risk during travel that influenced the choice of tourist destinations.

KEYWORDS

- **Tourist purchase decision**
- **perceived risk**
- **dimensions of perceived risks**
- **destination choice**

REFERENCES

Alba, J. W.; Hutchinson, J. W. Dimensions of Consumer Expertise. *J. Consum. Res.* **1987**.

Ankomah, P. K.; Crompton, J.; Baker, D. Influence of Cognitive Distance in Vacation Choice. *Ann. Tourism Res.* **1996**.

Bacharach, S. B. Organizational Theories: Some Criteria for Evaluation. *Acad. Manage. Rev.* **1989**.

Baloglu, S.; McCleary, K. W. U.S. International Pleasure Travelers' Images of Four Mediterranean Destinations: A Comparison of Visitors and Non Visitors. *J. Travel Res.* **1999**.

Basala, S. L.; Klenosky, D. B. Travel-Style Preferences for Visiting a Novel Destination: A Conjoint Investigation Across the Novelty-Familiarity Continuum. *J. Travel Res.* **2001**.

Bauer, R. A. Consumer Behavior as Risk Taking. In *Dynamic Marketing for a Changing World;* Hancock, R. S., Ed.; American Marketing Association: Chicago, 1960; pp 389–398.

Becker, C.; Murrmann, S. K. Methodological Considerations in Multi-Cultural Research. *Tourism Anal.* **2000**.

Bell, D. E.; Farquhar, P. H. Perspectives on Utility Theory. *Oper. Res.* **1986**.

Bettman, J. R.; Park, C. W. Effects of Prior Knowledge and Experience and Phase of the Choice Process on Consumer Decision Processes: A Protocol Analysis. *J. Consum. Res.* **1980**.

Cha, S.; McCleary, K. W.; Uysal, M. Travel Motivations of Japanese Overseas Travelers: A Factor-Cluster Segmentation Approach. *J. Travel Res.* **1995**.

Chandler, J. A.; Costello, C. A. A Profile of Visitors at Heritage Tourism Destinations in East Tennessee According to Plog's Lifestyle and Activity Level Preferences Model. *J. Travel Res.* **2002**.

Chen, J. S. A Comparison of Information Usage Between Business and Leisure Travelers. *J. Hospitality Leisure Mark.* **2000**.

Cheron, E. J.; Ritchie, J. R. B. Leisure Activities and Perceived Risk. *J. Leisure Res.* **1982**.

Cho, Y.-H. *Exploring Web-Based Virtual Tour Experience: The Effects of Telepresence on Destination Image.* Unpublished Ph. D., University of Illinois at Urbana-Champaign, Urbana-Champaign, 2002.

Choudhry, Y. A. Pitfalls in International Marketing Research: Are you speaking French like a Spanish cow? *Akron Bus. Econ. Rev.* **1986**.

Cohen, E. Contemporary Tourism-Trends and Challenges: Sustainable Authenticity or Contrived Post-Modernity? In *Change in Tourism: People, Places, Processes;* Butler, R., Pearce, D., Eds.; Routledge: New York, 1995; pp 12–29.

Cohen, E.; Cooper, R. L. Language and Tourism. *Ann. Tourism Res.* **1986**.

Cohen, E.; Cooper, R. L. Chapter 14: Language and Tourism. In *Contemporary Tourism: Diversity and Change;* Elsevier Ltd.: Oxford, UK, 2004; pp 205–227.

Coshall, J. T. The Threat of Terrorism as an Intervention on International Travel Flows. *J. Travel Res.* 2003.

Crompton, J.; Ankomah, P. K. Choice Set Propositions in Destination Decisions. *Ann. Tourism Res.* 1993.

Crouch, G. I.; Louviere, J. J. A Review of Choice Modeling Research in Tourism, Hospitality, and Leisure. *Tourism Anal.* **2000**.

Dellaert, B. G. C.; Ettema, D. F.; Lindh, C. Multi-Faceted Tourist Travel Decisions: A Constraint-Based Conceptual Framework to Describe Tourists' Sequential Choices of Travel Components. *Tourism Manage.* **1998**.

Ferber, R. The Problem of Bias in Mail Returns: A Solution. *Public Opin. Q.* **1948–1949**.

Fesenmaier, D.; Jeng, J.-M. Assessing Structure in the Pleasure Trip Planning Process. *Tourism Anal.* **2000**.

Fishburn, P. C. *Found. Expected Util.* Reidel: Donrdrecht, Holland, **1982**.

Goeldner, C. R.; Ritchie, J. R. B.; McIntosh, R. W. *Tourism: Principles, Practices, Philosophies.* John Wiley & Sons, Inc.: New York, 2000.

Gursoy, D.; Gavcar, E. International Leisure Tourists' Involvement Profile. *Ann. Tourism Res.* **2003**, *30*(4), 906–926.

Han, J.; Weaver, P. *Communication Problems in Foreign Travel.* Paper presented at the Eighth Annual Graduate Education and Graduate Students Research Conference in Hospitality and Tourism, Las Vegas, Nevada, 2003.

Hofstede, G. *Culture's Consequences: Comparing Values, Behaviors, Institutions, and Organizations Across Nations,* 2nd ed.; Sage Publications, Inc.: Thousand Oaks, California, 2001.

Howell, D. C. *Statistical Methods for Psychology*; Duxbury: Pacific Grove, CA, 2001.

Hudson, S.; Gilbert, D. Chapter Eight. Tourism Constraints: The Neglected Dimensions of Consumer Behavior Research. In *Consumer Psychology of Tourism, Hospitality and Leisure;* Woodside, A. G., Crouch, G. I., Mazanec, J. A., Oppermann, M., Sakai, M. Y., Eds.; CABI Publishing: New York, 2000; Vol. 1, pp 137–154.

Jacoby, J.; Kaplan, L. B. *The Components of Perceived Risk.* Paper presented at the Third Annual Conference, College Park, M.D. 1972.

Jeng, J.; Fesenmaier, D. Conceptualizing the Travel Decision-Making Hierarchy: A Review of Recent Developments. *Tourism Anal.* **2002**.

Jiang, J.; Havitz, M. E.; O'Brien, R. M. Validating the International Tourist Role Scale. *Ann. Tourism Res.* **2000**.

Kaplan, L. B.; Szybillo, G. J.; Jacoby, J. Components of Perceived Risk in Product Purchase: A Cross-Validation. *J. Appl. Psychol.* **1974**.

Kashyap, R.; Bojanic, D. C. A Structural Analysis of Value, Quality, and Price Perceptions of Business and Leisure Travelers. *J. Travel Res.* **2000**.

Klenosky, D. B. The "Pull" of Tourism Destinations: A Means-End Investigation. *J. Travel Res.* **2002**.

Laroche, M.; McDougall, G. H. G.; Bergeron, J.; Yang, Z. Exploring How Intangibility Affects Perceived Risk. *J. Serv. Res.* **2004**.

Lepp, A.; Gibson, H. Tourist Roles, Perceived Risk and International Tourism. *Ann. Tourism Res.* **2003**.

Mathieson, A.; Wall, G. *Tourism: Economic, Physical and Social Impacts;* Longman Inc.: New York, 1982.

Millman, A.; Pizam, A. The Role of Awareness and Familiarity with a Destination. *J. Travel Res.* **1995**.

Mitchell, V.-W.; Davies, F.; Moutinho, L.; Vassos, V. Using Neural Networks to Understand Service Risk in the Holiday Product. *J. Bus. Res.* **1999**.

Moutinho, L. Consumer Behaviour in Tourism. *Eur. J. Mark.* **1987**.

Moutinho, L. *Strategic Management in Tourism;* CABI Publishing: New York, 2000.

Nicolau, J. L.; Mas, F. J. Stochastic Modeling: A Three-Stage Tourist Choice Process. *Ann. Tourism Res. 32*(1), 2005.

Pearce, P. L. *The Social Psychology of Tourist Behavior*. Pergamon Press Inc.: New York, 1982.

Peter, J. P.; Ryan, M. J. An Investigation of Perceived Risk at the Brand Level. *J. Mark. Res.* **1976**.

Plog, S. A Carpenter's Tools: An Answer to Stephen L. J. Smith's Review of Psychocentrism/Allocentrism. *J. Travel Res.* **1990**.

Plog, S. *Leisure Travel: Making it a Growth Market...Again!* John Wiley & Sons, Inc.: New York, 1991.

Plog, S. Developing and Using Psychographics in Tourism Research. In *Travel, Tourism, and Hospitality Research: a Handbook for Managers and Researchers,* 2nd ed.; Ritchie, J. R. B.; Goeldner, C. R., Eds.; John Wiley & Sons, Inc. 1994.

Plog, S. *Vacation Places Rated*; Fielding Worldwide, Inc.: Redondo Beach, California, 1995.

Plog, S. The Power of Psychographics and the Concept of Venturesomeness. *J. Travel Res.* **2002**.

Plog, S. *Leisure Travel: A Marketing Handbook;* Pearson Prentice Hall: Upper Saddle River, New Jersey, 2004.

Reimer, G. D. Packaging dreams. *Ann. Tourism Res.* **1990**.

Richter, L. K. International Tourism and Its Global Public Health Consequences. *J. Travel Res.* **2003**.

Roehl, W. S.; Fesenmaier, D. R. Risk Perceptions and Pleasure Travel: An Exploratory Analysis. *J. Travel Res.* **1992**.

Schewe, C. D.; Calantone, R. J. Psychographic Segmentation of Tourists. *J. Travel Res.* **1977**.

Schiffman, L. G.; Kanuk, L. L. *Consumer Behavior,* 7th ed.; Prentice Hall: Upper Saddle River, New Jersey, 2000.

Schmoll, G. A. *Tourism Promotion: Marketing Background, Promotion Techniques and Promotion Planning Methods;* Tourism International Press: London, 1977.

Sonmez, S. F. *An Exploratory Analysis of the Influence of Personal Factors on International Vacation Decisions Within the Context of Terrorism and/or Political Instability Risk.* Unpublished Ph.D., The Pennsylvania State University, University Park, 1994.

Sonmez, S. F.; Graefe, A. R. Determining Future Travel Behavior from Past Travel Experience and Perceptions of Risk and Safety. *J. Travel Res.* **1998a**.

Sonmez, S. F.; Graefe, A. R. Influence of Terrorism Risk on Foreign Tourism Decisions. *Ann. Tourism Res.* **1998b**.

SPSS. SPSS for Windows (Version 11.5): SPSS Inc. 2002.

Swarbrooke, J.; Horner, S. *Business Travel and Tourism;* Butterworth-Heinemann: Oxford, UK, 2001.

Taylor, G. D. Styles of travel. In *Global Tourism,* 2nd ed.; Theobald, W. F., Ed.; Butterworth-Heinemann: Boston, 1998; pp 267–277.

Um, S.; Crompton, J. Attitude Determinants in Tourism Destination Choice. *Ann Tourism Res.* 1990.

Um, S.; Crompton, J. The Roles of Perceived Inhibitors and Facilitators in Pleasure Travel Destination Decisions. *J. Travel Res.* **1992**.

Verhage, B. J.; Yavas, U.; Green, R. T. Perceived Risk: A Cross-Cultural Phenomenon? *Int. J. Res. Mark.* 1990.

Vogt, C. A.; Andereck, K. L. Destination Perceptions Across a Vacation. *J. Travel Res.* **2003**.

Wei, L.; Crompton, J.; Reid, L. M. Cultural Conflicts: Experiences of US visitors to China. *Tourism Manage.* (December) **1989**.

Woodside, A. G.; Lysonski, S. A General Model of Traveler Destination Choice. *J. Travel Res.* 27(4), 1989.

Woodside, A. G.; Sherrell, D. Traveler Evoked, Inept, and Inert Sets of Vacation Destinations. *J. Travel Res.* 16(1), 1977.

WTO. *Concepts, Definitions and Classifications for Tourism Statistics*; World Tourism Organization: Madrid, Spain, 1995.

WTO. *WTO World Tourism Barometer;* World Tourism Organization: Madrid, Spain, 2005.

Yavas, U. Foreign Travel Behaviour in a Growing Vacation Market: Implications for Tourism Marketers. *Eur. J. Mark.* **1987**.

Yavas, U. Correlates of Vacation Travel: Some Empirical Evidence. *J. Prof. Serv. Mark.* **1990**.

Yuan, S.; McDonald, C. Motivational Determinates of International Pleasure Time. *J. Travel Res.* **1990**.

Zeithaml, V. A.; Bitner, M. J. *Services Marketing: Integrating Customer Focus Across the Firm,* 2nd ed.; McGraw-Hill Companies: Boston, Inc. 2000.

Zikmund, W. G. *Business Research Methods;* 6th ed.; Harcourt, Inc.: Orland, Florida, 2000.

Zimmer, Z.; Brayley, R. E.; Searle, M. S. Whether to Go and Where to Go: Identification of Important Influences on Seniors' Decisions to Travel. *J. Travel Res.* **1995**.

CHAPTER 6

COMMUNITY-BASED WASTE MANAGEMENT FOR SUSTAINABLE TOURISM IN BACKWATER REGIONS OF KERALA, INDIA

EMILDA K. JOSEPH

Christ College, Kattapanna, Kerala, India

CONTENTS

ABSTRACT

Tourism has grown into one of the world's major industries. As the growth of tourism depends on the sustainability of the environment, tourism has a major role to play in the conservation and protection of natural resources. Unless it is developed in a sustainable manner, the key objectives of sustainable tourism could not be achieved. Waste disposal is a serious problem in the areas where tourist arrivals and tourist activities are very high. Pollution of backwater regions due to tourism activities is a major concern and challenge for the tourism industry. Improper waste disposal would bring serious negative impacts on host community and destination. Local communities are being threatened due to improper waste management.

6.1   INTRODUCTION

Kerala in India is one among the unique destinations of travel lovers. Its unparalleled attraction makes Kerala the most popular tourist destination in the world. As the growth of the tourism activities depends upon the sustainability of the environment, tourism has a major role to play in the conservation of natural resources. But unfortunately, waste is the major challenge and problem to the backwater regions of Kerala, India, especially at Kumarakom and Kuttanadu in the districts of Kottayam and Alappuzha, respectively. These destinations, in one way or other, greatly seek to improve the life of the local communities through tourism, but waste disposal comes as a major threat to accomplish this goal in these destinations. Huge quantities of unscientifically dumped waste unbalance and spoil the pristine beauty of these tourist spots.

Lakes, beaches, backwaters, and houseboats are the unique selling point of Kerala's tourism industry. Most of the travelers are enchanted by the backwaters. It becomes the most enjoyable and not-to-miss tourist products in Kerala for the holiday and leisure trips of domestic and international tourists. Snake boat race, houseboat experiences, coir industry, marine products, and so on attract the tourists from all over the world. The inflow and outflow of national and international tourists create positive and negative impacts on the nature of the backwater regions. Houseboat tourism, that provides economic and sociocultural benefits to the local communities, is booming up in the backwater regions of Kerala, India.

But on the other hand, people living in the region become the victims of this ever-threatening problem of a poor waste management system. This directly or indirectly affects the groundwater, pure drinking water, and the eco-friendly life that a human being is bound to lead.

6.2 SUSTAINABILITY AND TOURISM

The word "sustainability" has become an important nomenclature in the field of the tourism industry as it is directly related to the available resources. It throws light on how this existing resource is used presently and how it will be used in the near future. Sustainable tourism has been developed to protect the natural beauty of the environment along with the creation of economic opportunities for local communities. It creates awareness among the people to conserve the environment as sustainable tourism is booming in many parts of the world. As the number of visitors to a destination increases, so does the curiosity and interest in visiting and experiencing new places and the new culture. Some of these destinations and places show how tourism activities, if not properly done, bring negative impact on the environment. Unethical practices of tourism activities may destroy the natural and cultural resources of the land that attracts the tourists. Excessive use of the environment to accommodate tourism activities may cause destruction of the ecosystem. Encroachment of builders, unsafe practices, and pollution due to waste and garbage and so on may bring negative impact on tourism.

It is very challenging to evaluate the negative impacts of the tourism activities on the ecosystem because the environmental impacts arise not only due to increase in a number of visitors but also due to various operations of tourism industry such as transportation, pollution, waste generation, and so on. Even though it is very difficult to evaluate the negative problems of the industry, it is the responsibility of each and every one who is involved in the tourism industry to protect the natural and cultural resources for sustainable tourism development.

Implementation of environment-friendly program creates a sustainable environment. It is better to practice solid waste management, energy saving measures, and recycling methods to reduce the negative impact on the destination or natural environment. Nowadays, customers are very well aware of the various responsibilities of the industry that would protect and conserve the natural ecosystem in which the industry operates. It is also essential to look into the changing customer preferences in choosing the most appropriate, eco-friendly, and sustainable products that would strengthen the environment and ecosystem. Habitats and sustainable products enliven the industry.

Different components such as local community, visitors, or tourists, and tourism industry in a destination must contribute to further sustainable development. When the products are more environmentally sensitive, to the business it means more profit, growth, and attention of the public because nowadays people are looking for the best natural and uncontaminated virgin products. The tourism enterprises do not often use sustainable practices to achieve the goals of the organization, but they consider it after they are financially stable or secure to reduce the risk of financial problems. Natural resources that are very crucial for protecting the environment and encouraging local livelihoods, such as fresh water, are also affected by various tourism activities. Recognizing these links is important to promote sustainable tourism in the coming future. At the same time, sustainability of the environment and nature protection through local awareness can have a positive effect on the destination. Legitimate tourism management practices promise both social and environmental benefits to the local community. It also needs the collaboration of sustainable development components as public and private agencies with the support of local communities.

The important factor to be remembered here is that if we want our economy to be developed in an unparalleled manner, so as to wipe off the poverty totally and to improve the livelihoods of local community, not only in this era but also forever, then we must make use of the available natural resources and cultural environment on which our tourism activities rely. Community participation in various tourism activities would lead us to attain sustainability in a destination. It will maintain a balance between economic sustainability and environmental sustainability. In such a way, sustainable tourism promotes environment-friendly tourism activities that would conserve the natural environment.

Sustainable tourism is not an isolated or peculiar type of tourism. To a certain extent, every type of tourism may make an effort to be more sustainable to the industry. Strengthening the tourism activities to be a nature-friendly one is not just in relation to controlling and subduing the harmful impacts of the industry. Tourism comes in a unique situation to promote local community, both economically and socially, to increase alertness in the preservation of the surroundings. Within the tourism industry, economic development and environmental protection should not be seen as divergent factors, rather they should be pursued hand in hand. Policies and performances must virtually support the benefits and diminish the expenses of tourism. The demands of tourists for water, marine resource, and wildlife have a distressing impact on the ecosystem. The local community, who are the victims, may be dispossessed of access to pure water and other resources. The unhealthy competition of houseboats is a major cause of pollution in the Vembanad Lake. The government and the Kerala Tourism department must take appropriate and strict measures to save tourism industry and its destinations otherwise the consequences will be horrible.

Responsible tourism has emerged as the need of the time in maintaining the uniqueness of backwater regions. To maximize the positive impacts of tourism and minimize the negative elements in the backwater regions, it is gaining wider acceptance across the destination. In India, Kerala is the pioneer in the field of responsible tourism and in Kerala, Kumarakom, the international backwater tourist destination, has the superiority of being the first destination in the country to have effectively implemented strategies in responsible tourism. This holistic form of tourism is providing tourists and the local community the supreme possible benefits from tourism with no cause of any environmental or social damage. Responsible tourism aims at protecting the environment with people participation, which vicariously benefits everyone socially and economically. Environmental protection initiatives may be incorporated to ensure sustainable tourism development.

6.3   THE BACKWATERS OF KERALA, INDIA

Backwater is "a part of a river not reached by the current, where the water is stagnant," or a body of water (as an inlet) that is out of the main current of a larger body, and Kerala, India showcases a lot of its charming backwaters. The backwaters of Kerala, India run through four major districts of Kerala, namely, Kollam, Alappuzha, Kottayam, and Kochi. Vembanad Lake, the largest backwater body of Kerala, India, runs through Alappuzha and Kottayam districts and opens out into the sea at the Kochi port. Backwaters of Kerala take every visitor to the most enchanting experience of *Kayals* (lakes), *Kettuvallams,* (houseboats), and countless lagoons. A journey along streams and waterways allows every tourist to take pleasure of unique life. Tourists can refresh themselves with natural best tender coconut that is found richly along the banks of Vembanad Lake. This amazing backwater is also blessed with charming natural rich islands. Snake boat races, local cuisine of steamed tapioca, and unique preparation of *Karimeen* (Green chromide or Pearl spot fish), unique classical dance forms and art forms of Kerala in India such as Kathakali, Kuchipudi, Mohiniyattam, and Bharathanatyam bring a major feast for the eyes of every visitor.

Some of the rivers flow down to join the vast stretches of backwaters and *canals* that interlace the heart of Alappuzha and the nearby regions of Kottayam. They support a prosperous wealth of fish and are also home to quite a lot of species, both inside and outside the water. Birds, both local birds, and migratory ones, find these water bodies ideal for feeding, nesting, and breeding. The local people look forward to these water bodies for food in the form of a variety of fish and also for livelihood. Traveling through the backwater villages, especially the ones in Alappuzha and Kottayam, the visitors would be treated with immense stretches of paddy fields, groves, swaying coconut trees, and several other peculiar types with their branches leaning over the water. Vembanad Lake is the largest lake in the state of Kerala in India, which covers an area of 200 km². Different major rivers and lakes that flow into this Vembanad Lake include Achencovil River, Manimala River, Meenachil River, Muvattupuzha River, Pampa River, and Periyar River. This lake also consists of islands such as Pathiramanal, Perumbalam, and Pallippuram. The world-famous Nehru Trophy Boat Race held in the Punnamada Lake at the Vembanad Lake makes a major contribution to the tourism industry. Kumarakom is one of the famous tourist spots around the Vembanad Lake. Various villages such as Punnamada, R-block, Nedumudi, Champakulam, and Kavalam play a major role in the tourism sector. The emergence of the tourism sector increased the value of the land, and the local people sold off their agricultural land to the tourism sector.

Women's participation in various tourism fields shows a paradigm shift from the traditional occupation. It is due to the increased number of houseboats, speedboats, and motorboats as the part of backwater tourism. But unless and until enough care is given, degradation of culture and mass collection of waste materials in these areas would be the aftereffect.

6.3.1 ALAPPUZHA

This destination is an important backwater destination of Kerala, India. It is known as the "Venice of East." It is famous for the boat race, beaches, marine products, coir industry, backwater tourism, and houseboat tourism. Kuttanadu—the rice bowl of Kerala, India lies in the lap of Alappuzha. Kuttanadu is one of the rarest places in the world where farming is done below sea level. With its web of waterways, Alappuzha is considered as the most striking destination of travel lovers. This destination is the spot for world-famous Nehru Trophy Boat Race conducted on the second Saturday in the month of August every year. The destinations such as Champakulam, Kavalam, Nedumudi, Pathiramanal, Punnamada, and R-Block are some of the famous tourist destinations of Alappuzha.

6.3.2 KOTTAYAM

Kottayam has many unique characteristics as it is surrounded by the Western Ghats on the east and the Vembanad Lake and paddy fields of Kuttanadu on the west. It is known by an enviable title: The land of letters, legends, latex, and lakes with panoramic backwater stretches, abundant green paddy fields, highlands, hills, and hillocks, rubber plantations, and birth/native places associated with many legends. Kumarakom, located on the Coast of Vembanad Lake, is the pride of this destination as this unique backwater destination is the best and the most important place in the world tourism map. Now it is considered as an international destination and is flooded with tourists from all over the world. This charming picnic spot provides boating facilities, houseboats, and motorboats, fishing, and other sightseeing experiences. Kumarakom is also famous for a bird sanctuary.

6.3.2.1 ATTRACTIONS

Alappuzha and Kottayam sketch unique attractions. Enormous stretches of backwaters and cruises on *Kettuvallams* (the traditional houseboat) could be seen here. This calm and quiet atmosphere makes every visitor fathom the natural beauty of backwater in a quite different way. Some of the main attractions include Champakulam, Kavalam, Pathiramanal, R-Block, Nedumudi, Punnamada, and Kumarakom.

6.3.3 CHAMPAKULAM

Champakulam is a small beautiful village and an important tourist destination in the Alappuzha district of Kerala, India. This village comes under the Kuttanadu region that is known as the rice bowl of Kerala. Champakulam is very famous for the Moolam Boat race, which is the oldest snake boat in the district of Kerala. This boat race is conducted on Moolam day of the Malayalam month Midhunam (i.e., in the month of July). The village is blessed with the natural beauty of backwater regions. There are a number of places where tourists can stay and experience the natural beauty of backwater regions.

6.3.4 KAVALAM

Kavalam is another main tourist attraction of Kerala in India, which is situated on the banks of the Vembanad Lake. This village is situated in the Kuttanadu region of Alappuzha district of Kerala. The natural scenic beauty of this place makes this destination unique. This destination is blessed with *Kayals* (canals) and lakes. Many tourists love to visit this place to experience the backwater regions.

6.3.5 PATHIRAMANAL

Pathiramanal is called "Sands of Midnight." This is the beautiful island located at the Shore of Vembanad Lake. This tourist spot is located at Muhamma Panchayath in the district of Alappuzha. This eco-friendly destination is only accessible by boat from Alappuzha. This place is the haven for rare migrating birds from different parts and corners of the world. A boat ride through serene waters will take you to this island that lies between the backwaters of Thaneermukkom and Kumarakom. According to a mythology that the people still believe, a young *Brahmin* divided the Vembanad Lake to perform his evening rituals and the water made way for the land to rise from below, thus creating the enchanting island of Pathiramanal.

6.3.6 R-BLOCK

R-Block is famous for wonders of the home-grown agricultural engineering know-how of Kerala and reminds the sightseer of the renowned dikes of Holland. Wide-ranging areas of land have been reclaimed from the backwaters and are protected by dikes built all around. Here, cultivation and habitation are made achievable four to ten feet below the sea level. A relaxed cruise along the canals that surround these *Kayals* is a memorable and unforgettable experience to any visitor coming to this beautiful place.

6.3.7 NEDUMUDI

The Nedumudi lies on the banks of the Vembanad Lake in Alappuzha District of Kerala, India. This beautiful tourist spot is entwined with lush green vegetation and numerous palms. The village presents itself as an ideal breakout for those who wish to spend a moment in the isolation of unspoilt nature. Its natural, quiet, and calm paddy fields with lakes and small canals create the best and nice tourist destination for travelers.

6.3.8 PUNNAMADA

This unique tourist destination is very famous for the Nehru Trophy Boat Race that is conducted on the second Saturday of August every year. The most popular and attractive attention of this boat race is the permutation of *Chundan Vallams* (snake boats). So, it is also known as snake boat race. During the month of August–September, this destination is crowded with thousands of tourists and a large number of competitors who participate in this boat race.

6.3.9 KUMARAKOM

Kumarakom, in India, is located 13 km away from Kottayam and is a quiet little village on the shore of Vembanad Lake in Kerala, India. It offers a wide diversity of flora, striking sightseeing, boating, and fishing experience. The bird sanctuary (Kumarakom Bird Sanctuary) here, which is spread across 14 acres, is a much-loved spot by the migratory birds and it is also a paradise for the ornithologist. Egrets, darters, herons, teals, waterfowls, cuckoo, wild duck, and migratory birds such as the Siberian Stork visit here in flocks and are attractions to the visitors. An enthralling backwater destination, Kumarakom offers visitors many other leisure options. It is one of the foremost travel destinations on the planet and a crown jewel of Kerala (India) tourism. The renowned backwaters of Kumarakom have brought visitors from far and wide to its shores. The dancing palm trees and the beautiful houseboats are just an added advantage which flourishes each visitor with an overwhelming experience.

6.4   WASTE MANAGEMENT

Waste Management remains the main problem for any natural destination. The problems we now face are as follows: (i) the amount of waste and (ii) the nature of the waste. Everything that we do creates leftovers and people living together create waste. The waste we create from every activity we perform is divided into three categories. It is organic, inorganic, or toxic. It can be further classified as solid, liquid, or gaseous, and each type needs special treatment. There is no greater task facing every single human being on the earth today than asking ourselves "How can I improve the environment?" and "How much waste am I creating today?" For every problem, there is a solution. We need to reflect on the past and see where and how these problems arise so that we can eradicate the dilemma in which we find ourselves now to make way for a cleaner, better, and healthier future. Proper waste management is the need of the time. The greatest example of handling waste is the "Zero Tolerance Policy" adopted by the Indian Government of no eating or drinking on the Metro railway system. This is a lesson for the world and look what has been achieved.

Nature is not nurtured by the people as it was intended in the beginning and natural resources are not utilized properly. Waste should not be considered as mere waste. The majority of the environmental resources are measured as unusable in our systems. If our ecosystem can be efficiently used, the quick exhaustion of natural resources can be solved and waste management problems could be solved as we would be able to reuse the waste, which in turn would also increase our income. Waste can be an important source of resource recovery. In economically progressing countries, resource improvement is common and generally happening at the local community level and reusable materials are frequently used as feedstock for reusing. If natural resources could be resourcefully and professionally used, the fast reduction of resources might be avoided and waste management problems could be solved (Wang et al., 2011).

The time-consuming centralized waste management approach is a crucial concern that needs to be reviewed in the upcoming decentralized waste management scenario. Due to the concerns about the prospective ecological impact caused, especially in the tourist destinations, both solid and liquid wastes have to be transported to the areas where scientific treatment or disposal would be possible.

6.5 COMMUNITY AND WASTE MANAGEMENT

Community-based tourism (CBT) presupposes the active participation of local communities in various projects of the industry for bringing up a better environment. The cooperation of local communities is of greater significance for tourism industry because it always deals with areas, regions, cultures, traditions, food, and so on. But it is very difficult to get the support and encouragement from the local communities to develop a proper sustainable destination. CBT and sustainable tourism are subsets of the concept of sustainable development (UNWTO, 2008). The UNWTO has guided many local communities to develop tourism under the principle of sustainability in and through the development of CBT projects (UNWTO, 2008). Tourism to be community-based or community-centered has to include the community from the very beginning of its various developments, starting with the planning processes. CBT initiatives that have employed an inclusive process from the onset of development have shown the greatest success (Cooper, 2004).

Recent studies have shown that in some regions of the Caribbean hotels and resorts produce more solid waste than all of the local residents combined (CAST/CTO, 1999). Nowadays, waste management is a growing issue in many countries. It becomes a great concern for the Central government, State government, Tourism departments, local authorities, researchers, local communities, and environmentalists. Total involvement of local people, who are living in and around the tourist destinations, is the need of the hour for an effective waste management system. Proper awareness and training should be given to the local communities in this regard. There should be enough waste bins in and around the destinations and training should be given to people to segregate the waste as degradable and nondegradable. The saying "cleanliness is next to godliness," must become practical in their lives. Health and hygiene must go hand in hand by making the surrounding areas neat and tidy. Most of the tourists are suggesting promotional ingredients keep the destinations clean, hygienic, and eco-friendly.

6.6   ROLE OF COMMUNITY IN TOURISM DEVELOPMENT

"The concept of CBT can be traced back and associated with alternatives development approaches formulated during the 1970s which were concerned with issues beyond strict economic reasoning, such as sustainability and empowerment" (Telfer, 2008). CBT activities may not be solely aiming at profit maximization for tourism investors, but they help in the promotion of healthy tourism practices. It directly deals with the various impacts of tourism on community and environment. "Community Based Tourism emerges from a community development strategy, using tourism as a tool to strengthen the ability of rural community organizations that manage tourism resources with the participation of the local people" (Community Based Tourism Hand Book, 2008).

Local communities could play an important role in the promotion of the various aspects of tourism. It is not only the responsibility of the tourism providers and visitors to take care of the environment, but the local residents also have an equal duty and responsibility to take care of their environment. The empowerment of local people is the main aim of CBT. The local community's relationship with the tourists generates economic growth, conservation of the environment, and benefits for local communities. CBT mainly looks upon community participation in various activities of the tourism industry. Many destinations use the community as the main strategy to protect the environment. The importance of CBT had a massive impact on the protection of the natural and cultural environment. CBT had a greater impact to remove the poverty from the local communities in rural villages. The community provides goods and services to the existing tourism business not only for a few but also for the mass tourism. Sustainable tourism should be community-based, giving the members of the community a full and fair chance of participating in various activities of tourism. There should be societal responsibility and environmental concern whenever we think about sustainable tourism.

The sustainable tourism is basically a community-based activity. Community members are related in all aspects of management of the resources that are the focus of tourism as well as management of their own life. CBT is derived from sustainable tourism, but it is not the same as sustainable tourism, though it is an overlapping concept. CBT is a form of sustainable tourism. Here, the local community has control over and is involved in its development, augmentation, and management with a major share of the benefits remaining within the community.

The community-based waste management initiatives have to prove their work when there is full support from the local authority and community-based organizations. Community-based waste management never addresses the environmental problems but it contributed to good health, good environment, and improved hygienic standards of local communities to a greater extent. By evaluating the community-based development in all stages, from beginning to the end, the result achieved so far indicates the enormous potential for the improvement of the sustainable environment through processes that are managed by communities.

6.7   REVIEW OF LITERATURE

The researcher reviewed the allied literature to identify the various components of community-based decentralized waste management for sustainable tourism in the backwater regions. The study enlightened the concept with clarity and distinction. The literature was thoroughly examined for making use of all elements in the fields, namely, the role of community in sustainable tourism, community-based decentralized waste management, the role of government in the promotion of sustainable tourism, backwater regions, and its various challenges.

6.8   ROLE OF COMMUNITY IN SUSTAINABLE TOURISM

Sustainable tourism is the key concept in tourism, and its effective and efficient implementation will expand tourism in any destination. However, the concern on the benefit that the poor gets has brought new light to community involvement and community participation in contemporary literature. In particular, sustainable development has become a way to address the long-term viability of income and employment in local communities. Prakobsiri (2007) says that the community should be the key principle in developing sustainable tourism in any destination. The community had the capacity to develop and promote sustainable tourism plans with the natural and cultural resources available in that destination. It satisfies their social, economic, and environmental needs. Participation of communities in diverse projects is essential for the development of tourist destinations.

Goodwin and Santilli (2009) said that communities should be judged on the basis of local economic development and living conditions. He also pointed out that without measuring the economic benefits, it was not possible to determine whether the community gained from the various tourism products. Community-based development delivers innumerable opportunities to the community as well as to the tourism industry. It is actually a new trend in the industry to reduce the negative impacts of the society and the tourist destinations, therefore making it more attractive and constructive (Prakobsiri, 2007). He also added that successful management of any problem that affected the sustainability of a destination could be solved through active community participation.

Goodwin and Santilli (2009) state that the governmental and nongovernmental organizations should encourage the local communities to take advantage of tourism by actively participating in it. Prakobsiri (2007) also gives a similar insight that community has a capacity to develop and promote sustainable tourism plans with the natural and cultural resources available in those destinations. The initiatives of the local communities should be judged on the basis of local economic development that reduces poverty. He also remarks that sustainable tourism takes into consideration the local community and environmental protection. Sustainable tourism consists of public and private participation, natural and environmental conservation, local benefits, the awareness program, and overall satisfaction of tourists. There are various economic opportunities created for local people in relation to the private sector, public sector, and various tourist departments (Gillian, 2004). Community participation and experience in community management is significant in the solid waste sector (Justine, 1996). Waste management is actually an ongoing process or system, which requires dynamic community participation. Local leaders, women, and youth have a special role to play in the community-based solid waste management. The dirty image and impression of waste are to be changed into a productive feeling—the "taste for waste" concept. To achieve this target, local government should supplement with innovative talks and motivational workshops to the communities.

All major communities in the backwater regions of Kerala (India) depend solely on Vembanad Lake for their livelihood (Priyadarsanan et al., 2008). So, for the constructive implementation of the solid waste management system, a vigorous community support is a must. Vembanad Lake is possible only through enlightening the local communities and informing the stakeholders of the various advantages it produces to the tourist spots even though Justine (1996) says that education alone does not seem to change the behavior of communities, rather the benefits of the solid waste services may be perceived by the target community. Chaudhuri (2009) postulated that sustainable tourism is an essential criterion for the development of the destination. Sociological understandings of local communities and their participation in various activities for the promotion of sustainable tourism is very crucial for spot developments. The commitment of communities, strategic planning, and the developing responsibility would add value to tourism experience (Richins, 2008). Communities that are located in the natural environment have a significant role to play in maintaining their original attraction in the midst of various developments.

Sustainable development is actually finding a solution for the better living of local communities without causing any harm to the natural environment (Slocum, 2010). It gives more attention to social, cultural, and economic value for long-term projects. She also talks about various constraints faced by the people for the economic participation, which make current or future tourism destinations more productive. The vision of environmental development in sustainable tourism includes best ecological practice, expansion in tourism, and an obligation of the community to the environment and destination (Richins, 2008). He also highlights the community participation in various tourism activities, the interdependence of members, community well-being, and a sense of community with the target group. Slocum (2010) states that communities can participate in various tourism activities that provide employment opportunities to them. But still, there are various constraints to economic participation of local communities, which include financial, educational, governmental, and community. In addition to this, ethnic and gender discrimination, cultural norms, and lack of social capital are also seen as constraints to economic participation of local community. Here, sustainable development becomes a way out for a better living without causing any problem to the natural environment. It gives more attention to social, cultural, and economic value for long-term projects. Himani and Shivangi (2009) perceive that sustainable development could concentrate on community participation and gender differences in relation to tourism. There should always be a holistic perspective on various dimensions of sustainable tourism.

The environment, local culture, and local communities should be preserved, but sometimes such development is difficult to obtain due to the lack of effective policies and methods (Murray, 2009). Tourism activities include policy making and planning of tourism activities (Goodson, 2000). So, there should be an educational system to train and improve the local community. It should concentrate on environment-friendly practices such as waste management, energy efficient devices, recycling, and use of organic materials. Proper waste management systems, appropriate sewage treatment measures, the creation of employment opportunities, more interdependence between communities, less violence, learning to live in harmony, a higher standard of living, and improved quality of holidays for the tourists are essential for the development of sustainable tourism in a destination (Moli, 2003). As a whole, the community plays a vital role in the promotion of sustainable tourism, or in other words, community-based development delivers a wide range of benefits to the tourism industry for the development of sustainable tourism. So participation of communities in various tourism projects is fundamental for the development of any tourist destination.

6.9   ROLE OF GOVERNMENT IN THE PROMOTION OF SUSTAINABLE TOURISM

The role of government in promoting sustainable tourism in a destination is very crucial. As said by Kunst (2011), the government should carefully analyze the existing practices of a destination and a dynamic process must be introduced for development. Therefore, authorities should encourage the domestic and foreign investors to invest more in the tourism industry to develop the infrastructure and other facilities that attract the tourists. The implementation of the developmental strategies must agree to the tourism strategy, which trims down the responsibility of the public sector in the tourism generation and advancement opportunities for ventures in the tourism sector. Csoban and Gathy (2005) highlight the 12 aims, which include economic viability, local prosperity, employment quality, social equity, visitor fulfillment, local control, community well-being, cultural richness, physical integrity, biological diversity, resource efficiency, and environmental purity, that are developed by the World Tourism Organization for the sustainable tourism in a destination. These aims create an opportunity for the local community to participate in various tourism advancements, boosting up the level of harmonization between government organizations in relation with the tourism industry, which takes the lead role in promoting the tourism and finally a full-fledged sustainable development in a destination.

Employment opportunities are to reinforce the future local job opportunities that are created by the process of the tourism development (Csoban and Gathy, 2005). Local enhancement is to ensure economic development in the host destination. For that reason, the government should implement laws, programs, plans, and educate local people to select an appropriate measure for the sustainable development of a destination together with the local enrichment (Gorica et al., 2012). Environmental sustainability, social sustainability, and economic sustainability are the three main components of sustainability. As said by Gorica, Kripa, and Zenelaj (2012), social impartiality gives an equal allocation of economic and social benefits to the local communities from the tourism industry. The government can either directly or indirectly get involved in the various sustainable development processes. Direct involvement can be through security, stability, laws, regulations, and providing infrastructure. Indirect involvement may be by providing proper support and incentives to the private enterprises, promoting natural and cultural resources, and so on. Active participation of local government brings economic benefits to businesses and at the same time, it provides employment opportunities to local people. Veron (2001) says that with the help of community participation, sustainable development can be achieved. Roseland (2000) also gives a similar insight on community-based sustainable development, which improved the social condition of Kerala (India).

Sustainable community development can be achieved when there is a change in our structure, values, and attitudes. Sustainability in future makes more perceptive rather than competitive. Sustainability of environment includes the development of the ecosystem, biological environment, and natural environment. If we want to achieve sustainability, then economic development and social development should improve natural environment for future generations (Veron, 2001). Stakeholders and community members share a common environment and different natural resources (Hasse, 2000). Therefore, community participation in various tourism activities increases their standard of living. Gorica et al. (2012) state that there should be active community participation to obtain community-based sustainable development. Second, there should be coordination between local government and civil society. Third, collective action should be taken for managing natural resources, and finally, there must be a need for coordination.

Ministry of Tourism (2011) addresses the various measures proposed to achieve sustainable tourism. They are as follows: (i) tourism criteria for hotels, tour operators, indicators for rural tourism, in which home stays are involved; (ii) market development assistance procedure will be enlarged to get the participation at the national level by conducting national seminars and workshops on sustainable tourism; (iii) participating and training different stakeholders under current schemes of the tourism ministry. Mei, Arcodia, and Ruhanen (2011) project that government has an important role in the promotion of tourism innovations, and it should be encouraged with enthusiasm. Sustainable tourism development in India includes some advancing niche tourism products in the field of adventure, medical, wellness, golf, polo, cruise sector, meetings, incentives, conferences, and exhibitions, spiritual travel, film tourism, eco-tourism, wildlife tourism, and caravan tourism (Ministry of Tourism, 2011). Private sector firms are very decisive for this innovation and development. Therefore, the government should support the private sector enterprises to bring development at the local level (Mei, Arcodia, and Ruhanen, 2011).

The government has to create an appropriate situation for investment through regulations and fiscal measures. So tourism projects need to be assisted at two different levels: first, at the time of making investment and second, at the time of operational stage (Seth, 2008). He also adds that the participation of the government sector may be more attractive to the investors. The government can help the tourism sector through manpower development by running hotels, giving tourism training in schools, and implementing various courses in different colleges. The extent of government concessions to tourism is basically linked with the importance a state attaches to the tourism sector compared with other sectors of the economy. Therefore, we can say that the government plays a major role in promoting sustainable development in a destination. Active participation of local government brings economic benefits to business, and at the same time, it provides employment opportunities to local people.

6.10 RESEARCH GAP

Though there have been a number of valuable studies on CBT, waste management and sustainable tourism, are the ever-growing threat of waste in backwater regions, which still persists. Reflecting with the reviews, it was barely visible that there is a dearth of studies that focused on community-based waste management for sustainable tourism in the backwater regions. So, this chapter substantiates the nuances and nitty-gritty to find out a most suitable waste management system for sustainable tourism and sustainable development. The chapter portrays potential areas that face the devastating side of tourism and demands good sustainable approach in building the regional capacity of the region. The prominence of related stakeholders is also inevitable, thereby, their role in a sustainable form of development is also captured.

6.11 NEED FOR THE STUDY

Community plays a major role in the promotion of sustainable tourism in a destination. A proper waste management system must be undertaken for the sustainability of tourism in backwater regions. The community must be educated and trained in the various methods of waste management, which helps in reducing pollution in the environment, water bodies, and backwaters. Thus, it will enhance the quality of the life of people and promote sustainable tourism.

People flock to visit the backwater regions of Kerala (India) as it is the unique selling point of Kerala tourism (India). Kumarakom, Pathiramanal, Punnamada, R-block, Nedumudi, Champakulam, and Kavalam are the most popular tourist centers in the backwater regions located in Kottayam and Alappuzha districts in Kerala (India). But high levels of pollution have been identified at these tourist spots. Thus, the longest backwater of Kerala, 'the Vembanad Lake' is highly polluted. Pollution of backwater regions due to tourism activities is a major threat and challenge to the tourism industry. So, community-based waste management is an initiative through which local community can minimize the waste that is dumped into the lake by creating proper awareness and community participation at various levels. It will, in turn, promote sustainable tourism in the backwater regions of Kerala (India).

The scope of the study covers the tourist destinations in Kerala (India), especially at Alappuzha and Kottayam and specifically in Kumarakom, Pathiramanal, Punnamada, R-Block, Nedumudi, Champakulam, and Kavalam, which are located on the banks of Vembanad Lake. Pathiramanal, Punnamada, R-Block, Nedumudi, Champakulam, and Kavalam are the villages in the Kuttanadu region of Alappuzha district, and Kumarakom is the Panchayath or village of Kottayam district. This chapter captures special focus on two paradigms; primarily, the importance of community-based waste management for the development of sustainable tourism, and various measures taken by the government to promote sustainable tourism in the backwater regions. This chapter cataloged only tourism-related aspects in the backwater regions and no other sectors are included. The sources of data collected for this research were divided into two categories: secondary data and Primary data. Secondary data were derived from the academic books, printed materials, newspapers, magazines, journals, articles, websites, and related research articles. Primary data were collected from the population and sample group under the area of investigation. Data from the local community, tourists, government officials, hotels, and resorts officials were collected through schedule questionnaire.

The structured questionnaire includes personal information, tourism-related experience in backwater regions, and factors influencing the respondent's decision-making while visiting backwater regions. Multiple choice questions, open-ended questions and rating, and the five rating scales were the criteria used. The questionnaires were used to collect data from the local community, tourists, government officials, and hotel and resort officials. The respondents were asked to answer the questions, and if they had any doubts, the researcher clarified the questions for them. The questionnaire was divided into four sets as follows: officials of the department of tourism, hotels and resorts, local communities, and domestic and international tourists. This exploratory endeavor concealed seven villages including one island located around the lake. The selection criteria of the represented villages are as follows:

1. The village must have places of tourist attraction, activities, or programs promoting tourism.
2. The village must be located on or close to the lake.
3. The village must have distinct occupational features that could be promoted as a tourist destination.
4. The village must receive direct impacts from tourism activities around the lake.
5. The village might be practicing some kind of waste management method.

As per the criteria, seven villages were chosen as the area of study, which are as given in Table 6.1.

TABLE 6.1   Districts and Villages Chosen for the Study.

Districts	Villages
Kottayam	Kumarakom
Alappuzha	Pathiramanal (Island)
Alappuzha	Punnamada
Alappuzha	R-Block
Alappuzha	Nedumudi
Alappuzha	Champakulam
Alappuzha	Kavalam

6.12   RESULTS AND SUGGESTIVE IMPLICATIONS

The factors of sustainable tourism such as local prosperity, economic viability, physical integrity, local control, and environmental purity can be achieved through waste management process. This includes economic development, community participation, reduction of waste material, healthy community, and a safe environment. Backwater regions face various problems of waste management due to tourism-related activities. They are (i) unplanned construction of tourism facilities such as hotels, resorts, homestays without proper waste management techniques, (ii) sewage or fuel spillage from boats create water pollution and pose a threat to aquatic life, (iii) mushrooming of houseboats, and (iv) dumping of plastic waste by tourists and local communities. Local communities in the backwater region face various problems of waste management due to tourism-related activities: (i) it degrades local surroundings and environment, (ii) growth of water hyacinth, giving the local communities a tough time, and (iii) huge quantity of nondegradable waste is dumped in a disorganized manner. Lack of community awareness and public participation is a major reason for improper waste management. Local communities, as well as the tourists, dispose the waste materials in a disorganized manner, sometimes in open drains, in any vacant plot of land available, or along the roadside.

The local community is affected by the huge volume of waste due to tourism activities that are indicated by a mean value of 4.30. The support from the local community is very much necessary, and the community should come forward to reduce the waste problems in the backwater regions. The unplanned construction of tourism facilities, dumping of waste materials from houseboats, and overcrowding of houseboats in the Vembanad Lake become a threat to both environment and the local community. The changes in the backwater regions due to improper waste management clearly point out that if the present situation continues, the destination will die out within years and it will affect the local communities and the tourism industry. The interaction with Government officials reveals that the government is focusing on the execution of practical guidelines for sustainable tourism by giving a special thrust to backwater tourism activities. Government officials are of the opinion that if they get active support from local communities, the promotion of sustainable tourism in the backwater regions would be much easier. Many schemes such as the Sewage Treatment Plant Kumarakom, pipeline composting, and Biogas plants are being implemented to extract the tourism potential of backwaters through sustainable tourism. New project on the sewage treatment plant aims at collecting waste materials from the houseboats by going directly to it.

In the present tourism scenario, the term 'Sustainable development' has become a major issue and is of importance among the environmentalists, academicians, sociocultural, and political outfits. However, like many other developing countries, we too are not being able to set up a model for the term "Sustainable." Improper allocation and management of funds, people, and other potential elements create chaos in this sector. Every tourist destination has a chunk of waste material which, if found out and recycled properly, could be made into 'taste for waste' valuable products that, in turn, may lead to sustainable development to an extent.

6.13   PROPOSITIONS FOR SUSTAINABLE DEVELOPMENT

To exterminate and negate the undesirable tourism impacts for quality community life, it is highly imperative that good mechanisms of waste management should not be considered as a highly critical aspect. The waste could be processed, recycled, and reused for the betterment of the community, which would help the local community in the economic growth. This, in turn, will promote a healthy environment, leading to tourist inflow. The government should issue strict rules to existing houseboat owners for the proper method of waste disposal. Strict actions must be taken against those who do not comply with the tourism norms. All unplanned construction that affects the sustainability of the backwater regions should be banned. Each and every house, houseboats, tourist destination, village, town, Panchayat, or municipality must have its own appropriate waste management method at or near the point of generation for sustainable tourism. Restrict or ban plastics and other nondegradable materials at the destination.

Use of plastic bags below the stipulated microns (plastic carry bags should be a minimum thickness of 40 µ) should be strictly banned or the use of plastic bags should be completely banned accordingly by the government. People are less aware of the benefits of community-based waste management systems. People need to be educated and trained about the benefits of this choice. Educate and train the local community and the general public on waste management, that is, segregation of waste at source into biodegradable (wet) waste and nonbiodegradable (dry) waste. There is a prominent requisite of proper directives, which must be given to the tourists through the concerned authorities for waste disposal and recycling process for efficient results.

6.14   CONCLUSION

Proper nurturing of backwater regions would improve the sustainability of the environment. It is high time to act against improper waste disposal otherwise the unique ecosystem may lose its entire beauty and ecological significance. Government agencies, voluntary organizations, individuals, and communities involved in the effort of preservation and conservation of the backwater regions are to be coordinated to maintain sustainable tourism. Waste management is a Herculean task, which can be achieved successfully only with the active support and participation of local communities. This would provide better income and employment opportunities to the communities. The people here become the ambassadors of tourism and become the part and parcel of promoting sustainable tourism in the backwater region. Waste management tackles the problem that brings negative impacts on tourism and the solid waste management. This system brings economic, social, health, and environmental benefits to the local communities. We need to wake up and make people conscious of the importance of keeping the environment clean, tidy, and eco-friendly. Each and every citizen should think that it is his/her duty and responsibility to keep the surrounding godly.

KEYWORDS

- **waste management**
- **sustainable tourism**
- **backwater regions**

REFERENCES

ACCCRN (Asian Cities Climate Change Resilience Network). M. G Post Graduate college, Gorakhpur and Gorakpur Environmental Action Group. *Decentralized solid waste management through community participation.* Asian Cities Climate Resilience Network: Gorakpur City, 2008.

CAST/CTO. Case study: Water, Energy and Solid Waste management in the hotel industry. *Caribbean alliance for sustainable tourism,* 1999; pp 1–8.

Business, Line. Decentralised Sewage Treatment: India. *Business Line,* 1, 2001.

CBT. Community Based Tourism—Principles and Meaning. Thailand Community Based Tourism Institute, 2008.

Chaudhuri, T. *Social Universe of a Protected Area: Community-based Ecotourism in Periyar Tiger Reserve;* Univercity of Washington: Cohen, Erik, 2009; pp 121–130.

Cooper, C.; Fletcher, J. *Tourism: Principles and Practice;* Prentice Hall: New York, 2004.

Csoban, K. V.; Gathy, A. B. Long-Term Government Responses to Sustainable Tourism Development: Principles and Strategies. *Appl. Studies Agribusiness Commer.* **2005,** 89–92.

Curb on Houseboats may Work out Well. *Deccan Chronicle.* (accessed Sept 11, 2013).

Efforts on for Decentralised Waste Disposal. *The Hindu,* June 17, 2008.

Experts Blame Fertilizer Discharge for Hyacinth Menace. *The Times of India.* (accessed Nov 6, 2012).

Fehr, M. Confirming decentralised Composting as a Definite Option in Urban Waste Management. *Int. J. Environ. Technol. Manage.* **2007**, *7*, 274–285.

Gillian, C. *Community-Based Tourism Initiatives in the Windward Islands: a Review of Their Impacts* (ISBN 1-890792-08-X) Caribbean Natural Resource Institute, 1–27, 2004.

Greens Say no to Seaplane Service in Kerala Backwaters. *The Times of India.* (accessed June 7, 2013).

Goodson, L. An Exploration into Gender and Local Residents Perceptions of Tourism and Community Participation. *Int. J. Tourism Res.* **2000,** 67–75.

Goodwin, H.; Santilli, R. Community-Based Tourism: a Success. *ICRT Occasional Paper,* **2009**, 1–37.

Gorica, K.; Kripa, D.; Zenelaj, E. The Role of Local Government in Sustainable Development. Economica, 2012, 8, 139–155.

Hasse, J. C. Tourism, Stakeholders and Sustainable Community Development: Theoretical and Methodological Reflections. *Int. J. Tourism,* **2000**, 67–75.

Himani, K.; Shivangi, G. Sustainable Tourism in India. *Worldwide Hospitality and Tourism Themes,* 12–18.

Human Waste Disposal in Kuttanadu Paddy Fields Causes a Health Concern. *The Times of India,* 2009. (accessed Feb 24, 2013).

Justine, A. Community-Based Solid Waste Management and Water Supply Projects: Problems and Solutions Compared a Survey of the Literature. *UWEP Working Document 2,* 1996.

K. Samu. *Environment/Climate Change.* Indian Social Institute: New Delhi, 2010.

Kunst, I. The Role of the Government in Promoting Tourism Investment in Selected Villages. *Inte. J. Tourism,* **2011**, 87–106.

Mei, X. Y.; Arcodia, C.; Ruhanen, L. A National Government's Tourism Innovation Initiatives: A Review of Tourism Development Policies in Norway. *Cauthe National Conference,* 2011.

Moli, G. P. Promotion of Peace and Sustainability by Community based heritage Eco-cultural Tourism in India. *Int. J. Humanit. Peace* **2003**, *19*(1), 40–45.

Panchayath to Approach Government on Pollution by Houseboats. *The Times of India.* (accessed Feb 6, 2013).

Pipeline. Decentralized Wastewater Treatment Systems. *Pipeline,* 1–10, 2000.

Prakobsiri, P. *A Model for Sustainable Tourism Development in Kwan Phayao lake rim Communities, Phayao Province, Upper Northern Thailand.* Doctoral Dissertation, Silpakorn University, 2007.

Priyadarsanan Adharma, R.; Seema, P.; Siddhartha, K.; Kiran, M. C.; Deepak, D. *Strengthening Communities and Institutions for Sustainable Management of Vembanadu Backwaters,* Kerala, 2008.

Roseland, M. Sustainable Community Development: Integrating Environmental, Economic, and Social Objectives. *Pergamon,* **2000**, *54*(2), 73–132.

Richins, H. Environmental, Cultural, Economic and Socio-Community Sustainability: A Framework for Sustainable Tourism in Resort Destinations. *Springer,* 2008, 787–800.

Saji, J. Integrated Water Resource and Solid Waste Management: Alappuzha. 32nd WEDC International Conference; Colombo: Sri Lanka, 2006; pp 52–55.

Sankar, K. A Propoal for Solid Waste Management. *Hand in Hand,* 2008.

Seshadri, A. *Decentralized Wastewater Management–An overview of community initiatives.* The Vigyan Vijay Foundation: New Delhi, 2005.

Seth, P. N. *Successful Tourism Management: Fundamentals of Tourism.* Sterling Publishers Pvt. Ltd.: New Delhi, 2008.

Simpson M. C. An Integrated Approach to Assess the Impacts of Tourism on Community Development and Sustainable Livelihoods. *Community Dev. J.* **2009,** *44*(2), 186–208.

Slocum, S. L. Sustainable Community Tourism Development: The Case of Tanzania. Ph.D. Thesis, Clemson University, 2010.

Sustainable Tourism Criteria for India Ministry of Tourism, Government of India. (accessed Nov 1, 2011).

Telfer, D. J. *Tourism and Development in the Developing World*; Routledge: London, 2008.

United Nations World Tourism Organization (UNWTO). Tourism and Community Development: Asian Practices, 2008; pp 1–13.

Veron, R. The New Kerala Model: Lessons For Sustainable Development. *World Dev.* **2001,** *29,* 601–617.

Vijayanagara Nagarikara Vedike. *Decentralized Solid Waste Management.* Vijayanagara Nagarikara Vedike: Bangalore, 2007.

Wang, J. Y.; Chang, V.; Lee, C. S.; Wang, X.; Stegmann, R. A *Decentralization-Based Approach for Urban Waste Management: Moving Towards Sustainable Resource Management.* Proceedings of the International Conference on Solid Waste 2011— Moving Towards Sustainable Resource Management, Hong Kong SAR, P.R. China, May 2–6, 2011, pp 98–101.

CHAPTER 7

CIVIL DISTURBANCES AND THE TOURISM SECTOR: AN IMPACT STUDY ON KERALA TOURISM, INDIA

SANDHYA HARIPRASAD[1] and BINDI VARGHESE[2]

[1]St. Micheals College, Cherthala, Kerala, India

[2]Christ (Deemed to be University), Bangalore, Karnataka, India

CONTENTS

ABSTRACT

The current chapter focused on assessing the impacts that are likely to be caused by civil instability and political disturbances on the hospitality sector of a destination. The pull factors that attract the tourists to visit a destination include the physical, social, and cultural aesthetics that are unique and distinct to the destination. The state of Kerala (India), promoted and marketed with the tagline "God's Own Country," can be rightfully contemplated as a pioneer state in the tourism and travel business of the country. Considered as a "year around destination," Kerala attracts around 10 million tourists throughout the year, contributing almost one-tenth of the mentions Gross Domestic Product (India Tourism Statistics, 2015). The success of a destination lies in the satisfaction of the customers and repeated visits, which are the end result of the varied tourism products, services, and hospitality extended toward them at the destination. Though the tourism sector of the state is very efficiently managed through a Private–Public Partnership Model, the political base of the state is highly influential. The political alliances in the state have been strengthened in such a manner that Kerala is subjected to hartals almost every fortnight. There are flash strikes and dawn-to-dusk hartals resulting in local businesses to shut down their activities affecting the day-to-day life of the people. The main objective of this paper is to assess the impact of civil disturbances on the tourism and hospitality sector of the state. The research lays its foundation on literature reviews focusing on various paradigms related to the topic, and the primary data collected through questionnaires form the base for data analysis and interpretation. Further, the study also aims at suggesting measures to curb the negative impacts caused by civil disturbances on the tourism and hospitality sector.

7.1   INTRODUCTION

Tourism is one of the predominant sectors of the economy of Kerala (India). The tourism industry in Kerala attracts millions of foreign and domestic visitors and garners revenue that totals to around 20,000 crores. Generating over a million employment opportunities and supporting the skilled and unskilled labor equally, the tourism industry is an inevitable contributor to the overall economic growth of the nation. Kerala (India) is a preferred destination for its luxurious ayurvedic spas, backwater resorts, exquisite home stays, hill-top bungalows, and beach properties. A unique feature of the service sector is that although the products and services offered are of high quality, a mere negligence in the hospitality or attitude can result in dissatisfaction among the tourists. Therefore, for a destination to emerge successfully, it not only has to promise quality services to the tourists but also has to deploy the right manpower with the right attitude and skill set to ensure the overall satisfaction of the customers. Similar is the case of Kerala tourism, which offers a wide range of products and services to the tourists, creating a unique and memorable experience to the visitors. Though the tourism industry is systematically managed and promoted throughout the state, external factors such as hartals and civil disturbances that lay beyond the capacity of the tour operators often result in an irate customer. Tourists visiting the state on a hartal day find themselves stranded in airports and railway stations with no means of transportation and accommodation.

The state comes to a sudden halt with total shutdown of shops, banks, offices, and other local businesses due to the political predicament. At this juncture, it becomes imperative to manage the situation and ensure a safe and memorable holiday at the destination. This study is primarily aimed to understand the impact of such civil disturbances on the tourism and hospitality industry. Through this study, an attempt is made to suggest measures to control the potential impact of such disturbances on the tourism sector and minimize the effects on the tourists. Although there are many studies undertaken on terrorism and political disturbances on a global scale, very little or none have been undertaken with special reference to Kerala tourism. The outcome of the study is to analyze the impact of civil disturbances on destination's competitiveness and thereby suggesting measures to curb these issues so that it does not impact the destination's appeal. Further, the study is also helpful in recommending various strategies and plans to minimize the impact of the political crisis on the tourism sector. The wide-ranging contribution of the study will be in developing measures by which tourists can be given support and aid at the time of hartals and strikes.

The findings indicated in the chapter can be particularly useful to policymakers and strategic decision makers in decisions relating to developing alternative means of assistance to the tourists during hartals and also taking preventive measures to ensure a hassle-free travel for the visitors.

7.2   REVIEW OF LITERATURE

The study forms a constructive base from the wide range of literature reviews pertaining to various paradigms related to destination competitiveness, branding, and marketing of tourist destinations, civil and political disturbances impacting tourism and destination management.

7.3   TOURISM DESTINATIONS AND DESTINATION BRANDING

A destination can be defined as a domain that comprises all the services and products a tourist consumes during his or her stay (Terzibasoglu, 2004, also cited in WTO, 2006). Therefore, a destination's appeal should be transformed into a unique and competitive destination brand, which expresses the reality of the destination (Hassan et al., 2009).

Destination branding is a fairly new concept in tourism research due to the complex characteristics of branding a place rather than a physical tangible product (Morgan et al., 2003; Pike, 2006). Destination branding is the DNA that communicates the unique attributes of a destination (UNWTO, 2007). A destination brand speaks about the core assets and distinct traits of the destination to the potential visitors, leading to the creation of a unique perception of the place. Destination branding, as discussed, is a complex process that involves numerous challenges. For the creation of a national brand, it requires the integration of tourism industry to create a balanced representation of the destination. "A brand refers to the essence, or core characteristics and features, of a product or destination which comprises of all activities and services thus making it distinctive and different from all its competitors" (Anholt, 2009).

In the highly competent modern world, destinations can be often seen competing with each other for achieving its share in the global market. Therefore, the creation of a favorable image for the destination is pivotal. This can only be achieved through the development of a powerful brand for the destination.

Destination brand is influenced by various internal and external factors. Although the external factors comprise the technological changes, sociocultural, economic, and political situation at the destination and the marketing and promotional efforts, the internal factors, on the other hand, are the perceptions of the tourists, their travel motivations, the brand personality, and the emotional value it communicates to the potential tourists (Kulkshetra, 2011). Although Ahworth (2005) believes that place branding cannot be understood through a single definition, there is some agreement to the definition that states branding is a process through which a new identity is created for a destination through the various social, cultural, and natural attributes of the destination. Furthermore, it is ascertained that a destination brand builds a dynamic relationship between the destination and how they are being perceived by the potential customers. It also creates a distinct relation and a harmony between the visitors and residents and their perception of the destination.

UNWTO (2008) has developed various brand-building models that can be used to establish the core essence and purpose of a brand. This further leads to obtaining a destination's brand essence and values, which are to be considered while marketing the brand. Therefore, destination brand is defined by Morgan et al. (2002) as "a corresponding tangible or intangible aspect of a destination that is visible or can be felt by customers and can differentiate one destination from another" (as cited in Kulkshetra, 2011).

7.4 DESTINATION MANAGEMENT—KERALA (INDIA) TOURISM

Carlsen (1999) debates that destination management and planning is extremely important due to the increasing competitiveness among destinations. The traditional methods of marketing and management have to be replaced with new and modern methods with effective application of advanced technology. Vajcnerova and Ryglova (2010) stress on the need to develop and maintain a deliberative system or an administrative body in the destination, which oversees and manages the activities at the destination, whereas other researchers like Zupanovic (2010) and (Žužić, 2012) debate on using cluster methods to form a separate body to monitor and evaluate the destination while carefully managing its resources. As the tourism sector is scattered and linked to many allied sectors, it creates a major setback to competition so as to bring about enhanced competitiveness within the destination, coordination, and good communication, ensuring that effective management of all the channels of distribution is very much essential (Zuzic, 2012).

Literature substantiates that destination management need not be of similar patterns in every destination. The style and pattern of destination management differ according to regions and countries and the scale and levels of operation. While in some countries it may be private-owned or public-sector undertakings, or a private–public partnership (PPP) model, in other countries, they are known as National Tourism Administrations, consortiums, and so on. Destination management is used so as to bring about increased destination competitiveness and at the same time to focus on the sustainability aspect. This is essential in bringing about collaboration amidst the various service providers to effectively manage the tourist demand (Vajcnerova and Ryglova, 2010).

Destination management in Kerala (India) is undertaken in a very systematic manner with the formation of a tourism board at the state level which is answerable to the national-level tourism development board that acts as the apex body to monitor and manage tourism in the country. Kerala State (India) Tourism Development Corporation—the government agency that oversees tourism prospects of the state—laid the foundation for the growth of the tourism industry. In the decades that followed, Kerala Tourism was able to transform itself into one of the niche holiday destinations in India. The tagline Kerala—"God's Own Country" was adopted in its tourism promotions and became a global brand. Kerala is regarded as one of the destinations with the highest brand recall. In 2010, Kerala attracted 660,000 foreign tourist arrivals as per the tourism statistics of the state (Kerala Tourism Policy, 2015, p. 7).

Formed in 1960 by the government of Kerala, Kerala Tourism Development Corporation (KTDC) became a separate commercial entity in 1970. The major objectives behind such a venture were to promote Kerala as a leading tourist destination by providing high-quality hospitality services to the tourists, provide adequate information to interested parties, and to ensure optimum return on investment to the government on the investment projects (Kerala Tourism Policy, 2015). This undertaking has been one of the most profitable ventures by the government of Kerala. KTDC manages the hotels, motels, resorts, and other accommodation facilities in the state. They have effectively categorized the hotels and resorts into premium, value, and budget category to cater to the needs of the various tourists (p. 11). The state's tourism agenda promotes ecologically sustained tourism, which focuses on the local culture, wilderness adventures, volunteering, and personal growth of the local population. Efforts are taken to minimize the adverse effects of traditional tourism on the natural environment and enhance the cultural integrity of local people. The state offers a diverse mix of tourism products including heritage, culture, traditions, adventure, and serene and beautiful nature.

A unique feature of the destination is that unlike other destinations like, for instance, Rajasthan, which promotes the various destinations within the state (Jaipur, Udaipur, etc.), the whole state itself is a tourism product (Vasudevan, 2008). Kerala gets a large share in the Indian market due to its competitiveness and unique brand image. According to World Travel and Tourism Council (WTTC) report (2000), Kerala was the first Indian state to become a partner state in the WTTC. Moreover, it attracts around 5.8 million tourists every year. Therefore, Kerala (India) as a brand has positioned itself in a very competent and unique manner. Tourists flock into the state throughout the year as the state has been recently declared as a "year around destination" (NDTV tourism destinations report, 2008). The monsoon season is promoted as the "dream season" as the state experiences heavy rainfall during this period (The Hindu, 2010). The state also attracts a lot of foreigners who desire to indulge in Ayurvedic massages and medicinal baths. Kerala's (India) cuisine is also quite popular among the foreign tourists due to its unique blend of spices and distinctive taste. Yet another attraction of the state is the festivals and fairs at destinations such as Onam, the harvest festival of Kerala, snake boat race, Thrissur pooram, and so forth, which attracts thousands of tourists to experience these cultural extravaganzas.

The state also has an amazing history to share depicting many palaces, old and heritage structures, temples, churches, mosques, forts and much more. The unspoiled coastline that offers pristine beaches pulls many tourists to the state to enjoy the sun, sea, and sand. The art and dance forms are another tourist attraction of Kerala (India). The very famous Ravi Varma paintings are a classic example of the same. Kerala's dance forms and music are also promoted and marketed effectively. This includes mohiniyattam, kathakali, theyyam, koodiyattam, ottam-thullal, and so forth. Koodiyattam is the only intangible asset from the state that has been listed in the United Nations Educational, Scientific and Cultural Organization (UNESCO) world heritage list (UNESCO HERITAGE LISTING, 2009).

7.5 POLITICAL AND CIVIL DISTURBANCES AFFECTING TOURISM SECTOR

Hartals can be termed "a violent challenge to the socioeconomic development of a destination" (Roy and Borsha, 2013). Hartals and lockouts not only affect one sector but the overall socioeconomic development of the destination also gets aggravated due to hartals. They result in huge losses to local businesses and undertakings, and hence the effect trickles down to all the sectors of the economy. A classic example of a country that has suffered huge losses due to hartals is Bangladesh.

The country faced a heavy loss of business and the economy was downtrodden due to frequent strikes and hartals in the country. Almost all undertakings, both public and private, had to be shut down resulting in depletion of resources and manpower; and Egypt, a destination primarily dependent on the tourism industry for its income, was largely affected due to the political disturbances. Many foreign tourists were stranded in the airports for hours with no food and water. Though the government made attempts to restore and control the situation, their attempts were in vain. There was a huge loss on the measures undertaken postcrisis to bring the economy back to its normal shape, which included a PPP model for managing and marketing the destination. Nasser (2012) in his study on political unrest affecting tourism in Egypt explains the impact of the Egyptian revolution due to canceling of fleets, canceled bookings for the travel agents and tour operators, public outrage and violence, and cease of the business of hotels and restaurants. Another example is Sri Lanka, which has been largely affected due to continuous political riots and disturbances since the 1970s (Venugopal, 2003). The unstable political system affected the growth and development of the various industries and businesses that were operating within the system. Agriculture, trade, and exports, and other small-scale businesses were the major income for the country. The country then restored its economy in the later years after the decline of the war in the early 2000s gained fair trade relations and international relations with many countries, thereby strengthening and rebuilding its economy (p. 27).

Therefore, it is evident that "Tourists are very sensitive to reports of violence and political unrest in potential holiday destinations" (Neumayer, 2004). "Tourism destinations and tourists have always been the soft targets for terrorist activities" (Paraskevas and Arendell, 2007). Tourists visit a destination for various reasons ranging from pilgrimages or leisure to official meetings and conferences. Tourists are often targeted for political and antisocial activities at the destination as they are normally the guests at the place. There is a connection between tourism and terrorism and sights instances were terrorism activities have aggravated the growth of tourism industry at a destination (Baker, 2014). The reviews substantiate that terrorist activities do not only affect the destination but also the neighboring destinations, resulting in a dramatic reduction in the tourist flow to the destinations. But, the shock resulting from the terrorist activity may be temporary and the destination can rebound back to its earlier form before there is a state of complete collapse of the tourism industry (p. 277).

Moreover, frequent exposure to political violence or disturbances at the destination results in the reduced fear for the local population and they tend to develop mitigation measures to protest against such circumstances. The risk perceptions related to traveling to a destination may result in travel anxiety toward that destination (Baker, 2014). It is noted that terrorism or political violence not only affects the tourism sector but also the allied sectors in tourism such as transportation, hotel and hospitality industry, restaurants, and shops that are directly or indirectly benefited from tourism (p. 173). Tourism, being an early casualty of internecine revolutions, warfare, or political disturbances, it will decline as the tourists tend to choose alternative destinations even if the major sightseeing points are secure and risk-free (Neumayer, 2004).

7.6   METHODOLOGY OF RESEARCH

This research was undertaken to understand the various impacts of political and civil disturbances on tourism and the economy of a destination. The study aims to apply a quantitative method of data collection. Primary data were collected using questionnaires. The sample for primary data included the public and private players in the tourism industry. The secondary data sources would be journals, newspaper articles, websites, and online travel blogs, case studies, previously undertaken research theses, and so forth. The study has adopted the impact assessment model used by Roy and Borsha (2013) to analyze the overall impact of political instability on the economic development of a country.

7.7   ANALYSIS AND FINDINGS

Roy and Borsha (2013) in their study on Bangladesh proposed an impact assessment model to study the impact of hartals on the overall economic development of the country. The flow diagram shows different sectors affected due to hartals, which include education, human right, tourism, transport, price level, small business, export, port, low-income people, local-level government, stock market, revenue collection, state property, gross domestic product (GDP) growth rates, and so forth. Through the impact assessment model, it was noticed that the sectors that were most affected due to hartals were the tourism, transport, and telecommunication sectors. There are various segments of the economy that were affected due to hartals, which further aggravates the overall socioeconomic development of the country. The impact assessment model was developed by collecting data from various sectors, reviewing and analyzing the positive and negative effects on each sector, the profits and losses caused to each sector, and assessing the degree of impact effectuated to each sector. Similarly, the impact assessment model is used to understand the impact of hartals on the tourism and allied sectors in Kerala. The sample for this investigation includes the travel agencies, tour operators, neli, and public tourism boards that operate throughout the state. Structured questionnaires were distributed to around 25 private travel agencies and five tour operators in Kerala (India). The major outcomes from the data collected are enlisted below. The tourists were also, most importantly, included in the study to understand their perception on hartals and the impact it has on the minds of the tourists.

7.8 TRAVEL AGENTS AND TOUR OPERATORS IN KERALA (INDIA)

Almost 50% of the employees in the travel agencies have 2–5 years of experience, and they handle around 200–500 tourists per month. A small portion of the total employee base (only 30%) have 5–10 years of experience and only a negligible portion (10%) have more than 10 years of experience. This shows that the skilled workforce employed are relatively young with an average of 5–6 years of experience. A competent and strong workforce with warm attitude helps in smooth running of the tourism industry and thus outruns the competition (Cornelissen, 2005). The majority of the employees are aware and have experienced difficulties in handling tourists during hartals. They had faced difficulties like canceling and rescheduling of flights and altering of tour plans. Hanna

(2013) states that alterations to travel plan can create tension and anxiety in the minds of the tourists, thus leaving a negative perception toward the destination even before undertaking the tour.

Although more than half of the total respondents have actually experienced and witnessed hartals and strikes in the state, a small portion of them are aware of hartals from media and newspapers while a negligible 5% of the respondents stated that they are not aware of the concept of hartals. The major portion of the sample includes travel agents and tour operators presiding out of the major tourist hubs of the state. Media plays an inevitable role in developing the image of a destination (Alvarez and Korzay, 2008). Potential tourists make the choice of destinations heavily relying on media and the internet. Positive image creation happens when the attractions and amenities of the destinations are advertised effectively. A negative image may be portrayed when events like war, terrorism, economic and social problems, natural hazards, and even disease outbreaks appear in the media (p. 42).

Civil disturbances affect the cost of business. This was strongly agreed by 50% of the workforce. The losses suffered on a hartal day are vast as it affects the whole of the economy. Roy and Borsha (2013) state that frequent civil disturbances leave an impact on the overall socioeconomic development of the place, affecting all major sectors ranging from agriculture to telecommunications and information technology. A majority of 79% agreed that hartals have negatively affected the way they feel about their job, resulting in less job satisfaction due to increasing customer complaints whereas the remaining opined that hartals do not negatively affect their passionate approach toward work.

Frequent disturbances often lead to higher absenteeism, refraining from work, lesser satisfaction, and poor quality of work (Atorough and Martin, 2012). Figure 7.1 depicts the effects of hartals on the employees of travel companies in Kerala (India). The managerial-level employees indicated that during hartals, there is an increasing level of absenteeism (25%), lateness to work (58%), idle time wasted during working hours (10%), and anxiety (7%) among the employees, resulting in less productivity (p. 53).

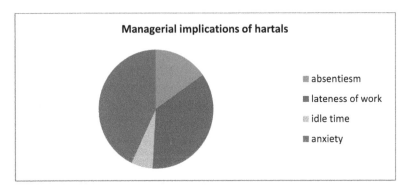

FIGURE 7.1   Managerial implications of hartals in travel organizations.

Of the overall workforce, more than half strongly feel that civil disturbances are a major reason behind increasing customer complaints resulting due to last-minute cancellations and alterations made to their travel plans. The other reasons for customer complaints were pointed out by the employees as the quality of products and services, cleanliness, and lack of proper infrastructure.

The private players in tourism industry strongly agree that civil disturbances and the frequency of hartals in the state have to be reduced. This statement was strongly supported by more than half of the total sample of travel professionals who were selected for the study. Hartals are often considered as the "voice of public" or a means of showing protest against the ruling government by the community. Hence, a portion of the population supports and considers hartals as a right of every citizen residing in the society (Roy and Borsha, 2013). A majority of the overall population have rated the efforts of stakeholders to control or minimize hartals in the state as very poor. Only a negligible portion of the sample (7%) stated that the efforts of private participants and other stakeholders in controlling the threat of hartals and strikes are satisfactory. González-Carrasco and Ruiz-Mezcua (2011) feel that an effective PPP model for destination management can ensure better utilization of resources and at the same time minimize the impact of political and social interferences in the society.

7.9   TOURISTS VISITING KERALA

The demographic profiling predominantly consists of the tourists visiting the state who belonged to the middle age group, which is less than 55 years old. It was noted that the total tourist volume of the state was dominated by female travelers over males. Domestic tourists tower over the international tourists. The majority of the tourists in the state primarily visit for leisure, honeymoon, and to enjoy the monsoon whereas the younger generation tourists, who were backpackers, students, adventure tourists, and businessmen, visited the state for official purpose.

With a bivariate correlation test, it was noted that the single travelers were mostly men traveling for adventure (13%), education purpose (27%), and business purpose (40%). The foreign tourists visiting the state were mainly backpackers. The most challenging problems faced by the tourists in Kerala (India) were safety and security concerns. The other challenges included quality of services, language barriers, and price of the products and services. The promotion and marketing of Kerala (India) is undertaken systematically. This is very evident as a majority of the tourists agreed that they came to know about the state through websites and word of mouth while a minority of the tourists stated that they were informed through advertisements in print media. Moreover, 89% of the tourists were aware of the brand name and tagline of Kerala tourism being "Kerala—God's Own Country" (India) whereas a negligible 11% were unaware of the same. Therefore, it clearly indicates that the role of media in promotion and marketing of the destination is very high. It also plays a major role in creating an image of the destination in the minds of the potential tourists (Alvarez and Korzay, 2008). A total of 69% of the tourists had experienced hartals during their visit to the state of which, more than half had to alter their travel plans and cancel bookings due to hartals. Others (23%) have not experienced hartals but are aware of it, and 8% of the tourists were unaware of hartals.

The tourists were satisfied with the services provided that includes climate (57%), local community cooperation (63%), hospitality and kindness of travel professionals (48%), knowledge of tour operators (48%), infrastructure (52%), heritage (60%), and landscape and beauty (70%). There was a lack of satisfaction in road connectivity (59%), safety and security (76%), cleanliness (64%), overcrowding at the destination (68%), and traffic congestion (64%). Although 59% of the tourists would surely recommend Kerala to their friends and relatives, 23% were doubtful about the same. A factor analysis was performed to understand the factors that contribute the most to tourist satisfaction in the state. The most contributing factor was landscape and scenic beauty (32%), heritage (28%), climate (12%), availability of tour operators and their knowledge (9%), and local community cooperation (6%) as depicted in Figure 7.2. The negative factors affecting the brand image of the destination were safety and security (30%), hartals (29%), infrastructure (20%), local traffic (10%), and overcrowding at destinations (11%).

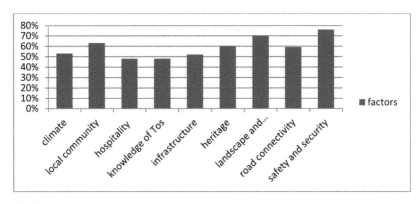

FIGURE 7.2   Factor analysis result.

7.10   GENERAL CONCLUSIONS AND RECOMMENDATIONS

In the year 2015–2016, there is an increase of around 77,000 foreign tourists and 54,000 domestic tourists, which is about 7.86% more than the previous year and thus contributes to an increase in total revenue generated up to INR 2204 crores. Tourism is a very well-established and systematically organized sector in the state. The repeated visitations to the state are also commendable as the authorities indicated that at least 7% of the tourists are repeat visitors to the state, which can be further improved by providing better quality products and services to the customers.

A significant trait of Kerala tourism is that the tourism industry in the state has been managed in a very professional manner. The highlight is that private firms are given their space to grow and develop themselves with adequate support from the state tourism boards. Thus, following a systematic PPP model of destination management, Kerala has emerged as a successful player in the global tourism market and is also renowned for its contribution toward the overall GDP of the country.

The results of this empirical study on Kerala tourism indicate that though the state is highly competent, Kerala tourism is not free from weaknesses. Antisocial activities, unhygienic conditions, and lack of tourists' information centers are the critical limiting factors that may hinder the growth of Kerala tourism. In the year 2015–2016, there were more than 35 hartals recorded in the state, causing a loss of more than 2 million rupees (The Hindu, February 2016). Furthermore, the travel agents and the allied sectors to tourism have faced a huge loss of resources and manpower. Therefore, efforts should be made to improve the infrastructure facilities that are essential for brand maintenance and enhancement of the quality experience for the visitors to Kerala.

Literature substantiates that when a destination reaches a stage in which tourists feel anxious about the safety and security at the destination, the tourism starts to decline. Hence, corrective actions have to be made at the right time so that the brand image of the state does not get hampered. But the good news is that if the situation is handled well, the destination can reverse its negative image by using proper promotion and marketing so that tourism can bounce back to its normal stature (Neumayer, 2004).

KEYWORDS

- **civil disturbances**
- **hartals**
- **destination image**
- **destination branding**

REFERENCES

Alvarez, M. D.; Korzay, M. Influence of Politics and Media in the Perceptions of Turkey as a Tourism Destination. *Tourism Rev.* **2008,** *63*(2), 38–46.

Atorough, P.; Martin, A. The Politics of Destination Marketing: Assessing Stakeholder Interaction Choice Orientations Toward a DMO Formation, Using the Thomas-Kilmann Conflict Mode Instrument. *J. Place Manage. Dev.* **2012,** *5*(1), 35–55. DOI: 10.1108/17538331211209031.

Carlsen, J. A Systems Approach to Island Tourism Destination Management. *Syst. Res. Behav. Sci.* **1999,** *16*(4), 321–327.

Cornelissen, S. Producing and Imaging 'Place' and 'People': The Political Economy of South African International Tourist Representation. *Rev. Int. Political Econ.* **2005,** *12*(4), 674–699.

González-Carrasco, I.; Ruiz-Mezcua, B. Sem-Fit: A Semantic Based Expert System to Provide Recommendations in the Tourism Domain. *Expert Syst. Appl.* **2011,** *38*(10), 13310–13319.

Haddad, C.; Nasar, A.; Ibrahim, H. A. How to Re-Emerge as a Tourism Destination after a Period of Political Instbility. *The Travel and Tourism Competitiveness Report,* 2015; 53–57.

Hanna, S.; Rowley, J. Practitioners Views on the Essence of Place Brand Management. *Place Branding Public Diplomacy Place Branding* **2012,** *8*(2), 102–109.

Naik. Opportunities and Challenges for Tourism in Kannur District of Kerala. *Int. J. Appl. Serv. Mark. Perspect.* **2013,** *2*(4), 632–637.

Nassar, M. A. Political Unrest Costs Egyptian Tourism Dearly: An Ethnographical Study. *Int. Bus. Res.* **2012,** *5*(10), 164–174.

Neumayer, E. The Impact of Political Violence on Tourism: Dynamic Cross-National Estimation. *J. Conflict Resolut.* **2004,** *48*(2), 259–281.

Paraskevas, A.; Arendell, B. A Strategic Framework for Terrorism Prevention and Mitigation in Tourism Destinations. *Tourism Manage.* **2007,** *28*(6), 1560–1573.

Pike, S. Destination Decision Sets: A Longitudinal Comparison of Stated Destination Preferences and Actual Travel. *J. Vacation Mark.* **2006,** *12*(4), 319–328.

Roy, M. B.; Borsha, F. H. Hartal: A Violent Challenges to the Socio-Economic Development of Bangladesh. *Int. J. Sci. Technol. Res.* **2013,** 2(8), 86–99.

UNWTO Handbook on Destination Branding, *UNWTO Market trends, Competitiveness and Trade in Tourism Services Report,* 2008.

Venugopal, R. The Global Dimensions of Conflict in Sri Lanka. *QEH Working Paper Series.* 2003; pp 1–33.

Vasudevan, S. The Role of Internal Stakeholders in Destination Branding: Observations from Kerala Tourism. *Place Branding and Public Diplomacy Place Branding* **2008,** *4*(4), 331–335.

World Economic Forum. *World Global Competitiveness Report,* 2006–2007, World Economic Forum, Geneva, 2007b. www.weforum.org/en/initiatives/gcp/.

WTTC. Competitiveness Monitor, *World Travel and Tourism Council,* 2004, www. wttc. org/frameset3.htm.

CHAPTER 8

ECOLOGICAL TOURISM POINTERS: ANALYSIS ON CONCEPTS, FRAMEWORKS, AND APPLICATIONS ON THE VEMBANAD LAKE OF KERALA, INDIA

SUJA JOHN

Christ (Deemed to be University), Bangalore, India

CONTENTS

ABSTRACT

The late twentieth century and the new millennium have witnessed a continued growth of a leisure society. As tourism progressed, the term sustainability came into vogue in 1980, taking into account the fact that there are limits on environmental resources and the ability of the biosphere to absorb human activities. The present study is confined to the Vembanad Lake, where backwater tourism of the state is flourishing, and Kuttanad regions consisting of Kottayam and Alappuzha Districts of Kerala, India. Development of tourism will be an apt solution for the revival of the region's economy. Backwater tourism in Kerala (India) is progressing in this region and has become the Unique Selling Point of Kerala Tourism industry, and international tourist arrivals have increased noticeably. But water contamination and loss of biodiversity continue to be a critical problem affecting the region, which, in turn, will certainly affect the growth of tourism. The study affirms that the conservation of ecological and biological diversity, usually shortened to biodiversity, is crucial in tourism development and priority should be given to its conservation by the National and State governments.

8.1   INTRODUCTION

The late twentieth century and the new millennium have witnessed a continued growth of a leisure society in which people have continued to value the significance of holidays, travel, and the experience of seeing new societies and their cultures. Tourism has now grown and become an integral part of the fabric of modern life. There are many constructive features of tourism—it stimulates economic growth and creates employment by providing incentives for protecting the environment and cultural heritage. Tourism also promotes peace, prosperity, and respect for human rights. Another feature of tourism is that it maximizes the positive economic, social, and cultural effects, and at the same time minimizes its negative social and environmental impacts.

8.2   CONCEPT OF SUSTAINABLE TOURISM DEVELOPMENT

The term "sustainability" came into vogue in 1980 at the World Conservation Strategy in which sustainable development was linked to conservation of living resources. Sustaining growth means achieving traditional objectives along with ecological and social sustainability. Barbier has defined social sustainability as "the ability to maintain desired social values, traditions, institutions, cultures or other social characteristics. It is to be understood as sustained growth or successful development." The World Commission on Environment and Development defines sustainable development as "development that meets the needs of the present without compromising the ability of future generations to meet their own needs." This concept implies that there are limits on environmental resources and the ability of the biosphere to absorb human activities. These limits are seen to have roots in technological inadequacies and inequitable social organization. Thus, sustainable development must entail a process of change in which the exploitation of resources, the direction of investments, the orientation of technological development, and institutional change are made consistently taking into account future as well as present needs.

The relationship between tourism and development is closely inter-twined. As George Perkins Marsh says in his book *Man and Nature* (1965), "Man is everywhere a disturbing agent, where he plants his foot; the harmonies of nature are turned to discords." Tourists' activities will have environmental impacts. Positive environmental impacts include heritage preservation, the establishment of national parks, wildlife resorts and bird sanctuaries, protection of beaches, and so forth.

Tourism improves those areas that were otherwise useless in terms of other forms of economic exploitation. The core issues that surround sustainable development are a balanced form of development that allows conserving the natural environment while allowing it to be exploited also so as to ensure economic growth. Tourism must be a community effort. Sustainable Tourism is vital reading for anyone seeking to understand the complexities associated with sustainable tourism development and how government and industries have responded to the challenges that the concept poses. Dealing with both conceptual issues and case studies, unique global perspective with multinational contributor team, and accessible yet rigorous treatment of a vital issue, "Sustainable Tourism" will be a welcome addition to the libraries of tourism industry professionals, individuals involved in the management of natural areas, tourism policy makers, tourism academics, and students with an interest in the future sustainability of tourism and the industry that supports it (Sustainable Tourism by Harris et al. (2002)). *Sustainable Practices in the Built Environment*, by Langston (2008), is an excellent book, primer for those in the construction industry who already have an interest in ecologically sustainable development and also for those who need to begin raising their awareness in this area.

This chapter deals with sustainability as it affects the construction industry and looks at the techniques and issues that designers, engineers, planners, and construction managers will have to deal with in their day-to-day activities. It covers methods of analysis such as environmental impact assessment and cost–benefit analysis as well as topics on design and energy regulation and conservation. *Two Way Track* (2005) published by Department of Environmental Heritage, Canberra, by Noel Preece and Penny van Oosterzee, identify and assess the potential long-term benefits and opportunities of strategically integrating biodiversity conservation requirements with the future needs of the nature-based and eco-tourism industry. It presents a national approach to formulating and implementing strategic plans to enable this integration. The need for an integrated approach, based on regional planning for biodiversity conservation and the development of tourism, has been recognized. This chapter recognizes that tourism must be ecologically sustainable, and that, for this to be successful, it must contribute to the long-term maintenance of ecosystems and species. Simply to "minimize impacts" is not enough as, with tourism growth, this will result in incremental damage and inevitable environmental deterioration.

8.3   AREA OF STUDY

The present study is confined to the Vembanad Lake, where backwater tourism of the state is flourishing, and Kuttanad regions consisting of Kottayam and Alappuzha Districts of Kerala, India. The Kuttanad region is renowned for its uniqueness. Paddy cultivation, the main crop of the region, has now turned less productive; thereby, the region's economy is in decline. It is highly necessary to supplement it with other means. Development of tourism will be an apt solution for the revival of the region's economy. From the tourism history of the region, it is evident that local tourism existed from the very ancient period onward. If it is properly marketed, it is quite sure that tourism will enhance the local economy as tourism has done wonders in other countries. In modern times, new forms of tourism activities were encouraged and innovative concepts were experimented with. In tune with the concept of houseboats of Kashmir, houseboats were introduced in the Vembanad Lake. This was a landmark in backwater tourism. The houseboats were provided with five-star hotel facilities. It was well-received from national as well as international tourists. The growth in the number of houseboats within a short span of time indicates its popularity with domestic tourists and, most importantly, with the international tourists. But water contamination continues to be a critical problem affecting the region, which, in turn, will certainly affect the growth of tourism.

To retain the momentum of growth and development of the tourism industry, it is highly essential to preserve the ecological balance and maintain the biodiversity of the region. *Two Way Track* (2005) by Noel Preece and Penny van Oosterzee suggests that simply to "minimize impacts" is not enough as, with tourism growth, this will result in incremental damage and inevitable environmental deterioration. There can be no net environmental deterioration if the industry is to be ecologically sustainable. Active management, which requires resources, is needed in all situations. Tourism has a significant responsibility to contribute to the management of the natural resources on which it is dependent. On the basis of the discussions and studies on backwaters with the prominent individuals, it is very clear that the growth potential of tourism in Vembanad region is unlimited. It is yet to be tapped using the latest business technologies. Like any other industry, tourism also needs good research, assessment of demand, product development, and tourists' feedbacks. Dr. U.K. Gopalan in the article titled "Inland Fishery" said that "there is no light still at the end of the tunnel" and remarked that the major environmental problem in Kerala is urban pollution. Loss of ecological resources and land degradation are also significant from the environmental angle.

The industrial pollution is an important contributor to the total pollution of Kerala backwaters. The United States Environmental Protection Agency's study on *Threats to Wetlands* (2001) warns, "Destroying or degrading wetlands can lead to serious consequences, such as increased flooding, extinction of species, and decline in water quality. We can avoid these consequences by maintaining the valuable wetlands we still have and restoring lost or impaired wetlands where possible."

8.4   PROBLEM STATEMENT

The Vembanad Lake is located in the central region of Kerala. The surrounding reclaimed portion of Vembanad Lake is known as Kuttanad.

The Lake has been formed due to the deluging of the rivers Achenkovil, Pampa, Manimala, Muvattupuzha, and Meenachil and its tributaries. The backwater tourism commenced and continued to grow in this region, the major tourist attractions being its biodiversity and scenic beauty. Backwater tourism in Kerala (India) is progressing in this region and has become the unique selling point (USP) of Kerala Tourism industry and international tourist arrivals have increased noticeably. Foreign tourists' appeal to quiet backwaters rose. International awareness was also directed toward the ecology of the Vembanad backwaters. Concurrently, international media responded to the ecological imbalances of the region. The international newspaper named The Observer, dated Sunday, August 14, 2005, published an article titled "Pollution threat to the backwater beauty of Kerala" by Dan McDougall. This is a clear indication that if not managed and maintained effectively, the ecological issues will lead to disastrous repercussions on the backwater tourism. The present tourism scenario will not be able to maintain the momentum if an immediate solution to the backwater contamination is not derived.

8.4.1   KUTTANAD TOURISM—APPEALING FACADES

The study has been divided into two different categories. The first part deals with the favorable factors for the tourism development in Kuttanad. The second part emphasizes on the ecology and biodiversity of the region. "The degree of fit between individuals and their environment depends on their expectations and motives for travel, as well as their ability to apply their actual experience on site to meet these requirements. As the degree of 'fit' increases, tourist's satisfaction also increases" Kingchan (1997). It has been observed that in addition to the scenic beauty and biodiversity, water temperature, air quality, noise level, and so forth are favorable factors for tourism development in the Kuttanad region.

8.4.1.1   WATER TEMPERATURE

Temperatures in the Kuttanad waters vary between 24 and 35°C. Water temperature is at a minimum during the monsoon season between July and September. From November onward, the temperature increases steadily, reaching a maximum in April. Temperatures are generally lower in upstream of Kuttanad and gradually increase toward the Vembanad Lake (Kuttanad Water Balance study, 2002).

8.4.1.2   AIR QUALITY

Air quality also plays an important role in tourism. People always prefer lesser polluted areas for spending holidays or their leisure time. The air quality in the surrounding area of the waterways is good as there are a few industries and only a few roads in the surrounding area.

8.4.1.3   NOISE

Noise levels are generally low in the vicinity of the waterways as there are few sources of loud noise, particularly from highways and factories. There may be activities such as rice harvesting, noises from loud radios, and sometimes festivals will also be the source of occasional noise in some locations. One of the major tourist attractions of the region is the absence of motor horns.

8.4.1.4   BOAT RACES

Vembanad backwaters are the venue of the Nehru Trophy Boat Race, and it can be taken as a milestone in the history of backwater tourism in Kerala. Though there are many boat races, this is the largest in Kerala. Chundanvallams or snake boats are decorated and those are rowed by around 115 people. These swift-moving Chundanvallams had been used as naval crafts of the ancient rulers of Kuttanad. In course of time, these were utilized for ceremonial and sports purposes. The race is held on the second Saturday in the month of August every year. Thousands of people gather to witness this festival.

8.4.1.5   WATER CRUISES

It is a fascinating experience to wander from village to village to explore the hinterlands. While passing through the villages, one can learn about the village economy and watch coir making, boat building, toddy tapping, and fish farming. The Press Information Bureau of Government of India has issued a special feature titled "Romancing with Kerala Backwaters." This shows the significance of Vembanad backwaters and cruising at the Lake.

8.4.2   OTHER FORMS OF AQUATIC TOURISM

The growth of different products in travel and tourism industry has led to the adding up of new products such as motorboat tourism, speed launch, water sports, and the houseboats, which have attracted the fancy of national and international tourists. Adventure-loving tourists have their options in the backwaters too. They can go for speed launches, which can be anchored wherever one feels like. Four- and six-seater speedboats are one of the best ways to enjoy the backwaters.

8.4.2.1   KETTUVALLOMS (HOUSEBOATS)

Houseboat Tourism has become the USP of Kerala tourism Industry. It is built in the traditional way of architecture, the Thachushastram. The design brings alive the memories of a past age with its features of a bygone era. Houseboats are eco-friendly and the packages are inclusive of food with options for Kerala and continental cuisines. It can be regarded as the indigenous version of the houseboats of Dal Lake in Kashmir.

The rooms of the houseboats provide all luxuries of a five-star hotel; in short, it is a floating palace. It is evident that backwater tourism is flourishing; it attracts tourists from all over the world. But the reality is that if the tourism industry has to thrive, it has to take care of the environmental hygiene. The aquatic environment is an attraction of the region and has to be protected from all sorts of pollution for further growth and development of the industry. Pizam (1978) found that "tourist satisfaction is the result of the interaction between a tourists' experience at the destination area and the expectations he had about that destination, when the weighted sum of total experiences compared to the expectations results in feelings of gratification, the tourist is satisfied; when the tourist's actual experiences compared to his expectations result in feelings of displeasure he is dissatisfied."

8.5   ECOLOGICAL PROTOTYPES

Ecology plays an imperative role in the promotion of tourism. Negligence may lead to environmental imbalances. The ecological impact has been quantified with relation to development. Vembanad region is a vast wetland ecosystem containing many smaller habitats. The rich biodiversity of the region attracts holidaymakers from all over the world. It can be said that it is a habitat of 150 varieties of fish species, three freshwater prawn species, and four species of mollusks.

Plant ecology in the Kuttanad area consists of remarkable diversity and abundance of local varieties of mango trees. Mango trees are supposed to have the capacity to absorb acidity from the soil and water. This is expected to be the reason for planting mango trees adjacent to wells. Mangrove forests were grown widely in Vembanad backwaters. The roots of mangroves aid in building up of dry land. It also provides food and shelter for an interesting range of animals which include fiddler crabs, mudskippers, herons, kingfishers, and mangrove snakes. The land is moist and marshy or even covered with water during the major part of the year. In this area, we can see the submerged plant species such as Chara, Nitella, Ceratophyllam, Utrichlaria, Hydrilla, and Potamojcton. In shallow waters, Aponogeton, Ludwigia, Limnophyla, Marsilia, Myriophyllaum, Hygrorhyxa, Jussciaea, Neptunia, Nymphaea, and Limnathamum can be commonly seen. There are other plants of commercial importance, which find applications in the making of herbal medicines. It is also used as fodder for domestic animals.

Water Hyacinth/*Eichornia crassipes* is a free-floating plant most commonly seen along the canals and waterways in abundance. This plant has nodes and small roots. Only one or two roots touch the ground and it reproduces rapidly by vegetative propagation. The growth of water hyacinth has become a major botheration of the people of Kuttanad. Lake water is full of water hyacinths that block water transportation. Due to its wild growth, the water becomes stagnant and a foul smell emanates. Water hyacinths have the quality to absorb many chemicals, including sewage and industrial wastes. Investigators are studying the possibility of making cattle feed on dried water hyacinths, but till now, no applications have been found here. This region is rich with diverse natural resources and is adequately opulent with multiple animal ecology, habitat ecology, water fauna, avifauna, and varied migrants.

Animal ecology is a subset of ecological dimensions and is a study of the interaction between animals and their environments. Domestic cattle such as cow, buffalo, sheep, and common poultry like chicken, duck, turkey, and geese are very common in Kuttanad. The habitat ecology deals with the various habitats of the biosphere. The details of the various habitats were collected from the Agriculture Research Station at Kumarakom.

The Vembanad supports the third largest population of waterfowl amounting to more than 20,000 in India. According to the Asian Waterfowl Census (1994–1996), Vembanad Lake supported 27 species 29,991 waterbirds in 1994, 33 species 21,416 waterbirds in 1995, and 35 species 21,724 waterbirds in 1996 (Centre for Water Resources Development and Management, PO Kunnamangalam, Kozhikode, August 19, 2002). Contemplating on the water fauna, the Vembanad Lake serves as a habitat for a variety of finfish, shellfish, a nursery of several species of aquatic life, and a transitional ecotone between sea and land. Many fish species depend on the wetland for food, spawning, and nursery. The common fish and mollusks and other aquatic species include Konju, Karimeen, Vala, different types of Carps, Cherumeen, tortoise, water snakes, rat snakes, migrating marine fish, and prawns. Other than these, two species of estuarine fish constitute the main part of it, namely Kuris. Envisaging the avifauna, both resident and migratory waterfowl are abundant in this region. Endangered species of waterfowl are as follows: (i) Spot-billed Pelican (*Pelicanus philippensis*), (ii) Oriental Darter (*Anlinga melanogaster*), (iii) Water Cock (*Galliere cincera*), and (iv) Black-billed Tern (*Sterna malnogaster*). Most common are crows/house crows as well as jungle crows, tree pies (Dendrocitta), babblers, seven sisters, and mynahs. Other birds such as bulbuls, magpie-robins, paradise flycatchers, King Crows or Drongo (Dicrurus), and tailorbirds are also common.

The Vembanad Lake supports the third largest population of waterfowl in India during the winter months. A total of 91 species of resident/locally migratory and 50 species of migratory birds are found in the Kol area. The birds come here from different regions, and they stay here for breeding and feeding. Vembanad Lake and the surrounding areas are the safe havens for migratory birds. It was, in fact, one of the richest bird habitats on the west coast of India. The aquatic or marsh birds, permanent dwellers or migrants, are abundant along the water bodies. The Kadal Kakka or terns is a subfamily of seabirds related to gulls and Thalassus, are abundant during the period from October to February. Thalassus also belong to the

Terns family. The paddy Oird or *Ardeola grayi* is found in the water-filled paddy fields. During the winter months, the migratory teals come to the shores from northern Asia. Teal breed on shallow freshwater pools and lakes bordered by dense vegetation. The large water bodies attract all types of marine birds and harbor an abundant brackish water fish fauna.

Main causes of environmental pollution in Vembanad Lake and Kuttanad region can be traced to waste and sediments deposited by deluging rivers, sewage from surrounding towns, water pumped from paddy fields with agrochemicals and pesticide wastages, oil spill from motorized boats and houseboats, the constraints due to the latrines of the natives which are open to the Lake, and the household waste deposits.

8.5.1   WASTE AND SEDIMENT DEPOSITS BY DELUGING RIVERS

Many towns of central Kerala carry a huge amount of sewage deposits into the Vembanad Lake. The river Pampa is one of these. The famous Hindu pilgrim center Sabarimala is situated on the banks of river Pampa. It is estimated that during the Sabarimala pilgrim season, nearly four million people cross the river Pampa to reach the hill shrine, and the river turns into a cesspool of human waste, raw sewage, and domestic and commercial garbage. All the wastes generated reach the river, which finally gets into the Vembanad waters. According to the Kerala State Pollution Control Board statistics, the coliform bacteria count in 100 ml of water in the Pampa at Sabarimala is 200,000. When the river reaches Edathuwa in Kuttanad, the count is 487,000. Other deluging rivers also release a huge volume of untreated sewage, including water that runs off construction sites and farmland and carries sediments and wastes to the lake. It is said that the bottom of Vembanad Lake is carpeted with plastic bags. Even though the tourism activities are being blamed for water contamination, in reality, the havoc is caused by the deluging rivers.

8.5.1.1   SEWAGE DISCHARGE FROM TOWNS

The urban areas in and around Kuttanad regions have no sewerage collection and treatment system. The sewage effluents from the municipalities of Kottayam, Thiruvalla, Changanassery, and Alappuzha, and other towns directly enter the Vembanad Lake through small canal outlets. Solid waste from medical colleges at Alappuzha and Kottayam also find a dumping ground in the Vembanad Lake.

8.5.1.2   WATER PUMPED FROM PADDY FIELDS WITH AGROCHEMICALS AND PESTICIDES WASTES

Monoculture is yet another reason for the havoc of the region. A hybrid variety of paddy cultivation requires the high quantity of fertilizer and pesticides and the wastewater that is pumped into the rivers nearby later reaches the backwaters. As the flow of the backwaters is restricted by the bund, the water remains stagnant and worsens the water contamination.

8.5.1.3   OIL SPILL FROM MOTORIZED BOATS AND HOUSEBOATS

The number of houseboats is proliferating. The main environmental hazard caused by the houseboat operation is the discharge of sewage and waste to the backwaters. About 300 houseboats are servicing in this region. The absence of suitable sewage disposal systems in the houseboats is a major problem of water contamination.

At present, the Department of Tourism has decided to set up eco-friendly sewage treatment plants of required capacities in the following places to treat the sewage pumped out from the houseboats. Oil spills from the houseboats is yet another environmental problem.

8.5.1.4   THE LATRINES OF THE NATIVES ARE OPEN TO THE LAKE AND THE HOUSEHOLD WASTE DEPOSITS

Sanitation facilities in Kuttanad are available only to one-third of the population. In Kuttanad, the toilet outlets are opened to the rivers and backwaters, leading to high-level water contamination. The said problem can be solved only by the construction of public latrines as the majority of the population belongs to the economically weaker section. Social awareness programs will also help to lessen the issue.

The Vembanad Lake and adjoining wetlands have suffered a grave loss with respect to diversity. Earlier, over 40,000 birds were seen in this area. At present, it is being reduced to half of that number. In 2003, only 66 species of birds were spotted in a bird count conducted by Kottayam Nature Society in association with the Forest Department in the Vembanad Lake. The droppings of birds stimulated the growth of the planktons—the nutrient of fish links. The sharp fall in the bird population has also trimmed the fish population in the area. Kuttanad can be an eco-friendly tourism spot if the society changes its attitude toward the resources and their utilization, they should also view the environment as a service provider. The failure to do so will lead to several environmental disasters. As environmental and social standards form an integral part of the tourism industry, accreditation standards are being set in the tourism industry at international levels and are bound to develop a positive and healthy relationship between humans and the environment.

Joseph Dougherty in his book on biodiversity and health comments that helping the rural poor to manage their resources more effectively will also help to ensure biodiversity. Moreover, while global economic forces may be driving the loss of biodiversity, the impacts of this loss are felt at the local level. The local knowledge that people have about their resources and how these resources should be managed provides a critical resource for all of the humanity. Indigenous people who live in intimate connection with biodiversity could provide much of the intellectual raw material for a shift to sustainable societies, provided they are empowered to act in their own self-interest. Thus, biodiversity and cultural diversity can be conserved together, enabling both to prosper. This is why biodiversity has become such a dominant theme in the global conservation movement.

8.6   SCIENTIFIC PROPOSITIONS AND IMPLICATIVE MEASURES

Sediment deposit is a serious concern. It will reduce the depth of the backwaters. Hence, the depth has to be maintained by dredging. This will keep up the water currents and will restore the natural way of flushing out to the sea and there will be better control of flood waters. The present system of dumping waste into the rivers and to the backwaters has to be prohibited. The usual practice of keeping the outlet of the toilets to the rivers and backwater is to be restricted by laws. This will reduce the water contamination of the region. Environmental awareness programs have to be organized for both the locals and the tourists for the effective maintenance of environmental and ecological balances. Specific policies and guidelines for ecotourism development, through a regulatory framework, maintain a balance between the negative and positive impacts of tourism through planning.

The main environmental hazard caused by the houseboat operation is the discharge of sewage and wastewaters directly to the backwaters. The absence of suitable sewage disposal system in the houseboats has led to contamination of water with an unacceptable level of coliform counts. The water is found to be unfit for swimming or fishing activities due to microbial contamination. The situation deprives the tourists of a most wonderful experience in backwaters. The problem is serious enough to adversely affect the growth and sustainability of the tourism industry based on backwaters. Therefore, installation of a suitable marine sanitation system for the safe discharge of sewage has become an absolute necessity. Abnormal growth of water hyacinths is a major threat to aquatic ecology. It also restricts the easy movement of houseboats, especially in the interior regions, and aqua tourism activities. Steps are to be initiated to control the wild growth of water hyacinths.

Monoculture paddy cultivation is done by using heavy agrochemicals and these are pumped into the backwaters. To keep up the ecological status and to save the habitat of a large-scale avian fauna of the backwaters, it is necessary to reduce the application of agrochemicals. Mangroves in the region, an important constituent of wetlands, are in a degrading condition. Therefore, mangroves at Pathiramanal and Kumarakom have to be protected. Tourism industry/government/academic-sponsored research has to be undertaken for the marketing and promotion of tourism. In turn, it helps and facilitates to understand the kinds of opportunities and interests the tourists are looking for. To attract high-yield tourists, the government should promote the introduction of more luxury and quality houseboats in line with the model of luxury houseboats at Dal Lake in Kashmir.

Rules and regulations have to be made to ensure safety and security for the tourists as tourist confidence is the primary requisite for the development of tourism. Regulations and guidelines need to be formulated to keep the backwater tourism eco-friendly and declare Vembanad backwaters as a Special Tourism Zone. Houseboats are to be fitted with bio-toilets and places for the deposit of garbage from the houseboats are be ensured. Even though Kuttanad is a land of rivers, aquatic sports and other tourism activities such as water skiing, water scooters, parasailing, airborne sailing, angling, and scuba diving are rare. These types of aquatic tourism activities require large capital investment. Hence, to promote such activities, foreign investments have to be promoted.

8.7 CONCLUSION

The conservation of ecological biological diversity, usually shortened to biodiversity, is crucial in tourism development and priority should be given to its conservation by the National and State governments. At the same time, tourism industry should adopt strategic thinking so as to develop tourism with benefits for everyone. Extend and diversify product offerings to improve yields and social values. If suggestions put forward are implemented, backwater tourism in Vembanad Lake can come out from its shell and enter the international market. In this study, a methodical approach has been engaged to comprehend the potential threats in the growth path of a fast growing and mushrooming business. Proven methods have been adopted to understand these problems. These observations are systematically analyzed with the help of industry experts and participants. Suggestions are made to ensure further growth and the health of the industry.

KEYWORDS

- Vembanad Lake
- backwater
- kuttanad
- biological diversity
- conservation

REFERENCES

Harris, R.; Griffin, T.; Williams, P., Eds. *Sustainable Tourism: A Global Perspective;* Routledge, 2002.

Kingchan, K. Tourist Satisfaction in Relation to a Holiday in Thailand. Greend. The Development and Evaluation of Activity Schedules for Tourists on One-Day Commercial Reef

Trip [sC]. Published by the Coop-erative Research Centre for Ecologically Sustainable Development of the Great Barrier Reef, 4. 1997.

Langston, C., Ed. Sustainable Practices in the Built Environment; Routledge, 2008.

Marsh, G. P. Man and Nature; University of Washington Press, 1965.

Pizam, A. Tourism's Impacts: The Social Costs to the Destination Community as Perceived by its Residents. J. Travel Res. 1978, 16(4), 8–12.

Preece, N.; James, D. E.; Van Oosterzee, P.; Department of the Environment, Sport and Territories, Australia, Biodiversity Unit. *Two Way Track: Biodiversity Conservation and Ecotourism: An Investigation of Linkages, Mutual Benefits and Future Opportunities;* Dept. of the Environment, Sport and Territories: Canberra, ACT, 2005.

U.S. Environmental Agency. *Threats to Wetlands (Rep.);* Virginia: U S Environmental Agency, 2001.

CHAPTER 9

MANAGING A HERITAGE CITY FOR TOURISM AND THE CONTRIBUTION TO THE REGIONAL DEVELOPMENT: A CASE OF DARASURAM IN KUMBAKONAM, TAMIL NADU, INDIA

K. SELVA KUMAR

Army Institute of Hotel Management and Catering Technology, Bangalore, India

CONTENTS

ABSTRACT

This current chapter deals with Darasuram at Kumbakonam in Tamil Nadu, which is transforming into a heritage city. Examining the impact of the recent growth of cultural activities in the city, this chapter focuses on the destination with its specific forms of tourism (cultural, heritage, historical, leisure, etc.). Moreover, it is of high significance for the destination managers and marketing bodies to shape the destination image. Consequently, it is crucial for developing a marketing and urban development strategy, with the purpose to provide appropriate tourism products, in accordance with demands and desires caused by additional sociocultural identity. Hence, the need for a permanent investigation on various categories and market segments is of high regard.

9.1   INTRODUCTION

Modern perspectives look at the city as more than a mere focus on people and think it as a hub of trade, culture, information, and industry. Because of increasing urbanization, cities play ever more important roles in their country's economic development and may perform a vital function in global or regional networks. As such, cities are increasingly challenging one another to attract visitors, investors, and residents, and to host international events or corporate headquarters (UN-Habitat, 2006). Therefore, researchers provide a growing attention to the city as a subject of study. Kumbakonam (Tamil Nadu, India) is one of the most well-known cities along with Tamil Nadu and it is renowned because of its Mahamaham event. In the seventh century, it had been the capital of Chola kings. Kumbakonam (Tamil Nadu, India), the renowned brow area of Southern India, is usually picturesquely found around both the streams, Cauvery and Arasalar. Kumbakonam will be the brow town of Southern India tucked within the Thanjavur area of Tamil Nadu. The location is usually renowned because of the Mahamaham event that may be framed after with 12 many years from the Mahamaham tank located in the center from it. The location is usually renowned because of metal shipwrecks. It is mainly an industry area to the primarily agriculture-centered villages adjoining it. In addition, betel leaves tend to be developed in Kumbakonam given that it is also referred to as Kumbakonam Vettrilai (in Tamil).

Kumbakonam (Tamil Nadu, India) is often a hectic, dirty, and business-oriented hub, nestled down the Cauvery Pond, a few 37 km northeast of Thanjavur. Many temples or wats tend to be scattered around the area along with this. It is the excellent bottom to check out the exceptional Chola temples nearby or head far east to the resort cities of the Cauvery Delta. As a result, the document looks at the procedure through which Kumbakonam is usually modifying right traditions town and investigates the effect of the latest growth of national activities from the town in other locations of progress.

9.2 STUDY AREA

Darasuram or Dharasuram is a panchayat town located 3 km from Kumbakonam in Thanjavur District, Tamil Nadu, India. The town is known for the Airavateswara temple constructed by the Rajaraja Chola II in the 12th century AD. The temple is a recognized as a United Nations Educational, Scientific and Cultural Organization (UNESCO) world heritage monument.

9.3 HERITAGE CITY: A CULTURAL PERSPECTIVE LITERATURE REVIEW

It is generally recognized that the identity of a city is closely related to the remains of its past. Historic buildings are often an important aspect of the ambiance of inner city neighborhoods and sometimes even characteristic for the city as a whole, as is witnessed in, for example, Rome, Jerusalem, Cairo, and Delhi. This built heritage is part of the cultural capital of cities, and the importance of this asset has in recent years been stressed by many authors (e.g., Fusco Girard and Nijkamp, 2009; Throsby, 2001). In general, urban economists have stressed the importance of urban amenities for the attractiveness of inner cities as a place of residence or creative business

(Brueckner et al., 1999; Glaeser et al., 2001). A historic center is probably the most important example of such an amenity. Cultural products and cultural industries create new employment opportunities and make a significant addition to the conventional methods for the conservation of cultural heritage (Bayliss, 2004). Changes in consumption trends in the 1980s led to the appeal of the unique and special rather than the commonplace, and the tendency toward niche markets have increased the economic value and expanded the market share of products with a potent cultural dimension. Thus, with the attractive investment opportunities offered by the cultural industries, the private sector has steadily increased its investment in this area. Cultural industries have also strengthened local and regional economies with their contribution to creativity, innovation, and efficiency (Berg et al., 2001).

In this way, cultural industries boost the attractiveness of cities as places to live, work, visit, and spend leisure time in; and consequently, spatial arrangements nurturing these industries make up the central axis of urban development strategies (Darlow, 1996).

9.4   RESEARCH METHODS

The research embraces together the primary and secondary data sources. The major data and information pertaining to the research study have been accumulated from the primary sources. The main sources of primary data were personal visits to Darasuram Temple and their observation. The secondary sources, the main source of secondary data, were the Ministry of Tourism, Govt. of India, including the Dept. of Tourism and Culture, Govt. of Tamil Nadu and its cognate departments, books, journals, portals, and newspapers.

9.4.1   WHAT MAKES A HERITAGE CITY?

In today's highly competitive tourism marketplace, cities have to work hard to differentiate themselves and create a positive image (Morgan et al., 2004; Baker, 2007; Trueman et al., 2008). Kumbakonam (Tamil Nadu, India) has a powerful image as a temple city, shopping, and designer lifestyles; to date, however, the marketing strategies and activities at Kumbakonam are ignored with its broader cultural heritage and focused on the business market. Destination heritage is an arena in which the inheritance could be dealt commendably, while one can connect, understand, value the resources, and preserve the cultural resources.

The Cauvery river delta was first recognized by the Chola rulers, as an ideal place to settle, as it was rich in alluvial soil that was best suited for agriculture. They set up their capital at Uraiyur in Tiruchirappalli. Kumbakonam (Tamil Nadu, India) was the second capital of Cholas, who ruled since the third century. It was developed as a religious center and was organized around several temples. Most of the old Shiva temples, mandapam, and padithore belong to this period. The Pandyas of Madurai came into power in the thirteenth century. Hoysalas ruled from the fourteenth century onwards and were overpowered by the Vijayanagar kings who appointed Nayakas to rule the region. The Nayakas made additions to the existing Shiva temples and made new Vaishnava temples. Art, architecture, crafts, literature, music, and dance were patronized by Chola, Nayaka, and Maratha rulers in the region. Later, the city was recognized for its importance as a center for handicrafts and artifacts. There are more than 180 temples in Kumbakonam, six of which particularly attract a large number of devotees every year. As a result, Kumbakonam has a significantly high floating population and pilgrimage tourists.

9.5 CULTURAL PROPERTIES OF KUMBAKONAM: AIRAVATESVARA TEMPLE (TAMIL NADU, INDIA)

Monuments with cultural significance are usually among popular tourism attractions. In particular, when monuments have the status of World Heritage Sites (WHS), the international visibility of the sites as tourism attractions is increased. Airavatesvara Temple is a Hindu temple of Dravidian architecture located in the town of Darasuram near Kumbakonam. This temple, built by Rajaraja Chola II in the 12th century CE is a UNESCO WHS along with the Brihadeeswara Temple at Thanjavur and the Gangaikondacholisvaram Temple at Gangaikonda Cholapuram; altogether, they are referred to as the Great Living Chola Temples.

Temples: The prominent temples in Kumbakonam (Tamil Nadu, India) include Adi Kumbeswarar temple, Sarangapani temple, Somessar temple, Nageswaran temple, Ramaswamy temple, Chakkarapani temple, and Pana Pureeswarar temple.

Religious Institutions: Kumbakonam is home to the famous Maharaja Kala Shre Govindha Theekshidar Veda Kavya Pada Salai that is engaged in training youth in Vedic literature and other religious activities. Sankara madam, Govinda Kudi, and Ahobila madam are other major institutions in Kumbakonam.

Environmentally Sensitive Areas: These include the numerous holy tanks and riverfront areas and include the renowned Mahamaham tank (famous for its Mahamaham festival held every 12 years during which devotees throng to Kumbakonam to take a holy dip in the tank), Porthamarai Theertham, Paga Theertham, and Ghats of River Cauvery and Arasalar.

Minor Heritage Areas: These include the traditional settlements of various social groups. The traditional houses are linear and endowed with architectural features including the Columnar Thinai, Madam, Muttrum, and so forth.

9.5.1 HISTORY AND CULTURE IN KUMBAKONAM (TAMIL NADU, INDIA)

Kumbakonam has a prominent place in history as the capital of the Chola Empire and the city dates back to the Sangam period and was ruled by the Early Cholas, Pallavas, Medieval Cholas, Later Cholas, Pandyas, Vijayanagar Empire, Madurai Nayaks, Thanjavur Nayaks, and Thanjavur Marathas. The town reached the zenith of its prosperity during the time when it was a prominent center of European education and Hindu culture, and it acquired the cultural name, the "Cambridge of South India." In 1866, Kumbakonam was officially constituted as a municipality, which today comprises 45 wards, making it the second largest municipality in Thanjavur district. Kumbakonam is known as the "Temple Town" due to the prevalence of a number of temples here for which it is noted and attracts people from all over the globe. The main products produced are brass, bronze, copper, and lead vessels, silk and cotton cloths, and pottery.

9.5.2 ARTS AND CULTURE FESTIVALS

The contribution of festivals to economic and social development can be evaluated on two levels—the international and the local. Organizing a festival that will attract international visitors contributes to boosting the visibility and image of that city. As long as the festivals include original and high-quality art and cultural events, they can be a symbol for the city and become one of its traditions (Garcia, 2004). This would then expand the viewer profile of the festival to an international level and lead to an increase in the number of visitors coming to that city. On a local level, these festivals are important in raising the quality of life in the city, facilitating social integration, and supporting the development of artistic production. Festivals are also among one of the most important fields of cultural investment utilizing the latest technologies.

9.6   SYNERGY BETWEEN CULTURE AND TOURISM IN KUMBAKONAM (TAMIL NADU, INDIA)

Culture and tourism are often viewed together as a critical combination that attracts both visitors and investment to the area. Culture is instrumental in creating a unique image for the destination, whereas tourism generates income that is necessary for the support and maintenance of the cultural products and heritage assets. Urban tourists have more discretionary income, incur in greater expenditures, and have higher education levels, coupled with interest in cultural affairs (ETC, 2005). Therefore, cities increasingly aim to become competitive in the cultural tourism market through their ability to provide better goods and services. In this sense, Kumbakonam has rich resources that include its cultural, historical, and heritage sites, which are paramount to boost the attraction of the city. The competitiveness of the city is derived from its history, architecture, heritage, and vibrant modern culture, its diversity, as well as the existence of various cultural attractions such as temples, religious institutions, art galleries, fairs, and festivals throughout the year. In addition to culture the city has also expanded its infrastructure and superstructure significantly in recent years, with the construction of an infrastructure, meeting facilities, and a greater hotel capacity.

The market for luxury hotels is corporate travelers, meetings and incentive participants, and up-market cultural tourists. Some city hotel chains have residences fully equipped to cater to business and corporate travelers. Along with the international chain hotels, local investors have also invested in luxury and other category hotels in Kumbakonam. Recently, a new budget type of 'city hotel' concept, with moderate rates but complemented by corporate facilities, has been introduced. This restructuring of the city's infrastructure and superstructure affects business, meetings, and urban tourism demand. These various tourism types are related to each other, creating a synergy between the demand components. A few of the significant places near Kumbakonam are: Konerirajapuram, a small village, well-known due to the colossal Nataraja symbol made up of bronze, which is biggest in the world; Tiruvidaimarudur (10 km in south to Kumbakonam) is just about the nearly all famed Shaivite revolves; Pattiswaram (8 km from Kumbakonam, one of several Shiva temples connected with great antiquity, along with mythological as well as historical interest, although not a lot is known outdoors); and Thiruveragam, popularly known as Swamimalai, a small village 10 km west to Kumbakonam city throughout Thanjavur district, north of the a couple waterways, Arasalar as well as Cauvery, and is also well-known with the forehead connected with the almighty Muruga, possesses quite a few festivals famed typically the most popular getting, Valli Kalyana festival which usually lures big crowds of supporters as well as visitors.

9.6.1   MAHAMAHAM FESTIVAL (DIVINE TIME TO PURIFY)

The antiquity of the Mahamagam is reasoned from the structural and epigraphical examples. The roof of the Gangatirtha mandapam conveys the sculptural representation of Tulapurushardava. It is trusted that Govinda Dikshitar subjected himself to the occasion and gave the gold for the building of the 16 mandapas. The visit of Krishandevaraya amid 1445 is recorded in an engraving in the gopuram of Nagalpuram, a town in Chengalpattu locale. That Krishnadevaraya went to the occasion is likewise recorded in the engraving found in the Shiva sanctuary in Kuthalam. The festival as a tourism event also affects the cultural and social realm. On one hand, it can be instrumental in presenting local cultural traditions and customs to visitors, thereby preserving and diffusing the heritage.

On the other hand, exposing local culture to attract visitors can similarly threaten continuity through pressures of commercialization (Saleh and Ryan, 1993; Senior and Danson, 1998; Waterman, 1998). In India, festivals and holy baths attract the attention of the public and draw lakhs of people to the water bodies at a time. This holy bath, which takes place in four places once in 12 years, is called as Kumbhamela, namely, Holy Prayag (the Ganga Yamuna confluence) in Allahabad, the Ganga in Haridwar, the Sipra River in Ujjain, and the Godavari in Nasik. Mahamaham is another important festival of a similar kind. This festival was first celebrated in the early Sangam period. It is identified by the Sangam literature. The festival has been very famously celebrated in the 20th century A.D. The Mahamagham festivals have celebrated nine times in this same century (1909, 1921, 1933, 1945, 1956, 1963, 1980, 1992, and 2004). The Mahamagham tank is on the 6 acre. The tank boundary is the southern side 470 ft, northern side 580 ft, eastern side 285 ft, and western side 500 ft. The Mahamagham tank is shaped for the pottery.

9.7   ECONOMIC AND PHYSICAL DEVELOPMENTS IN KUMBAKONAM (TAMIL NADU, INDIA)

Kumbakonam is a special grade municipal town and the second biggest in terms of administrative status in the Thanjavur district. It is located 313 km away from Chennai on the South, 90 km from Trichy on the East, and 40 km from Thanjavur on the Northeast. The town is a religious center with the presence of a large number of temples. It has gained importance as a commercial and industrial (small-scale) center during the last quarter of the nineteenth century. Kumbakonam is also home to a well-known bronze handicraft cluster. The Tamil Nadu Handicraft Development Corporation (Poompuhar) was set up in Swamimalai to train artisans and foster this art. The city corporation plan points out that in spite of a market among hotels, temples, and offices, the art of bronze sculptures has not been leveraged to its full potential and indicates that there is significant export potential especially to the markets of Singapore and Malaysia. The important commercial activities of the town are arecanut products, brass vessels, and textiles.

9.8   GAP ANALYSIS

The current chapter examines most pertinent aspects that are critical and crucial for a heritage destination to represent itself as an attractive tourist destination. Hence, the nitty-gritty involved in the destination appeals as a WHS that is of extraordinary regard and is of great potential.

9.8.1   STATUS OF EXISTING INFRASTRUCTURE SERVICES IN KUMBAKONAM TOWN LEVEL

The anchors in assessing the infrastructure parameters—pilgrimage amenity center, parking, shops/kiosks, accommodation/hotels, drinking water facility, solid waste management, tourist information centers, trained guides, information signages, seating/resting, garden/parks, security, restaurant, street lightings, and so forth—are either of very poor ambience or sometimes do not exist in the destination. These aspects are critical and crucial for a destination to portray as an attractive tourist destination. Hence, the nitty-gritty involved in the destination appeal as a WHS that is of high regard and of great potential.

9.8.1.1   BOTTLENECKS AT THE REGION

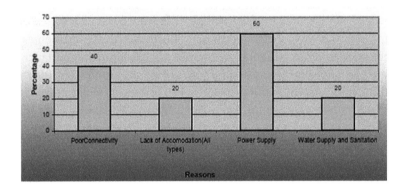

9.8.1.2   SOURCE RESULT OF MARKET RESEARCH BY CUSTOMER EFFORT SCORE

It is revealed that there is a deficiency of power supply (60%) at the region, following which, poor network (40%) has been recognized as the greatest bottleneck, trailed by the absence of an accommodation (20%), and water supply and sanitation (20%) issue, as demonstrated graphically in the accompanying.

9.9 INTRODUCING VOLUNTEERING PHENOMENON

The voluntary sector comprises all the activities and accommodations provided on the substratum of volunteering, that is, unpaid work accomplished within the context of a formal business (public or private) or an association. Volunteering can have its source in a positive posture that finds that availing people or accommodating society can lead to a higher degree of life gratification. It engenders the community participation within this context of "positive attitude" and "life satisfaction" through the concept and types of value. Volunteering is one of the key factors in the prosperity of events. It takes the strenuous exertion and support from community volunteers to ascertain that a festival or event runs smoothly. Directional boards and signs should be placed at sundry corners of the temple so that Free Individual Tourists may eschew facing quandaries in proceeding further by guiding themselves. Furthermore, all the ingressions in the detailed map of the temple of immensely colossal size should be placed so that devotees/tourists without any avail can guide themselves. Online reservation should be made available through website and the internet for visit, darshan (to visually perceive), offering poojas (worship) and prayer, and for availing other facilities of the temple. Camera and T.V. facilities must withal be made available for having darshan to optically discern the main deities so as to eschew rush outside the sanctum sanctorum particularly at the time of offering poojas.

Acclamation for the pedestrian pathways around the temple is of imperative nature. The endowment of shaded walkways around the temple and path for pedestrians are a basic and imperative requirement of a historically significant destination. Public utilities like street lighting at the main ingression to the temple and public accommodation facilities at the town are also presented in a trivial condition. It is also essential to develop and engender light and sound shows exhibiting the history, culture, and tradition of a temple and ensuring that the heritage museum inside the temple involute is of high regard. Other parameters include strengthening of connecting link road in and around Darasuram and promoting utilization of sustainable technology (alternative energy, recycling, etc.). Temple administration and regime take initiatives to commence spiritual retreat centers are also highly significant. It is also germane to encourage companies to provide information to tourists on cultural activities that subsist in the destination and to establish cognizance programs for the care of heritage and reverence for local customs.

9.10   CONCLUSION

The tourist facilities have additionally contributed to regional economic development by enhancing the tourism product, reaching to distant tourism markets, and connecting visitors to local businesses that accommodate their desiderata; they accompany cash into the association in several ways and accommodate opportunities for businesses and borough enterprises to abet in association accessory initiatives. Local and municipal regime plays a paramount role with deference to pilgrimage tourism for the region. In addition, the orchestrating, development, promotion, marketing, and implementation of these products and accommodations can sustain cultural tourism as an economic activity that can ameliorate standards of living for people in the region. This chapter addresses the critical shortages of resources, infrastructure, and skills among tourism stakeholders, business, practitioners, communities, and so forth, and offers some strategies as recommendations to ameliorate the regional market with incipient cultural products and accommodations. This analysis may be the commencement point for further research about pilgrimage and heritage tourism development, marketing, and promotion on the region of Kumbakonam.

GLOSSARY

Adikumbashwara: Also known as "Lord of the Pot" famous temple in Kumbakonam dedicated to Lord Shiva.

Ahobila Matam: Ahobila Matam is a Sri Vaishnava religious institution established 600 years ago in a place called Ahobilam by Srimad Athivan Satakopan.

Arasalar: The River Arasalar is a tributary of Cauvery.

Cauvery Delta: Cauvery Delta Zone lies in the eastern part of Tamil Nadu between 10.00 and 11.30 North latitude and between 78.15 and79.45 longitudes.

Chola kings: The Chola Dynasty was a Tamil dynasty, which was one of the longest ruling in some parts of southern India, from third century BC to until the 13th century AD.

Mahamagham Festival: The Mahamagham festival that comes on once in 12 years when Jupiter passes the constellation of Simha or Leo.

Nayaks: The Nayaks were subordinates of the imperial Vijayanagara emperors and were appointed as provincial governors by the Vijayanagar Emperor who divided the Tamil country into three Nayakships, namely, Madurai, Tanjore, and Gingi.

Govinda Dikshitar: Govinda Dikshitar was a scholar, philosopher, statesman, and musicologist. He served as a minister under Achuta Nayak and Ragunatha Nayak, the rulers of Tanjore in the 16th century.

Vettrilai: The Betel (Piper betle) is the leaf of a vine belonging to the Piperaceae family.

KEYWORDS

- **tourism**
- **culture**
- **Kumbakonam**
- **cities**
- **economic development**
- **world heritage**

REFERENCES

Action Plan for the Provision of Basic Amenities and Infrastructure Development Works in Kumbakonam Town for the Mahamagham Festival, 2004.

Darlow, A. Cultural Policy, and Urban Sustainability: Making a Missing Link? *Plann. Pract. Res.* **1996,** *11*(3), 291–301.

Fusco Girard, L; Nijkamp, P. Eds. *Cultural Tourism and Sustainable Local Development;* Ashgate: Aldershot 2009.

G.O. (4D) No.8. The Government of Tamil Nadu. October 15, 2003. (accessed Dec. 5, 2011).

Garcia, B. Urban Regeneration, Arts Programming and Major Events: Glasgow 1990, Sydney 2000 and Barcelona 2004. *Int. J. Cultural Policy* **2004,** *10*(1), 103–118.

Identification of Tourism Circuits across India Interim Report-Priority Circuit Tamil Nadu, IL&FS Infrastructure Development Corporation Ltd (IL&FS IDC), appointed as the National Level Consultant (NLC) by Ministry of Tourism.

UN-Habitat. State of the World Cities Report 2006/2007, United Nations Human Settlements Programme. 2006.

PART II

Operational and Managerial Perspectives in the Service Sector

ORGANIZATIONAL CULTURE AND EMPLOYEE MOTIVATION AMONG THE TOURISM PROFESSIONALS IN KARNATAKA, INDIA

TOMY K. KALLARAKAL

Christ (Deemed to be University),Bangalore, India

CONTENTS

ABSTRACT

The productivity and effectiveness of any organization depend mainly on the performance level of the employees in the organization. Human behavior scientists over the years have conducted various studies and have concluded that the performance of employees in any organiza- tion depends largely on their motivational behavior. Reviews of related literature confirm the role of various factors in the motivational behavior of employees pertaining to organizational culture. The major objective of this chapter is to ascertain the relationship between motivational behavior and organizational culture of tourism employees and finding out whether differences in demographic variables would account for significant differences in motivational behavior. The population of the study consisted of 323 employees of the public sector, the private sector, and multinational companies working in travel agencies, tour operations, airlines, and hotels and resorts in Bangalore. The study unravels organizational culture and its influence on the motivational behavior of employees working in the tourism sector. This chapter unleashes certain nuances that influence organizational culture and the intricacies of the motivational behavior of the employees of the travel industry. Therefore, in the Indian context, based on the results of the present study, there is a need for a thorough revamping of the existing practices in the tourism organizations to raise the motivational behavior of these employees and thereby help these organizations to deliver quality service.

10.1   ORGANIZATIONAL CULTURE

The concept of organizational culture is fairly recent. Culture has become a common subject in international business research (Gerhart and Fang, 2005) as well as in academic textbooks and the popular press. With the increasing globalization and mobility of the global labor force, such emphasis is appropriate. The concept of organizational culture provides a framework for systematically analyzing, understanding, and interpreting human experiences in organizations (Tierney, 1988). It reflects the national, regional, local, and leaders' influences on the employees of an organization. In general, organizational culture exists at various levels. On the surface are visible artifacts and observable behaviors—the way people dress and act, and the symbols, stories, and ceremonies that organization members share. The visible elements of culture, however, reflect deeper values in the minds of organization members. These underlying values, assumptions, beliefs, and thought processes are the true culture. Moreover, organizational culture represents a three-tier model. The tiers belong to the unconscious, semiconscious, and conscious levels depending on the contributing factors. At the unconscious level, factors such as values, beliefs, and assumptions are present. At the level of semiconsciousness, people will find components such as attitude and artifacts. At the conscious level of culture, one may find norms, behaviors, practices, rituals, and so forth. Institution building for an organization may be viewed as a proactive process that generates new values for the organization as well as for the society (Kundu, 2009).

Organizational culture can be viewed as a process through which organizations solve problems (Jelinek et al., 1983; Kuh and Whitt, 1988). Cameron and Quinn (1999) suggest that organizational culture type can be used to understand a variety of organizational phenomena. It is concerned with how employees perceive the characteristics of an organization's culture and not with whether they like them. Culture performs a number of functions within an organization. First, it has a boundary defining role, that is, it creates distinctions between an organization and others. Second, it conveys a sense of identity for the organization members. Third, culture facilitates the generation of commitment to something larger than one's individual self-interest. Fourth, it enhances the stability of the social system. Culture is the social glue that helps to hold the organization together by providing appropriate standards for what employees should say and do. Finally, culture serves the attitudes and behaviors of employees.

Organizational culture is both a product and a process, the shaper of human interaction, and the outcome of it (Jelinek et al., 1983). Thus, culture could be viewed not only as a process (e.g., patterns) to help solve organizational problems noted but also as a product of the problem-solving process. As a response to the environment, organizations respond to pressures for innovation and are also a product of the innovation process.

10.2   MOTIVATIONAL BEHAVIOR

Motivation is a basic psychological process (Luthans, 1998) and an important element of organizational behavior. This energizing force has implications in the form of direction, intensity, and duration of behavior of employees, and Viteles (1962) postulates "Motivation as an unsatisfied need which creates a state of tension or disequilibrium, causing the individual to move in a goal-directed pattern towards restoring a state of equilibrium, by satisfying the need." Motivated people are in a constant state of tension, this tension is relieved by drives toward an activity and outcome that is meant to reduce or relieve such tension. Motivation has been a difficult concept to properly define in part because there "are many philosophical orientations toward the nature of human beings and about what can be known about people" (Pinder, 1998). Although the term defies definition, Kleinginna and Kleinginna (1981), through an extensive multidisciplinary review, identified approximately 140 attempts to define motivation.

Dubrin (2000) pronounces the "why" of behavior—the reason people do things. The key elements in this definition are an intensity of efforts, persistence, and direction toward organizational goals and needs. Decenzo (2001) stated that motivation is the result of the interaction between the individual and the situation. Certainly, employees differ in the motivational drive, but an individual's motivation varies from situation to situation, from culture to culture. Robbins (2001) defined motivation as the willingness to exert high levels of efforts to reach organizational goals, conditioned by effort's ability to satisfy some individual needs.

10.3   REVIEW OF RELATED LITERATURE

This chapter emphasizes two integrated constituents in designing the organizational roles and the entire process of leading people through understanding organizational behavior and its culture.

10.3.1   MOTIVATIONAL BEHAVIOR

As the level of motivation varies among individuals from time to time, maintaining a highly motivated workforce has become the most challenging task. Achievement, affiliation, influence, control, extension, and dependence in the context of motivational behavior have been studied by Pareek (2003).

Various studies confirm that intrinsic factors are more motivating than extrinsic factors (Myers, 1964; Pinder, 1976; Eskildsen et al., 2004; Cameron and Pierce, 1994; Venkatesh, 1999; Nawab et al., 2011; Dysvik and Kuvaas, 2008; Cınar et al., 2011; Grant, 2008; Grant and Berry, 2011) and that motivation is to be studied in relation to individual needs (Dixit, 1971; Schmidt, 1976; Zinovieva et al., 1993; Bénabou and Tirole,

2003; Nygard, 1975; Nohria et al., 2008). Individuals were highly motivated by achievement, recognition, and advancement in their profession. These needs are dominant in the motivational hierarchy and are significant in determining satisfaction. The need for achievement motivation was stressed by all. Abdel-Halim (1980), Kovach (1995), and Nandi (2008) are of the opinion that it is not money but interesting work that motivates workers–. Employment relationship was considered to be more important than pay. Jurkiewicz et al. (1998) and Grant (2008) did comparative studies on motivation in public and private organizations and concluded that the motivation of public service employees can be enhanced by connecting them to their prosocial impact.

Academicians and researchers on organizational behavior relate the causes of a behavior of individuals with motivation along with other factors such as perception, personality, attitudes, and learning. While recognizing the central role of motivation, many organizational behavior theorists think that it is important to reemphasize behavior (Meyer et al., 2004). Gardner et al. (2011) in a study on "The impact of motivation, empowerment, and skill enhancing practices on aggregate voluntary turnover" examined the collective commitment as a mediator of motivation, empowerment, and skill-enhancing practices, and aggregate voluntary turnover. Cinar et al. (2011) in their study explored the effectiveness of intrinsic and extrinsic factors on employee motivation, which one was more effective and compared them according to demographic characteristics of employees. The study by Grant and Berry (2011) substantiated on prosocial motivation that strengthened the association between intrinsic motivation and independent creativity ratings and indicated that perspective mediated this moderating effect. Ayuppa and Kong (2010) focused on two forms of interdependence, namely, task interdependence (works execution) and outcome interdependence (compatibility of coworkers' performance), whereas work motivation looked at employees' cooperation and collective effort. Furthermore, initiated task interdependence was found to have a significant relationship with employees' cooperative manner. Yazici (2010) reconnoitered whether Project Management Maturity related to perceived organizational performance and how an organization's cultural orientation was a contributing factor.

Lavanya and Murthy (2009), in an exploratory study on the "Dimensions of Small-Scale Entrepreneurs," suggested that small-scale entrepreneurship played a significant role in the economic development of the country. Therefore, the development of motivation in individuals was a crucial input to entrepreneurship. The conclusions drawn from the empirical study showed that the direct support from their family members (in the form of finance) encouraged small-scale entrepreneurs to start their new ventures, which was a healthy signal for the economic development of the country. Garg and Rastogi (2006) brought out the positive impact that a well-designed job could have on the motivations of employees, and thereby, employee satisfaction and the quality of performance. The need to design jobs to reduce stress is mechanisms to enhance motivation and satisfaction of employees for improved performance and global competency. Lee-Ross (2005) identified a gap in the area of cross-cultural research in organizations and compared the attitudes and work motivation. Hobson et al. (2004) brought out the long-term benefits of a strategy introduced to help supervisors respond effectively to employees confronted with stressful, family-related/personal life events. The benefits included enhanced employee motivation, commitment, loyalty, and performance.

Meyer et al. (2004) embrace an integrative framework in which commitment was presented as one of the several energizing forces for motivated behavior. Naquin and Holton (2003) brought out the limitation in the traditional conceptualization of motivation as motivation to learn or motivation to train. Bénabou and Tirole (2003) indicated how performance incentives offered by an informed principal (manager, teacher, and parent) could adversely impact an agent's (worker or child) perception of the task or of his own abilities. A meta-analytic seminal work (Parker et al., 2003) indicated that the psychological climate operationalized an individual's perceptions of their work environment, but had significant relationships with individuals' work attitudes, motivation, and performance. Benabou and Tirole (2002) conducted a study on self-confidence and personal motivation. The study weighed the benefits of self-confidence in enhancing motivation against the risks of overconfidence. The study concluded that while "positive thinking" could improve welfare, it could also be self-defeating. Erez and Isen (2002) premeditated the influence of positive effect on the components of expectancy motivation. Huddleston et al. (2002) studied the influence of firm ownership and demographic variables of age, gender, education, and job tenure on the work motivation and job attitudes. The results indicated that demographic and firm ownership variables were a factor in workers' preference for reward, effort performance expectation, job satisfaction, organizational commitment, and work motivation.

While going through the literature on motivational behavior, it is explored that many variables of motivational behavior have been discussed in the existing literature, and there are not many studies done on the variables of motivational behavior such as achievement, affiliation, influence, control, extension, and dependence identified by Pareek (2003), especially in the context of tourism employees in India.

10.3.2 ORGANIZATIONAL CULTURE

Lin and McDonough (2011) reconnoitered how strategic leaders created an organizational culture within which the contradictory forces for exploration and exploitation vie. DuPlessis et al. (2011) in their seminal work indicate the large gap between the current and preferred culture, which generates a lot of stress and frustration. Huhtala et al. (2011) examined whether the associations between managers' perceptions of ethical organizational culture and their occupational well-being were indirectly linked to ethical strain. From the study, it emerged that the managers' perceptions of the ethical culture prevailing in their organizations were associated with their occupational well-being, both directly and indirectly. Schroeder (2010) used the organizational culture perspective to investigate the degree to which team improvement featured a change in team culture. McClure (2010) aimed to review three recognized culture types—bureaucracy, supportive, and innovative—and developed a model describing how intra-organizational conflict mediated the relationship between these cultures and market orientation. Liu et al. (2010) examined how flexibility orientation negatively moderated the effects of coercive pressures and positively moderated the effects of simulated pressures. Lok et al. (2005) probed on the relationship between perceptions of organizational culture, organizational subculture, leadership style, and commitment. The perceived organizational subculture has a strong relationship with commitment. Furthermore, the relative strength of specific types of leadership style and specific types of a subculture with commitment are examined. Both innovative and supportive subcultures have a clear positive relationship, whereas bureaucratic subcultures have a negative relationship.

Contemplating through the literatures on organizational culture, inferences reveal the various dimensions of organizational culture such as 'sensemaking actions,' 'sense giving actions,' shared perceptions, autonomy/independence, external orientation, interdepartmental coordination, human resource orientation, improvement orientation, ethical values, involvement, adaptability, mission, consistency, hierarchy, clan, adhocracy, shared meanings and so others are all studied as a social phenomenon. Culture is reflected in the ways adopted to deal with the basic phenomenon. But in the case of organizations existing in the modern world, addressing these basic phenomena alone may not be enough to gauge whether an organization has a strong or a weak culture.

In trying to identify whether these cultural dimensions affect the motivational behavior of employees in the modern organizations, confining the dimensions of culture to these basic phenomena alone may not be sufficient. Similarly, it is pragmatic that the literature has not addressed the various aspects of organizational culture such as internal, ambiguity tolerant, context sensitive, narcissistic, future orientated, individualistic, inner-directed, universal, role bound, androgynous, power parity, expressive, conserving, assertive, and expanding as identified by Pareek (2003) in explaining the motivational behavior of tourism employees. This chapter establishes a bilingual relationship between the dimensions of motivational behavior (i.e., achievement, affiliation, influence, control, extension, and dependence) and organizational culture (internal, ambiguity tolerant, context sensitive, narcissistic, future orientated, individualistic, inner-directed, universal, role bound, androgynous, power parity, expressive, conserving, assertive, and expanding).

10.4 CLUSTER ANALYSIS FOR ORGANIZATIONAL CULTURE

The cluster analysis is done to identify the prominent cultures prevailing in the tourism industry. The primary function of cluster analysis is to classify those aspects with homogenous scoring into one cluster or group. This is also a factor reducing technique for the purpose of better understanding of 15 aspects of organizational culture as given below.

Aspects of Organizational Culture.

Internal (INT)	Ambiguity Tolerant (AMBT)	Context sensitive (CON)	Narcissistic (NAR)	Future-oriented (FO)
Individualistic (IND)	Inner-directed (ind)	Universal (UNI)	Role bound (RB)	Androgynous (AND)
Power parity (PP)	Expressive (EXP)	Conserving (CON)	Assertive (ASS)	Expanding (EXP)

This chapter deals with Regression analysis to find out the significant predictors of the dependent variable, motivational behavior, and the independent variable. Organizational culture along with a cluster analysis of organizational culture is used to identify the predominant culture prevailing in the tourism organizations. The methodological outline in this chapter deals with Correlation analysis of variables under motivational behavior and organizational culture. Measuring the relationship between dimensions of motivational behavior and organizational culture aspects in all segments of tourism industry business divulges an imperative need for a cluster analysis to be carried over to understand the predominant organizational culture across the industry.

10.5   THE IMPLICATIVE MEASURES

This chapter deals with propositions concerning the motivational behavior of employees working in the tourism sector in Bangalore, India. It indicates that employees of private sector organizations in the tourism industry want to involve themselves in the decision-making process, especially on matters that affect their welfare. These employees want their organizations to be prepared to face the uncertainties that may arise in the future such as the change in government policies, economic recession, and calamities that may have a direct influence on their business. Hence, the perplexities can be addressed effectively with alternative plans ready to meet the eventualities that may arise in the future. In the case of public sector undertakings in the tourism industry, no aspect of organizational culture has any influence on any of the dimensions of motivational behavior. In this context, lack of a sense of ownership is a concern and there seem to be no shared beliefs among the employees. There could be a deliberate attempt from the side of the managements to initiate discussions with the employees so that the concerns of the employees are addressed. The only organizational culture aspect that seems to have a relationship with the motivational behavior of employees working in multinational companies in the tourism industry is Ambiguity Tolerant. It implies that employees of multinational companies want to look at different ways of solving problems. They want to feel free to express opinions and ideas which may be different from that of their "boss."

Employees of multinational companies in the service sector expect to have minimal rules, regulations, and procedures. Organizations could increase tolerance to ambiguity by equipping their employees to creatively and innovatively respond to situations. The field study conducted reconnoiters the fact that the motivational behavior of employees working in travel agencies are greatly influenced by Future-oriented and Ambiguity-tolerant aspects of organizational culture. It implies that employees give a lot of importance to planning for their future tasks. At the same time, they want to look at different ways of solving problems. This may be very evident in the nature of work of the employees of travel agencies who, in spite of planning well in advance, may have to come up with new perspectives at the last moment like a change in the travel plan due to events that are beyond the control of the customer or the service provider. Employees of travel agencies prefer to have a closely knit social framework in their workplace. The individualistic culture may result in more of competitive strategies, which may be seen as a reason for the negative motivation. Tourism sector should engage more of affiliation strategies rather than control strategies.

In the case of employees working in tour operations business, a significant positive relationship is found between the achievement, control, and extension dimensions of motivational behavior and the universal aspect of organizational culture. At the same time, it is observed that, employees of tour operations want to work under the closely knit social framework and the employers could create more avenues to work in teams rather than as individual members for effective results. In contrast to the notion of the general public about the airlines business, it was explored that, there is no significant relationship between organizational culture and motivational behavior of employees working in airlines. But there is a lack of achievement motivation and a tendency to withdraw from the peer group interactions among the employees working in airlines. In the case of employees working in hotels and resorts, a momentous positive relationship is found between the universal aspect of organizational culture and motivational behavior. It infers that employees of these organizations can be motivated if the managements of these organizations are able to balance the needs and aspirations of their employees with those of their other stakeholders. The managements could ensure that the needs and aspirations of their employees are taken care of while satisfying the needs and aspirations of the other stakeholders.

The future-oriented aspect of organizational culture is an optimistic significant predictor for affiliation dimension of motivational behavior. Therefore, the managements of tourism organizations should ensure that their organizations are not firefighting organizations; instead, they should plan well in advance to deal with issues that may arise in future to enhance the affiliation of their employees. The Individualistic aspect of organizational culture is a negative significant predictor for Affiliation dimension of motivational behavior. Managements of tourism organizations could ensure that their employees cultivate a "we" feeling concept among them and they have a closely knit social framework to enhance their affiliation, along with a desire to maintain a high degree of interdependence among their employees so that they can make an impact on others and help to develop people. In case the managements of tourism organizations fail to enhance the degree of interdependence among their employees, they will not be in a position to create an urge to change among their employees.

The narcissistic aspect of organizational culture is a positive significant predictor for Control dimension of motivational behavior. Here, the managements of tourism organizations could ensure that their employees do not engage themselves in self-seeking behavior so that they enhance their desire for orderliness and also take corrective actions when needed. The future-oriented aspect of organizational culture is an optimistic significant predictor for Dependence dimension of motivational behavior. Hence, the managements of tourism organizations can assure and encourage a culture that is not fire-fighting; instead, they should plan well in advance to deal with issues that may arise in future so that these employees can seek help from others, if needed, in their own development. These measures taken by the managements can inculcate a concern for excellence among the tourism employees and move these employees to new projects or reshaping existing business, it would result in the lack of orderliness among the employees. The field survey also explored that there is no significant difference in the motivational behavior of male and female employees engaged in the tourism industry with respect to any of the dimensions of motivational behavior. It means that gender does not influence motivational behavior. The manager and supervisory cadre employees of tourism industry differed significantly with regard to their affiliation and extension dimensions of motivational behavior. The supervisors had a higher affiliation and extension dimension score as compared with managers. This implies that the supervisory cadre employees of tourism industry had a concern for establishing and maintaining a close and personal relationship with others in the organization. Further, they also demonstrated a concern for others and to be useful to others including the society.

A significant difference is observed between male and female employees of the tourism industry with regard to their context sensitive, expressive, and conserving aspects of organizational culture. It is denoted that the female employees working in the tourism industry expect the rules of the organizations to be worked out in detail but while applying these rules, they want special considerations to be given to special circumstances in special cases. Similarly, the female employees would love to help in preserving and refining the traditions and legacy of the culture of their organization. On the other hand, the male employees would like to be more creative and be allowed to experiment and to innovate. There is a significant difference among employees of private sector, public sector, and multinational companies with respect to influence and control dimensions of motivational behavior. Employees of public sector undertakings are apprehensive to make an impact on others and an urge to develop people. They also have a desire to work under bureaucratic guidelines and to remain informed on important matters.

Managements of public sector undertakings need to create facilities for their employees to play the role of mentors for the junior staff. These managements should ensure a proper scalar chain with regard to the flow of information and it should be strictly followed. Managements of private and multinational companies have to create sufficient avenues in their organizations to enable employees to have more interaction with them and create appropriate systems for the proper flow of communication. There is a noteworthy variance among employees of travel agencies, tour operations, airlines, and hotels and resorts with respect to Influence dimension of motivational behavior. Managements of travel agencies, tour operations, and airlines could initiate appropriate corporate social responsibility initiatives to address this dimension of the motivational behavior of their employees.

This contemporary research also revealed that the role of qualification of the employees in the tourism industry does not have any significant influence on the motivational behavior of employees. Hence, hiring employees with higher educational qualifications alone may not be sufficient to ensure higher motivation of employees in the tourism industry. Managements have to ensure that qualified employees are adequately compensated. The experience of the employees in the current organization does not have any substantial influence on the motivational behavior of employees in the tourism sector. It infers that length of service alone may not be sufficient to ensure higher motivation of employees in the tourism industry. Managements should also ensure that experienced employees are adequately compensated.

There is a significant difference among employees of private sector, public sector, and multinational companies of the tourism industry with respect to ambiguity tolerant, context sensitive, and power parity aspects of organizational culture. Further, it is established, that employees of private sector undertakings had higher power parity scores than employees of multinational companies. It denotes that the employees of private sector undertakings love to work in unpredictable situations and express opinions and ideas which may be different from that of their bosses. Similarly, employees of public sector undertaking wish to have rules and regulations in place, but while applying these rules, they want consideration to be given to special circumstances in special cases. Further, employees of private sector undertakings are willing to accept a hierarchical order in their organizations.

Managements of private sector undertakings could encourage their employees to work in unpredictable work situations and allow them to express opinions which may be different from that of their superiors. Managements of public sector undertakings need to allow their employees to interpret the meanings of events, phenomena, and behavior in the context in which they occur. Similarly, managements of private sector undertakings have to purposely create a little more of hierarchy and power distance among the members of the organization.

It was also inferred that there is a significant difference among employees of travel agencies, tour operations, airlines, and hotels and resorts with respect to a number of organizational culture aspect scores, namely, internal, context sensitive, future-oriented, inner-directed, androgynous, power parity, expressive, and conserving. On comparing the mean scores, it is found that employees of travel agency had higher internal aspect scores than employees of tour operations. Similarly, employees of airlines had higher context sensitive aspect scores than employees of tour operations. Further, employees of travel agency had higher future-oriented aspect scores than employees of tour operations. Similarly, employees of travel agency had higher inner-directed aspect scores than employees of hotels and resorts. Further, employees of airlines had higher inner-directed aspect scores than employees of hotels and resorts. Similarly, employees of hotels and resorts had higher androgynous aspect scores than employees of travel agencies. Further, employees of travel agency had higher power parity aspect scores than employees of airlines. Similarly, employees of tour operations had higher expressive aspect scores than employees of airlines.

Further employees of hotels and resorts had higher expressive aspect scores than employees of airlines. Similarly, employees of airlines had higher conserving aspect scores than employees of a travel agency. It implies that employees of travel agencies would like to have some say in influencing the vital matters of the organization. They also give importance to long-term planning and working for the future. They set internal standards and their behaviors are directed by such standards. Employees of travel agencies love to work under a well-defined hierarchy. Employees of airlines love to interpret the various events, phenomena, and behaviors which occur in their organizations in the context in which they occur. These employees also set internal standards for their behavior. Employees of airlines wish to preserve and refine the traditions and legacy of their culture that has a high sense of discipline. Employees of hotels and resorts value interpersonal trust very highly and they desire harmony and friendship. Similarly, employees of tour operations look for opportunities to experiment and to innovate. Managements of travel agencies should allow their employees to express their opinions while making decisions on matters which affect them. The policy makers of these organizations should plan well in advance the tasks to be done in future, the managements of travel agencies should allow their employees to set standards for themselves and be guided by such standards. Proper authority structures should be created in such organizations with a delegation of authority. Managements of airlines should ensure that the rules of their organizations are worked out in detail, but while applying them, special considerations may have to be given in special cases. Airlines could also allow their employees to set internal standards and be guided by such standards. Discipline should be seen as a major trait of these organizations. Managements of hotels and resorts should cultivate harmony and friendship within the organizations and the managements of tour operations should provide their employees with opportunities to experiment and innovate.

It was inferred that there is no significant difference among employees of tourism industry possessing different educational qualifications and various aspects of organizational culture. It implies that tourism industry does not regard educational qualifications in creating a good organizational culture. Tourism organizations, while dealing with employees with 8 or more years of service in their organization, should allow these employees to apply the rules pertaining to them according to the background of each and every case. This may look a bit too difficult, but this is what can affect their motivational behavior.

10.6 CONCLUSIONS

The role of tourism in the national economy is proven without any doubt. All the components of tourism industry such as travel agency, tour operations, airlines, and hotels and resorts play a significant role in transforming the economy of a nation. In spite of the fact that these organizations do generate sufficient Foreign Exchange Earnings and create employment opportunities for various categories of people, the importance that they deserve has not been attributed to them by the governments and other allied sectors. The role of organizational culture in affecting the behavior of the employees is emphasized in various literatures available. The importance of these constructs is very high in the context of the tourism industry as it is a constellation of various service sectors.

Being the constituents of a large industry, it is expected that the tourism organizations share a common culture to mutually complement the growth of the industry. The study reveals that most of the organizations in the tourism industry hold Internal and Narcissistic aspects of organizational culture reflecting the sad state of affairs being prevalent in these organizations. There is a lack of future orientation to create a strong culture aligned with the value systems of the founders. This, in most of the cases, has resulted in a negative motivation among the employees as evident in the study. Though there is a strong achievement and affiliation motivation, the prevailing culture does not support to the extent to which they expect the organizations to facilitate. This, in a way, echoes the present state of affairs of this industry that is finding it hard to retain efficient employees and ensure continued high level of productivity. Most of the employees seem to be desirous of having a stable and secure job that will support their lifestyle. There could be deliberate efforts by the organizations to be aware of the fact that a strong organizational culture has a high impact on the motivational behavior of employees. Such a strong cultural environment would be highly motivating and rewarding for each and every employee of the organizations. This chapter also echoes some predominant cultural aspects such as Internal and Narcissistic aspects that are extremely imperative for organizations to establish enhanced stability and continued employment.

KEYWORDS

- **motivational behavior**
- **organizational culture**
- **tourism employees**

REFERENCES

Abdel-Halim, A. A. Effects of Higher-Order Need Strength on the Job Performance-Job Satisfaction Relationships. *Pers. Psychol.* **1980,** *33*(2), 335.

Ayuppa, K.; Kong, W. The Impact of Task and Outcome Interdependence and Self-Efficacy on Employees' Work Motivation: An Analysis of the Malaysian Retail Industry. *Asia Pac. Bus. Rev.* **2010,** *16*(1–2), 123–142.

Benabou, R.; Tirole, J. Self-Confidence and Personal Motivation. *Q. J. Econ.* **2002,** *117*(3), 871–915.

Bénabou, R.; Tirole, J. Incentives and Prosocial Behavior. Institute d'Économie Industrielle (IDEI). 2003; *IDEI Working Papers 389.*

Cameron, J.; Pierce, W. D. Reinforcement, Reward, and Intrinsic Motivation: A Meta Analysis, Rev. *Educ. Res.* **1994,** *64*(3), 363–423. DOI: 10.3102/00346543064003363.

Cameron, K. S.; Quinn, R. E. *Diagnosing and Changing Organizational Culture;* Addison Wesley: Reading, MA, 1999.

Cınar, O.; Bektas, C.; Aslan, I. A Motivation Study on the Effectiveness of Intrinsic and Extrinsic Factors. *Econ. Manage.* **2011,** 1822–6515.

Decenzo, D. *Human Relations: Personal and Professional Development*, 2nd ed.; Prentice Hall. 2001.

Dixit, L. M. Employee Motivation and Behavior: A Review. *Indian J. Soc. Work* **1971**, *32*, 17–24.

DuBrin, A. J. *Applying Psychology: Individual and Organizational Effectiveness.* Prentice Hall: New Jersey, 2000.

DuPlessis, A. J.; Visagie, J. C.; Wijnbeek, D. Maxweber S Theory Re-visited: Modern Organization Culture Stimulating Productivity Interdisciplinary. *J. Contemp. Res. Bus.* **2011**, *2*(12), 15–30.

Dysvik, A.; Kuvaas, B. The Relationship Between Perceived Training Opportunities, Work Motivation, and Employee Outcomes. *Int. J. Train. Dev.* **2008**, *12*(3), 1360–3736.

Erez, A.; Isen, A. M. The Influence of Positive Affect on the Components Expectancy Motivation. *J. Appl. Psychol.* **2002**, *87*(6), 1055–1067.

Eskildsen, J. K.; Kristensen, K.; Westlund, A. H. Work Motivation and Job Satisfaction in the Nordic Countries. *Employee Relat.* **2004**, *26*(2), 122–136.

Gardner, T. M.; Wright, P. M.; Moynihan, L. M. The Impact of Motivation, Empowerment, and Skill-Enhancing Practices on Aggregate Voluntary Turnover, the Mediating Effect of Collective Affective Commitment. *Pers. Psychol.* **2011**, *64*, 315–350.

Garg, P.; Rastogi, R. New Model of Job Design: Motivating Employees Performance. *J. Manage. Dev.* **2006**, *25*(6).

Gerhart, B.; Fang, M. National Culture and Human Resource Management: Assumptions and Evidence. *Int. J. Hum. Res. Manage.* **2005**, *16*(6), 971–986.

Grant, A. M. Employees Without a Cause: The Motivational Effects of Prosocial Impact in Public Service. *Int. Publ. Manage. J.* **2008**, *11*(1), 48–66.

Grant, A. M.; Berry, J. W. The Necessity of others is the Mother of Invention: Intrinsic and Prosocial Motivations, Perspective Taking and Creativity. *Acad. Manage. J.* **2011**, *54*(1), 73–96.

Hobson, C. J.; Kesic, D.; Rosetti, D.; Delunas, L.; Hobson, N. G. Motivating Employee Commitment with Empathy and Support During Stressful Life Events. *Int. J. Manage.* **2004**, *21*(3), 332–337.

Huddleston, P.; Good, L.; Frazier, B. The Influence of Firm Characteristics and Demographic Variables on Russian Retail Worker's Work Motivation and Job Attitudes. *Int. Rev. Retail Distrib. Consum. Res.* **2002**, *12*(4), 395.

Huhtala, M.; Feldt, T.; Lämsä, A.; Mauno, S.; Kinnunen, U. Does the Ethical Culture of Organizations Promote Managers' Occupational Well-Being? Investigating Indirect Links via Ethical Strain. *J. Bus. Ethics* **2011**, *101*, 231–247. DOI 10.1007/s10551-010-0719-3.

Jelinek, M.; Smirch, L.; Hirsch, P. Introduction: A Code of Many Colors. *Adm. Sci. Q.* **1983**, *28*, 331–338.

Jurkiewicz, C. L.; Massey, T. K.; Jr. Brown, R. G. Motivation in Public and Private Organizations: A Comparative Study. *Publ. Prod. Manage. Rev.* **1998**, *21*(3), 230–250.

Kleinginna, P. R. J.; Kleinginna, A. M. A Categorical List of Emotion Definitions with Suggestions for a Consensual Definition. *Motiv. Emotion* **1981**, *5*(4), 345–379.

Kovach, K. A. Employee Motivation: Addressing a Crucial Factor in your Organization's Performance, *Employee Relat. Today* **1995**, *22*, 93–105.

Kundu, K. Influence of Organizational Culture on the Institution Building Process of an Organization. *Curie J.* **2009,** *2*(4), 48–57.

Lavanya, L. K.; Murthy, B. E. V. V. N. The Dimensions of Small-Scale Entrepreneurs: An Exploratory Study. *South Asian J. Manage.* **2009,** *16*(2), 91–108.

Lee-Ross, D. Perceived Job Characteristics and Internal Work Motivation. *J. Manage. Dev.* **2005,** *24*(3), 253–266.

Liu, H.; Weiling, K.; Kee· W. K.; Jibao, G.; Huaping, C. The Role of Institutional Pressures and *Organizational Culture* in the Firm's Intention to Adopt Internet-Enabled Supply Chain Management Systems. *J. Oper. Manage.* **2010,** *28*(5), 372–384.

Lin, H.; McDonough III, E. F. Investigating the Role of Leadership and Organizational Culture in Fostering Innovation Ambidexterity. *IEEE Trans. Eng. Manage.* **2011,** *58*(3), 497

Lok, P.; Westwood, R.; Crawford, J. Perceptions of Organizational Subculture and Their Significance for Organizational Commitment. *Appl. Psychol. Int. Rev.* **2005,** *54*(4), 490–514.

Luthans, F. *Organizational Behaviors;* 8th ed.; Irwin McGraw-Hill: New York, 1988.

McClure, R. E. The Influence of *Organizational Culture* and Conflict on Market Orientation. *J. Bus. Ind. Mark.* **2010,** *25*(7), 514–524.

Meyer, J. P.; Becker, T. E.; Vandenberghe, C. Employee Commitment and Motivation: A Conceptual Analysis and Integrative Model. *J. Appl.* **2004,** *89*(6), 991–1007.

Myers, M. S. Who are your Motivated Workers? *Harv. Bus. Rev.* **1964,** *42*, 73–88.

Nandi, J. K. Achievement Motivation Amongst Front Line Managers, The ICFAI University. *J. Organ. Behav.* **2008,** *7*(3).

Nawab, S.; Ahmad, J.; Shafi, K. An Analysis of Differences in Work Motivation Between Public and Private Sector Organizations. *Interdiscip. J. Contemp. Res. Bus.* **2011,** *2*(11), 110–127.

Nohria, N.; Groysberg, B.; Lee, L. E. Employee Motivation—A Powerful New Model. *Harv. Bus. Rev.* 2008.

Nygard, R. A Reconsideration of the Achievement-Motivation Theory. *European Journal of Social Psychology,* **1975,** *5*(1), 61–66.

Pareek, U. *Behavioral Process at Work;* Oxford &IBH: New Delhi, 2003.

Parker, C. P.; Baltes, B. B.; Young, S. A.; Huff, J. W.; Altmann, R. A.; Lacost, H. A.; Roberts, J. E. Relationships between Psychological Climate Perceptions and Work Outcomes: A Meta-Analytic Review. *J. Organ. Behav.* **2003,** *24*, 389–416.

Pinder, C. C. Additivity versus Non-Additivity of Intrinsic and Extrinsic Incentives—Implications for Work Motivation, Performance and Attitudes. *J. Appl. Psychol.* **1976,** *61*(6), 693.

Pinder, C. C. *Work Motivation in Organizational Behavior;* Prentice Hall: Upper Saddle River, NJ, 1998.

Robbins, S. P. *Organizational Behavior: Concepts, Controversies, Applications,* 9th ed.; Prentice Hall: U.S.A., 2001.

Schmidt, G. L. Job Satisfaction among Secondary School Administrators. *Educ. Adm. Q.* **1976,** *12*(2), 68–86.

Schroeder, P. J. Changing Team Culture: The Perspectives of en Successful Head Coaches. *J. Sports Behav.* **2010,** *33*(1), 63–88.

Tierney, W. G. Organizational Culture in Higher Education: Defining the Essentials. *J. Higher Educ.* **1988,** *59*(1), 2–21.

Venkatesh, V. Creation of Favorable User Perceptions: The Role of Intrinsic Motivation. *MIS Q.* **1999,** *23,* 239–260.

Viteles, M. S. *Motivation and Morale in Industry;* Allied Pacific Private Sector: Bombay, 1962.

Yazici, H. J. The Role of Project Management Maturity and Organizational Culture in Perceived Performance. *Proj. Manage. J.* **2010,** *40*(3), 14–33.

Zinovieva, I. L.; TenHorn, L. A.; Roe, R. A. Motivation in Post-Socialist Industrial Organizations. *Eur. Work Organ. Psychol.* **1993,** *3*(3), 251.

CHAPTER 11

EMPLOYEE ENGAGEMENT IN TRAVEL ORGANIZATIONS IN INDIA: THE INFLUENCE OF PSYCHOLOGICAL CLIMATE ON EMPLOYEE ENGAGEMENT AND ITS INFLUENCE ON INTENT TO STAY

GINU GEORGE

Arya Systems, Hyderabad, India

CONTENTS

ABSTRACT

Employee engagement (EE) is becoming very vital in the recent years because organizations with engaged employees tend to out-perform than employees who are disengaged. The outcomes of engaged employees are higher performance, lower turnover, increased profitability, and much more. However, there are some ignorant industries that neglect the importance of having engaged employees. Hence, it is necessary to conduct more research on EE, which creates more awareness in the organizations about the prominence of focusing on EE and also augment the existing literature. The current research was conducted on employees working in travel organizations that are set up in Bangalore. The study considered one factor influencing EE [psychological climate (PC)] and another variable that is considered as the outcome of EE (intent to stay). Results indicated that PC has a significant and positive relationship between EE, and with respect to outcome variables, it was determined that higher the engagement level, the higher the intent to stay.

11.1   INTRODUCTION TO TOURISM

People across the world perceive tourism as one of the major social events. Tourism emerges as a natural urge within every individual and the outcome of it could be either to have a new experience or a desire to get pleasure or to learn something from the travel experiences. Hence, tourism takes place for different purposes such as entertainment, religious, business, or it can even happen as part of education in which people travel with a desire to gather information about the customs and culture in other parts of the globe. As a result, the purpose of traveling changes from person to person. People often have a misconception about the concept "tourism" as the sole intention of traveling, but it includes many other aspects such as transportation, attraction, accommodation, and food. Moreover, without all these, the experiences of an individual become incomplete. The industry that provides all of these services is termed as travel and tourism industry.

11.1.1   INTRODUCTION TO TRAVEL AND TOURISM INDUSTRY

Travel and tourism industry is one of the most people-oriented service industries, which comprises a range of sectors providing varied services that are essential for tourism. The sectors that constitute travel and tourism industry are classified differently by different authors. Tribe and Airey (2007) explained that travel and tourism industry comprises transportation, catering services, accommodation, cultural services, recreation and management, tour operators and travel agents, convention services, and many miscellaneous tourism services (such as tourism equipment, visa processing, and issuing services). According to Dun and Bradstreet research, the components constituting travel and tourism industry are travel agents, tour operators, transportation, attraction, tourist information and guiding services, accommodation, and catering. Irrespective of the type of classification, a "travel experience" to a tourist can be provided only when there is complete integration among these sectors.

Customers have no choice but to meet these intermediaries at different points of travel, starting from buying a travel package from the travel agent followed by insurance company, ground transport to and from the airport, airport handling agents, airport services (shops, food and beverage outlets, and bureau de change), the airline on all legs of the journey, immigration and customs services, local ground transportation, the hotel, tour services at the destination, companies and individuals selling a diversity of goods and services at the destination (retail, food and beverage, entertainment, culture and heritage, financial, etc.), emergency services at the destination (medical, police, and legal), and service providers on return (such as photography processing and medical) (Baum, 1997). So, it can be said that all these intermediaries, irrespective of how small, have the ability to "make" or "break" the tourist experience.

11.1.2   ECONOMIC CONTRIBUTION OF TRAVEL AND TOURISM INDUSTRY IN WORLD

According to World Travel and Tourism Council (WTTC) (2015), some of the key facts are that the total contribution of travel and tourism to Gross

Domestic Product (GDP) was United States Dollar (USD) 7580.9 billion (9.8% of GDP) in 2014 and is predicted to rise by 3.7% in 2015, and to rise by 3.9% p.a. to USD 3593.2 billion (3.3% of GDP) by 2025. In 2014, the total contribution of travel and tourism to employment, including jobs indirectly supported by the industry, was 9.4% of total employment (276,845,000 jobs). This is expected to rise by 2.6% in 2015 to 283,983,000 jobs and rise by 2.3% p.a. to 356,911,000 jobs in 2025 (10.7% of total employment). Visitor exports generated in 2014 was USD 1383.3 billion (5.7% of total exports). This is predicted to grow by 2.8% in 2015 and increased by 4.2% p.a. from 2015 to 2025 and by USD 2140.1 billion in 2025 (5.6% of total). Travel and tourism investment was expected to have attracted USD 814.4 billion in 2014. It is also expected to rise by 4.8% in 2015 and further rise by 4.6% p.a. over the next 10 years to USD 1336.4 billion in 2025.

11.1.3   ECONOMIC CONTRIBUTION OF TRAVEL AND TOURISM INDUSTRY IN INDIA

According to WTTC (2015), some of the key facts are that the total contribution of travel and tourism to GDP was INR 7642.5 billion (6.7% of GDP) in 2014 and is forecast to rise by 7.5% in 2015, and to rise by 7.3% p.a. to INR 16,587.2 billion (7.6% of GDP) in 2025. In 2014, the total contribution of travel and tourism to employment, including jobs indirectly supported by the industry, was 8.7% of total employment (36,695,500 jobs). This is expected to rise by 1.8% in 2015 to 37,365,000 jobs and rise by 2.0% p.a. to 45,566,000 jobs in 2025 (9.0% of total employment). Visitor exports generated INR 1224.4 billion (4.1% of total exports) in 2014. This is predicted to grow by 5.2% in 2015 and by 6.3% p.a. from 2015 to 2025 to INR 2377.2 billion in 2025 (4.2% of total). Travel and tourism investment in 2014 was INR 2107.2 billion or 6.2% of total investment. It is expected to rise by 9.3% in 2015 and further rise by 6.5% p.a. over the next 10 years to INR 4337.8 billion in 2025 (6.9% of the total).

11.2 THE ROLE OF TOURISM INDUSTRY AS COMPARED WITH OTHER INDUSTRIES AND ITS CONTRIBUTIONS TOWARD ECONOMY

a) The contribution of travel and tourism industry toward GDP: According to WTTC 2011 data, it is indicated that travel and tourism generated $ 121 million of India's GDP in 2011. This industry's contribution to GDP is larger than that of education and mining sectors.

b) The contribution of travel and tourism industry toward employment: According to WTTC 2011, with respect to employment, it generated 39.3 million jobs in India in 2011 and this industry employs more people than the communication services, automotive manufacturing, and mining sectors. In this industry, GDP expanded 229% between 1990 and 2011 whereas the total economy expanded 279%.

c) The contribution of travel and tourism industry toward exports: Economic development is directly related to exports of the country. When a country exports increase at a faster rate as compared with imports, it clearly indicates that the economy is developing in a healthy way. On the other hand, when exports become volatile, it can negatively affect the process of economic development. Lower exports mean low foreign exchange and lower foreign exchange, which in turn, means reduced purchasing power of a nation in the international market. Travel and tourism industry is a significant source of exports in India and ranks the second position after manufacture of chemical industries. Exports of travel and tourism industry also exceed the exports of agriculture, mining, automotive manufacturing, financial services, construction, and education.

d) Travel and tourism has huge scope and benefits for other industries: This is one of the industries that provides an opportunity to create linkages with other sectors of the economy such as communications, utilities, petroleum products, mining, financial services, hotels and restaurants, other community services, agriculture, transport and storage, and wholesale and retail. WTTC in its 2011 reports pointed out, "for every $1 million in travel and tourism sales, $ 189,000 of gross value added is generated in the agriculture and in the case of wholesale and retail sector the gain is $ 109,000.

e) Tourism leads to development in rural areas: It is a fact that most of the tourist attractions are not in the city centers but are located in the rural areas. As a result, tourism allows rural people to get their share of the benefits generated due to tourism development and this also leads to balanced and sustainable forms of development.

f) Demand for tourism is a continuous process: When compared with any other product or service, the demand for tourism is a continuous process as people across the world keep traveling every day. If a vacation is taken today, it will not bring down the demand for the holiday next year, next month, or next weekend. This means that the potential market for tourism will continue to grow.

11.2.1 INTRODUCTION TO TRAVEL AGENCY

A travel agency is a private retailer or a service agency providing tourism-related services to the travelers on behalf of the suppliers such as airlines, car rentals, hotels, railways, cruise lines, and package tours. Travelers are of different types consisting of single travelers, family travelers, group travelers, business travelers, senior travelers, and backpackers. Travel organizations become very important for these travelers as they help in providing suggestions about ideal holiday destination, designing of the itinerary, selling them to the tourist, and also making all the other arrangements such as transportation and accommodation based on the needs of the customer. Thus, Bhatia (1983) points outs that travel agents play a vital role in the entire process of developing and promoting tourism. With the development of technology, people from all parts of the world have access to the internet and through that one can find the best offers available and plan their vacations accordingly. Thus, many people resist from taking the help of travel organizations. Though this is true to an extent, many still fail to realize that approaching a travel agent makes one's vacation more organized and the difficulties they face will be lesser when compared with a trip that is self-planned. When approaching a travel agent, customers play the role of an informer and need to provide information on the type of hotel, mode of transportation, activities, and any other special needs they require. Once all the details are provided, then travel organizations design the itinerary accordingly. The role of travel organizations is immense, especially when customers are busy with work and family and have no time to research and select the best plan for their vacation. In addition to this, a travel agent is the one who is closely connected with the industry and as a result, they are more aware of all the offers that exist than the customer. Hence, travel agents with their dedicated team can provide good hotel accommodation, transportation facilities, and other services at a reasonable cost. Thus, the benefits customers obtain by trusting travel agents are as follows: it saves time, they receive reasonable discounts, get personalized service, and continuous support till the trip ends. However, this is possible only if customers are able to find the right and authorized travel agent.

There are many small, medium, and large-scale travel outlets that prevail across the country who call themselves as travel agents. Hence, it becomes important for people to choose the trusted and recognized agency. This can be ensured by selecting a travel agent who displays a logo of International Air Transport Association (IATA) as it is one of the bodies that has the power to grant approval to run a travel agency after an intense check on the professional competence and financial reliability (Seth and Bhat, 2003). The other authorized bodies are Travel Agents Association of India, Travel Agents Federation of India, Indian Association of Tour Operators, Universal Federation of Travel Agents Association, and American Society of Travel Agents.

Looking at the cost factor of travel organizations, it was explained by Seth et al. (2003) that travel organizations work on the basis of the commission they receive from their suppliers such as airlines, hotels, motels, and car rentals, and they do not generally charge a fee from their clients. However, travel organizations cannot charge commissions from all suppliers, for example, when clients are booking train tickets through travel organizations, it cannot get the commission from Indian railways. In such instances, travel organizations charge a service fee from their clients. The rate at which travel organizations charge commission from clients differs from country to country and in the case of India, the norms are laid by IATA.

11.2.2 ROLE OF TRAVEL ORGANIZATIONS IN COMPARISON WITH HOTEL AND AIRLINE INDUSTRY

Chowdhary and Prakash (2008) stated in their article that for keeping tourist as a focal point, there are three main players, they are government, tour operators or travel agency, and tour guides, who are directly or indirectly connected with the tourist. The role of a government in tourism is to promote the country or the region as a tourist destination with the required infrastructure. The role of a tour guide is to explain about the destination to the tourist by creating an experience as they are the ones who accompany the tourist. However, the effort of the government in promoting a destination will not be complete unless there is an intermediary to organize and sell the destination to the tourist. It applies to tour guides in the same way as they will not be able to provide their services to tourists without the help of the travel agents. Nowadays, there exist a large number of unauthorized tour guides who cheat the tourist, and to avoid such risks, the travel agents themselves arrange for tour guides. The tour guides are arranged on the basis of the requirements of the tourists such as language, subject expertise, or any other. The services like accommodation and transportation for the tourist are generally taken care of by travel agents or tour operators. Thus, it is evident that it is a travel agent who comes first in contact with the tourist and the effect of sales of tourism products takes place through these travel agents.

11.2.3   HUMAN RESOURCES IN TRAVEL ORGANIZATIONS

Travel and tourism industry is one of the employment generating sectors in developed as well as in developing nations and the employment opportunities are both direct and indirect. According to Kusluvan (2003), direct employment consists of setting up businesses such as hotels, car rentals, and travel organizations, and indirect employment is in the form of producing goods and services for businesses, which in turn supplies services to visitors or travelers directly. As already stated, the travel and tourism industry is always considered as the most labor-intensive sector when compared with other industries (International Labor Organization and World Trade Organization). It was also said by Kusluvan (2003) that this is the only sector which claims to "employ more employees per dollar invested compared to other industries."

Employees play a very important role in all industries but their role in travel and tourism industry is more significant as this is the only industry in which employees' and customers' contact are intense. However, the relationship between customers and employees are more evident in travel agency because the contact between them does not stop with selling a package but it extends throughout the trip and ends only when customers completes their trip. Thus, travel organizations need tourism professionals specializing in different operational and managerial functions as their job description consists of tour planning and itinerary designing, travel information, reservation and ticketing services, destination counseling, sales and marketing, finance and accounts, conferences and conventions, visa and travel insurance, foreign exchange services, and many more.

Employees hired in travel organizations can modify the quality of services offered and consequently the whole atmosphere of the company. Therefore, it is very important to pick, upbeat and dedicated workers at all levels in a travel agency as the contentment of a travel by the tourist begins and ends with the travel agents who are the first and the last with whom the tourist interacts. With professional knowledge and experience, it is not only sufficient to promote tourism but also to ensure that employees should be committed to their work and organization. When employees are content and engaged in their work, then they are able to do the best at work and to their customers. It is the job of human resource (HR) managers to ensure that right people are chosen for work and also continuous measures need to be taken to make the employee committed and engaged in their work and organization.

There are many problems prevailing in travel and tourism industry such as low wages, shortage of skilled employees, unsocial working hours, shift patterns, overrepresentation of women and ethnic minorities in low-level operative position, with high pay with higher status and more skilled jobs being filled by men, undeveloped policies, poor or nonexistent career structure, use of seasonal employment, overreliance on informal recruitment methods, lack of good HR management practices, little or no trade union presence, high level of labor turnover, and difficulties in recruitment and retention of employees (Keep and Mayhew, 1999; Kusluvan et al., 2010). The very reason for this being more prevalent in travel and tourism industry is because the HR managers of tourism and hospitality organizations are constantly directed to short-term issues such as recruitment, selection, and basic training rather than long-term areas that could conceivably offer more development and career progression for existing employees. The abovementioned problems, if prevail, in the long run, can lead to low productivity, high operating cost, low customer loyalty, high labor turnover, and so on, which will develop a negative image of the company and the industry as a whole.

11.3   NEED FOR THE STUDY

With the realization that travel and tourism industry is a labor-intensive sector, it is essential to measure and understand the extent to which employees are engaged in the organizations. In a study titled "Preparing for take-off," conducted by Hay Group along with Centre for Economics and Business Research (2013), it was predicted that attrition rate in 2013 for India will be 26.9%, which stood the top when compared with Russia, Indonesia, Brazil, United States, China, and the United Kingdom, and further the attrition rate in India is expected to go up to 27.5% in 2014. The study determined that in India, one in four employees changes the job and the reasons for leaving the job were, 55% of employees in India felt that the compensations that they receive are not fair and 48% of them felt that the other benefits they receive are not sufficient to meet their needs.

There were also other issues that the study pointed out such as 37% of the employees felt there is a lack of career opportunities in the company they work, 39% of them said less learning and developmental opportunities, and 36% of them said there is less supervisory coaching. The research also highlighted the finding that around 5.5 m employees felt that these factors were predictors of employee engagement (EE). Thus, when employees are not engaged, they leave the organization, which leads to increase in attrition. Janani (2014) stated that when an organization faces staff turnover, the outcomes of it are unnecessary wastage of managers' time in activities such as recruiting, selecting, and placing, the time lag in meeting customer demands, increase in training expenses, and so on. The author also stated that the "replacement cost can reach as high as 50–60% of an employees' annual salary." One of the ways suggested by the author to tackle these issues is by keeping employees engaged every day by ensuring that their anxieties and vulnerabilities are addressed promptly and efficiently. Thus, without any doubt, it is very important that all companies across all industries need to measure EE on regular intervals so as to ensure they are engaged, this is more important in travel and tourism industry as it as a huge contribution toward the economic development of India. The study also aims at determining whether psychological climate (PC) influences EE and also tries to find out whether EE has any influence on intent to stay which is considered as the outcome variable. According to the Human Resource Management International Digest, "creating a retention-rich organization that attracts, engages and builds lasting loyalty among the most talented employees is a key to success in the modern globalized economy."

11.4 REVIEW OF RELATED LITERATURE

11.4.1 EMPLOYEE ENGAGEMENT

The concept EE has gained a lot of attention among academicians, companies, HR consultancy firms, and various other research-based institutions. Khan (1990) was the first to develop this concept, which was then called as personal engagement and personal disengagement. Personal engagement was explained as "harnessing of organization members' selves to their work roles;" in engagement, "people employ and express themselves physically, cognitively and emotionally during role performances;" and personal disengagement means "uncoupling of selves from work roles;" in disengagement, "people withdraw and defend themselves physically, cognitively and emotionally during role performances" (p. 694). The concept was later reconstructed as 'Employee Engagement' that was coined by a consulting firm name Gallup in 1999 and started applying at a business level. Thereby, Buckingham and Coffman (1999) defined EE as, "a fully engaged employee as one who could answer yes to all 12 questions on Gallup's workplace questionnaire." There were many other researchers who also contributed in the evolution of EE (Maslach and Leiter, 1997; Schaufeli and Bakker, 2001; Schaufeli et al., 2001; Harter et al., 2002; May et al., 2004; Robinson et al., 2004; Saks, 2006; Macey and Schneider, 2008; Soane et al., 2012).

11.4.2 PSYCHOLOGICAL CLIMATE

PC is a concept that was operationalized on certain assumptions and based on these, it is defined as "individual's internalized representations about situational conditions within the organization and its subunits, tends to emphasize conditions that are relatively immediate to individual experience and reflects a cognitive transformation and structuring of these conditions into perceived situational influences" (Jones and James, 1977, p. 4). A year later, the concept was redefined by James et al. (1978, p. 786) as

"The individual's cognitive representations of relatively proximal situational conditions, that reflect psychologically meaningful interpretations of the situation." Two decades later, Brown and Leigh's (1996) study on PC was the next most quoted study after Jones and James (1977). According to Brown and Leigh (1996), PC consisted of six dimensions such as supportive management, clarity, and self-expression based on psychological safety, and dimensions such as contribution, challenging, and recognition were based on psychological meaningfulness.

When employees perceive more positively about PC, they tend to engage more in their work and toward their organizations. Some of the studies that were conducted in determining the relationship between PC and EE study by Conning (2009) on 175 samples, which included people working in different government contracting and private industries between the age group of 25–45 years. To measure PC, the study used PC scale of Brown and Leigh (1996) and findings of the research were that when employees positively perceive about PC, it leads to higher engagement, in turn, exhibiting work addiction risk behavior. Though organization sees work addiction as an advantage, in this study, authors have suggested that in long run it can have a negative impact on the quality of work they do and on the organization.

A study by Thayer (2008) aimed at determining the relationship of PC with EE and organizational citizenship behavior. The research was conducted on employees working in different sectors in the United States. By using Brown and Leigh's PC scale, the study proceeded in analyzing the relationship and with the help of regression, it was found that PC is a strong predictor of EE. Hence, there exists a positive relationship between the two variables.

One of the recent studies that was conducted was by Strydom (2014), which was on 177 employees working in hospitality organizations in New Zealand, and the findings confirmed that PC is correlated and also determined it as being a predictor to work engagement. The subdimensions of PC used in the study of Strydom (2014) were supervisor support, organizational support, which was most strongly correlated with work engagement, following the interpersonal conflict, workgroup cooperation and friendliness had a moderate relationship and lastly, regulations and organization had a small relationship with work engagement.

From the reviews, it was found that all the studies proved that there exists a positive relationship between PC and EE. Hence, the PC is a positive predictor of EE.

11.4.3   INTENT TO STAY

In today's world, there exists a stiff competition as each company strives to get the right person for the right job and ensuring that these employees remain with the organization, in the long run, become a difficult task. This is mainly due to a rapid growth of companies across all sectors, which provides employees with the wider option to select a company that offers better pay and perks compared with the present one. The rate at which employees enter and exit from a company is very fast and in HR context, this is termed as "staff turnover," "labor turnover," or "employee turnover." Labor turnover is a process in which staff leaves the organization or the organization asks the employee to leave. Thus, turnover could be either voluntary or involuntary. Voluntary turnover happens when employees decide to leave the organization on their own due to various jobs and organization-related factors, whereas involuntary turnover takes place when the organization removes an employee due to poor performance, death, or accident (Ongori, 2007).

Employees' decision to remain or quit the organization is termed as "intention to stay" (IS) or "intention to quit" (IQ). Therefore, turnover intention is "a mental decision prevailing between an individual's approach with reference to a job to continue or leave the job" (Jacobs and Roodt, 2007). Thus, from the definition, it could be understood that a prolonged intention to leave in the minds of the employees will lead to taking the decision of leaving the organization.

There are many factors that influence employees' IS and IQ; one such factor is EE. Studies have shown that EE as a negative relationship with IQ, wherein employees who are highly engaged very rarely think about leaving the organization and thus increase retention (Lee and Shin, 2005; Cawe, 2006; Hewitt, 2010; Ngobeni and Bezuidenhout, 2011; Pieterse-Landman, 2012; Soane et al., 2012), as a result, EE predicts IQ or intent to stay, therefore managers must ensure that employees are engaged so as to make their intentions more positive about the organization (Andrew and Sofian, 2012).

11.5 RESEARCH FRAMEWORK

The main purpose of this study is to empirically test the model that will enrich the understanding of whether PC has any influence on EE. Similarly, the model also tries to examine the kind of relationship EE has on intent to stay.

11.5.1 METHODOLOGY OF THE RESEARCH

The study collected data from 433 employees, working in both national and international travel organizations, set up in Bangalore were considered for the study. The research used both primary and secondary sources. Primary data were collected on the basis of a survey method and secondary data were gathered from articles, thesis, books, and websites. Questionnaires were used to collect the data from these employees. The data were analyzed with the help of statistical tools to derive inferences from the data collected.

11.6 DISCUSSIONS OF THE RESULTS

11.6.1 PSYCHOLOGICAL CLIMATE AND EMPLOYEE ENGAGEMENT

Many studies have brought confusion by referring to organization climate, collective climate, organization culture, and PC as being the same. There are many other studies, however, which brought in clarity and proved that there is a distinct difference between these constructs. The meta-analysis conducted by Parker et al. (2003) portrays the constructs such as organization climate, collective climate, and organization culture are measured at group level whereas PC is measured at an individual level. Conferring to James et al. (1978); Rousseau (1988) "Psychological climate was defined as a molar construct which consists of items measuring individual perception about their organizational structure, process, and events" (as cited in Parker et al., 2003). Luthans and Avolio (2003) in their seminal work confer on a decisive and a supportive ambiance is required for employees to have a sustainable growth. An organization, to grapple with the fluctuating market and fierce competition, calls for a positive work environment. The competition has become so strong that the organizations are finding it a challenge to manage their employees effectively and efficiently. Thus, it is becoming tougher to attract and retain efficient employees (Kataria et al., 2013). The organization's expectations from their employees are also growing day by day.

The best way to tackle this scenario is by providing employees a positive and fulfilling work environment that satisfies the employees and helps the organization to flourish in the present scenario. Thus PC can have an important effect on employees and leads to many positive individual- and organization-level outcomes such as job satisfaction, higher performance, organizational commitment, job involvement, employee motivation, and psychological well-being (Parker et al., 2003). This chapter measures the PC at an individual level and tested its relationship with EE.

From the analysis, it can be inferred that if the employees' perception of their work environment is satisfactory, the overall mean stands as 3.79 on a scale of 5. PC consisted of six subconstructs—supportive management, role clarity, contribution, recognition, self-expression, and challenge. When analyzed at a subconstruct level, it was determined that the employees feel the work given to them are more challenging and interesting as it was rated highest having a mean score of 3.95 on the scale of 5. These days, it has become important to give a challenging and interesting job to keep the employees going, which many organizations fail to provide. Employees often try to see whether their skills, experience, and education are matching with their job role. The general problem that prevails in most of the organizations is either an overqualified employee is provided with less challenging work or an underqualified employee is given a job that is more than his or her skill, either of the situations can lead to dissatisfaction and lower productivity.

The analysis made leads with an inference that the employees are given challenging jobs for the very reason that the nature of tourism industry is such that the services provided to each customer are different and unique. The main job role of employees working in these organizations is to plan and sell itineraries to their customers. These travel agents need to discuss with their customers about the destination they wish to travel, mode of travel, dates on which they will be traveling, their budget, and the type of accommodation they would wish to stay in. These discussions can be long and differ from customer to customer. Hence, it becomes important for the travel agents to actively listen, understand the customer requirements, and plan the trips according to their demand. The travel agents need to be cautious and give attention to all aspects while planning the travel for their customers.

Their job also calls for a lot of responsibilities as they are involved in planning the itinerary, executing them, and getting the feedback from their customers. There could be instances in which these employees are confronted with complaints from customers regarding their travel and thus they should have the ability to resolve such complaints. Therefore, the role of travel agents is more challenging than any other industry and this is what many employees expect from their job. Supportive management and role clarity is the next highest rated construct having a mean score of 3.83.

Supportive management plays a vital role in all organizations irrespective of the size. Organizations cannot be successful and profitable just by having a well-defined strategy and resources but should also have a supportive management. Supportive management can harness, guide, and motivate the team and individuals to engage in delivering the company objectives. Similarly, with respect to role clarity, it is important for the management to inform the employees clearly the way the job is to be done, the level of responsibility involved in the job, and the rules and regulations related to the performance. Many employees work in an environment of total ambiguity, which greatly impacts the employee productivity and overall performance of the organization. In the current study, the employees working in a travel organization are highly satisfied with their management and the clarity they have with respect to the job they do. The other constructs measuring PCs, such as contribution, recognition, and self-expression, were also found to be perceived positively by the employees having a mean score ranging between 3.6 and 3.78.

11.6.2 EMPLOYEE ENGAGEMENT AND INTENT TO STAY

Employees leaving organizations is becoming very common and labor turnover rates are found to be high in the service industry, and this is more visible in travel organizations. The two main negative outcomes of high labor turnover are increased operational cost and time-consuming process as time has to be given for recruiting, selecting, and placing employees in the vacant positions. Controlling labor cost has become a primary concern these days for organizations as it increases operational cost, thus affecting the revenue of the company. There are many strategies that companies can adopt to retain the employees in the organization. One such strategy is that the companies can make their employees engaged in the organization. The current study measured the influence of EE on intent to stay and it was found that there is a positive relationship between these two constructs. The current findings support previous studies; a study by MacMinn (n.d.) found that the attrition rate can be decreased by 66% by engaging the employees in the organization. There are many companies focusing on EE as a strategy to reduce labor turnover, one such report about a call center named KFFS initiated engagement programs to reduce their employee turnover from 52 to 34% (Work Foundation, 2014). Thus, measuring EE and introducing programs that help in increasing engagement level becomes very important in every industry and company.

11.6.3 PRACTICAL IMPLICATION

The results derived from the study enlighten the practitioners about how vital EE is in travel organizations. The implications of the findings are on the practitioners, policymakers, HR managers, or managers of the companies as they are the ones who are involved in developing strategies and programs to ensure that employees are always engaged in their organization.

The first construct PC has proved to be one of the vital predictors of EE and employees working in any organization have some basic expectation about their organization work environment. Though the results indicated that the employees perceived more positively about the climate, the mean score is ranging between 3.77 and 3.95. Without a doubt, the level of challenge involved in the job is high but areas like recognition given to their employees for the good work that one has done needs to be focused on more. The policy maker can adopt either a monetary or nonmonetary benefit after reviewing the type of work an employee has completed efficiently. Employees always expect some kind of recognition from their managers for the hard work they have put in. It could either be some incentives, words of appreciation, mementos, gift card, and things like that which always drive them to do better in the future. Thus, to understand how employees perceive about their work climate becomes the manager's responsibilities to regularly measure on PC, which would help them to understand the prevailing condition, initiate and implement remedies that will help them to mitigate any problem that prevails. It also becomes important to train the managers and other higher authorities on the importance of being supportive to their subordinates and help them in the difficulties related to work. IS, which is considered as the outcome variable of EE, explains that organizations can automatically control turnover and retain efficient employees if EE is high.

11.6.4   SUMMARY OF THE STUDY

EE is an approach carried out in the workplace by providing the right work conditions for the employees in the organization. As discussed in the previous chapters, EE is driven by various individual and organization-related antecedents. Many studies have been carried out to determine the relationship between the various factors and outcomes of EE and the findings are proved to have a positive relationship. In one of the recent programs, Conely (n.d.) shared an insight from a research conducted on EE by Leigh Branham. The research explained four basic needs every leader needs to take care of at work to attain EE.

They are—developing trust among employees, having hope on employees, creating a sense of worth among the employees by providing appropriate reward and recognition, and the last one is to develop a challenging work that will help the employees to grow (Vora, 2015). It was also mentioned by Conley (n.d.) that there is an epidemic of workers who are not interested and actively disengaged in the work they do. The findings were also supported by a recent survey that was conducted by Deloitte indicating that only 20% of employees are happy and productive in their work and the remaining, which are estimated to a size of 23 million of employees, being "actively disengaged." Engagement level differs from industry to industry and country to country. In a research conducted by Dale Carneige Training (2015) on a sample size of 1200 consisting of executives, individual contributors, managers, and chief executive officers across the country found that employees engaged in India stood at 46%, which was higher than the global average of 34% and that of 30% of the United States.

The reasons indicated for the above scenario are that the education level of employees in India is much higher than that of United States and that the education is directly linked to EE. The study also revealed few other facts like 61% of them are willing to work overtime without any extra incentives, 58% of employees were very confident as there was job clarity, and 58% of them felt that their work is important for the success of the organization. Sector-wise analysis indicates that the healthcare sector has the most engaged employees, whereas employees working in local government and education sector were less engaged. The size of the organization also played a pivotal role where organizations with more than one lakh employees are highly engaged in comparison with small companies with an employee size of 500–10,000.

In today's competitive world, EE is becoming a key business driver for organizational success. Organizations leverage on EE to have a cutting edge against the competition. Kaye and Jordan-Evans (2003) stated, " the challenge today is not just retaining talented people but fully engaging them, capturing their minds and hearts at each stage of their work lives." Thus, organizations having engaged employees result in achieving business targets, better staff morale, increase in revenue and profit, high attendance rate, low absenteeism, higher productivity, hire better candidates, and retaining them (Duncan, n.d.; Kular et al., 2008; Lockwood, 2007; Markos and Sridevi, 2010).

11.7   CONCLUSION

From the study, it can be concluded that the employees in travel organizations are engaged to a greater extent, and it is also very clear that there is one specific step to attain EE across any organizations or industries. It is a challenge and difficult task to ensure that employees are always engaged but this has become a necessity to withstand unstable and uncertain competition. Thus, it is said that EE is considered to be a double-edged weapon (Chitra and Badrinath, 2012) to withstand competition. Therefore, managers, supervisors, or concerned HR managers are encouraged to constantly measure employees' perception of work climate, the psychological capital of employees, on the engagement level, and to invest in the strategies and practices. This will enable organizations to maintain the engagement level of the employees and withstand the unstable market more competently.

KEYWORDS

- **employee engagement**
- **psychological climate**
- **intent to stay**

REFERENCES

Andrew, O. C.; Sofian, S.; Individual Factors and Work Outcomes of Employee Engagement. *Proc.-Soc. Behav. Sci.* **2012**, *40*, 498–508.

Baum, T. Making or Breaking the Tourist Experience: The Role of Human Resource Management. In *The Tourist Experience—A New Introduction;* Ryan, C., Ed.; Cassell: London, 1997; pp 92–111.

Bhatia, A. K. *Tourism Development: Principles and Practices*, 2nd ed.; Sterling Publishers: New Delhi, 1983.

Brown, S. P.; Leigh, T. W. A New Look at Psychological Climate and its Relationship to Job Involvement, Effort, and Performance. *J. Appl. Psychol.* **1996**, *81*(4) 358.

Buckingham, M.; Coffman, C. *First, Break All the Rules;* Simon and Schuster: New York, 1999.

Cawe, M. Factors Contributing to Employee Engagement in South Africa (Master's thesis, University of the Witwatersrand, Johannesburg). 2006. http://citeseerx.ist.psu.edu/viewdoc/download?doi=10.1.1.453.5315&rep=rep1&type=pdf.

Chitra, K.; Badrinath, V. Employee Engagement—Need of the Hour—A Special Focus on Bank Employees. In *Management Issues in Emerging Economies (ICMIEE)*, Conference Proceedings of 2012, 2012, pp 110–114.

Chowdhary, N.; Prakash, M. Challenges of Tourist Guiding-An Assessment of Situation in India. 2008. space.iimk.ac.in/bitstream/2259/.../28802+Dr.+Nimit+Chowdhary.pdf.

Conning, K. M. E. Psychological Climate and Work Addiction Risk: Do the Perceptions of Our Organizations Matter? Master Thesis, East Carolina University, United States. 2009. http://thescholarshipecu.edu/bitstream/handle/10342/2223/Conning_ecu_0600M_10053.pdf?sequence=1&isAllowed=y.

Duncan, D. 7 Great Benefits of Engaging your Staff. PARiM Workforce Software. 2015. http://parim.co/7-great-benefits-of-engaging-your-staff.

Harter, J. K.; Schmidt, F. L.; Hayes, T. L. Business-unit-level Relationship Between Employee Satisfaction, Employee Engagement, and Business Outcomes: A Meta-analysis. *J. Appl. Psychol.* **2002**, *87*(2), 268.

Hewitt, A. Trends in Global Employee Engagement. 2010, www.aon.com/attachments/thoughtleadership/TrendsGlobal_Employee Engagement_Final.pdf.

Jacobs, E.; Roodt, G. The Development of a Knowledge Sharing Construct to Predict Turnover Intentions. *Aslib Proc.: New Inf. Perspect.* **2007**, *59*(3), 229–248.

James, L.; Hater, J.; Gent, M.; Bruni, J. Psychological Climate: Implications from Cognitive Social Learning Theory and Interactional Psychology. *Pers. Psychol.* **1978**, *31*, 783–813.

Janani, S. Employee Turnover: Present Scenario of Indian IT Industry. *Indian J. Appl. Res.* **2014**, *4*(3), 254–256.

Jones, A. P.; James, L. R.; Bruni, J. R.; Sells, S. B.; Hornick, C. W. *Psychological and Organizational Climate: Dimensions and Relationships.* 1977. http://www.dtic.mil/dtic/tr/fulltext/u2/a042202.pdf.

Kahn, W. A. Psychological Conditions of Personal Engagement and Disengagement at Work. *Acad. Manage. J.* **1990**, *33*(4), 692–724.

Kataria, A.; Garg, P.; Rastogi, R. Does Psychological Climate Augment OCBs? The Mediating Role of Work Engagement. *Psychol.-Manager J.* **2013**, *16*(4), 217.

Keep, E.; Mayhew, K. The Assessment: Knowledge, Skills, and Competitiveness. *Oxford Rev. Econ. Policy* **1999**, *15*(1), 1–15.

Kular, S.; Gatenby, M.; Rees, C.; Soane, E.; Truss, K. Employee Engagement: A Literature Review. (KBS Working Paper; No. 19). Kingston Business School: Kingston-upon-Thames, 2008.

Kusluvan, S. *Managing Employee Attitudes and Behaviors in the Tourism and Hospitality Industry;* Nova Publishers: New York, 2003.

Kusluvan, S.; Kusluvan, Z.; Ilhan, I.; Buyruk, L. The Human Dimension a Review of Human Resources Management Issues in the Tourism and Hospitality Industry. *Cornell Hospitality Q.* **2010**, *51*(2), 171–214.

Lee, K. E.; Shin, K. H. Job Burnout, Engagement and Turnover Intention of Dietitians and Chefs at a Contract Food Service Management Company. *J. Community Nutr.* **2005**, *7*(2), 100–106.

Lockwood, N. R. Leveraging Employee Engagement for Competitive Advantage. *Soc. Hum. Resour. Manage. Res. Q.* **2007**, *1*, 1–12.

Luthans, F.; Avolio, B. J. "Authentic Leadership: A Positive Developmental Approach", In *Positive Organizational Scholarship,* 1st ed.; Cameron, K. S., Dutton, J. E., Quinn, R. E., Eds., Barret-Koehler: San Francisco, 2003; pp 241–261.

Macey, W. H.; Schneider, B. The Meaning of Employee Engagement. *Ind. Organ. Psychol.* **2008**, *1*(1), 3–30.

MacMinn, M. *How to Know Whether Your Employees are Truly Engaged—Co.tribute.* n.d. https://cotribute.com/blog/how-to-know-whether-your-employees-are-truly-engaged/.

Markos, S.; Sridevi, M. S. Employee Engagement: The Key to Improving Performance. *Int. J. Bus. Manage.* **2010**, *5*(12), 89.

Maslach, C.; Leiter, M. P. *The Truth About Burnout: How Organizations Cause Personal Stress and What To Do About It;* Jossey-Bass: San Francisco, 1997.

May, D. R.; Gilson, R. L.; Harter, L. M. The Psychological Conditions of Meaningfulness, Safety and Availability and the Engagement of the Human Spirit at Work. *J. Occup. Organ. Psychol.* **2004**, *77*(1), 11–37.

Ngobeni, E. K.; Bezuidenhout, A. Engaging Employees for Improved Retention at a Higher Education Institution in South Africa. *Afr. J. Bus. Manage.* **2011**, *5*(23), 9961–997.

Ongori, H. A Review of the Literature on Employee Turnover. *Afr. J. Bus. Manage.* **2007**, *1*(3), 49–54.

Parker, C. P.; Baltes, B. B.; Young, S. A.; Huff, J. W.; Altmann, R. A.; Lacost, H. A.; Roberts, J. E. Relationships Between Psychological Climate Perceptions and Work Outcomes: A Meta-analytic Review. *J. Organ. Behav.* **2003**, *24*(4), 389–416.

Pieterse-Landman, E. The Relationship Between Transformational Leadership, Employee Engagement, Job Characteristics and Intention to Quit. Doctoral Dissertation, Stellenbosch University, South Africa, 2012.

Robinson, D.; Perryman, S.; Hayday, S. *The Drivers of Employee Engagement;* Institute for Employment Studies: Brighton, 2004.

Rousseau, D. M. The Construction of Climate in Organization Research. In *International Review of Industrial and Organizational Psychology;* Cooper, C. L., Robertson, I. T., Ed.; John Wiley and Sons: England, 1988; pp 139–159.

Saks, A. M. Antecedents and Consequences of Employee Engagement. *J. Manage. Psychol.* **2006**, *21*(7), 600–619.

Schaufeli, W. B.; Bakker, A. B. Work and Well-being: Towards a Positive Occupational Health Psychology. *Gedrag and Organisatie,* **2001**, *14*(5), 229–253.

Schaufeli, W. B.; Martinez, L.; Marque's- Pinto, A.; Salanova, M.; Bakker, A. B. Burnout and Engagement in University Students. A Cross Nation Study. *J. Cross Cultural Psychol.* **2002**, *33*(5), 461–481.

Seth, P. N.; Bhat, S. S. *An Introduction to Travel and Tourism;* Sterling Publishers: New Delhi, 2003.

Soane, E.; Truss, C.; Alfes, K.; Shantz, A.; Rees, C.; Gatenby, M. Development and Application of a New Measure of Employee Engagement: The ISA Engagement Scale. *Hum. Resour. Develop. Int.* **2012**, *15*(5), 529–547.

Strydom, A. Psychological Climate, Work Engagement, Intention to Leave and Organizational Citizenship Behavior in Small Hospitality Businesses. Master Thesis, University of Waikato, New Zealand. 2014. http://researchcommons.waikato.ac.nz/bitstream/handle/10289/8654/thesis.pdf?sequence=3&isAllowed=y.

Thayer, S. E. Psychological Climate and its Relationship to Employee Engagement and Organizational Citizenship Behaviors. Doctoral Dissertation, Capella University, United States, 2008.

Travel and Tourism Economic Research. WTTC. 2016. http://www.wttc.org/media/files/reports/economic%20impact%20research/countries%202016/india2016.pdf.

Tribe, J.; Airey, D. *Developments in Tourism Research;* Elsevier Science: Amsterdam, 2007.

Vora, T. Employee Engagement: 4 Basic Human Needs. 2015. http://qaspire.com/2015/09/29/employee-engagement-4-basic-human-needs/ (accessed Dec 14, 2015).

Work Foundation. Constrained at Work. 2014. http://www.theworkfoundation.com/DownloadPublication/Report/350_Con.

CHAPTER 12

CAN FOREIGN EXCHANGE VOLATILITY REALLY INFLUENCE TOURIST INFLOW IN INDIA?

K. J. ANSON[1] and AVIN THALIATH[2]

[1]Department of Commerce, Christ (Deemed to be University), Bangalore, India

[2]Department of Hotel Management, Christ (Deemed to be University), Bangalore, India

CONTENTS

ABSTRACT

In the current context, the currency becomes an important medium of exchange, unlike our own historical times. In the years of 2007 and 2008, a very important event changed the phase of international markets as we see it today. The subprime lending crisis that took place in America had its ripples spread far and wide consuming every other global market, including India. This not only affected the industries but also the domestic currencies in the global context. This has opened up both threats and opportunities for our markets. Tourism products are consumed from the point of supply that forms a major part of the expenditure for a tourist. Thereby this sector is a big contributor toward the economy. But tourism as a sector is not one of the most prioritized sectors in India; therefore, tourism becomes an area of discussion in this chapter. Second, keeping all other variables constant, is there an influence of foreign exchange volatility on foreign tourist arrivals?

12.1 INTRODUCTION

The inquisitiveness of man has led us far and beyond our traditional boundaries. Earlier, this quest was in search of newer pastures and resources, which later on transformed into conquests of empires. As time passes by, we try to understand our past by revisiting these mesmerizing structures of glory, which talks about our culture, traditions, and lifestyle. But this has changed, according to the World Tourism Report as quoted by Nanthakumar et al. (2007), stating "international tourism encompasses the activities of visitors who make visits across their own residential area to the international borders and remain there for more than 24 h. The main reasons for traveling are leisure, businesses, conventions, seminars, meetings, study abroad, religious purposes as well as sports or games."

Tourism sector is one of the potential drivers of the economy as it has a long-run relationship with economic growth through different channels (Balaguer and Cantavella-Jorda, 2002), primarily by way of employment opportunities, economic expansion, significant foreign exchange earnings and a central role in stimulating industries directly as well as indirectly (Schubert and Brida, 2009). Therefore, there is also an intense competition between destinations far and wide to attract tourists. This also depends on few prominent factors such as economic, political, and social stability (Agiomirgianakis et al., 2014).

Traditionally and even now to have a better balance of payment position, developing countries often focus on export trade, which usually adds comparatively less value to the overall economic stability and this is where tourism has become a savior (Durbarry, 2004). Tourism as such provides a competitive advantage, globally for small economies by providing the volume to overcome insufficient market demand, thereby ensuring higher efficiency and economies of scale while decreasing the cost per unit of production. It also increases competition by encouraging new entrants in the market, thereby resulting in a positive impact on the price levels of goods and services. Finally raising the standard of living and improving the quality of life (Croes, 2006). This link between economic growth and that of development in the tourism industry has been interesting areas of research and has recently attracted considerable attention. As per the World Tourism Organization barometer, "International tourist arrivals grew by 4.4% in 2015 to reach a total of 1184 million in 2015. Some 50 million more tourists (overnight visitors) traveled to international destinations around the world last year as compared to 2014."

Moreover, this marks the sixth consecutive year of above-average growth. The report further states that the demand was strong but had mixed results due to foreign-exchange fluctuations, decrease in oil prices, and other commodities that led to an increased disposable income in importing countries but weakened demand in export-oriented countries. It was also noticed that there were increased concerns over safety and security with a rise in terrorist activities. When we consider facts of India with reference to the tourism sector, The World Travel and Tourism Council states that India will be a tourism hotspot from 2009 to 2018, having the highest 10-year growth potential. As per the Economic Impact Report 2015, India ranks ninth in terms of real growth total contribution to GDP at 7.5%, whereas India ranks the fourth in terms of long-term growth for the 2015–2025 period at 7.3% total contribution to GDP. This shows, how prospective it is to capitalize this sector. The majority of the research work that is empirical in nature is in lines with understanding the long-run growth prospects through tourism or TLGH (Tourism-Led Growth Hypothesis) (Gunduz and Hatemi, 2005; Katircioglu, 2009; Lean and Tang, 2010; Tang, 2011; Brida et al., 2010; Katircioglu, 2009, 2010; Brida et al., 2008). Moreover, TLGH considers multiple variables that are interconnected to the growth aspect such as accommodation, transport, and infrastructure. Studies that focused on small economies state that specialization is beneficial for growth (Brau et al., 2007; Lanza et al., 2003), and this would result from an increase in tourist consumption of nontraded goods (Hazari and Sgro, 1995). Despite these research findings, there are very few growth models including tourism as a sector and analyzing the impacts of changes in tourism growth on long-run economic growth (Schubert and Brida, 2009).

The subprime-lending crisis that took place in America had its ripples spread far and wide consuming every other global market, including India. This not only affected the industries but also the domestic currencies in the global context. This has opened up both threats and opportunities for our markets. Tourism products are consumed from the point of supply that forms a major part of the expenditure for a tourist. Thereby this sector is a big contributor toward the economy. But tourism as a sector is not one of the most prioritized sectors in India; therefore, tourism becomes an area of discussion in this chapter. Second, keeping all other variables constant, is there an influence of foreign exchange volatility on foreign tourist arrivals?

12.2   LITERATURE REVIEW

Stability in currency regime had always encouraged better trade. De Vita and Kyaw (2013) found a positive impact on the volume of international tourist arrivals from the effect of common currency. Less-flexible exchange rates are expected to promote international trade and tourism via reduced uncertainty in international transactions, eliminated transaction costs, and enhanced transparency of the markets (Santana-Gallego et al., 2010). However, this is not conclusive evidence as Gil-Pareja et al. (2007) found a moderate effect of the currency union on tourism for the members of the Economic and Monetary Union.

A currency union or a common currency not just removes exchange rate volatility among members but also reduces transaction costs of trade and tourism and thereby creating an avenue for macroeconomic policies. Rose (2000) states "entering a currency union delivers an effect that is over an order of magnitude larger than the impact of reducing exchange rate volatility from one standard deviation to zero." This is possible to understand as hedging strategies are usually not used in the case of tourism. Furthermore, López-Córdova and Meissner (2003) add that "gold standard countries traded up to 30% more with each other than with nations, not on gold." This implies that stability in foreign exchange is more profitable for countries than otherwise. Tracing back to history, the fall of Bretton wood system, triggered what we see currently as volatility in exchange rate regime. Though in the latter years there was an attempt made to unify currencies in the Eurozone, which resulted in the formation of Euro, thereby encouraging a better exchange of wealth with no long-run sustainability, resulting in the Eurozone crisis.

Falk (2013) has made an attempt to study the euro crisis, which led to a strong appreciation of Swiss franc since 2008 and its sensitivity on tourism demand in Austrian mountain villages and has found that there was an increase in the number of nights spent by Swiss tourist by the depreciation of euro against Swiss franc, and the Swiss tourists are more sensitive to upward changes in Swiss franc. There are several studies that indicate the relationship between foreign trade and exchange rate volatility. Some of which brought a very new perspective (Rose, 2000), two countries sharing the same currency trade three times as much as they would with different currencies. This would call in for a stable foreign exchange but, in reality, is a currency union possible for a country such as India? Therefore, it is needless to say that the emphasis is still on export orientation to improve the balance of payment position.

There is also a lack of literature pertaining to the effect of foreign exchange volatility in the Indian tourism sector. Therefore, allusions from literature available for different economies will be used to draw rationality toward this concept in the Indian context. The concept of foreign exchange volatility creates a sense of uncertainty. Dumas (1978) and Adler and Dumas (1980, 1984) defined exchange rate exposure as "the measure of what one has at risk," whereas risk is the "statistical quantities that summarize the probability," of a currency value deviation from the originally anticipated value. Yap (2012) tried to find the effect of exchange rate volatility and increasing uncertainty in tourists coming to Australia from the following nine countries of origin, namely China, India, Japan, Malaysia, New Zealand, Singapore, South Korea, the United Kingdom, and the United States of America from 1991 to 2011. The study concluded that fluctuation in exchange rate creates spillover effects on tourist who are coming to Australia, and the effect differs from stronger or weaker, which depends on the tourist-generating country that creates these tourism inflows into Australia. Cheng et al. (2013) state that as US dollar depreciated it increased tourist receipts without affecting tourism expenditure or the import spending. Furthermore, foreign tourists are more sensitive to the exchange rate than US tourists going abroad, whereas US tourists are more sensitive to income (Cheng et al., 2009).

Hong Kong is known as "Asia's most popular travel destination" that has a unique culture blending along with Western lifestyles and Chinese traditions. The year 2000 marked as a significant one, placed Hong Kong the 14th in the World Tourism Organization's top destinations with a growth rate of 15.3%, whereas the world and regional average growth rates in the same year were 74 and 14.5%, respectively. The important factor that determined the demand for Hong Kong tourism was the costs of tourism in Hong Kong (Song et al., 2003). Adler and Dumas (1984) state that corporations, including those with no foreign accounts, are also exposed to foreign exchange risk. The United States depends on Japanese tourist, to a great extent to correct its trade deficit with Japan.

Therefore, it can be stated that there is a significant relationship between exchange rates and economic development. This also implies on the sectoral contribution (Beer, 1993). Over the recent past, international tourism is slowly being recognized to have a positive long-run economic growth through different channels in the economy. It is also called tourism-led growth hypothesis, a term coined by Balaguer and Cantavella-Jorda (2002). As tourism is a high contributor in terms of foreign exchange, at least one of three developing countries has made tourism as a priority sector (Durbarry, 2004). For instance, countries such as Singapore, Thailand, Malaysia, and many more heavily depend on revenue generated from tourism. That is, countries that increase expenditure on tourism have shown considerable improvement in terms of the potential benefits that they receive (Sinclair, 1998). This further implies the sectoral priority of these countries. There are several advantages of using tourism as a development strategy—first, natural and sociocultural attractiveness of the tourism destination; second, locally produced products command higher prices when sold to tourist than in terms of their exports, and this also implies the perishable goods as well (Mihalic et al., 2002).

Research studies on the impact of foreign exchange volatility on tourist inflows have concluded that there is a negative effect of foreign exchange volatility on the number of tourist arrival to the country (Agiomirgianakis et al., 2015; Aktaş et al., 2014). Furthermore, individuals have a tendency to adapt their activities in terms of expenditure and destination and will still continue to travel (Figuerola, 1992). But this view is contrary to the views proposed by Webber (2001), who states that in 40% of the cases, the tourists abandon the idea to travel to a country because of the exchange rate volatility. In addition, the significant determinant of the long-run tourism is the degree of variation in the foreign exchange rate but in some cases, exchange rate volatility might also be associated with political instability or social unrest in the destination country deterring tourists from this destination.

Therefore, exchange rate regimes that are more stable or less flexible tend to attract more tourists (Santa-Gallego et al., 2010). This is more so an impact on spending than on arrivals (Saayman and Saayman, 2013). Introspecting from the perspective of the Indian context, the exchange rate policy in India has seen a huge shift from the traditional currency union emphasized by the gold standard what we currently follow, which is the Peg system. The opening-up of the Indian market to global accessibility created the market-driven exchange rate system that has ensured stability in the Indian economy. In terms of volatility, the policy authorities have allowed depreciation of the currency as long as it required and intervened when the markets appeared unstable. Research on tourist arrivals and their sensitivity toward exchange rates variation have reached different conclusions about positive effects and negative effects, strong relationship, and a weak relationship between the two variables depending upon the statistical analysis done on the different time period. In this study, we try to assess how the existing foreign exchange situation in Indian will encourage tourist inflow, though tourism not being a priority sector in India. The current value of the Indian rupee is comparatively lower than what it used to be during the 2007–2008 term. This calls for an understanding of how tourism could be capitalized on being a significant contributor toward the economy.

12.3 OBJECTIVES

The current chapter primarily makes an attempt to analyze the foreign exchange volatility and its influence on foreign tourist inflows. This can contribute to determining the degree of impact and further generate implicative measures for framing propositions and strategies.

12.4 RESEARCH METHODOLOGY

Data: Secondary source comprising BIS-effective exchange rate index collected from the bank for international settlements and foreign tourist arrivals are sourced from the ministry of tourism, Government of India.

The data are collected from 2010 to 2015. The framework of data is monthly.

Variables: The two variables used in this study are the BIS-effective exchange rate index and foreign tourist arrivals. The data have been seasonally adjusted by using TRAMO SEATS method.

Analysis tools: The data are analyzed by using unit root test (augmented Dickey–Fuller (ADF)), generalized autoregressive conditional heteroske-dasticity (GARCH) model, and Johansen cointegration. The test is applied as Granger and Newbold (1974) stated that the "levels" of many economic time series are integrated (or nearly so), and if these data are used in a regression model then a high value for the coefficient of determination (R2) is likely to arise, even when the series are actually independent of each other. They also demonstrated that the associated regression residuals are likely to be positively autocorrelated, resulting from a very low value for the Durbin–Watson statistic.

The GARCH models evaluate the volatility of the exchange rate (effective exchange rate index). Cointegration tests are used to establish a relationship and finally VECM to understand the adjustment towards disequilibrium.

12.4.1 ANALYSIS

Unit root test: By using the ADF Test, it was found that the market during the observation period was stationary at first difference, which means that the markets were stationary at 1-degree lag. Table 12.1 signifies that the t-statistic is highly significant because it is negatively higher than all critical values, and the probability factor is also highly significant as it is below the critical point that is 0.05%, which means that there are no predictable patterns in the observation using the first difference lag. The DW stat signifies that there is no autocorrelation.

The equation of unit root test is expressed as follows:

$$\Delta R_t = a_o + a_2 t + \sum_i^k \beta_i + \varepsilon_t$$

TABLE 12.1 Unit Root Test Results of Foreign Tourist Arrivals.

Null hypothesis: D(LFTA_SA) has a unit root			Prob.*
Exogenous: Constant			
Lag length: 0 (automatic—based on SIC, maxlag = 11)			
Augmented Dickey–Fuller test statistic		−14.00740	0.0001
Test critical values:	1% level	−3.527045	
	5% level	−2.903566	
	10% level	−2.589227	
Durbin-Watson stat	2.117633		

*MacKinnon (1996) one-sided p-values.

Table 12.2 signifies that the t-statistic is highly significant because it is negatively higher than all critical values, and the probability factor is also highly significant since it is below the critical point that is 0.05%, which means that there are no predictable patterns in the observation using the first difference lag. The DW stat signifies that there is no autocorrelation.

TABLE 12.2 Unit Root Test Results of Effective Exchange Rate Index.

Null hypothesis: D(LREER) has a unit root			Prob.*
Exogenous: Constant			
Lag Length: 0 (Automatic—based on SIC, maxlag = 11)			
Augmented Dickey–Fuller test statistic		−6.001246	0.0000
Test critical values:	1% level	−3.527045	
	5% level	−2.903566	
	10% level	−2.589227	
Durbin–Watson stat	1.970390		

*MacKinnon (1996) one-sided p-values.

The unit root test results prove that both real effective exchange rate and foreign tourist arrivals are nonstationary at level series, and they become stationary at the first difference. Therefore, Johansen cointegration is used to establish the relationship between these two variables instead of regression.

12.4.2 GENERALIZED AUTOREGRESSIVE CONDITIONAL HETEROSKEDASTICITY MODELING

In principle, one should adopt a GARCH type of volatility estimator. Hence, we use GARCH model to analyze the data set. The GARCH model can be specified with GARCH (p, q), where p is the order of the GARCH terms of δ^2, and q is the order of the ARCH terms of $\in^2$. The model can be given as

$$\delta_t^2 = \alpha_0 + \alpha_1 \in_{t-1}^2 + \cdots + \alpha_q \in_{t-q}^2 + \beta_1 \delta_{t-1}^2 + \cdots + \beta_p \delta_{t-p}^2$$
$$= \alpha_0 + \sum_{i=1}^{q} \alpha_i \in_{t-i}^2 + \sum_{i=0}^{p} \beta_i \delta_{t-i}^2$$

The model of conditional volatility is referred to as GARCH (1, 1).

If the GARCH error coefficients (α_1) are high then it means that there exists an intensive reaction of volatility in the market, if the GARCH lag (β_1) coefficients are high then it means that there is a slow reaction of volatility in the market or it takes a long time to react to the market (Table 12.3 and 12.4).

TABLE 12.3 Test Results of GARCH Model.

GARCH = C(2) + C(3)*RESID(−1)^2 + C(4)*GARCH(−1)

Variable	Coefficient	Std. Error	z-Statistic	Prob.
C	81.12340	0.212421	381.8986	0.0000
	Variance Equation			
C	3.362638	2.382825	1.411198	0.1582
RESID(−1)^2	1.276922	0.707282	1.805392	0.0710
GARCH(−1)	−0.301043	0.201779	−1.491947	0.1357

If the GARCH error coefficients (α_1) are high and the GARCH lag (β_1) coefficients are low, then it means that the volatility tends to be spikier. Thereby this is reflected in Figure 12.1, where it depicts that the market is persistent to volatility. Therefore,

$$(\alpha_1) + (\beta_1) = 1$$

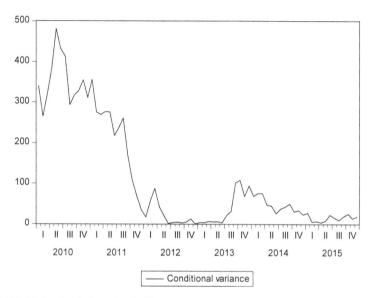

FIGURE 12.1   Depiction of volatility.

TABLE 12.4   Johansen Cointegration of Real Effective Exchange Rate and Foreign Tourist Arrivals.

Unrestricted Cointegration Rank Test (Trace)				
Hypothesized		Trace	0.05	
No. of CE(s)	Eigenvalue	Statistic	Critical Value	Prob.**
None*	0.223193	19.95289	15.49471	0.0099
At most 1	0.035947	2.526044	3.841466	0.1120
Trace test indicates 1 cointegrating eqn(s) at the 0.05 level				

*Denotes rejection of the hypothesis at the 0.05 level
**MacKinnon–Haug–Michelis (1999) *p*-values

Unrestricted Cointegration Rank Test (Maximum Eigenvalue)				
Hypothesized		Max-Eigen	0.05	
No. of CE(s)	Eigenvalue	Statistic	Critical Value	Prob.**
None*	0.223193	17.42684	14.26460	0.0153
At most 1	0.035947	2.526044	3.841466	0.1120
Max-eigenvalue test indicates 1 cointegrating eqn(s) at the 0.05 level				

*Denotes rejection of the hypothesis at the 0.05 level
**MacKinnon–Haug–Michelis (1999) *p*-values

TABLE 12.4   *(Continued)*

Unrestricted Cointegrating Coefficients (normalized by b'*S11*b=I):	
FTA	REER
−1.17E−05	−0.063451
2.30E−07	−0.102105

Unrestricted Adjustment Coefficients (alpha):

D(FTA)	34521.59	4579.991
D(REER)	−0.180832	0.244488
1 Cointegrating Equation(s):	Log likelihood	−983.8478

Normalized cointegrating coefficients (standard error in parentheses):

FTA	REER
1.000000	5423.455
	(2075.96)

Adjustment coefficients (standard error in parentheses):

D(FTA)	−0.403882
	(0.10139)
D(REER)	2.12E−06
	(2.0E−06)

If two variables are not stationary, running a regression could result in a spurious regression. For there to be a long-run relationship between the variables they must be cointegrated. The result rejects the null hypothesis of no cointegration between foreign exchange volatility and foreign tourist inflow. Further accepting the alternate hypothesis, it implies that there is a long-run relationship between foreign-exchange volatility and foreign tourist inflow. The vector error correction model is also calculated, which implies the speed of adjustment towards the long-run relationship.

Equation

$$D(FTA) = C(1)*(FTA(-1) + 5423.45490155*REER(-1) - 1027331.23167)$$
$$+ C(2)*D(FTA(-1)) + C(3)*D(FTA(-2)) + C(4)*D(REER(-1))$$
$$+ C(5)*D(REER(-2)) + C(6)$$

	Coefficient	Std. Error	*t*-Statistic	Prob.
C(1)	−0.403882	0.101387	−3.983554	0.0002
C(2)	0.560330	0.110728	5.060405	0.0000
C(3)	0.027906	0.130915	0.213159	0.8319

	Coefficient	Std. Error	t-Statistic	Prob.
C(4)	7124.042	6549.577	1.087710	0.2809
C(5)	−4013.906	6489.447	−0.618528	0.5385
C(6)	4642.616	8994.080	0.516186	0.6075
R-squared	0.387772	Mean dependent var	5809.391	
Adjusted R-squared	0.339182	S.D. dependent var	88553.08	
S.E. of regression	71985.43	Akaike info criterion	25.28926	
Sum squared resid	3.26E+11	Schwarz criterion	25.48353	
Log likelihood	−866.4793	Hannan–Quinn criter.	25.36633	
F-statistic	7.980551	Durbin–Watson stat	1.946405	
Prob (F-statistic)	0.000007			

The test statistics is significant and also shows that the time series tested above, which is foreign-exchange volatility and foreign tourist arrivals, adjusts to disequilibrium, thereby establishing a long-run relationship between both.

12.5   CONCLUSION

Tourism products are consumed from the point of supply that forms a major part of the expenditure for a tourist. Thereby this sector is a big contributor toward the economy. Researchers state that exchange-rate volatility signals risk associated with the destination and thereby refraining those to visit or even cancel their trips. Therefore, the study primarily focused on the influence of exchange rate volatility on foreign tourist inflows. The test results show that variables are cointegrated, emphasizing that there exists a long-run relationship between foreign tourist arrivals and foreign-exchange volatility but also that the variable adjusts themselves toward disequilibrium. Therefore, implying that the fluctuation in tourists is related to foreign-exchange volatility and a stable currency standard could further boost the income earned through this sector. The current context of Indian rupee, which has depreciated ever since 2007–2008 subprime crisis to touch a figure of rupees 66.83 against 1 US dollar, calls for the revival of tourism sector reforms to attract foreign tourist, thereby creating a secondary support system to sustain the balance of payment position in India.

KEYWORDS

- foreign-exchange volatility
- tourism receipt
- tourism-led growth hypothesis

REFERENCES

Adler, M.; Dumas, B. The Exposure of Long-term Foreign Currency Bonds. *J. Financ. Quant. Anal.* **1980**, *15*(04), 973–994.

Adler, M.; Dumas, B. Exposure to Currency Risk: Definition and Measurement. *Financ. Manage.* **1984**, 41–50.

Agiomirgianakis, G.; Serenis, D.; Tsounis, N. Exchange Rate Volatility and Tourist Flows into Turkey. *J. Econ. Integr.* **2014**, *29*(4), 700–725.

Agiomirgianakis, G.; Serenis, D.; Tsounis, N. Effects of Exchange Rate Volatility on Tourist Flows into Iceland. *Proc. Econ. Finance* **2015**, *24*, 25–34.

Aktaş, A. R.; Ozkan, B.; Kaplan, F.; Brumfield, R. Exchange Rate Volatility: Effect on Turkish Tourism Incomes. *Manage. Stud.* **2014**, *2*(8), 493–499.

Balaguer, J.; Cantavella-Jorda, M. Tourism as a Long-run Economic Growth Factor: The Spanish Case. *Appl. Econ.* **2002**, *34(7)*, 877–884.

Beer, P. S. An Econometric Model of Demand for Tourism in Nepal.MA (Economics) Unpublished Thesis Submitted to Dalhousie University, Halifax, NS Canada, 1993.

Brida, J. G.; Pereyra, J. S.; Risso, W. A.; Devesa, M. J. S.; Aguirre, S. Z. The Tourism-led Growth Hypothesis: Empirical Evidence from Colombia, 2008.

Brida, J. G.; Lanzilotta, B.; Lionetti, S.; Risso, W. A. The Tourism-led Growth Hypothesis for Uruguay. *Tourism Econ.* **2010**, *16*(3), 765–771.

Cheng, K. M.; Kim, H.; Thompson, H. The Exchange Rate and US Tourism Balance of Trade, 2009.

Cheng, K. M.; Kim, H.; Thompson, H. The Real Exchange Rate and the Balance of Trade in US Tourism. *Int. Rev. Econ. Finance* **2013**, *25*, 122–128.

Croes, R. R. A Paradigm Shift to a New Strategy for Small Island Economies: Embracing Demand Side Economics for Value Enhancement and Long Term Economic Stability. *Tourism Manage.* **2006**, *27*(3), 453–465.

De Vita, G.; Kyaw, K. S.; Role of the Exchange Rate in Tourism Demand. *Ann. Tourism Res.* **2013**, *43*, 624–627.

Dumas, B. The Theory of the Trading Firm Revisited. *J. Finance* **1978**, *33*(3), 1019–1030.

Durbarry, R. Tourism and Economic Growth: The Case of Mauritius. *Tourism Econ.* **2004**, *10*(4), 389–401.

Falk, M. Impact of Long-term Weather on Domestic and Foreign Winter Tourism Demand. *Int. J. Tourism Res.* **2013**, *15*(1), 1–17.

Figuerola, M. *Teoría económica del turismo.* Alianza Editorial: Madrid, 1992.

Gil-Pareja, S.; Llorca-Vivero, R.; Martínez-Serrano, J. A. The Effect of EMU on Tourism. *Rev. Int. Econ.* **2007**, *15*(2), 302–312.

Glick, R.; Rose, A. K. Does a Currency Union Affect Trade? The Time-series Evidence. *Eur. Econ. Rev.* **2002**, *46*(6), 1125–1151.

Gunduz, L.; Hatemi-J. A. Is the Tourism-led Growth Hypothesis Valid for Turkey?. *Appl. Econ. Lett.* **2005**, *12*(8), 499–504.

Katircioglu, S. Testing the Tourism-led Growth Hypothesis: The Case of Malta. *Acta Oecon.* **2009a**. *59*(3), 331–343.

Katircioglu, S. T. Revisiting the Tourism-led-growth Hypothesis for Turkey using the Bounds Test and Johansen Approach for Cointegration. *Tourism Manage.* **2009b**, *30*(1), 17–20.

Katircioğlu, S. Research Note: Testing the Tourism-led Growth Hypothesis for Singapore– an Empirical Investigation from Bounds Test to Cointegration and Granger Causality Tests. *Tourism Econ.* **2010**, *16*(4), 1095–1101.

Lean, H. H.; Tang, C. F. Is the Tourism-led Growth Hypothesis Stable for Malaysia? A Note. *Int. J. Tourism Res.* **2010**, *12*(4), 375–378.

López-Córdova, J. E.; Meissner, C. M. Exchange-rate Regimes and International Trade: Evidence from the Classical Gold Standard Era. *Am. Econ. Rev.* **2003**, *93*(1), 344–353.

Mihalič, T. A. N. J. A.; Sharpley, R.; Telfer, D. J. *Tourism and Economic Development Issues;* Channel View Publications: Clevedon, UK, 2002; pp 81–111.

Nanthakumar, L.; Ibrahim, Y.; Harun, M. Tourism development policy, strategic alliances and impact of consumer price index on tourist arrivals: the case of Malaysia, 2007.

Page, J. P. Tourism Management, Managing for Change. *Butterworth- Heinemann.* 2003, 51 p.

Rose, A. K. One Money, One Market: the Effect of Common Currencies on Trade. *Econ. Policy* **2000**. *15*(30), 08–45.

Saayman, A.; Saayman, M. Exchange Rate Volatility and Tourism-revisiting the Nature of the Relationship. *Eur. J. Tourism Res.* **2013**, *6*(2), 104.

Santana-Gallego, M.; Ledesma-Rodríguez, F. J.; Pérez-Rodríguez, J. V. Exchange Rate Regimes and Tourism. *Tourism Econ.* **2010**, *16*(1), 25–43.

Schubert, S. F.; Brida, J. G. A Dynamic Model of Economic Growth in a Small Tourism-Driven Economy. In *Chapter in the Book, Advances in Tourism Economics: Impact Analysis;* Matias, Á., Nijkamp, P., Sarmento, M., Eds.; Physica-Verlag: Heilderberg, 2009.

Sinclair, M. T. Tourism and Economic Development: A Survey. *J. Develop. Stud.* **1998**, *34*(5), 1–51.

Song, H.; Wong, K. K.; Chon, K. K. Modeling and Forecasting the Demand for Hong Kong Tourism. *Int. J. Hospitality Manage.* **2003**, *22*(4), 435–451.

Tang, C. F. Is the Tourism-led Growth Hypothesis Valid for Malaysia? A View from Disag-gregated Tourism Markets. *Int. J. Tourism Res.* **2011**, *13*(1), 97–101.

Webber, A. Exchange Rate Volatility and Co integration in Tourism Demand, *J. Travel Res.* **2001**, *39,* 398–405.

Yap, G. C. L. An Examination of the Effects of Exchange Rates on Australia's Inbound Tourism Growth: A Multivariate Conditional Volatility Approach. *Int. J. Bus. Stud.* **2012**, *20*(1), 111–132.

CHAPTER 13

CELEBRITY ENDORSEMENT: SOLVING THE DESTINATION MARKETING PUZZLE: AN INDIAN PERSPECTIVE

ROSMA MARY JOLLY

St. Mary's College, Thrissur, Kerala, India

CONTENTS

ABSTRACT

Celebrity endorsement is one of the major forms of advertising in which a business organization makes use of famous individuals or well-known organizations to boost consumer interest in the product and/or services that they want to sell. Nowadays, every company is trying to bring in a brand ambassador for their brands. Slowly, the trend of tying up with a celebrity to promote has moved toward promoting tourism destinations. Travel and tourism are one among the largest service sectors in India. The main aim of this industry is to develop and promote tourism, maintain and increase the competitiveness of India as a tourist destination, improve and expand existing tourism products to ensure employment generation and thus bringing about economic growth to India. The current chapter finds out the opinion of the consumers toward celebrity endorsement in influencing them at the time of decision making. The chapter also investigates the various motivating factors of the endorsers taken into consideration to visit the advertised destination. For this, the most important factors of celebrity endorsement were taken as a note of thorough extensive literature reviews. Making an inspection on the Swatch Bharat scheme and the involvement of celebrities gives more relevance to the study. Three main economic indicators such as gross domestic product, foreign direct investment, and foreign exchange were evaluated to find the effect of Swatch Bharat scheme. The data used were partially primary and secondary so that all the aspects could be identified and covered. The data were analyzed with the help of statistical package for the social science SPSS with tests such as one-sample t-test, ANOVA, chi-square test, Friedman test.

13.1   INTRODUCTION

Advertising is the process by which companies increase sales, create awareness, and promote their products, services, and ideas. This can be done by using different mediums such as TV, radio, the internet, and so forth. It helps one to identify the specific product from the clutter and make the customer more focused on their need to buy the product. Advertising has become a vital part of the corporate world today, and thus companies are allocating massive part of their revenues to the advertising budget. In the research of Liu et al. (2007), they suggest that promotion of a brand is one of the best effective advertising strategies that are currently available. Using celebrities provides a great deal of help to the companies to create unique ads and engender a positive effect on the attitude and sales intention towards the brand (Ranjbarian et al., 2010). The link between a brand and a product has a positive impact on how the consumers purchase the products and are predominantly facilitated by the use of four major endorsers—the CEO, celebrity, expert, and the archetypal consumer (Liu et al., 2007). However, the statistics claim that as much as 25% of the chief media trailers and advertisement are endorsed by celebrities (Erdogan et al., 2001), and this is the main emphasis upon which this chapter is based.

13.1.1 INTRODUCTION TO ADVERTISING

According to American marketing association "advertising is any paid form of non-personal presentation and promotion of ideas, goods, and services by an identified sponsor." Advertising is the process by which companies increase sales, create awareness and promote their products, services, and ideas. Advertising has the power to persuade, the power to influence the mind, and shape destiny. It has the power to change markets and improve profit margins. Advertising has short- (conveying new information, building awareness, enhancing credibility, etc.) and long-term power (conveying brand image, attaching emotional values to the brand, building a positive reputation, etc.) (Jerry, 2008). Advertising can be broadly divided into four categories—product advertising, service advertising, public service advertising, and institutional advertising. The main participants are advertisers, advertising agency, artists, and target audience. Some of the commonly used advertising media are television, print, radio, the internet, mobile, hoarding, and direct mail. Advertising agency places a very important role in creating, planning, and handling advertisements.

13.1.2 HISTORICAL DEVELOPMENT OF CELEBRITY ENDORSEMENT

The use of celebrities in advertisements is not a recent phenomenon (Kaikat, 1987). The history of celebrity endorsement of products dates back to the 1760s. Josiah Wedgwood, the founder of the Wedgwood brand of pottery and chinaware, also called the father of the modern brand (Robert and Ignatius, 2003), used royal endorsements and other marketing tools to make an impression about the name of his firm that helped to create a brand that had a worth far beyond the attributes of the product. From the late nineteen celebrities have been endorsing products in full fledge. One such instance of celebrity endorsement from the early days is when Queen Victoria was associated with Cadbury cocoa (Shearman, 1985). In 1979, celebrity endorsers used in commercials were estimated as one in every six advertisements (Howard, 1979). By 1988, estimates were one in five (Motavalli, 1988). Looking into the early 1930s, athletes were the major endorsers, but during 1945, film icons such as Charlie Chaplin were preferred more. When color TVs became popular that is during 1965, TV personalities and entertainers started becoming popular. Researchers Robert Clark and Ignatius Horstmann of Boston University studied a collection of 1000 endorsement advertisements from 1920 to 1970 and found that they were predominantly used by cigarettes, beauty products, beverages, and audio equipment (Clark and Horstman, 2003).

13.1.3 CELEBRITY ENDORSEMENT

Definition: "Celebrity is an omnipresent feature of society, blazing lasting impressions in the memories of all who cross its path" (Kurzman et al., 2007). Kamins (1989) defined a celebrity as an individual who is known to the public for his/her achievements in areas other than that of the product class endorsed. Thus celebrities mostly include a person who consumes the product, an expert in the product class that is endorsed, or the president of a company. A celebrity endorser is "an individual who enjoys public recognition and who uses this recognition on behalf of a consumer good by appearing with it in an advertisement" (McCracken, 1989, p. 310). People are ready to buy the products on the basis of its benefits and features, but when clutter comes into picture, it makes consumers difficult to differentiate, so the use of celebrities is useful. Agrawal and Kamakura (1995) concluded that the advertisements by using celebrities are more effective than the advertisements using noncelebrity, which shows a great contrast between celebrity and noncelebrity. Some studies prove that the use of appropriate celebrities helps increase a positive attitude on consumers.

13.1.4   CELEBRITY ADVERTISING IN INDIA

In India, celebrity endorsement is successful because consumers have the perception that if a brand is endorsed by a celebrity, it has superior quality as it is endorsed by a credible source. Celebrities in India are thought to be very good examples of reference groups. Populations of more than 1 billion, people in India need something or someone to look up to and move on. India is a country where people are driven away by film stars, cricketers, politicians, and even criminals. People feel a sense of security, respect, expertise, and above all, someone they aspire to be at a higher level in their lives (Sheikh, 2002). Factors that have helped celebrity endorsement work out well in India are familiarity and high reliability toward the celebrity.

13.1.5   TOURISM MARKETING

Tourism can be classified as an important element of the service industry of the economy. Tourism marketing can be defined as "the managerial process of anticipation and satisfying existing and potential visitor wants more effectively than competitive suppliers or destinations." The management of exchange is driven by profit, community gain, or both; either way, long-term success depends on a satisfactory interaction between customers and suppliers (Lumsdon, 1997, p. 25). Marketing services govern on five principles that make the marketing of services more difficult than that of the products of consumers or industries. These five underlying principles are intangibility, perishability, heterogeneity, inseparability, and lack of ownership (Ferrell and Hartline, 2005). The major elements that constitute or help the marketer when marketing a product or service are together called as marketing mix. The 8P model by Morrison (2002) is a famous model that is suitable for tourism marketing (Lawton and Weaver, 2005). The 8Ps consist of place, product, people, price, packaging, programming, promotion, and partnerships.

13.1.6   CELEBRITY ENDORSEMENT IN TOURISM INDUSTRY

The service industry is finding it difficult to bring in creativity and differential among the products that are being advertised. Penetration into the market and gaining the awareness of the consumers has become a challenging one. One way out of this problem is to make effective use of celebrity endorsers. Researchers have identified that celebrity endorsement can add to a higher advertisement ratings and product acceptance. But making use of services of the celebrities can be similar to a double-edged sword. So it is very important that the right celebrity is selected to endorse the product. To help create a destination image, some studies have identified four characteristics that can be looked into to create a good image of the destination. These four characteristics are complexity, multiplicity, relativity, and dynamics. Essentially, celebrities are made by the audience who are willing to read about them or see them on television (Boorstin, 1992). Thus, they become desirable marketing tools (Gamson, 2001). Celebrities have great market appeal, and celebrity endorsement has been found to increase the likelihood of consumers choosing the endorsed product or brand (Agrawal and Kamakura, 1995 after Heath et al., 1994; Kamin et al., 1989). Some of the benefits of using celebrities in tourism advisements are given: capturing the audience's attention (Misra and Beatty, 1990), adding credibility to the product or brand (Agrawal and Kamakura, 1995; Misra and Beatty, 1990), making the advertisement or product easier to remember (Agrawal and Kamakura, 1995), making the brand easier to recognize (Agrawal and Kamakura, 1995), assisting in achieving positive attitudes towards the brand (Agrawal and Kamakura, 1995; Misra and Beatty, 1990).

13.2   DETERMINANTS OF CELEBRITY ENDORSERS FOR TOURIST DESTINATIONS

When a celebrity endorses a product successfully, consumers will evaluate the endorsement positively, feeling it is credible, believable, and appealing (Ohanian, 1990, 1991). Consequently, people would tend to like the advertisement, brand name, enhanced advertisement recall, increase product liking, and other positive effects may occur (Brown and Stayman, 1992). Thus to bring a positive attitude toward the products endorsed by celebrities, some traits are necessary. The main determinants discussed in this chapter are expertise, trustworthy, celebrity product match, similarity, credibility, familiarity, liability, transfer of meaning.

13.2.1 EIGHT MAJOR DETERMINANTS OF CELEBRITY ENDORSEMENT

After doing an extensive review of the literature, the determinants of a celebrity endorsement for a tourist destination were brought under eight heads. These determinants were summarized from factors of celebrity endorsement of the product as no much study was done in relation to tourist destinations.

a) Expertise: Effective endorsement can be made only if the celebrity has an acceptable level of expertise. Till (2004) stated that celebrity experience should be a key variable for organizations interested in the value of celebrities. Expertise may include competence or qualification of the celebrity. When a celebrity achieves a higher level of expertise, he is considered to be more persuasive, and this, in turn, helps one to positively alter the consumer's attitude. The importance of expertise is clearly true in the case of tourism and hospitality endorsements because consumers are unaware of the services provided, and an additional opinion of an expert helps them to make a buying decision. According to Pornpitakpan (2003), perceived expertise is created by many factors; chief among them is the celebrity experience.

b) Trustworthiness: In the framework of celebrity endorsement, trustworthiness can be thus defined as honesty, integrity, and believability of an endorser as perceived by the target audience. Trustworthiness can be the confidence and the acceptance the listener has toward the celebrity and the message in the advertisement (Erdogan et al., 2001, p. 40). Trustworthiness that is built on consumer's association with the endorsed brand has been considered an integral component of celebrity product advertisement framework. Thus, consumer consumption experience is a function of consumers' perception of how reliable the celebrity is (Ohanian, 1990; Silvera and Benedikt, 2003). The need for trustworthiness is very much important for hospitality/tourism destination endorsements as the transactions in these sectors are high in the quality of experience (Ibok and Ibok, 2013). Experience qualities are those that can understand during or only after consumption (Ibok and

Ibok, 2013). Hence, a celebrity endorsing the tourist destination or a hotel will be considered reliable to stand for the destination even if the consumer has not visited the destination.

c) Similarity: It is the third attractiveness concept and the S in TEARS (trustworthiness, expertise, physical attractiveness, respect, and similarity) model. It represents the degree to which an endorser matches an audience in terms of age, gender, ethnicity, and so on. "Similarity" is an important factor because people tend to prefer individuals who share with them common features or traits (Shimp, 2010). Similarity is described as "a supposed resemblance between the source and the receiver of the message" (McGuire, 1985). People can be influenced more easily by an endorser who is similar to them. If the celebrity and the consumer have common factors like common interests or lifestyles, a better cohesiveness is created (Erdogan, 1999). Companies also try to create empathy using celebrities (Belch and Belch, 2001). By using empathy, companies try to create a bond between the celebrity and the consumer (Ibok and Ibok, 2013). Moreover, the level of persuasiveness is increased by using similarity (Ibok and Ibok, 2013).

d) Transfer of meaning: The meaning transfer is based on the idea that celebrity endorsers bring their own figurative meaning to the endorsed product and in the endorsement process. The cultural meanings that the celebrities have will go beyond the person and are passed on to the products (McCracken, 1989; Brierley, 1995). Advertisers hold the belief in employing the celebrities for endorsement of the products that consumer consume images of celebrities and advertisers hope that consumer will also consume products endorsed by celebrities. Hirschman (1980) states that symbolic meanings are generated and familiarized to the customers through the production process. McCracken (1986) argues that advertising is one of the ways to forward meanings of personality to products.

e) Familiarity: It is the supposed resemblance as the knowledge that a celebrity endorser possesses through exposure (Erdogan, 1999; Belch and Belch, 2001). Companies should be very careful while choosing a celebrity; companies should make sure to what extent consumers are familiar with the celebrity. The more familiar the consumer is the celebrity, the more positive the effect will be (Hoekman, 2013). It is also well known that consumers, who are more familiar with a celebrity and are more exposed to a celebrity, will automatically like a celebrity more; this is called the mere exposure effect (Zajonc, 1968). Familiarity is effective when there are no longer delays in between the advertisements shown. The effect decreases when there are long exposures of the celebrity and when there are shorter delays between the exposures (Bornstein, 1989).

f) Likeability: Likeability is the "affection for the source as a result of the source's physical appearance and behavior" (McGuire, 1985, p. 239). McGuire (1985) also states that when people like the celebrity, they will also like the accompanying brand and therefore celebrities are used in commercials and advertisements.

g) The match between celebrity and product: Several studies (Cooper, 1984; Forkan, 1980) show that the match-up congruence between celebrity endorser and the product or company is of major importance. This correspondence results in a better recall of the commercial and brand information and will positively affect the transfer influence with regard to the personification of the brand (Rockney and Green, 1979). Advertising a product via a celebrity, who has a relatively high product congruent image, leads to greater advertiser and celebrity believability if you would compare it with a less congruent product/celebrity image (Kotler, 1997). The match-up consists of two central terms: the perceived fit and the image of the celebrity (Misra, 1990). When a celebrity has a good image and fits to the product and company, this will lead to greater believability and so effectiveness. By uniting those aspects, you create two advantages, working together for the product (Erdogan, 1999). Celebrities become most effective in advertisements when a match is established between them, and the product they are endorsing. Greater acceptance and believability is formed when the celebrity endorser's image and values are similar to the product or service that they are endorsing.

h) Physical attractiveness: Many studies have portrayed a vision between celebrity's physical attractiveness and attitude changes of consumers (Caballero and Pride, 1984; Chaiken, 1979; Kahle and Homer, 1985). A positive effect on the consumers is created by the attractiveness of the celebrity endorsers. Target viewers can recall, recognize the celebrities mush easily on the basis of the attractiveness of the celebrities. They are more liked by the audience due to attractiveness. Attractiveness also entails concepts such as intellectual skills, personality properties, a way of living, athletic performances, and skills of endorsers (Erdogan, 1999). Physical attractiveness suggests that a celebrity determines the effectiveness of persuasion as a result of that consumer wanting to be similar to the endorser and wanting to identify themselves with that endorser (Cohen and Golden, 1972). When there is a match between brand and celebrity, attractiveness becomes less important, and thus the company might choose a less-attractive celebrity (Fig. 13.1).

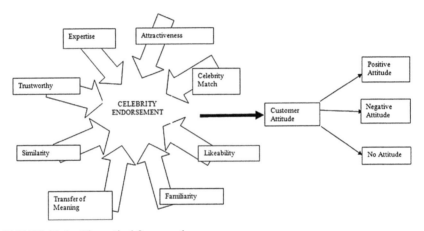

FIGURE 13.1   Theoretical framework.

13.3   SCHEME OF RESEARCH PROJECT

Quantitative data analysis is a very helpful way in the evaluation of data because it delivers quantifiable and easily understandable outcomes. Quantitative data can be investigated in a variety of different means. This type of data analysis is mainly used when the respondents are large in number. It is mainly carried out with the help of questionnaires. This type of data analysis, unlike qualitative analysis, uses statistical data processing (Fig. 13.2).

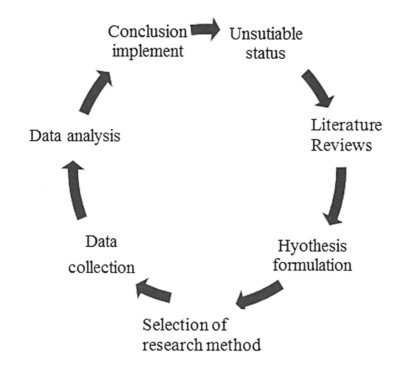

FIGURE 13.2   Scheme of research project.

13.3.1   *METHODOLOGY FRAMEWORK*

13.3.1.1   *UNSUITABLE STATUS*

A problematic area of concern, a state to be developed upon, a difficulty to be removed or a disconcerting question that exists in a researcher's literature, in a model, or in a real situation that points to the need for meaningful understanding and deliberate inquiry. Celebrities are almost always attracted to people especially in India where they and their words are worshiped as Gods. It is a recent trend in which the tourism industry is also roping in celebrity endorsement to boost up the frequency of visiting a particular destination, for easy recall and for creating awareness. Many places such as Gujarat, Australia, and so on have used this strategy and have achieved good results, but whether celebrity endorsement is really an effective tool for marketing destinations or what are the factors that should be looked into to make an effective tourism advertisement is a major concern. This study will examine the effectiveness of using celebrities to market a tourism destination among different occupations in Bangalore and to verify if the celebrities are really influencing these people in deciding their tourist destination.

13.4   LITERATURE REVIEW

A literature review is an account of what has been published on a topic by accredited scholars and researchers. In writing the literature review, your purpose is to convey to your reader what knowledge and ideas have been established on a topic, and what are their strengths and weaknesses. The purpose of a review is to analyze critically a segment of a published body of knowledge through summary, classification, and comparison of prior research studies, reviews of literature, and theoretical articles.

13.5   HYPOTHESIS FORMULATION

A hypothesis is a particular statement used for prediction. It describes in actual terms what one expects in his/her study. There is no prescribed form of preparing a hypothesis, and possibly the purpose of the study is to discover some specific area more carefully in order to develop some precise hypothesis or forecast that can be verified in future research. A single research work may have one or many hypotheses. This chapter mainly deals with two hypothesis, they are as follows:

H1: There is a significant difference between occupation and perception of getting attracted to a destination, recognizing and recalling, identifying destination details, and then visiting the destination when endorsed by a celebrity.

H2: All factors of the celebrity endorser influence the customers to visit the advertised destination.

13.6   SELECTION OF THE RESEARCH METHOD

Research methods are meant as the different ways and means of steering a research that may comprise conducting of experiments, surveys, and so on. It can be understood that research methods usually involve finding solutions to a research problem. There are many types of research methods. Malhotra and Birks (2000, p. 76) divide conclusive research design into further two categories: Descriptive research (used to describe some functions or characteristics) and Causal research (used to research cause and effect relationships); in this chapter, descriptive research is done that mainly involves research v/s analytical data. Descriptive research helps scholars create data that can give a detailed explanation of the composition and features of related groups. These groups could be customers, employees, organizations, or other service providers (Neenlankavil, 2007, p. 134).

13.7   DATA COLLECTION

Data collection is the process of collecting and quantifying information on variables of concern, in a predetermined organized technique that helps and allows one to answer detailed research questionnaire, testing of hypothesis, and evaluation of outcomes. In this chapter, the data were collected from primary data, that is, questionnaire in which the respondents were divided into five equal portions 50 from IT employees, 50 from teachers, 50 from businessmen, 50 students, and 50 other people such as HR people, people in advertising, doctors, and people in the medical field, and so on. Contents of the questionnaire were validated by experts' opinion both from academic and industry. Secondary data were collected from journals, books, newspapers, and so on. A structured questionnaire was developed with the help of suggestions given by the experts. As mentioned, the first section of the questionnaire consisted of nominal scale, which was used to collect demographic information of the respondents, and the second includes a five-point Likert scale to understand the views of respondents toward tourism advertisement A pretest was done on the questionnaire that was first prepared to take a sample size of 30 before the final use in the study. The main aim of pretesting was to determine the suitability of the type of questions and its content and to incorporate the corrections in the final questionnaire. Thus, reliability and the validity of the questionnaire were thus established.

13.8   DATA ANALYSIS

Data Analysis is the method of systematically doing statistical techniques to describe, shorten, and evaluate data. According to Shamoo and Resnik

(2003), various analytic procedures "provide a way of drawing inductive inferences from data and distinguishing the signal (the phenomenon of interest) from the noise (statistical fluctuations) present in the data." This study mainly deals with one sample t-test and chi-square.

13.9   CONCLUSION IMPLEMENT

The conclusion part of a project provides an effective and useful ending to the report. The content in the conclusion should have a direct relation to the objectives of the project report as indicated in the introduction, and thus summing up the essentials of your work. This section gives an overall idea of the report and a brief summary of the major findings and suggestions.

13.10   ANALYSIS AND INTERPRETATION

The analysis and interpretation picture on the different analysis done to attain the objectives, the various analytical tools that are used to prove the hypothesis of the study and the inferences from tests.

13.10.1   ASSESSING THE INFLUENCE OF CELEBRITY ENDORSED TOURISM ADVERTISEMENTS ON CONSUMER DECISION-MAKING

Consumer decision-making is a process by which individuals interact with their relevant internal and external environment factors to decide about the purchase of products/services (Pavleen, 2006). The destination product is complex and not subject to the degree of control and management often available for other products (Crouch 2000, p. 69). Thus, the process of decision-making of the consumers for services is slightly different from that of products. Kotler (1998) identifies that, when involved in a purchase decision, the consumer transmits the stages of (1) need recognition, (2) information search, (3) evaluation of alternatives, (4) choice of product or service, and (5) post-purchase evaluation. However, a significant advantage of Kotler's model is that the buying decision process is likely to originate long back, that is, in advance to the actual purchase of the product and continue after purchasing has occurred, signaling that marketers need to pay attention to the entire buying process rather than just on the purchase decision (Kotler, 1998).

First, at the need recognition stage, the consumers feel they have to take a break from their daily routine and go for a trip, at this stage. They start thinking about which place to go. When the respondents were asked, they came out with the opinion that if the destination was endorsed by a celebrity, they could easily recognize and recall the destination. Thus, celebrity endorsed destination advertisements, if done, helps the marketers thought not immediately but at the time when the consumers are at the stage of need recognition. Consumers will easily recognize the celebrity and link the destination with the celebrity, thus giving more preference to the particular destination endorsed. Following the need recognition stage, information search is the stage in the process in which the consumer gets aroused to search for more details of the destination. At this stage usually, the consumers go in active search for more details on the destination, or they increase their attention to the relevant information sources such as advertisements. Thus, at this stage again if the advertisements are endorsed by celebrities, more weight will be there. Once all the information has gathered, the consumers start to evaluate the different alternative solutions. In this stage, the consumers will evaluate all the alternatives by examining each attribute of the tourist destination, give specific levels to those attributes according to the importance. Here the respondents that consist of teachers, medical representatives, and so on of the study communicated that they may or may not pay attention to the details or specifications of the celebrity-endorsed destination when evaluating the attributes, but it was shocking to know that businessmen and usual students took special note of the attributes of the celebrity-endorsed advertisement. IT employees communicated that they took note of a destination attributes not because the destination was advertised by a celebrity.

13.10.2   ATTRIBUTES OF CELEBRITIES THAT HELP ATTRACT CUSTOMERS TOWARD TOURISM DESTINATION ADVERTISEMENTS

When taking into consideration, the different pros and cons of tying up with a celebrity, it becomes crucial to find the best and the apt celebrity to endorse a product/service. As not many studies have been done to list out the attributes that a celebrity should have when endorsing a tourist destination, this chapter tries to find out some prominent factors to build an effective celebrity-endorsed tourism destination advertisements.

13.11   MODELS FOR CELEBRITY ENDORSEMENT

13.11.1   TEARS MODEL

The TEARS model can be considered as a tool that can be used for evaluating potential celebrities, so that the most effective celebrity can be used for endorsement. The model is based on mainly two attributes credibility and attractiveness (Ohanian, 1990; Till and Busler, 2000). Shimp (2007) divides the two attributes into five subattributes. Two of these pertain to credibility and three to attractiveness, together creating the acronym TEARS, which stands for Trustworthiness (T), Expertise (E), Physical Attractiveness (A), Respect (R), and Similarity (S). Here in this chapter other than respect, all other factors are considered. The factor Respect was not taken into consideration on the basis of the prequestionnaire circulation and factor analysis. Shimp (2007) divides Credibility into two separate, but related, subattributes: Trustworthiness and Expertise otherwise called as source creditability model. Again Shimp (2007) divides attractiveness into three separate subattributes: Physical attractiveness, Respect, Similarity otherwise called as source attractiveness model. It is contended that the effectiveness of a message depends on similarity, familiarity, and liking for an endorser (McGuire, 1985). Researchers say that attractiveness is not only the physical appearance of the celebrity, but it includes many other factors such as lifestyle, intellectual qualities, familiarity, and others. Thus with reference to the model, six factors were borrowed and inculcated into this study—Trustworthiness, Expertise, Physical Attractiveness, Similarity, Familiarity, and Liking.

13.11.2   PRODUCT—MATCH MODEL

Match-up hypothesis is defined as the consistency between the characteristics of a celebrity endorser, and the attributes of the product that they endorse (Misra and Beatty, 1990). According to Erdogan (1999), the Product Match-up Hypothesis maintains the messages conveyed by celebrity image, and the product message should be congruent for effective advertising. Furthermore, Erdogan (1999) states that advertising a product with a celebrity who has a relatively high product congruent image leads to a greater advertiser than an advertisement with a less congruent product/spokespersons image. He again adds that if celebrities do not have a proper match with the product consumers will tend to believe that the celebrities were paid a handsome amount of money to endorse the product. Thus as the model was found to be of great importance, the attribute was considered in the context of a destination advertisement.

13.11.3 MCCRACKEN'S MEANING TRANSFER MODEL (1989)

McCracken defines this transfer as the translation of the meaning of celebrity to a product, service or brand. The McCracken model makes it possible to explain how celebrities transmit an extensive set of associations with the brands they endorse. Therefore, before companies select celebrities to represent their brands, they need to ensure that the person conveys the right meaning (Fleck-Dousteyssier and Korchia, 2006). The consumers admire celebrities maybe because the celebrity is physically attractive or maybe he has done what the consumer wants to view but this is not always the case, consumers also look into the fact that the celebrity provides meanings of the product or service to the consumer. Thus, with the reference of the above three models and with pretesting of questionnaire, eight attributes were come up for the study. With these factors, a cross-case analysis was done to find out the reactions of the different occupation group toward these celebrity attributes.

13.12 CROSS-CASE ANALYSIS

Cross-case analysis is an analysis that includes a check of more than one case; this can be either a variable- or case-oriented analysis. Here each of the occupational group is analyzed with each of the celebrity endorsement attributes to find which occupational group favors to which attribute, thus helping the marketer at the time of target marketing of a destination (Fig. 13.3).

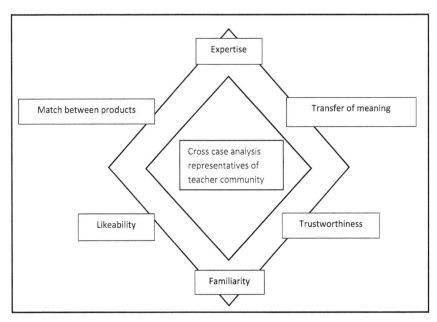

FIGURE 13.3   Cross-case analysis of representatives of teacher.

The teacher representatives felt that some of the major attributes that a celebrity endorser should have when endorsing a tourist destination are expertise in his/her own field; the teacher fraternity also felt that it is very important to have a match between the product and the celebrity, the endorser should be familiar and trustworthy and preferably likable and ultimately pointed out the importance of transfer the message and the meaning of the advertisement. The teacher respondents felt that physical attractiveness of the celebrity has no much role to play in their preferential factor list (Fig. 13.4).

The student's representatives also felt the same as that of the teachers. They emphasized on the expertise of celebrities, the match between the product and the celebrity, familiar and trustworthy and preferably likable and the importance of transfer the message and the meaning of the advertisement accurately. Again it was found that physical attractiveness of the celebrity did not make much effect on the group (Fig. 13.5).

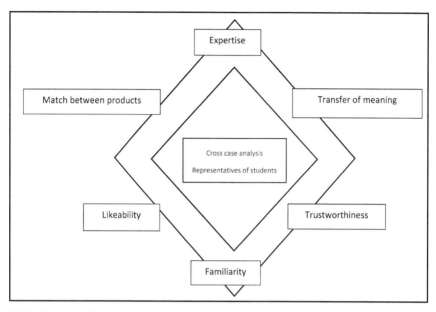

FIGURE 13.4   Cross-case analysis of representatives of students.

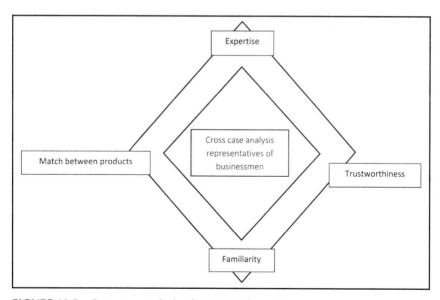

FIGURE 13.5   Cross-case analysis of representatives of businessmen.

The businessmen representatives had a slightly different opinion. They highlighted on the expertise of the celebrities, the match between the product and the celebrity, familiar and trustworthy but they didn't feel that likable and transfer of meaning of the advertisement was necessary for a celebrity endorsing a destination. Again physical attractiveness of the celebrity did not make any effect on the group (Fig. 13.6).

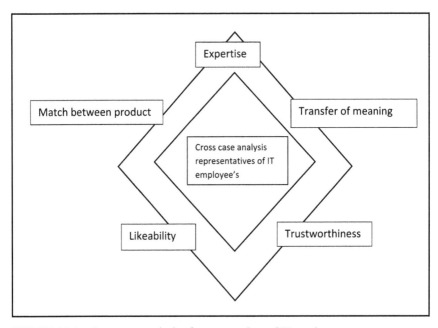

FIGURE 13.6   Cross-case analysis of representatives of IT employee.

IT employee's representatives felt the same as that of the teachers and students except they felt familiarity is not an important attribute for endorsing a destination. Physical attractiveness of the celebrity also did not make any effect on the group (Fig. 13.7).

The "other" group included HR people, people in advertising, doctors, people in the medical field, and so on. They felt the same as that of the teachers and students. They emphasized on the expertise of the celebrities, a match between the product and the celebrity, familiar and trustworthy and preferably likable and the importance of transfer of meaning of the advertisement accurately. Here also physically attractive.

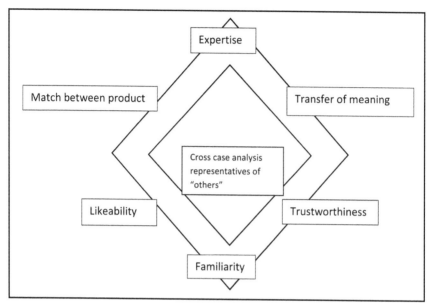

FIGURE 13.7   Cross-case analysis of representatives of "others."

13.13   IMPLICATIONS FOR CELEBRITY ENDORSEMENT

Some of the major implications that can be drawn from this chapter are given below:

- The destination advertisement would be more appealing to the consumers if there is a match between the destination and the celebrity. For example, if the destination to be promoted is Kerala. It is better to select an endorser who is a native of Kerala and a person who loves traveling this would give a more genuine feeling to the customers.
- As the chapter finds out that physical appearance has very little or no impact on the decision-making process, it is better for the organizations not to invest money on celebrities, just on the basis of beauty.
- It would be better if the advertisers try to create a combination of noncelebrity advertisement and celebrity advertisements for a tourist destination because, when compared, consumers agreed that

better convincing, more weight, and enhancement of belief of want satisfaction can be done with noncelebrity advertisement, and the benefit of using a celebrity endorsement is making better choice among the different destinations and better product recognition.

- Another implication made from the chapter was that as the students' community were more attracted toward celebrity destination endorsements, any destination having educational benefits or fun type views/experiences such as water theme parks, and so on, the advertisement would be more impactful if done by a celebrity.
- It is suggested that celebrities who have multiple endorsements (two or more products) is not much preferred by the customers as they feel the overall credibility of the celebrity is lost.
- After a detailed study of Swatch Bharath, it was found that the celebrity advertising strategy has helped to increase the gross domestic product rate and the foreign exchange rate. Here the strategy was a bit trickier, in which celebrities were involved with no cost as it was for a social cause but the publicity boosted up as more than six celebrities were involved.
- One major inference is that the use of a celebrity during advertising of a product does not necessarily lead to a positive in the decision-making; however, the use of a celebrity does help the respondents to notice the advertisement and also gives a glamorous effect to the advertisements.
- With the literature review, it can also be concluded that celebrity endorsement can be either used for a new product or for a mature product so that the destinations can differentiate from that of its competitors.
- The study also concludes that celebrities with a good image in the public will be able to boost the acceptance of the product among the customers and helps the customers to easily recall and remember the advertisement.

13.14 CONCLUSION

Celebrity endorsers are used by advertisers to differentiate and position their products or services from their competitors. It has become a trend nowadays to rope with a celebrity endorser and endorse their place and differentiate the destination from that of their competitors and to create direct awareness of their product by showcasing their own unique selling propositions. This study helps one to understand the response of tourists in Bangalore toward celebrity endorsement and to explore the effect of celebrity endorsers on them. The research results suggest that celebrity endorsement helps to bring in awareness about the destination, recognize the place, and helps one to recall by creating an association with the celebrity. Thus, it should be understood that celebrity endorsement helps one to create awareness but need not directly translate the awareness to visiting the destination or building a liking to the destination. Celebrity endorsement as found in the study may help the consumer to filter choices from the too many destinations he has in mind to visit. Billions of money is spent when celebrities are used. So it is very important for the marketers to choose the right celebrity and to use these celebrities in the right way. One major finding from the research is that a combination of celebrities, the unique attributes of the destination and with some experienced tourists would help in translating the awareness to visiting the destination.

KEYWORDS

- celebrity endorsement
- tourism destination advertisements
- expertise
- trustworthiness
- similarity
- familiarity
- likeability
- match between the celebrity
- transfer meaning
- physical attractiveness

REFERENCES

Ahmed, A.; Mir, F. A.; Farooq, O. Effect of Celebrity Endorsement on Customers' Buying Behavior; a Perspective from Pakistan. *Interdiscip. J. Contemp. Res. Bus.* **2012**, *4*(5), 584–592. http://search.proquest.com/docview/1115314157?accountid=38885.

Amos, C.; Holmes, G.; Strutton, D. Exploring the Relationship Between Celebrity Endorser Effects and Advertising Effectiveness. *Int. J. Advertising* **2008**, *27*(2), 209–234. http:// hull.aug.edu/thoughtleadership/research/Amos Holmes Strutton-IJA-2008.pdf.

Dimed, C.; Joulyana, S. *Celebrity Endorsement-Hidden Factors to Success;* Jonkoping University: Sweden, 2005. http://hj.divaportal. org/smash/get/diva2:3943/FULL-TEXT01.pdf.

Erdon, Z. Celebrity Endorsement: A Literature Review. *J. Mark. Manage.* **1999**, *15,* 291–314. https://desn310.wikispaces.com/file/view/CelebrityEndrosementModels_01. pdf.

Glover, P. Celebrity Endorsement in Tourism Advertising: Effects on Destination Image. *J. Hospitality Tourism Manage.* **2009**, *16*(1), 16–23. http://www.freepatentsonline.com/ article/Journal-Hospitality-Tourism-Management/229992198.html.

Hoekman, M. *Celebrity Endorsement;* Tilburg University: Netherlands. 2013. http://arno. uvt.nl/show.cgi?fid=115680.

Ibok.; Ibok, N. Factors Determining the Effectiveness of Celebrity Endorsed Advertisements: The Case of Nigerian Telecommunication Industry. *Am. J. Bus. Manage.* **2013**, *2*(3), 233–238.

Kumar, A. *Celebrity Endorsement and its Impact on Consumer Buying Behavior.* Bournemouth University, 2010. http://ssrn.com/abstract=1802531.

Malik, A.; Sudhakar, B. Brand Positioning Through Celebrity Endorsement-A Review Contribution to Brand Literature. *Int. Rev. Manage. Mark.* **2014**, *4*(4), 259–275. http:// www.econjournals.com/index.php/irmm/article/viewFile/946/pdf.

Mehta, A. Celebrities in Advertising. In *The Advertising Business: Operations Creativity Media Planning Integrated Communications;* Jones, J., Ed.; SAGE Publications, Inc.: New York, 1999; 193–209.

Norman, S.; Pettersen, M. A Qualitative Study Investigating Australian Tourism Companies' Promotional Efforts on the Japanese Market. Master Dissertation, FEK, 2008, 61–80. www.diva portal.org/smash/get/diva2:238334/FULLTEXT01.

Pandey, V. Impact of Celebrity Endorsement on Young Generation Through TV Advertisement. *VSRD-IJBMR,* **2011**, *1*(4), 226–231. http://www.vsrdjournals.com/MBA/ Issue/2011_6_June/3_Vivek_Kr_Pandey_Researc h_Article_June_2011.

Ranjbarian, B.; Shekarchizade, Z.; Momeni, Z. Celebrity Endorser Influence on Attitude Toward Advertisements and Brands. *Eur. J. Soc. Sci.* **2010**, *13*(3), 399–407.

Rashid, Z.; Nallamuthu, J.; Sidin, S. Perceptions of Advertising and Celebrity Endorsement in Malaysia. *Asia Pac. Manage. Rev.* **2002**, *7*(4), 535–554. http://apmr.management.ncku.edu.tw/comm/updown/DW0904302290.pdf.

Reid, R. D.; Bojanic, D. C. *Hospitality Marketing Management;* John Wiley and Sons, INC.: New Jersey, NJ, 2009. http://books.google.co.in.

Shimp, T. *Advertising, Promotion, and Other Aspects of Integrated Marketing Communications;* South-Western, Cengage Learning: South Calafornia, CA, 2010. http://abufara.

com/abufara.net/images/abook_file/Advertising,%20Promotion,%20and%20other%20
aspects%20of%20%20Integrated%20Marketing%20Communications-Terence%20A.
Shimp-2010.pdf.

Thomas, J. Advertising Effectiveness. Decision Analyst, Inc. 2008. http://www.decision-
analyst.com/publ_art/adeffectiveness.dai.

Van, d. V. Celebrity Endorsement Effectiveness for Print Destination Advertising. *Eur. J.
Tourism Res.* 2009, *2*(2), 186–189.

Waldt, V. D.; Loggerenberg, M. V.; Wehmeyer, L. Celebrity Endorsements Versus Created
Spokespersons in Advertising: A Survey Among Students. *South Afr. J. Econ. Manage.
Sci.* **2009**, *12*(1), 100–114.

Yannopoulos, P. Celebrity Advertising: Literature Review and Propositions. *World Rev.
Bus. Res.* **2012**, *2*(4), 24–36.

Zafar, Q. Impact of Celebrity Advertisement on Customers' Brand Perception and Purchase
Intention. *Asian J. Bus. Manage. Sci.* n.d., *1*(11), 53–67. www.ajbms.org.

CHAPTER 14

TALENT DEVELOPMENT IN THE TOURISM INDUSTRY: A DELIBERATION ON THE OPEN SOURCE TALENT IN GOA, INDIA

CHERYL POORNIMA SMITH E VENAN DIAS[1] and
VENAN BONAVENTURE DIAS[2]

[1]Assistant Professor, S.S. Dempo College of Commerce and
Economics, Goa, India

[2]Founder, Antonios Services, Goa, India

CONTENTS

ABSTRACT

Current chapter defines, examines, and explores the constructs of talent development (TD) in the tourism industry. TD mostly connects with an availability of open source talent that is obtainable in form of graduates who possess a certain level of inbuilt talent. The models developed over a period of time are critically examined to identify any research gaps. This chapter attempts to address research questions associated with the important constituents of TD, external influxes, and facilitators associated with TD, activities to be undertaken by the support systems to promote and position the TD internationally and interventions taken up by the Indian Government toward TD. The first part of the chapter explains the generalized management models of TD, the second part of this paper focuses on TD with a special emphasis on open source TD in tourism. The chapter also explores the various dimensions in which TD has become a reality starting with cultural tourism, intrinsic development, and development programs by institutions, globalization, environmental factors, international institutional approach, and steps taken by Indian government towards TD in tourism.

14.1   INTRODUCTION

"Talent is the innate ability, aptitude, or faculty, especially when unspecified; above average ability" (The Collins English Dictionary, 2015). Talent development (TD) has been extensively studied and a part of research and theory building since the early 1980s. The construct was fairly novel at that time because it was studied in comparison to the century-old myth that talents would develop without any efforts spontaneously (Chan, 2010). Thus, embedding itself deep in the aspects of pedagogy, inviting curiosity from various child psychologists including Dr. Howard Gardner who gave the concept of multiple bits of intelligence. It may be termed natural or nurtured, in which intrinsic and extrinsic influences are observed (Ceci and Williams, 1999). To provide further clarity (Gagne, 2007) differentiates that talent translates to systematically developed skills, whereas gifts are natural abilities. Chambers et al. (1998) indicated that the construct TD has not received much attention that it deserves. TD to be successful, and earn its rightful role in organizations, needs to be considered a separate entity that complements talent management, rather than embedded in talent management (Manikoth, 2010). Often this construct is loosely associated with talent management that is more of a strategic human resource concept, whereas it has to be studied as a unique construct, because it lies at the boundary when an individual makes entry into an organization due to the talent he already possesses, it may be effected through facilitators and could be intrinsically present.

As defined by Garavan et al. (2011), TD focuses on the planning, selection, and implementation of development strategies for the entire talent pool to ensure that the organization has both the current and future supply of talent to meet strategic objectives and that development activities are aligned with organizational talent management processes. This definition is a little narrow in approach as it considers existing talent pool. The individual's self-development activities are completely ignored. The definition is oriented toward strategic goals of the organization. Gilbert et al. (2001) identified eight common TD elements as commitment, confidence, desire, focused connection, genetics, ongoing learning, opportunity, and support systems. Ceci and Williams (1999) debated about the genetic attributes or nature versus the environmental factors or nurture and their contribution to the development of talent.

Somewhere there has to be a blend of the two if talent was predominantly natural or genetically determined, then the facilitators can do very little to develop talent. By birth, important talent elements may be present in an individual, namely personality and intelligence (Cohen, 1999). If we consider the premise that talent is developed by nurturing the abilities, acquiring expertise, and pursuing excellence, then the facilitators will be critical to the development of talent (Bloom, 1985; Ericsson, 1996).

14.2 RESEARCH METHODOLOGY

The current research was undertaken with an objective to describe the role of TD and thereby, to support substantially, a descriptive study was executed on 447 students from various vocational schools and colleges. The sample was widespread on vocational to postgraduate students from Goa and from varying disciplines. The objectives of the descriptive research discussed in the chapter deal with the tourism-based influencers of TD through literature review. To conceptualize either side of the coin, there has been an initiative to examine the intrinsic and extrinsic factors of TD. The attempt also is laid to profile the potential tourism–based open source talent available in Goa. The methodology in research employs mechanisms to determine the awareness of a course influences individuals to work in the tourism industry and thereby, to determine if there is a significant difference between vocational students and graduates in the perception to supplement their studies with a professional course.

14.2.1   RESEARCH GAP

Lacuna of awareness of sustainable TD opportunities and support systems for open source talent in Goa is the major reason for the youth not to choose careers in the tourism industry. Hence the research question addresses the support systems that create an opportunity to develop sustainable open-source tourism based talent pool in Goa. An individual develops his skill sets by joining formal education and also through certification courses. The human resource development process starts way before the candidate joins an organization. This TD is undertaken by the individual through the support of family, through scholarships, supporting government inter-ventions, while working in a different role or also while pursuing formal education. However, the lack of awareness that any discipline taken for studies can be a part of tourism industry can cause many youths to miss out on the opportunities that they have available as an open source talent. This chapter explores all the factors that contribute toward the intrinsic development and extrinsic support through policies, scholarships, and initiatives, locally and globally.

14.3   SKILLS AS AN INTEGRAL PART OF TALENT

Is there a relationship between skills and talent? If talent is based on ability, we need to question if skills are also part of talent. Natural talent is the inherent talent owned by an individual (Brady et al., 2008). Frymire (2006) specified that hiring individuals with the brainpower (both natural and trained) and especially the ability to think creatively was the greatest challenge rather than finding or hiring cheap workers. Creativity cannot be suggested in instruction or taught during training, whereas it is possible to narrate instances of creativity to individuals during a classroom session and application of this creativity in a real-life situation or a job situation can lead to the ability to use the skill.

The public policy governs the manner in which skills are developed in a country especially through training this is also a high skill employment business environment (Brown et al., 2001). A 2005 survey in India demonstrates that being fluent in English, a business language, increased men's hourly wages by 34% relative to those who speak no English, as high as the return to completing secondary school and half the return to completing an undergraduate degree. Being able to speak a little English raised wages by 13% (Azam et al., 2010). Learning is however not a talent whereas executing the learning can be termed talent substantiating this claim; we can say that sustaining skills after acquiring the skills are important. The Society of Corporate Meeting Professionals was founded over 30 years ago to serve as a vehicle for corporate meeting professionals to interact with their peers, to gain advanced knowledge, and to develop enhanced professional skills. This unique partnership among the membership of corporate planners, hotel/convention center/service professionals, independent planners, and students provides an atmosphere to achieve a high level of professional excellence.

14.3.1   TALENT DEVELOPMENT THROUGH CULTURAL TOURISM

Cultural elements by Goeldner and Ritchie (2012) in tourism are developed through special activities. Infrastructure used namely theaters, libraries, museums, and other national institutions might not be created with tourism in mind; however, they have the ability to attract tourist. Museums and monuments are important features of a tourist's itinerary. At times specialized knowledge has to be acquired to explain such tourism products to tourists, expert knowledge, information, and ideas can be acquired from abroad. There could be a need to introduce special courses, not only for the locals but also for foreigners. Guides should have language skills, and information should be technologically available as well as through local people. Education plays an important role in "rescue" efforts of traditional skills that are used to produce authentic products. An example is of Fred Harvey founder of Fred Harvey Company; he was instrumental in encouraging Indians to continue attractive crafts, which were marketed by him in his hotels, restaurants, and gift shops. Tourism experiences can be created by offering services that require skills and level of education.

Traditional TD was done in isolation from the workplace; processes such as training are extremely effective at imparting technical competencies (Lahti, 1999; Hirsh, 2009). The term "generic competencies" emphasizes a range of qualities and capabilities that are important in the workplace. Skills included are problem-solving and analytical skills, communication skills, teamwork competencies and skills to identify access and manage knowledge. Generic competencies also include personal attributes such as imagination, creativity, and intellectual rigor and personal values such as persistence, integrity, and tolerance (Garavan et al., 2009; Sandberg, 2000).

14.3.2   PROGRAMS TO ENABLE TALENT DEVELOPMENT

The four categories of programs that can enable TD are formal programs, relationship-based developmental experiences, job-based developmental experiences, and Informal/nonformal developmental activities (Conger, 2010; McCall et al., 1988; Byham et al., 2002; Garavan et al., 2009). Other schools of thought have suggested a 70:20:10 strategy in which 70% of TD takes place through work activities; 20% through relationships and 10% through formal development activities (Wilson et al., 2011). Formal TD programs cover a broad spectrum of strategies including conceptual and skill-based development programs, personal growth development programs, feedback-based development interventions, and action focused development interventions (Conger, 2010).

14.3.3   GLOBALIZATION AND TALENT DEVELOPMENT

Frank and Taylor (2004) indicated that the challenge to TD is the increasingly complex and ever-changing economic landscape. Although Fernandez-Araoz (2007) credited globalization as a factor for multinationals to pursue talent from anywhere in the world, to that matter they have expanded their talent base outside their current headquarters. With globalization set in, it is also essential to develop a global mindset (Marquardt and Berger, 2003). The question remains whether the international certification that offers career development be also implied to TD? Does it actually nurture talent that is available in its raw form? Lewis and Heckman (2006) criticize the concept of TD as it is neither strategic in its approach to develop the inherent talent, nor there is clarity on the resources required to uncover this talent. Contrastively Ashton and Morton (2005) support the concept that everyone has the potential to develop their talent, and impress that it can be measured and managed. They were also of the opinion that talent strikes a balance between performance of not only the present but also the past. They also link it to the future as it has got a scope for being identified and developed.

14.3.4 ENVIRONMENTAL FACTORS THAT FACILITATE TALENT DEVELOPMENT

It is critical to evaluate the role of government in facilitating TD through its various policy measures. The proper role is considered to be both a catalyst and a challenge for innovation (Gathungu and Mwangi, 2012). Turbulent environment gives a competitive advantage and a dynamic capability to renew competencies to be attuned to the changing environment (Teece et al., 1997; Teece, 2007). Speaking about the severe shortage of talent in the travel and tourism industry, Scowsill (2015) stressed the need for a stronger coordinated effort between the private sector, educational establishments, and government.

14.3.5 INTERNATIONAL INSTITUTIONAL INTERVENTION TOWARDS TALENT DEVELOPMENT

World Travel and Tourism Council (2015) suggests that companies and government need to implement and promote proactive talent supply management policies together with education. They need to develop stronger and coordinated talent efforts. Australia Government (2012) identified that labor and skills are a crucial component in the tourism supply chain. Enhancing the quality of service is pivotal in building a region's reputation, both domestically and globally, and making it competitive in the international marketplace. It ensures that once tourists visit your destination, they will want to return and bring others with them. Developing more tourism infrastructure; hotels, resorts, transportation, tourist destinations, and other amenities is not enough to meet the needs of this rapidly expanding industry in China. The government and private enterprises must invest in tourism and hospitality education to fill the critical gap in workers who understand international best practices. China has invested billions of dollars in infrastructure but now is the time to invest in human resources and skills development. It is also observed that governments who have succeeded in aligning the skills to productivity, employment, and development were successful as they were able to match the demand to supply of skills, encouraged both enterprise and workers to adapt to change, and also built and sustained competencies for future labor market needs (ILO, 2010). Singapore: Training Industry Professional in Tourism Scheme to support companies in employee upgrading and TD. National Association of Travel Agents Singapore (NATAS) accreditation aimed at encouraging tourism professionals to upgrade skill sets through certified courses.

14.3.6   TALENT DEVELOPMENT IN THE INDIAN TOURISM SCENARIO

Skills can be developed on the basis of talent that an individual possesses. India noticed that a significant number of workers were employed with low levels of productivity and income. The challenges faced were high dropout rates, lack of formal education, and also shortage of teaching faculty. To deal with these challenges, India adopted an ambitious National Skills Development, Policy in 2009. Its main aim, in the words of the Union Minister of Labour and Employment, is to empower all individuals through improved skills, knowledge, and internationally recognized qualifications to give them access to decent employment and to promote inclusive national growth. It was envisaged, among other things, to increase vocational training capacity to 15 million students over the 11th Five Year Plan period (2007–2012). Though the planning commission has now been abolished, the present government also has initiated skill building initiatives after the World Youth Skills day observed all over the country on July 15, 2015 (ILO, 2010). Gujarat has intervened in training and skill development for employees engaged in providing tourism services through 335 Kaushalya Vardhan Kendras providing vocational skills to rural youth in various sectors including tourism. Technical skills and soft skills development initiatives were undertaken for ticketing staff and tour guides under this scheme. KPMG (2013) suggested that a provision of additional training institutes to be made, thereby enhancing capacity of existing ones along with introduction of short-term courses providing specific skills directed at hospitality and travel trade sector employees may be required.

14.3.7 INTRINSIC FACTORS DRIVING TALENT DEVELOPMENT

It is increasingly recognized that employees are responsible for managing their own development to prepare themselves for future career and job changes (Simmering et al., 2003). Accelerated TD programs focus on ensuring that talent is competent to perform, and there is a strong emphasis on accelerating the learning curve. Such programs are premised on a highly motivated learner; ongoing intensive training, extensive use of simulation tools, structured projects, and experiences to drive learning and self-managed development processes. Critical objectives that drive accelerated development include the enhancement of knowledge and skills (Lombardo and Eichinger, 2000). Garavan et al. (2011) have identified the major gap in their understanding of individual characteristics that facilitate self-directed learning, the nature of self-development behavior and the influence of group and organizational factors that facilitate self-development in the context of TD. Smith-Dias et al. (2016) suggested that if an organization still follows traditional HR excellence and tries to implement the emerging sustainability aspect, they may consider the Open Source Talent to some extent. Low cost may be involved; however, they do not make any investment in such talent.

Individuals of varying talent types interact with the organizations in which balance-sheet employees are the ones on whom the organization may have a higher degree of control, than the Open Source talent on whom the organization may have a lower degree of control, whereas the level of control reverses when the individual tries to develop their talent as indicated in Figure 14.1. The TD focus of both individual and organization is different in comparison.

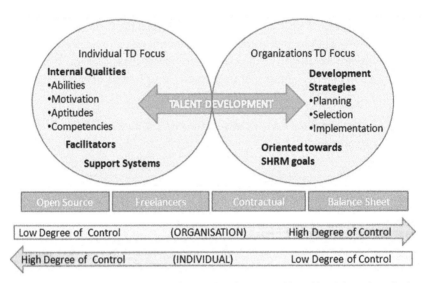

FIGURE 14.1 A conceptual view of talent development: either side of the coin and talent development the individual and organization perspective.
Source: Authors.

In Table 14.1, profiles of the students are based on gender, age, and family status; the discipline of study starts from 12th to postgraduation levels, whereas the last row denotes the family income group of the students. The research postulated a certain hypothesis and a detailed statistical investigation portray the research testing of the hypothesis. H_{al}: The awareness of a tourism-based professional course does influence the open source talent to take up a career in the tourism industry (Table 14.2).

TABLE 14.1 Data Analysis of Tourism-Based Open Source Talent in Goa.

		Frequency of respondents			Percentage
		Male $n=133$	Female $n=314$	Total $n=447$	100
Age	<15	8	5	13	2.90
	15–20	64	203	267	59.73
	20–25	59	100	159	35.57
	25–30	0	2	2	0.44
	30–35	2	1	3	0.67
	>35	0	1	1	0.22

TABLE 14.1 *(Continued)*

		Frequency of respondents			Percentage
		Male ***n*=133**	**Female** ***n*=314**	**Total** ***n*=447**	**100**
Family status	Single	117	305	422	94.40
	Married	7	8	15	3.35
	Others	9	1	10	2.23
Education	10th standard	23	4	27	6.04
	12th standard	33	114	147	32.88
	Graduate	65	182	247	55.25
	Vocational	3	1	4	0.89
	Post graduate	9	13	22	4.92
Discipline in 12th Std.	Vocational general	26	1	22	4.92
	Commerce	59	164	223	49.88
	Science	1	3	4	0.89
	Arts	45	143	188	42.05
	Vocational T&T	2	3	5	1.11
Discipline in graduation	N/A	38	39	77	17.22
	B.Com.	41	124	165	36.91
	B.B.A. specialization	3	5	8	1.78
	B.A.	51	146	197	44.07
PG discipline	N/A	113	291	404	90.38
	M.B.A.	2	4	6	1.34
	M.Com.	13	10	23	5.14
	M.A.	3	7	10	2.23
	PGDBA	2	1	3	0.67
	MTM	0	1	1	0.22
Family income	50k–1 lakh	86	236	322	72.03
	1 lakh–3 lakhs	32	58	90	20.13
	3 lakhs–5 lakhs	6	9	15	3.35
	>5 lakhs	9	11	20	4.47

TABLE 14.2 Awareness of a Tourism-Based Professional Course and Choice of a Career in the Tourism Industry.

		Do you want to make a career in the tourism industry?		Total
		Yes	No	
Are you aware of International Air Transport Association course?	Yes	85	54	139
	No	72	236	308
Total		157	290	447

The chi-square statistic with a value 59.9752, in which the result is highly significant at $p < 0.05$, and thereby, the investigation proves the awareness of a tourism-based professional course does influence the open source talent to take up a career in the tourism industry. Hence, the alternative hypothesis is accepted. H_{a2}: There is a significant difference in the perception of vocational and graduate students with regards to supplementing studies with a professional tourism-based course (Table 14.3).

TABLE 14.3 Cross Tabulation: By Type and Perception. Importance to supplement education with a professional course? (*Source:* Authors, 2016.)

		Is it important to supplement education with a professional course?		Total
		Yes	No	
Type	Vocational	0	27	27
	Beyond vocational	324	96	420
Total		324	123	447

The chi-square statistic with a value 75.6941, in which the result is highly significant at $p < 0.05$, and thereby, the investigation proves the significant differences in the perception of vocational and graduate students with regards to supplementing studies with a professional tourism–based course. Hence, the alternative hypothesis is accepted.

14.4 CHALLENGES AND SHORTAGE OF DEVELOPED TALENT IN TOURISM

Speaking of talent pool, it is very difficult to find a right fit many times. The demand for talent may surpass the supply. WTTC (2015) has indicated some economy-wide reasons for talent shortages: according to the Manpower Group talent shortage survey. The main reasons employers had difficulty filling jobs in 2014 include are as follows: (in descending order) lack of technical competence (hard skills), lack of applicants, lack of experience, lack of workplace competence (soft skills), looking for more pay than is offered, undesirable geographic destination, poor image of business sector/occupation and lack of applicants willing to work in part-time/contingent roles. It is clear that many of these reasons correlate closely with the factors identified specifically for travel and tourism.

14.5 FINDINGS AND DISCUSSION

The current chapter with a critical evaluation and assessment brought into light the imperative need for the tourism TD process and has been understood with the statistical evaluation that very little has been done in terms of tourism TD process integrating some of the cultural tourism aspects. WTTC's initiatives are sustained to identify challenges in the industry, even though tourism is the largest export earner in the world and has a multidisciplinary approach. A study conducted on students of various disciplines in Goa revealed that awareness of the professional course in the tourism industry will influence them to take up a career in the tourism industry, whereas there was a significant difference in the perception of only vocational and beyond vocational course students about supplementing their education with a professional tourism-based course. A further study on what motivates the young students to develop their talent in the tourism industry is also suggested.

14.6 CONCLUSION

After examining the literature on TD, it is evident that one school of thought defines it in terms of natural ability that gets translated into developed competencies and skills by the intervention of facilitators, by support systems as in educational institutions, through governments and international institutions. Open-source talent is largely available and should be explored; however, it requires some amount of trust from the organization that hires such talent. However, tourism is not confined only to four walls of an agency; it can transcend culturally into museums, heritage homes, and art galleries. Talented people are required to run such tourist hotspots; for such purposes, open source talent will be a suitable option.

KEYWORDS

- talent development
- strategic human resource management
- talent development models
- talent management
- open source TD in tourism

REFERENCES

Ashton, C.; Morton, L. Managing Talent for Competitive Advantage: Taking a Systemic Approach to Talent Management. *Strategic HR Rev.* **2005**, *4*(5), 28–31.

Auguste, B.; Kihn.; Miller, M. Closing the Talent Gap: Attracting and Retaining Top-third Graduates to Careers in Teaching. McKinsey and Company: New York, NY, 2010. http://mckinseyonsociety.com/downloads/reports/Education/Closing_the_talent_gap.pdf.

Australia Government. Tackling Labor and Skills Issues in the Tourism and Hospitality Industry. And the hospitality talent gap, China Business Review, 2012.

Azam, M.; Chin, A.; Prakash, N. The Returns to English Language Skills in India. Institute for the Study of Labor (IZA) Discussion Paper 4802. Bonn, 2010.

Bloom, B. *Developing Talent in Young People;* Ballantine: New York, 1985.

Baum, T. Skills and Training for the Hospitality Sector: A Review of Issues. *J. Vocational Educ. Train.* **2002,** *54*(3), 343–364. DOI: 10.1080/13636820200200204.

Brady, C.; Bolchover, D.; Sturgess, B. Managing in the Talent Economy: The Football Model for Business. *BerkeleyHaas* **2008**, *50/4*(Summer 2008), 54–73.

Brown, P.; Green, A.; Lauder, H. *High Skills. Globalization, Competitiveness and Skill Formation;* Oxford University Press: Oxford, 2001.

Byham, W. C.; Smith, A. B.; Paese, M. J. *Grow Your Own Leaders: How to Identify, Develop, and Retain Leadership Talent;* Development Dimensions International and Prentice Hall: Upper Saddle River, NJ, 2002.

Ceci, J. C.; Williams, W. M.; Eds. *The Nature-nurture Debate: The Essential Readings.* Blackwell: Malden, MA, 1999.

Chambers, E. G.; Foulton, M.; Hanfield-Jones, H.; Hankin, S. M.; Michaels III, E. G. The War for Talent. *McKinsey Q.* **1998**, *3,* 44–57.

Chan, D. W. Talent Development from a Positive Psychology Perspective. *Educ. Res. J.* **2010**, *25*(1).

Cohen, D. B. *Stranger in the Nest: Do Parents Really Shape their Child's Personality, Intelligence, or Character?* John Wiley and Sons: New York, 1999.

Collins Dictionary. Meaning of the Word Talent. 2015. http://www.collinsdictionary.com/dictionary/english/talent.

Conger, J. A. "Developing Leadership Talent: Delivering on the Promise of Structured Programs", In *Strategy-Driven Talent Management;* Sitzer, R., Dowell, B. E., Eds.; Jossey-Bass: San Francisco, CA, 2010; pp 281–312.

Dakhli, M.; de Clercq, D. Human Capital, Social Capital, and Innovation: A Multi-country Study. In *Entrepreneurship and Regional Development 16;* Employment Studies: Brighton, 2004; pp 107–128.

Ericsson, K. A.; Ed. *The Road to Excellence: The Acquisition of Expert Performance in the Arts and Sciences, Sports and Games;* Lawrence Erlbaum: Mahwah, NJ, 1996.

Fernández-Aráoz, C. Making People Decisions in the New Global Environment. *MIT Sloan Manage. Rev.* **2007**, *49*(1), 17–20.

Frank, F. D.; Taylor, C. R. Talent Management: Trends that will Shape the Future. *Hum. Resour. Plann.* **2004**, *27*(1), 33–41.

Frymire, B. The Search for Talent; Business and Society. The Economist, 8498, 11. (2006, October 7).

Gagne, F. From Gifts to Talents: The DMGT as a Developmental Model. In *Conceptions of Giftedness,* 2nd Ed.; Sternberg, R. J., Davidson, J. E., Eds.; Cambridge University Press: New York, NY, 2005; pp 98–119.

Gagne, F. Ten Commandments for Academic Talent Development. *Gifted Child Quarterly* **2007**, *51,* 93, Sage Publications, 2009. DOI: 10.1177/0016986206296660.

Garavan, T. N.; Hogan, C.; Cahir-O'Donnell, A. *Developing Managers and Leaders: Perspectives, Debates, and Practices in Ireland;* Gill and Macmillan: Dublin, 2009.

Garavan, T. N.; Carbery, R.; Rock, A. Mapping Talent Development: Definition, Scope, and Architecture. 2011. http://www.emeraldinsight.com/2046-9012.htm.

Gathungu, J. M.; Mwangi, J. K. Dynamic Capabilities, Talent Development and Firm Performance. *DBA Afr. Manage. Rev.* **2012**, *2*(3), 5.

Gilbert, W.; Akers, J.; Barton, D.; Beati, B.; Blancfield, J.; Campbell, C.; Conway, M.; Creighton, K.; Curran, R.; Davis, J.; Flores, I.; Johnson, A.; Johnson, M.; King, C.; Marchbanks, G.; McGee, M.; Moore, K.; O'Sullivan, K.; Pagsanjan, R.; Powell, M.; Sholiton, M.; Vela, M.; Walton, T.; Zuk, I. Elements of Talent Development Across Domains. *J. Excellence* **2001**, *5,* 63.

Goeldner, C. R.; Ritchie, J. R. B. Tourism Principles, Practices, Philosophies, 12th Ed.; John Wiley and Sons, Inc.: Hoboken, New Jersey, 2012, pp 216–398.

Hirsh, W. Talent Management: Practical Issues in Implementation, Institute for 2009.

ILO. A skilled workforce for strong, sustainable, and balanced growth: A G20 training strategy, 2010.

Kemple, J. J.; Herlihy, M. C.; Smith, J. T. Making Progress Toward Graduation. Evidence from the Talent Development High School Model. 2005, p 29.

Lahti, R. K. "Identifying and Integrating Individual Level and Organizational Level Core Competencies." *J. Bus. Psychol.* **1999**, *14*(1), 59–75.

Lewis, R. E.; Heckman, R. J. Talent Management: A Critical Review. *Hum. Resour. Manage. Rev.* **2006**, *16*, 139–154.

Lombardo, M. M.; Eichinger, R. W. "High Potentials as High Learners." *Hum. Resour. Manage.* **2000**, *39*(4), 321–330.

Lynch, D. Can Higher Education Manage Talent? Inside Higher ED. 2007. https://www.insidehighered.com/views/2007/11/27/lynch.

Manikoth, N. N. *Talent Development in the New Economy;* The George Washington University: USA, 2010.

Manpower Group. Talent Shortage Survey Results, 2014. http://www.manpowergroup.co.uk/media/137404/2014_talent_shortage_wp_us2.pdf.

Marquardt, M.; Berger, N. O. The Future: Globalization and New Roles for HRD. *Adv. Dev. Hum. Resour.* **2003**, *5*(3), 283.

McCall, M.; Lombardo, M.; Morrison, M. *The Lessons of Experience: How Successful Executives Develop on the Job;* Lexington Books: Lexington, MA, 1988.

OECD. OECD Skills Outlook 2013: First Results from the Survey of Adult Skills, OECD Publishing, 2013, DOI: 10.1787/9789264204256-en.

Patterson, F.; Kerrin, M.; Gatto-Roissard, G. *Characteristics and Behaviours of Innovative People in Organizations;* City University: London, 2009.

Sandberg, J. "Understanding Human Competence at Work: An Interpretative Approach." *Acad. Manage. J.* **2000**, *43*(1), 9–25.

Scowsill, D. Global Talent Trends and Issues for the Travel and Tourism Sector. Oxford Economics for the World Travel and Tourism Council, 2015.

Simmering, M. J.; Colquitt, J. A.; Noe, R. A.; Porter, C. "Conscientiousness, Autonomy Fit, and Employee Development: A Longitudinal Field Study." *J. Appl. Psychol.* **2003**, *88*(5), 954–963.

Smith-Dias, C. P. V.; Radha, P.; Dias, V. B. Emerging Trends in the Talent Economy: A Special Emphasis on Talent Development and Talent Management. *Anushandhan Interdiscip. Res. J.* **2016**, *6*(1), 73–78.

Sondergaard, L.; Murthi, M. *Skills, Not Just Diplomas: Managing Education Results in Eastern Europe and Central Asia.* The World Bank: Washington, DC, 2012.

Subotnik, R. F.; Jarvin, L. Beyond Expertise: Conceptions of Giftedness as Great Performance. In *Conceptions of Giftedness,* 2nd ed.; Sternberg, R. J., Davidson, J. E., Eds.; Cambridge University Press: New York, NY, 2005; pp 343–357.

Tannenbaum, A. J. Giftedness: A Psychosocial Approach. In *Conceptions of Giftedness;* Sternberg, R. J., Davidson, J. E., Eds.; Cambridge University Press: New York, NY, 1986; pp 21–52.

Teece, D. J. "Explicating Dynamic Capabilities: The Nature and Micro Foundations of Sustainable Enterprise Performance." *Strategic Manage. J.* **2007**, *28*(13), 1319–1350.

Teece, D. J.; Pisano, G.; Shuen, A. "Dynamic Capabilities and Strategic Management." *Strategic Manage. J.* **1997**, *18*(7), 509–533.

The World Economic Forum, cited in The Hospitality Talent Gap, China Business Review, n.d. http://www.chinabusinessreview.com/the-hospitality-talentgap/.

Wilson, M. S.; Van Velsor, E. A New Terrain of Leadership Development: An Indian Perspective. In *Towards the Next Orbit: Corporate Odyssey;* Verma, S. Ed.; Sage: Delhi, 2011.

WTTC. Global Talent Trends and Issues for the Travel and Tourism Sector. Oxford Economics for the World Travel and Tourism Council, 2015.

CHAPTER 15

ROLE OF TOURISM EDUCATION IN MEETING THE COMPETENCY EXPECTATIONS OF THE TOURISM INDUSTRY IN INDIA

NAGARJUNA G.

Department of Travel and Tourism, Mount Carmel College, Bangalore, India

CONTENTS

ABSTRACT

Education is one of the strongest foundations, which enables an individual to develop his competency and skills. Education also helps in making a positive contribution toward the creation of wealth and quality of life. An educational institution that transforms the life of the individual and also makes him contribute for the welfare of the society and organization he or she works for. An education institution also needs to adapt to the changing pace of the economy that will meet the workplace skills and knowledge requirements. The organization looks for those candidates who can contribute to the growth and development of the organization through his or her ability and skills. Education institution has to develop skills and abilities among the students that meet the competency expectations of the organization. The tourism industry is also called as people-oriented industry depends on the skilled human resources. An individual with necessary tourism knowledge, skills, and abilities makes a huge difference in terms of growth and development of tourism sector. Tourism education can play a major role by providing quality human resources that meet the competency requirements of the industry. It is the responsibility of the tourism education to imbibe necessary skills and abilities among students that will help not only the growth of individual but also the development of tourism sector as it depends on quality human resources. The main objective of the study is to understand that what skills and abilities are needed to be developed by students that will meet the competency expectations of the industry. The study is conceptual in nature. This study is mainly based on the review of various literatures on tourism industry expectation on competencies. The study is conceptual in nature. The study also suggests tourism education incorporate necessary skills and abilities in curriculum and extra curriculum that will meet the necessary competency requirements of the industry.

15.1   INTRODUCTION

Tourism education can be dated back to the 1960s when key changes started to take place in the field of tourism education. In the year 1960, tourism developed as a distinct discipline and offered subjects for study as a diploma course, degree course and also for research. Tourism education emerged in four stages of development. They are industrial, fragmented, benchmark and mature stage. During the industrial stage, tourism programs concentrated on vocation and content, and it was mainly dominated by economists. Tourism programs were designed as per the need of tourism sector. In this stage, there is a close link with the industry and its employers. Degree programs were focused on the practice and operation of the industry. The growth of tourism as an activity and the popularity of vocational education programs influenced and encouraged the educationists to launch tourism programs. The main aim of the tourism programs was to provide skilled human resources for the tourism sector. The curriculum is highly uncertain in its fragmented form that has led to tourism education to become a subject for debate. Subjects from other disciplines also started to make their mark on tourism. There are debates and uncertainty about the content of the tourism curriculum, and this stage was called as a fragmented stage. In the United Kingdom (UK), an effort was made to consider the fundamental contents of subjects for degree level studies, including tourism. A broad codification was developed to consider what to study in tourism, and it was generally related to J. Jafari's 'knowledge platform'. But so far it has not been able to achieve a universal agreement about the curriculum. This period was called as 'Benchmark Stage' (Airey, 2008).

The development of tourism education started with a growing field of practice and debates about the curriculum that reflects the preoccupations of those writing about tourism education featured by uncertainties about how much provision, that is, what is the balance between practice and theory, and about the overall curriculum. In that case, tourism education can be considered as immature. However, there has been a drastic improvement in tourism education by correlating new inquiries with the existing inquiries and engaging in debates and self-criticism. This shows that tourism education is moving toward a new stage of development. The concern of tourism education is not about mitigating or questioning its existence, it is about wider debates more akin to the social sciences generally. Tourism education may be considered as moving toward a mature stage (Airey, 2008).

15.2 TOURISM EDUCATION IN INDIA

In 1972, the first tourism course was started at the undergraduate level by the college of Vocational Studies, University of Delhi. Tourism department of government and airlines organized airline ticketing and tour guiding programs to achieve specific skill requirements of the sector. In 1983, Ministry of Tourism, Government of India established Indian Institute of Tourism and Travel Management (IITTM) as an apex body for the tourism education. In 1989, IITTM started its regional chapter at Bombay and Trivandrum. It started offering management development programs in tourism and Diploma in Tourism Management. At Present, IITTM has its regional chapters in Bhubaneswar, Calcutta, Goa, Lucknow, and Trivandrum. It offers diploma and training programs at Gwalior and all in its regional offices. It provided assistance in curriculum design, especially for the master-level programs in tourism administration (MTA), which was started in the year 1991 at Kurukshetra University (Jithendran and Baum, 2000).

Importance of tourism in economic contribution and requirements of skilled human resources has influenced many universities and colleges to start tourism courses from certificate level to doctoral level. Various colleges affiliated to universities started offering undergraduate and post-graduate tourism programs. Certificate and diploma level programs are offered by vocational higher secondary schools and technical training institutes. To get admission at the undergraduate level tourism programs, one has to complete higher secondary education. One of the most common postgraduate programs is MTA, which is a two-year full-time program (Kuruvilla et al., 2011).

15.3   HUMAN ASSETS IN TOURISM SECTOR

Travel and tourism sector currently employing 31 million people, which is expected to meet 40 million and 43 million by 2019 and 2022, respectively (NSDC, 2009). Ticketing, travel counseling, marketing and sales, finance department, foreign exchange, and so on are the few functional areas in tourism that require essential skills such as communication skill, interpersonal skills, knowledge of the product, knowledge of various destinations, technical skill, and so on. The National Skill Development Corporation (NSDC) estimates that there will be 7.2 million employment generation by the year 2022. The employment generation in hotel category excluding motels is expected to increase 1.9 million in 2012, 2.9 million by 2018, and 4 million by 2022. Human resource requirements in restaurants are estimated around 0.72 million. Travel agencies and tour operators sector accounts for 55% of all the employees in this sector. A total of 0.13

million people were employed by the travel trade in the year 2008, and this number has grown to 0.16 million by 2012. Travel trade is estimated to be employed 0.3 million people by the end of the year 2022 (NSDC, 2009).

15.4 EDUCATIONAL APTITUDES IN TOURISM

Tourism educational competency depends on its ability in providing quality education and contributing skilled manpower to meet the expectations and requirements of the tourism sector. According to WTO tourism education system during its education process has to consider the skills and competencies that meet the expectations of both external and internal consumers. Tourism education needs to adapt as per the changing requirements of the tourism industry and has to calculate right kind of skills in the individuals (WTO, 2004).

15.5 ACADEMIA AND RECRUITMENT FOR THE LEISURE INDUSTRY

Education institutions are a source of recruitments for the tourism industry. One such instance is Association of Tourism Trade Organizations, India (ATTOI, 2013). ATTOI take various measures to create awareness about tourism opportunities and its growth. It also supports students to opt for higher studies in tourism education with the help of educational institutions. The tourism sector always looks for the individuals who have completed their course in tourism education. The websites of tourism organization such as SOTC in the career column of their website mentioned the qualifications required for the post of senior manager sales as graduates, diploma/ PG in travel, and tourism management. In a similar instance, Cox and King (2012) also advertized opportunities for graduates and International Air Transport Association (IATA), qualified for their job requirements.

15.6 TOURISM AND INDIAN SCENARIO

Travel and tourism is considered as one of the largest service sectors in India. This sector will be contributing 7.7% to the National Gross

Domestic Product between the period of 2013 and 2022, 1.6% of the total employment (Travel and Tourism Competitiveness Report, 2013). It has been noted that tourism sector has produced US $ 100 billion in 2008, and it is expected to increase US $ 275.5 billion by 2018. As per the World Travel and Tourism Council report, India will be a tourism hotspot from 2009 to 2018, having the highest ten-year growth potential (Lalnunmawia, 2013). By keeping the above facts in consideration, it is essential for the tourism sector to maintain the quality and demand to remain competitive. The skilled human resources are very much essential to meet the quality of services and demand of the consumers.

15.7   PURPOSE OF THE STUDY

Tourism is a very much a service segment, and its chief functionality relies on the manpower and human resources. The individual approach and superiority in services is identical and much essential to content the consumers, and the success of leisure industry is closely associated and depended on the same. The academia and travel education can incidentally add to the success of leisure industry by providing excellence in manpower training as per the market expectations.

15.8   OBJECTIVES

The main objective of the study is to understand that what skills and abilities are needed to be developed by students that will meet the competency expectations of the industry. As the objective states, it is essential to understand competency expectations of the industry so it is easy to deliver what tourism industry expects. This objective is measured by reviewing various articles that emphasize on the competency expectations of the tourism industry.

To suggest tourism education, imbibe necessary skills and abilities in the students that will meet the competency expectations of the industry. Based on the review, competency expectations are identified. So its tourism education needs to fulfill the competency requirements of the industry. This objective is measured by suggestion tourism education to meet the competency requirements of the industry.

15.9   REVIEW OF LITERATURE

The intention of this study is to understand how tourism education can play an important role in meeting the competency requirements of the tourism industry. So, in order to deliver the quality education that meets the competency expectation of tourism industry, it is essential to understand what skills and abilities are actually tourism industry is looking for. The review of literature helps in understanding the competence expectations of the tourism industry. Various reviews were collected from various books, journals, and online sources such as EBSCO, ProQuest, Google Scholar, and so on. The industry requires youngsters who are skilled and ready to meet its growing demands. They must also be ready to face global competition but in reality, it is not happening. A skilled workforce is required for a strong, sustainable, and balanced growth. Both soft skills and job competencies are essential to make a good impression during job interviews, but the current young workforce does not possess such soft skills. Soft skills such as time management, written communication, personal skills, stress management, and transferable skills such as the capability to deal with the internal politics of the industrial organization and the ability to sell oneself have to be considered while formulating the tourism education curricula (DNA, 2013; Singh, 2005).

The competencies that play a major role in building a student's career at the global level are the openness to new perspectives and influences, cross-cultural sensitivity, inquisitiveness, cross-cultural negotiations, international adjustment and adaptability, emotional intelligence, managing uncertainty, and complexity in international business environments and self-management (Vance and Paik, 2011). Cultural and basic language skills are required to cater to the large and growing sources of tourists. Management skills are also essential for meeting the future demands of a tourism organization. Management competencies are defined as "a combination of observable and applied knowledge, skills and behaviors that create a competitive advantage for an organization" (ILO, 2011; Littlejohn and Watson, 2004; Nath and Raheja, 2001). In today's scenario, professionals are giving more importance to interpersonal skills (Ricci and Kaufman, 2007; Tsai et al., 2006). The most desired competencies include communication skills, professional appearance, guest service skills, understanding of industry expectations, pride in self, and the ability to work with people to complete administrative tasks (Tesone and Ricci, 2005). Moreover, problem-solving, self-management, and interpersonal skills are considered as most important skills (Raybould and Wilkins, 2005). Computer skills, language skills, the ability to work in a team, and take up the role of a leader and knowledge pertaining to the tourism and hospitality industry have a major impact on one's career success (Lertwannawit et al., 2009). An enthusiastic, well educated, committed, and well-trained workforce is important for the tourism industry (Jiang and Tribe, 2009).

Chung-Herrera et al. (2003) have identified the link between future hospitality leaders and leadership competencies. A list of 99 skills or competencies that contribute to leadership success has been suggested. Self-management was considered as most important, and this consisted of flexibility and adaptability, ethics and integrity, time management, and self-development. The second important competency was strategic positioning comprising commitment to quality, managing stakeholders, awareness of customer needs, and concern for community. Leadership, interpersonal skills, and industry knowledge were factors that were ranked lower by respondents, whereas Kay and Russette (2000) in their study on 'hospitality management competencies' found that the competencies in the leadership domain represented the majority of skills designated as 'Essential Competencies'.

They found that a number of essential competencies fall under all five of 'Sandwith's Competency Domains' (i.e., interpersonal, leadership, conceptual—administrative, technical, and creative). Interpersonal skills and leadership are important competencies that are applicable to both functional and management level. Professional competencies emphasize on creativity, humanity, flexibility, sharing with employees, and communication between the management and the labor force. The employers are looking for a more flexible and adaptable workforce because it helps the organization to respond to the changing market and customer needs (Horng and Lu, 2006; Cox and King, 2006). The tourism employers are emphasizing on general transferable skills and practical skills, but this contradicts with the expectations of educators who are developing a course curriculum that is more conceptual and full of tourism-specific material (Singh, 2005). The tourism industry is looking for specific knowledge, academic know-how, and competencies of managers and employees as well as overall vocation-oriented competencies (Zehrer et al., 2006; Barrie, 2006). The employers are looking for overall intellectual ability and concentrate on flexibility, language skills that include good use of

English and other foreign languages, oral and written communication skills, outgoing personalities and people skills, IT competencies, ability to convert classroom theory into practice, the potential to complete tasks with little guidance, and the motivation to go beyond what is asked (Singh, 2005; Daugherty, 2002). Different authors used different methodologies to identify various competency expectations of the tourism industry. It ranges from basic operation and communication skills to changing requirements of the organization and customer need, that is, adaptability. They also mentioned that these competencies also help in the development of student career and help them to work at the global level. The quality human resources are very much essential for sustainable growth of tourism organization.

15.10   RESEARCH GAP

The main aim of the study is to identify the role of tourism education in meeting the competency expectations of the tourism industry. All the previous studies concentrate only on competency requirements of the industry, but how to meet these competency requirements are never addressed before. So the present study is aimed at finding out what are the steps tourism education has to undertake in order to meet the competency requirements of the tourism industry by providing quality human resources.

15.11   FINDINGS OF THE STUDY

Reviews substantiate that tourism industry requires those candidates who possess skills such as time management, written communication, personal skills, stress management, and transferable skills such as the capability to deal with the internal politics of the industrial organization and the ability to sell oneself to make a good impression during job interviews. Openness to new perspectives and influences, cross-cultural sensitivity, inquisitiveness, cross-cultural negotiations, international adjustment and adaptability, emotional intelligence, managing uncertainty and complexity in international business environments and self-management helps in building student career at a global level. Basic language skills and interpersonal skills are required to cater to the large and growing sources of tourists.

Professional appearance, guest service skills, understanding of industry expectations, pride in self and ability to work with people to complete administrative tasks. Computer skills and ability to work in a team is also required to grow as a leader. Innovative skills are also essential to solving the problems. Self-management was considered as most important, and this consisted of flexibility and adaptability, ethics and integrity, time management, and self-development by the hospitality leaders. Apart from the review of literature, a small survey was conducted among tourism professionals to find out the competency expectations of the tourism industry. Mean values of the importance of tourism skill sets from the perception of Tourism professional were analyzed. In the result, the mean value ranged from 3.59 to 4.71. According to tourism professionals, the first three important skills and abilities were relationship management skills, team working skills, and oral communication, and the least important skills were considered to be organizational ability, research skills, and academic grades. The tourism professionals also highly valued adaptability at work (4.51), customer-service skills (4.51) and leadership ability (4.51), confidence and problem-solving skills (4.47). Second, tourism professionals equally valued skills such as marketing and sales skills (4.43), networking ability (4.43) and written communication (4.39), negotiation skills (4.39) and decision making (4.35), practical skills (4.35), and work ethics (4.35). Finally, relevant work experience (4.23) and creativity (4.19) were found to be perceived more important than event management skills (4.15) and industry knowledge (4.15). Critical thinking (4.07) was given little importance when compared with computer skills (4.06) by the tourism professionals. To respond to changing needs of the market and customer needs organization looks for an adaptable and flexible workforce. The students need to develop skills and abilities that meet the requirements of the tourism organization.

15.12 SUGGESTIONS

Apart from curriculum design, the tourism education has to give more importance to cocurriculum and extra curriculum activities that will enhance the skills and abilities of students. Cocurricular activity hours enhance the knowledge of the students. It is a perfect platform that brings out a whole new world both inside and outside of the classroom. Various activities help students to develop skills and knowledge that are much expected by the industry. The various benefits of cocurricular activities in students' association as follows:

Networking: The easy and best way to network with students who have similar interests is joining a student Association. It can help them with their career, hobby, or anything that are passionate about.

Social skills: As a student has to learn how to talk to other people from different cultures and countries, as an international student, it is an opportunity to build some social skills.

Professional experience: If students join professional chapter student association, the students will get exposed to a lot of professional careers and help build professionally. For example, if they join American Marketing Association will help them in getting the feel of a professional career.

Personality development: Communication skills will improve in the individual due to interaction with different people. A student may learn even more if he/she is on the executive board. They learn to balance education and organizational work focusing on their goals.

Leadership skills: In the events, if the student becomes a coordinator and takes up the responsibility or challenge to be a leader, they will learn what it takes to be a leader.

Alumni networking: Student Associations usually try to bring in alumni and ask them to share their experiences. It provides an opportunity for them to learn from seniors who have graduated and help them to get connected. It helps them with job search and mentoring.

Organization and management skills: Many of us are not familiar how an organization works and how to manage everything. If they are in the event coordinating board, they will get to learn how fundraising works, how finances work, how to market for the event, how to work as a team. It helps them in the long run of their career or if they are opening their own ventures (Kumar, 2013).

15.13 CONCLUSION

The role of tourism in the national economy is proven without any doubt. All the sectors of the tourism industry such as travel agency, tour operations, airlines, and hotels play a significant role in transforming the economy of a nation. These organizations generate foreign exchange earnings and create employment opportunities, and, at the same time, its development and growth depend on the human resources. These sectors rely more on the human resources for their day-to-day operation. Though technology plays a significant role in this sector, human capital is very much essential for the survival of the organization. Tourism industry requires skilled workforce in order to meet the growing demands, and the development of the skilled workforce for the tourism industry is the responsibility of tourism education. Quality education in tourism is a platform for the sustainable development of the industry. Education institutions have to build skills and knowledge among human resources to meet the various diverse needs of an organization. The knowledge and skills are very much essential to perform the task effectively in this sector.

KEYWORDS

- **competency**
- **skills**
- **knowledge**
- **human resources**
- **tourism education**

REFERENCES

Airey, D. Tourism Education Life Begins at 40. *Teoros Revue De Recherche En Tourisme* **2008,** *27*(1), 27–32. http://teoros.revues.org/1617.

ATTOI. Tourism Education, 2013. http://www.attoi.org/tourismeducation.html.

Barrie, S. Understanding What We Mean by the Generic Attributes of Graduates. *Higher Educ.* **2006,** *51*(2), 215–241.

Chung-Herrera, B. G.; Enz, C. A.; Lankau, M. J. Grooming Future Hospitality Leaders: A Competencies Model. *Cornell Hotel Restaurant Admin. Q.* **2003,** *44*(3), 17–25.

Cox, S.; King, D. Skill Sets: An Approach to Embed Employability in Course Design. *Educ. Train.* **2006,** *48*(4), 262–274.

DNA. Why is Young India Under Skilled? http://epaper.dnaindia.com/story. aspx?edorsup=Sup&queryed=860009&querypage=9&boxid=36289&id=17260&eddat e=2013-Oct-16,&ed_date=2013-Oct-16,&ed_code=860009&wintype=popup (accessed Oct 16, 2013).

Daugherty, S. How to Prepare for Success Using Internships and Co-ops. *Black Collegian* **2002,** *33(1),* 109–113.

Horng, J. S.; Lu, H. Y. Needs Assessment of Professional Competencies of f&b/hospitality Management Students at College and University Level. *J. Teach. Travel Tourism* **2006,** *6*(3), 1–26.

ILO. *Toolkit on Poverty Reduction Through Tourism*, 2011. http://www.ilo.org/wcmsp5/groups/public/---ed_dialogue/---sector/documents/instructionalmaterial/wcms_162289.pdf.

Jiang, B.; Tribe, J. Tourism Jobs—short Lived Professions': Student Attitudes Towards Tourism Careers in China. *J. Hospitality, Leisure, Sport Tourism Educ.* **2009,** 8(1), 4–14.

Jithendran, K. J.; Baum, T. Human Resources Development and Sustainability—The Case of Indian Tourism. *Int. J. Tourism Res.* **2000,** *2.*

Kay, C.; Russette, J. Hospitality-management Competencies. *Cornell Hotel and Restaurant Administration Quarterly,* **2000,** *41*(2).

Kumar. Eight Reasons Why Should You Join Student Organizations in us Universities? How Many to Join? What Kind of Student Organizations to Join? 2013. http://redbus2us.com/8-reasons-why-should-you-joinstudent-organizations-in-us-universities-how-many-to-join-what-kind-of-student-organizations-to-join/.

Kuruvilla, A.; Moira, P.; Jacob, R.; Mylonopoulos, D.; Kuruvilla, A.; Weng, R. *Tourism Curriculum in Greece and India—a Comparative Analysis*. 7th International Conference on Education, Greece, July 2011.

Lalnunmawia. Development and Impact of Tourism Industry in India, 2013. http://www.trcollege.net/articles/74-development-and-impact-of-tourism-industry-in-india.

Lertwannawit, A.; Serirat, S.; Pholpantin, S. Career Competencies and Career Success of Thai employees in Tourism and Hospitality Sector. *Int. Bus. Econ. Res. J.* **2009,** *8*(11), 65.

Littlejohn, D.; Watson, S. Developing Graduate Managers for Hospitality and Tourism. *Int. J. Contemp. Hospitality Manage.* **2004,** *16,* 408–414.

Nath, R.; Ralieja, R. Competencies in Hospitality Industry. *J. Serv. Res.* **2001,** *7*(1), 25–33.

National Skill Development Corporation. Human Resources and Skill Requirements in the Tourism, Travel, Hospitality and Trade Sector (2022)—A Report, 2009. http://www.nsdcindia.org/pdf/tourism.pdf.

Raybould, M.; Wilkins, H. Over Qualified and Under Experienced: Turning Graduates into Hospitality Managers. *Int. J. Contemp. Hospitality Manage.* **2005,** *17*(2/3).

Ricci, P.; Kaufman, T. Managerial Expectations for New Hires: Similarities Between Vacation Ownership and Traditional Lodging. *J. Teach. Travel Tourism* **2007,** *7*(2), 35–49.

Singh, R. Tourism Curriculum Designing for Bridging the Gap Between Industry and Education Needs. In *Advancement in Tourism Theory and Practice: Perspective from India;* George, B. P., Swain, S. K., Eds.; Abhijeet Publications: Delhi, 2005.

Tesone, D.; Ricci, P. Toward a Definition of Entry-level Job Competencies: Hospitality Manager Perspectives. *Int. J. Hospitality Tourism Adm.* **2005,** *7*(4), 65–80.

Tsai, F.; Goh, B.; Huffman, L.; Wu, K. Competency Assessment for Entry Level Lodging Management Trainees in Taiwan. *Chin. Econ.* **2006,** *39*(6), 49–69.

Vance, C. M.; Paik, Y. *Managing a Global Workforce: Challenges and Opportunities in International Human Resource Management,* 2nd ed.; M.E. Sharpe: Armonk, NY, 2011.

World Tourism Organization. *TedQual Certification System. Volume I. Executive Introduction,* 2004. http://www.themis.ad/english/products/portfolio/tedquaLeng.pdf.

Zehrer, A.; Siller, H.; Altmann, A. A Module System in Tourism and Leisure Education—Theoretical and Practical Perspectives. In Imagining the future of travel and tourism education, proceedings of the ISTEE Conference 2007 in Las Vegas (US). Hu, C., Ed.; 2006.

CHAPTER 16

SOCIALLY RESPONSIBLE INVESTMENT: A NEW PARADIGM IN THE TOURISM AND HOSPITALITY SECTOR: AN INDIAN SCENARIO

GOWRI SHANKAR R. and ARJUN B. S.

Assistant Professor, Christ (Deemed to be University), Bangalore, India

CONTENTS

ABSTRACT

A socially responsible investment refers to investing in companies on the basis of financial returns and environment, social, and governance (ESG) practices. Companies subscribe capital from general public and invest the same in business operations. These business activities should be aligned with the expectations of the investors. These days investors are not only keen on monetary returns but also would like to contribute socially and environmentally. In most industries, corporate social responsibility standards and practices have been developed by the private sector to respond to external pressure. In tourism, however, the use of codes of conduct and certification is not widespread and is not based on yet upon agreed international standards. Under this concern, investors would reflect their personal values, moral behavior, environmental interest, and others in their investment choice. This study, however, made an effort to analyze the attitude of individual investors toward socially responsible investment with special reference to tourism and travel companies.

16.1   INTRODUCTION

Over the period of years, there has been growing awareness among investors in the field of socially responsible investment (SRI), which was previously known as an ethical investment and responsible investment. According to Social Investment Forum, nearly 11% socially responsible investment is that type of investment available to companies that follow societal and environment benefit practices. SRI is termed by other names including "ethical investing," "green investing," "targeted investing," "values-based investing," "sustainable investing," and nowadays just "responsible investing" (White, 1995; Cowton, 1998; Cranston, 2004; Petersen, 2005). Wood and Urwin (2010) discuss numerous ways to express the same content such as "SRIs," "social investments," "responsible investment," and "ethical investment." The major remarkable difference between SRI and conventional investing is that former considers monetary returns as well as social, ethical, and environmental practices, latter considers only monetary returns. The SRI is gaining importance both in practitioners and academicians.

16.2 SOCIALLY RESPONSIBLE INVESTMENT

SRI funds pass two forms of benefits for investors—one is through monetary returns based on systematic financial analysis that matches or exceed returns on classical investments and the other through social and environmental benefits that are added value from investment portfolios (Williams, 2013). The former gives benefit to only one but later can spread the benefit to many. SRI is defined in multiple ways by the authors and researchers as it grows over the period of time. Generally, the term SRI refers to a set of approaches that include social, approaches to investment decisions ethical and environmental considerations in addition to conventional financial screening criteria (Cowton, 1999; Schueth, 2003). An investment process that considers the social and environmental effects of investments, both positive and negative, within the context of rigorous financial analysis (Social Investment Forum, 2001), it considers financial, social, and environment criteria's invest action. Further, World Economic Forum (2013) has termed SRI as investing in a manner that takes into account the impact of investments on wider society and the natural environment, both today and in the future.

This process of investing contrasts with conventional investment approaches in which decisions are purely based on monetary returns. It is a long-term business success while contributing towards economic and social development and a healthy environment and stable society. Companies are expected to give stable returns without involving themselves in poor corporate governance or bad environmental practices. SRI is closely associated with corporate social responsibility (CSR) and environmentally sustainable practices. From an economic perspective, it addresses externalities, which are the costs or benefits that arise from company activities that are not priced into the shares. SRI allows investors to make positive economic decisions by taking into account not only financial but also the nonfinancial management of risk. SRI has got the different meaning of its scope. Social investing is an investment strategy in which an investor considers social factors while investing either excluding or including the specific stocks. Negative screening (excluding) of the stocks of companies involved in military weapon manufacturing, tobacco products, alcohol, gambling activities, and so on, whereas positive screening includes social welfare activities, CSR benefits, fair benefits to labor and employees, community development, customer-friendly initiatives, and so on. Sustainable investing approach focuses on excluding those companies that have a relatively negative impact on the environment such as agricultural chemicals, hazardous waste, and o on or because the companies do nonenvironmental practices such as poor waste management, causing pollution, absence of recycling system, and so on and emphasizing companies that have a relatively positive impact on the environment.

16.3   IMPORTANCE OF SOCIALLY RESPONSIBLE INVESTMENT

Investing socially and ethically on a global level not only helps one to support the clean tech revolution but also provides valuable portfolio. Companies focused on environmental and social issues make the best corporate citizens and may provide the greatest long-term opportunities. This philosophy is taking the hold among investors not only within our culture but around the world. You now have the chance to capitalize on the worldwide growth and support of SRI and help advance the green and sustainable technologies of tomorrow. As the scope of SRI is wide, stakeholders such as investors, government, suppliers, employees, customers, and employees will be benefited through it.

16.4   SOCIALLY RESPONSIBLE INVESTMENT AND TOURISM

Lending institutions generally evaluate the environmental and social performances of their clients before they invest or offer financial services. This practice has become common in sectors such as agriculture business, oil, gas, mining, information technology, and other sectors that have a significant contribution to gross domestic product. However, in the recent past, this concept has got much momentum in tourism and hospitality sector. This trend originated partly from the growth in SRI, but more importantly, from the changing risk profiles that banks have witnessed in their mainstream investments. This has been the case particularly with project finance in which the use to which proceeds are put is fully defined and can, therefore, be linked to specific investments. As the financing is clearly traceable, banks are not ready to fund or invest in projects that are perceived to be detrimental to the environment or society.

16.4.1 THE EQUATOR PRINCIPLES

A major step forward came in 2002 with the emergence of The Equator Principles that were developed by a range of commercial banks with assistance from the International Finance Corporation, the private equity arm of the World Bank. The principles are a set of guidelines to help financial institutions manage environmental and social issues in finance lending. Signatories to the Equator Principles "will not provide loans directly to projects where the borrower will not or is unable to comply with our environmental and social policies and processes." Projects are categorized according to risk, and those with the highest risk (category A and some category B projects) require an environmental impact assessment to be carried out which will form the basis of an environmental management plan. In parallel with the emergence of the eliminating poverties (EPs), a number of banks including HSBC, Goldman Sachs, JP Morgan, Citibank, and others began to develop their own environmental and social policies, some of which are more exacting than the EP requirements, to address areas of risk. These focus on a range of environmental and socioeconomic concerns such as forestry, access to clean water, infrastructure development, and biodiversity protection and are increasingly being applied across all the bank's products and services.

16.4.2 SUSTAINABILITY PROTOTYPE AND TOURISM

To some, the travel and tourism industry was ahead of the financial sector in recognizing the need to embrace environmental and socioeconomic issues, because it had to survive for a long term. Protection of the environment heritage, culture, and local economies is so fundamental to tourism that the industry ignores such issues at its peril. Global environmental events such as the World Summit on Sustainable Development (WSSD) spurred the world, including the travel and tourism industry, into action. It was at WSSD that the World Tourism Organization (WTO) launched the sustainable tourism-eliminating poverty (ST-EP) initiative). The industry increasingly recognized the importance of local economic development and the social aspects of tourism. International award schemes such as the responsible tourism awards (sponsored by First Choice in 2005) and the WTIC Tourism for Tomorrow Awards are encouraging greater customer discernment and expectation in this area.

As more hotels and tour operators start to look "beyond the footprint" and examine their supply chains, sourcing policies, and the cumulative impacts of tourism in specific areas, the need for more sophisticated environmental and social management within the tourism sector will increase. If tourism development is real to be more sustainable in the future, it will require sustainability to be "designed-in" from project inception and to ensure that everyone involved follows sustainable principles.

16.5   FINANCE AND TOURISM—A FUTURISTIC PREVIEW

CSR, with its "stakeholder" duties of greater transparency and disclosure, is now firmly on the business agenda. Today, many companies (though only a handful of tourism businesses) publish full CSR reports and engage in "stakeholder dialog" to demonstrate their commitment to sustainability. Worldwide, around 4000 companies have so far published sustainability or "nonfinancial" reports. The drivers for this form of disclosure vary, but there is increasing evidence that this information is being used by the financial sector (especially SRI funds) to gauge company performance and as the basis for engagement on specific issues. The evolution of solutions and good practices that align financing and tourism development/operations could prove a powerful engine for change as is clear from the case studies supporting this article. Areas that are likely to be the early focus of attention include the following:

1.   Protection of natural habitats, cultural assets, and ecosystem services. The self-interest that the tourism sector has toward the protection of its natural and cultural assets seems likely to be underpinned by a similar commitment on the part of banks to finance projects in which there has been an assessment of risks to such assets. Companies that fail to protect assets or are sited so that they (or ancillary assets) negatively affect, for example, coral reefs or areas of cultural significance, may well struggle to obtain finance.

2.   Greenhouse gas emissions and global warming from transport, construction, and power generation. Many banks have commitments regarding greenhouse gas emissions, both in their own operations and in their investments. They are also increasingly active in carbon trading and financing energy-efficient investments.

Opportunities for linking energy efficiency and renewable energy options in hotel and tourism development may signal a growing opportunity for financing. Hotel and resort developments that are built with sustainable issues in mind will have an advantage over others in terms of lower operating costs, higher residual values, and potentially lower insurance premiums.

3. Economic development and poverty alleviation. The globalization of the financial services industry has created fierce competition for the small pool of large corporate clients in emerging and transition economies. The volume and range of financial products available to microenterprises and small- and medium-sized enterprises (SMEs) should substantially increase. Ways in which tourism can support these moves (i.e., through committing to service agreements that allow small companies to secure loans) are a potentially significant mechanism for spreading economic benefits into local communities and helping toward the achievement of poverty alleviation.

16.6 SUSTAINABLE TOURISM: CRITICAL ISSUES

From energy consumption and sourcing to poor working conditions and tax avoidance, there are many areas to consider. A socially responsible investor tries to balance the profit margin of the company and also the wealth and welfare benefits of the stakeholders and that too when it comes to tourism sector, this kind of investment strategy is little complicated.

The tourism sector is heterogeneous, and it brings variety of stakeholders under its umbrella such as hotels, resorts, and travel services. However, there are few pressing issues that affect the whole sector. External threats such as climate change, resource depletion, and health and wellness, have an impact on a companies' attractiveness. Here are the core issues an SRI into the tourism sector should consider:

16.6.1 CARBON AND OTHER EMISSIONS

Even though the tourism sector may not be one of the major greenhouse gas contributors, the development of international air travel and air traffic has contributed to its carbon footprint.

16.6.2   ENERGY CONSUMPTION AND WATER WASTE

Out of the entire service sectors, tourism sector tends to have high-energy consumption levels, particularly at hotels. A strong relation is usually observed between a hotel's star rating and the energy consumption per room. Luxury services such as a heated pool, spa, golf, or laundry services all increase energy consumption and also a contributor to water waste. Theme parks in recent days are a major user and contributor of water waste. As an SRI, one should appreciate the value of all the resources and should invest in companies that safeguard resources or reuse the resources.

16.6.3   JOB CREATION AND CONTRIBUTION TO LOCAL ECONOMY

The leisure industry contributes the major income to the sector, but if it generates the income by involving communities into the ambit of this sector then SRI investors will be more interested to invest their surplus money as it creates ample of jobs to the local bodies and individual.

16.6.4   WORKING CONDITIONS

Meet and Greet is the basic tagline of this sector, but when there are tough working conditions, poor remuneration, and misuse of labor, then it will lead to devastating effects on the revenue generation itself.

16.6.5   RESPONSIBLE SOURCING

SRIs should definitively consider companies' purchasing criteria, with a special focus on the boarding and lodging segment.

16.6.6   FRANCHISING AND HOTEL NETWORK VALUES

Franchising is a good business model, but it fails when it is not monitored. As a customer, it is very difficult to fight against the franchise operator when they change and localize the food supply without ensuring the safety values. SRIs should consider how these can be improved in terms of supply and manage risks.

16.6.7   HEALTH AND WELLNESS

The entire hotel chains and restaurants provide attractive food but are they explaining the side effects of such foods? Some food chains even find an alternative method of cooking, but the nutrition or the health component is still questionable. So SRI investors should look into the other dimensions of the same.

16.6.8   FOOD SAFETY

Food safety is the alarming concern everywhere. Any tourist who visits a place in search of foods, all the food joints in the destination need to be certified and monitored by the SRI investors before they invest so that the companies and food joints have a moral fear in their commitment.

16.6.9   E-SECURITY

As the level of educated tourist inflow into the country is increased, the security of their data is a big concern. Physical security is taken care at the destination through various means, but the data security is still a concern. As an SRI investor, one should try to figure a way out to protect the data of the clients in a best possible way.

16.6.10   TAX AVOIDANCE

The complex structure and the number of departments involved in the tourism sector are relatively more, and the governing rules are also a concern, and due to this nature, there is a possibility of tax avoidance.

16.7   SOCIALLY RESPONSIBLE INVESTMENT PRACTICES IN THE INDIAN SCENARIO

A decade ago, a set of nonfinancial issues such as climate change, human rights, and extinction of few biomasses and governance were raised at the international level. Unfortunately, business is one among the major contributions for these issues.

As a sign of change, many financial institutions and investors have started funding and investing in social and ethical manners that restrict the company indulging in nonenvironmental and nonethical practices. Concurrently, this also encourages corporates to do their business activities in a responsible way. It results in lining the companies to operate in socially acceptable manner. In the context of India, the Securities and Exchange Board of India (SEBI) mandated that from March 31, 2012, the top 100 listed companies must submit Business Responsibility Reports (BRRs) as part of their annual reports, providing information about their sustainability performance. This initiative of the SEBI helps the investor to understand different companies approach sustainability. Another crucial development in India is the Companies Act of 2013 that states that the companies which have a net worth of Rs 500 crore or a turnover of Rs 1000 crore or net profit of Rs 5 crore need to spend at least 2% of its average net profit for the immediately preceding three financial years on CSR activities. It mandates companies to design and implement CSR policies.

SRI is creating vibes in the field of global investment in many countries. For India, it is not even in the infant stage, as many of the investors are not aware of SRI concept and its importance. SRI is yet to make an impact in India, spreading across the globe. Investment patterns are emerging concepts in Muslim countries such as Malaysia, Indonesia, and India (Murtaza and Rana, 2013). ABN Amro Sustainable Development Fund was the first SRI fund to accumulate to invest in companies with good environment, social and governance values (Menon, 2007). Past articles and research works are reviewed to understand the concept of the study, and the same is projected under different heads based on its area.

16.8   CRITICAL REVIEWS ON SOCIALLY RESPONSIBLE INVESTMENT

In Rosen et al. (1991) socially responsible investment behavior of companies were identified more in environmental and labor relations issues and practices. In White (1995), Cowton (1998), Cranston (2004), and Petersen (2005), SRI is termed by a number of other names including "ethical investing," "green investing," "targeted investing," "values-based investing," "sustainable investing," and nowadays just "responsible investing."

In Renneboog et al. (2008), the most important difference between socially responsible investing and traditional investing is that SRI sets out investment criteria, not only with a monetary point of view but also takes into account social, environmental, and ethical aspects in the investment process. In Nilsson (2009), it is not a charity, and SRI is an investment not only considering financial criteria. In Eccles et al. (2008), corporate governance, infrastructure development, sustainability, black economic empowerment, gender empowerment issues, and employee relations are the most important ESG issues. The attitude and behavior of SRI investors are visibly exemplified by Estes and Hosseini (1988), as gender is the most important factor influencing the confidence while taking decisions in investment. Women are less confident than men. Rosen et al. (1991) concluded that compared with other investors SRI investors are younger and better educated. In Williams (2005), social responsibility investors are more concerned about social aspects, and they are more likely to punish organizations for poor social performance. In Glac (2008), if the SRI investors had sufficient information, they would have engaged more in SRI. In Schueth (2003), the investors invest their money to work in a manner that is closely aligned with their personal values and priorities. In addition, invest capital to work in ways that support and bring positive change in the society. Dilla et al. (2013) showed a significant direct relationship between specific environmentally responsible attitudes and SRI holdings. Borgers and Pownall (2014) show that investors are opinioned that they would like to exclude the companies operate in the weapons industry and companies that violate human rights amendments from their investment list. Hutton et al. (1998), McLachlan and Gardner (2004), and Diouf and Hebb (2013) emphasized upon the sociodemographic factors influences, the behaviors and attitudes of investors and portrayed that the young- and high-level of educates have more awareness about social investment. It is perceived that women are more concerned to invest in a responsible stock compared with men. In the study of Dilla et al. (2013), New Ecological Paradigm scale has been used to measure the relationship of basic environmental attitudes with the specific attitude toward environmentally responsible investment. The result showed that there is a significant direct relationship between specific environmentally responsible attitudes and SRI holdings. The study of Williams (2005) analyzed the approaches of socially responsible investors and conventional investors across six countries. The result shows that social responsibility investors are more concerned about social aspects, and they are more likely to punish organizations for poor social performance.

Though traditional investors believe that a good social performance directs to a good financial performance, they do not appear to follow this through in their portfolios. The study of Tripathi and Bhandari (2015) was focused on evaluating the performance of socially responsible stocks portfolios of India. Sharpe ratio, Treynor ratio, and absolute rate of return tools were used to analyze the data. The result shows that ESG and GREENEX Index provided positive returns and also outperformed NIFTY and SENSEX during the crisis period. The study of Nybom (2012) attempted in investigating the decision-making process of potential investors in selecting SRI. It is found that individual financial advisors influence more in decision-making process, and investors have a higher level of education. The article by Cumming and Johan (2007) studied institutional investor allocations to the socially responsible asset class. This study proposed two elements influence socially responsible institutional investment in private equity: internal organizational structure, and internationalization. It compared socially responsible investment across different asset classes and different types of institutional investors (banks, insurance companies, and pension funds). It is found that socially responsible investment in private equity is also more common among institutional investors. The result of Ainul Azreen Adam and Ainul Azreen Adam (2012) study shows that investors' attitude, subjective norm, and moral norm have a positive effect on intention which, in turn, certainly affects behavior toward social responsibility investment. Investor's personal standards are also found to influence the interest and behavior to invest in SRI. The study of Richard Hudson and Roger Wehrell (2005) stated that SRI investors have mainly two goals: to have market-based returns and to make companies act in a socially responsible way. The study concludes that lenders can influence microentrepreneur to act in a more responsible way toward society. Shauki (2012) in their study used structural equation modeling to measure the relationship between different variables. The result says that attitude, subjective norm, and moral norm of investors have a positive effect on behavior toward SRI. Investors' personal standards are also found to influence the intention and behavior to invest in SRI. In addition, they stated that this will enable Malaysian authorities as well as fund management companies to launch effective marketing strategies and develop SRI products.

Socially responsible stocks can bolster the CSR law, According to the company's act of 2013, a CSR committee has to be constituted if any company has a net worth of Rs. 500 crore or more, or a turnover of Rs. 1000 crore or more or a net profit of Rs. 5 crores or more during any financial year.

In this chapter, Schueth (2013) provides the concepts and practices of socially and environmentally responsible investing in the United States. It describes that the group of investors feels to employ their money to work in a manner that is closely associated with their personal values and priorities. Other groups feel to put their money to work in ways that encourage and improve the quality of working life for a social cause. In the paper of Martin and Moser (2012), the main objective lies to examine the response of investors toward green disclosures by the managers of the company. This chapter has highlighted that though investment on green practices has not made an impact on the future cash flows, but investors have responded positively toward green disclosures. Rhodes (2010) discusses the challenges in screening the stocks considering the social and ethical factors. It states that irregular availability of ethical and social benefit information leads to the complexity in defining investment screens.

In the study of Beal et al. (2005), the authors have identified that financial returns, nonwealth reasons, and social changes are three motives of social investors. In this article, the authors depicted that investors feel happy in investing socially responsible stocks and give more importance to ethical practices of the company compared with financial returns. In their study, Jansson and Biel (2014) investigate psychological drivers and financial motives that may influence major Swedish investments institutions to adopt SRI and the conventional investors (NON-SRI). The article considered the following major factors for investment: psychological factors and financial beliefs that impede or promote professional investors within investment institutions to adopt socially responsible investments.

Many studies have been conducted to analyze the general attitude and behavior of investors toward ESG (ethics, social, and governance) in various manufacturing and trading sectors, but very few studies have been found in the service sector especially in tourism and hospitality sector. This study analyzes the general attitude of investors toward SRI. This chapter delves with a detailed explanation about the various tools that are used to analyze this study. The significance of each variable and construct that has been found to be relevant to the present study, through the literature reviews, has been critically analyzed with the support of various statistical tools. The chapter also provides an overview of the operational definitions, sample size, techniques, sources of data, methods of data collection, and the various techniques used to analyze the data.

16.9 RESEARCH PARADIGM

Socially responsible investment has a wide scope as it consists of ethical practices, the type of products a company produces, relationship with employees, environmental objectives and effective corporate governance. The financial return was the major reward or expectation by an investor in selecting a stock. But over the past few decades, investors are considering and thinking beyond financial returns. SRI is the integration of ethical, environmental, and social concerns into the investment decision and incorporates convention investment initiated with the expectation that it will take a certain period of time before it generates a positive cash flow. Disclosure of social responsibilities information may strengthen and develop a positive image in the minds of the public minds. The effect of CSR may have a positive impact on the investor to develop the belief that long-time consistency or additional cost may reduce the resources of the company. The purpose of the study is to help investment fund managers, portfolio makers, mutual fund managers, brokers, institutional investors, tour operators, travel agencies, hoteliers, and investment agencies to understand the opinion and preferences of investors in a better way. The main objective of this paper is to analyze and understand investor's awareness about SRI and their opinion in buying those stocks.

16.10 METHODOLOGICAL PREVIEW

The sources of data collected for this study are divided into primary and secondary data. Primary data were collected with the help of structured questionnaire that was circulated among the investors. The questionnaire included the respondents' demographic information, awareness on investment opportunities, specific social and environmental items. A five-point Likert scale was used to get the required information. Secondary data were collected from printed materials, newspapers, journals, articles, websites, and research articles. Various statistical tools and techniques are used to analyze the data and to prove the hypothesis with the help of statistical package SPSS 20.

16.11 RESULTS AND DISCUSSIONS

One of the predominant objectives was to study the awareness among investors about socially responsible stocks, and the statistical method applied was the descriptive statistics (mean) and factor analysis to analyze. One of the hypotheses postulates the awareness among investors about SRI.

Mean Score of Types of Investments.

Awareness of investment types	Mean score
Bank deposits	3.47
Postoffice deposits	3.20
Mutual funds	2.71
Share market	2.89
Bullion market	2.21
Real estate	3.12
Provident fund (PF)	2.69
National savings scheme	2.35
Insurance	3.36
Socially responsible investment	1.90

It is inferred that selected investors have a greater awareness of bank deposits over other investment avenues, followed by insurance and post office deposits. The mean score of SRI is 190, which is least compared with others. This means selected investors are less aware of the SRI. Hence, this hypothesis can be rejected.

Factor Analysis of General Awareness and Attitude of Socially Responsible Investment: Kaiser–Meyer–Olkin (KMO) and Bartlett's test.

KMO measure of sampling adequacy		.560
Bartlett's test of sphericity	Approx. chi-square	474.392
	Degree of freedom	136
	Sig.	.000

Kaiser–Meyer–Olkin (KMO) measure of sampling adequacy: This measure varies between 0 and 1, and values closer to 1 are better. A value of .6 is a suggested minimum, and, in this case, it is .560 which means the data are adequate and not minimum.

Bartlett's test of sphericity: This tests the null hypothesis that the correlation matrix is an identity matrix. An identity matrix is that in which all of the diagonal elements are 1, and all off diagonal elements are 0. In this test, we can reject this null hypothesis.

These two are put together to provide the minimum pass standard for factor analysis.

Table Factor Analysis and Loading: General Awareness and Attitude of Socially Responsible Investment.

Communalities		
	Initial	Extraction
I have never heard of socially responsible investment (SRI) before	1.000	.824
I have never thought about buying SRIs	1.000	.873
I would buy SRIs if my retirement plan offered that option	1.000	.787
I would buy SRIs if it carries Tax exemption	1.000	.770
I would buy SRIs if I had more information on how to do it	1.000	.726
I would buy SRIs if it is more profitable	1.000	.626
I would buy SRIs though it yields fewer returns	1.000	.679
I recommend others to be a part of SRI	1.000	.712
Generally, RIs are less attractive	1.000	.767
I invest in both SRI and conventional investment (which are not responsible investment)	1.000	.731
Even if it is less profitable, I will go for SRI	1.000	.739
I don't believe in SRI	1.000	.820
I take pride in my investments	1.000	.786
My investments make me feel good about myself	1.000	.754
Do you think SRI is "unique selling points" of a company?	1.000	.584
It is not appropriate to express one's social and environmental beliefs through investing	1.000	.467
I feel good about the SRIs I own	1.000	.703

Extraction method: principal component analysis.

Communalities: This is the proportion of each variable's variance that can be explained by the factors (e.g., the underlying latent continua).

Extraction: The values in this column indicate the proportion of each variable's variance that can be explained by the retained factors. Variables with high values are well represented in the common factor space, whereas variables with low values are not well represented.

Total Variance Explained.

Component	Initial Eigen values			Extraction sums of squared loadings			Rotation sums of squared loadings		
	Total	% of variance	Cumulative %	Total	% of Variance	Cumulative %	Total	% of variance	Cumulative %
1	2.876	16.915	16.915	2.876	16.915	16.915	2.320	13.644	13.644
2	2.499	14.702	31.617	2.499	14.702	31.617	1.959	11.524	25.169
3	2.139	12.583	44.200	2.139	12.583	44.200	1.825	10.734	35.903
4	1.500	8.822	53.022	1.500	8.822	53.022	1.806	10.624	46.527
5	1.255	7.380	60.402	1.255	7.380	60.402	1.669	9.819	56.346
6	1.057	6.217	66.620	1.057	6.217	66.620	1.391	8.184	64.530
7	1.024	6.023	72.643	1.024	6.023	72.643	1.379	8.113	72.643
8	0.983	5.780	78.423						
9	0.815	4.794	83.217						
10	0.520	3.060	86.277						
11	0.497	2.923	89.200						
12	0.440	2.591	91.791						
13	0.395	2.326	94.117						
14	0.313	1.840	95.957						
15	0.268	1.579	97.536						
16	0.217	1.279	98.815						
17	0.201	1.185	100.000						

Extraction method: principal component analysis.

Factor: The initial number of factors is the same as the number of variables used in the factor analysis. However, not all 17 factors will be retained. In this research, only the first seven factors are retained.

Initial eigenvalues: Eigenvalues are the variances of the factors. As we conducted our factor analysis on the correlation matrix, the variables are standardized, which means that each variable has a variance of 1, and the total variance is equal to the number of variables used in the analysis, in this case, 17.

Total: This column contains the eigenvalues. The first factor will always account for the most variance (and hence have the highest eigenvalue), and the next factor will account for as much of the leftover variance as it can, and so on. Hence, each successive factor will account for less and less variance.

% of Variance: This column contains the percentage of total variance accounted for by each factor.

Cumulative %: This column contains the cumulative percentage of variance accounted for by the current and all preceding factors. For example, the seventh row shows a value of 72.643. This means that the first seven factors together account for 72.643% of the total variance.

Extraction sums of squared loadings: The number of rows in this panel of the table corresponds to the number of factors retained. In this research, it is decided that seven factors be retained, so there are seven rows, one for each retained factor.

Rotation sums of squared loadings: The values in this panel of the table represent the distribution of the variance after the varimax rotation. Varimax rotation tries to maximize the variance of each of the factors, so the total amount of variance accounted for is redistributed over the seven extracted factors.

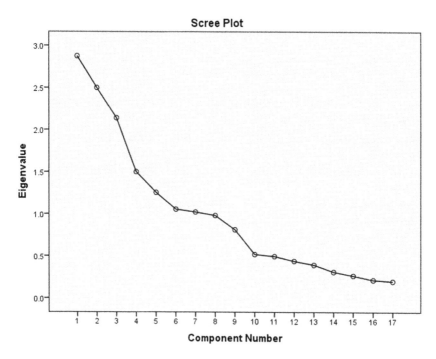

The scree plot graphs the eigenvalue against the factor number. From the seventh factor on, the line is almost flat, meaning each successive factor is accounting for smaller and smaller amounts of the total variance.

Rotated Component Matrix[a].

	Components						
	1	2	3	4	5	6	7
I have never heard of SRI before	−.115	.868	.112	.182	.054	.072	.064
I have never thought about buying SRIs	−.046	.924	.005	.004	.101	.007	−.080
I Would buy SRIs if my retirement plan offered that option	−.159	.010	.860	−.018	.140	.031	.043
I would buy SRIs if it carry's Tax exemption	.195	.128	.817	−.143	.156	.026	.055
I would buy SRIs if I had more information on how to do it	.171	.096	.090	.037	.789	−.235	.037

Rotated Component Matrix[a]. (*Continued*)

	Components						
	1	**2**	**3**	**4**	**5**	**6**	**7**
I would buy SRIs if it is more profitable	−.082	.062	.172	−.127	.735	.134	.111
I would buy SRIs though it yields fewer returns	−.068	−.091	−.356	.715	.103	−.096	.094
I recommend others to be a part of SRI	.782	−.103	.040	−.004	.226	−.041	−.186
Generally, SRIs are less attractive	.076	.186	.166	.780	−.220	−.146	−.145
I Invest in both SRI and conventional investment (which are not responsible investment)	.238	−.236	.318	.062	.337	.577	−.260
Even if it is less profitable I will go for socially responsible investment	.569	−.343	−.165	.255	−.422	.166	.003
I don't believe in SRI	.032	.120	−.001	−.090	−.165	.876	.032
I take pride in my investments	.040	−.096	.113	.034	.134	−.017	.862
My investments make me feel good about myself	.624	.175	−.045	−.020	.001	−.075	.571
Do you think SRI is "unique selling points" of a company?	.433	.093	−.027	.598	−.044	.150	.070
It is not appropriate to express one's social and environment beliefs through investing	−.015	.147	−.252	.412	−.020	.328	.322
I feel good about the SRIs I own	.789	−.104	.071	.100	−.046	.121	.197

Extraction method: principal component analysis.
Rotation method: varimax with Kaiser normalization.
[a]Rotation converged in seven iterations.

Factor: The columns under this heading are the rotated factors that have been extracted. Seven factors were extracted. These are the factors that mostly represent the general awareness and attitude of the investors. These factors can be named as social consciousness, SRI illiteracy, SRI financial plan, uniqueness of SRI, SRI preferences, and SRI opinion.

Factor 1: Social consciousness

Social Consciousness	Factor loadings
I recommend others to be a part of SRI	.782
Even if it is less profitable I will go for SRI	.569
My investments make me feel good about myself	.624
I feel good about the SRIs I own	.789

Factor 2: SRI illiteracy

SRI illiteracy	Factor loadings
I have never heard of SRI before	.868
I have never thought about buying SRIs	.924

Factor 3: SRI Financial Plan

SRI financial plan	Factor loadings
I would buy SRIs if my retirement plan offered that option	.868
I would buy SRIs if it carries tax exemption	.924

Factor 4: Uniqueness of SRI

Uniqueness of SRI	Factor loadings
I would buy SRIs though it yields less returns	.715
Generally SRIs are less attractive	.780
Do you think SRI is "unique selling points" of a company	.598

Factor 5: Uniqueness of SRI

SRI preferences	Factor loadings
I would buy SRIs if I had more information on how to do it	789
I would buy SRIs if it is more profitable	.735

Factor 6: SRI opinion

SRI Opinion	Factor loadings
I invest in both SRI and conventional investment (which are not responsible investment)	.577
I don't believe in SRI	.876

16.12   SUMMARY OF FINDINGS

It is found that nearly 69% of the investors are aware of the bank deposits and its importance. Although 67.2% of them aware of insurance policies that are offered by the companies, followed by post office (3.20) and real estate (3.12) as their mean scores. Remaining investment avenues are not much popular among the respondents. Even SRI is not popular as only 38% of the respondents are aware of this. Factor analysis has been conducted to identify those factors that are highly considered by the investors. In general, attitude of SRI, 17 items were considered, out of which more than 15 items were grouped and named under the heads of social consciousness, SRI illiteracy, SRI financial plan, uniqueness of SRI, SRI preferences, and SRI opinion.

16.13   SUGGESTIONS

Stakeholders of tourism and hospitality sectors similar to tour operators, travel agencies, hoteliers, and regulatory bodies must take an effort to popularize importance of SRI in their respective domain. On the other hand, investors can reshape and rejuvenate the society by using SRI as a tool. As the concept of SRI is emerging in developing countries such as India, there is a requirement of initiatives from government bodies, policymakers, corporate houses, and individual investors. SRI conforms to a particular profile of investors, as they think nonfinancial returns as well. This study used a small group of a sample size of individual investors including those with knowledge of SRI and those without to determine their attitude. The aim of this research was to understand the awareness and attitude of Investors toward SRI. SRI is an emerging concept in Indian financial system. A few studies have been done in this area. Further research can be taken by extending the sample size and wide geographical scope. SRI pertains to different stakeholders like investors, government bodies, employees, general public, institutional investors, and much more. Moreover, specific sector studies have not been conducted widely.

KEYWORDS

- **socially responsible investment**
- **attitude**
- **social**
- **sustainable environment practices**
- **corporate social responsibility and tourism**

REFERENCES

Barber, B. M.; Odean, T. Boys will be Boys: Gender, Overconfidence, and Common Stock Investment. *Q. J. Eco.* **2001,** *116*(1), 261–292.

Beal, D. J.; Goyen, M.; Philips, P. Why do We Invest Ethically? *J. Invest.* **2005,** *14*(3), 66–78.

Bennet, E.; Selvam, M.; Indhumathi, G.; Ramkumar, R. R.; Karpagam, V. Factors Influencing Retail Investors Attitude Towards Investing in Equity Stocks: A Study in Tamil Nadu. *J. Modern Acc. Auditing* **2011,** *7*(3), 316–321.

De Cleene, S.; Sonnenberg, D. *Socially Responsible Investment in South Africa*; 2nd Ed.; African Institute of Corporate Citizenship: Johannesburg, 2004.

Derwall, J.; Koedijk, K.; Ter Horst, J. A Tale of Values-Driven and Profit-Seeking Social Investors. *J. Banking Finance* **2011,** *35*(8), 2137–2147.

Dilla, W. N.; Janvrin, D. J.; Perkins, J. D.; Raschke, R. Investor Attitudes, Investment Screen Use, and Socially Responsible Investment Behavior. Investment Screen Use, and Socially Responsible Investment Behavior, 2013. (accessed May 2, 2013).

Diouf, D.; Hebb, T. Exploring Factors that Influence Social Retail Investors' Decisions: Evidence from Desjardins Fund. *J. Bus. Ethics* **2013,** 1–23.

Eccles, N. S.; Nicholls, S.; De Jongh, D. The State of Responsible Investment in South Africa. *Pretoria: UNISA Centre for Corporate Citizenship.* 2008. 5 August 2008. http://www.unisa.ac.za/contents/colleges/col_econ_man_science/ccc/docs/State%20of%20 responsible%20In vestment%20in%20South%20Africa.pdf.

Estes, R.; Hosseini, J. The Gender Gap on Wall Street: An Empirical Analysis of Confidence in Investment Decision Making. *J. Psychol.* **1988,** *122*(6), 577–590.

Hejazi, R.; Hesari, S. *Investor's Reaction to the Disclosure Types of Corporate Social Responsibilities,* 2nd International Conference on Social Science and Humanity. IACSIT Press: Singapore, 2012; Vol. 31; http://www.ipedr.com/vol31/027-ICSSH 2012-S10023. pdf. (accessed Jan 23, 2013).

Herringer, A.; Firer, C.; Viviers, S. Key Challenges Facing the Socially Responsible Investment (SRI) Sector in South Africa. *Investment Anal. J.* **2009,** *70*(69), 11–26.

Hutton R. B.; D'Antonio, L.; Johnsen T. Socially Responsible Investing. *Bus. Soc. Mag.* **1998,** *37*(3), 281–306

IFC. Towards Sustainable Responsible Investments in Emerging Markets. Prepared by Enterprising Solutions Global Consulting. October. Investors Must Navigate the

Minefield of Socially Acceptable Offerings. Business Day survey: pension fund investments, 2003, 29 April: 18.

Jansson, M.; Biel, A. Investment Institutions' Beliefs About and Attitudes Toward Socially Responsible Investment (SRI): A Comparison Between SRI and Non-SRI Management. *Sustainable Dev.* **2014,** *22*(1), 33–41.

Martin, P.; Moser, D. V. Managers' Green Investment Disclosures and Investors' Reaction. AAA, 2012.

McLachlan, J.; Gardner, J. A Comparison of Socially Responsible and Conventional Investors. *J. Bus. Ethics* **2004,** *52*(1), 11–25.

Nilsson, J. Segmenting Socially Responsible Mutual Fund Investors. The Influence of Financial Return and Social Responsibility. *Int. J. Bank Mark.* **2009,** *27*(1), 5–31.

Renneboog, L.; Ter Horst, J.; Zhang, C. Socially Responsible Investments: Institutional Aspects, Performance and Investor Behavior. *J. Banking Finance* **2008,** *32*, 1723–1742.

Rhodes, M. J. Information Asymmetry and Socially Responsible Investment. *J. Bus. Ethics* **2010,** *95*(1), 145–150.

Rosen, B. N.; Sandler, D. M.; Shani, D. Social Issues and Socially Responsible Investment Behavior: A Preliminary Empirical Investigation. *J. Consum. Affairs* **1991,** *25*(2), 221–234.

Schueth, S. Socially Responsible Investing in the United States. *J. Bus. Ethics* **2003,** *43*(3), 189–194.

Slapikaite, I.; Tamosiuniene, R. Socially Responsible Mutual Funds–A Profitable Way of Investing. *Ann. Alexandru Ioan Cuza University–Economics* **2013,** *60*(1), 202–214.

Social Investment Forum. Report on Socially Responsible Investing Trends in the United States. Social Investment Forum Research Program: Washington DC, 2001.

Sustainability and International Finance Corporation. Developing Value: The Business Case for Sustainability in Emerging Markets.

Viviers S. A Critical Assessment of Socially Responsible Investing in South Africa. Unpublished Doctoral Thesis, Nelson Mandela Metropolitan University, Port Elizabeth, 2007.

Woods, C.; Urwin, R. Putting Sustainable Investment into Practice: A Governance Framework for Pension Funds. *J. Bus. Ethics* **2010,** *92*, 1–19.

CHAPTER 17

SOCIOCULTURAL IMPACTS OF THE NAMDAPHA ECOCULTURAL FESTIVAL ON THE LOCAL RESIDENTS OF MIAO, INDIA

PINKY JACOB

Product Support Specialist at TravelClick, Melbourne, Australia

CONTENTS

ABSTRACT

Tourism worldwide is gaining popularity. Tourism is used as a tool for synergizing conservation of biodiversity and also community development. Festivals and events can support and promote tourist destination to brand and attract tourists. There is extensive literature and research done on tourists but very few of local residents and its sociocultural determinants along with environmental impacts pertaining to tourism activities. The current chapter is exploratory in nature, and the emphasis is laid on the residents of the Miao region and attempts to measure their perceptions toward sociocultural impacts of the Namdapha Ecocultural Festival. However, in order to profoundly analyze the complexities of attitudes formation in regards to the festival, it is endorsed to demeanor a longitudinal study (a repeated study of the same elements over a period of time). This chapter attempts to bring forth the impact of tourism on a destination and also the ways in which the local residents or the community plays a foremost role in achieving sustainable tourism development.

17.1   INTRODUCTION

Tourism is a dynamic, evolving, consumer-driven force and is the world's largest industry if all of its interrelated components are placed under one umbrella. Tourism, the world's largest industry, offers the greatest global employment as well as development prospects. In recent decades, the concept of tourism has broadened into holistic interpretations that have given rise to the modeling of tourism as a system. Scholarly articles disseminate recommended many tourism models, and the key results of this holistic and interrelated models include tourism is not a discipline; instead, it is a multidisciplinary field and is generated by two major powers—demand and supply. Any attempt to define tourism and describe its scope fully must consider the various groups that participate in and are affected by this industry. The tourism industry is constantly on the move with the development and creation of new attractions, destinations, and innovative products. But the industry as a whole has recognized the importance of conserving, preserving, and protecting the environment and its natural resources. Sustainable tourism, responsible tourism, ecotourism, natural, green tourism, cultural tourism are the jargons that are predominantly used in any tourism sector. Even the tourists have become vocal about their role in preserving environment because tourism is too important to mankind to let it continue to drift.

The trend is right now to "experience" the various tourism products, for example, cultural, local traditions, volunteer, and so forth rather than just visiting them. The various service providers and suppliers have developed innovate itineraries to attract this kind of tourists. Many unexplored destinations are attracting a good share of tourists and contributing to the development of their nations—for example, Azerbaijan, Turkey, Slovakia, and much more. Various theme-based hotels and resorts are getting popular among new-generation tourists. Events have long played an important role in human society. The tedium of daily life, with its constant toil and effort, was broken up by events of all kinds. In most societies, the slightest excuse could be found for a good celebration although traditional celebrations often had strict rituals and ceremonies. In the modern world, some of the historic driving forces for events have changed. Many events play a contemporary role in attracting tourists (and thus tourist income) to a particular place. Historic, traditional folk ceremonies, and rituals, in practice, are recent innovations or recreations. People travel from one country to another to witness the pomp and splendor of festivals and also to be a part of the ceremonies.

One of the main characteristics of an event is its uniqueness. It does have many other characteristics in common with all types of services, and in particular with hospitality and leisure services of many kinds. Historically, social events have played an important role in human society by breaking the dullness of daily life filled with constant hard work and effort. Before the industrial revolution, daily routine activities were regularly mixed with festivals and carnivals all over the world. Some of the historic driving forces for events have changed in the modern world, and today many events play a contemporary role in attracting tourists and tourist income. Some of the key factors attributing to the growth of festivals have been the potential of development in terms of repositioning, revitalization, and economic restructuring.

In recent years, festivals have gained greater importance in tourism strategies. It is one of the world's largest and fastest growing industries in the economy and has been adopted by many destinations as a way to promote and rejuvenate tourism as well as to revitalize the local economy. On a global basis, there is unprecedented interest in festivals at events at the international and national level, in cities and towns, villages, and so forth. Everyone wants to celebrate their particular form of culture, tradition differences or similarity with others. Festivals and events can help promote tourist destination and attract tourists. No matter what the reason is for hosting a festival or event, there is a wide range of customers, and festivals are therefore a significant and integral segment of the leisure industry. Festivals are evolving as a mounting and exciting sector of tourism and leisure businesses and are seen to have significant economic, sociocultural, and political impacts on the destination area and host groups. Most public festivals are viewed as cultural celebrations bringing in tremendous development in tourism.

Today many cities all over the world are supported by the government to position themselves through high-profile events as event destinations. One such festival is Namdapha Ecocultural Festival celebrated every year at Miao, Changlang District. The year 2004 saw the start of the Namdapha Ecocultural Festival. It is held for 3 days at Miao between January and February, and it brings together all the tribes of the region. The festival is based on the twin objectives of promoting the rich cultural heritage of the people of the district and also to preserve the environment. In this ecocultural festival, held on February 5, 2010, several NGOs and private agencies took part including Oil India Limited India. The venue was filled with over 162 stalls and cultural troupes belonging to different communities of the state.

This 3-day event became very popular this year, with a singing sensation of a popular reality show performing on a concluding day. Several other local artists and groups also gave a boost to the celebration. The festival included traditional food items and exhibitions put up by different government departments as well as private agencies. In addition, various games, sports, dance, and fashion shows of different communities were also showcased. A large number of senior delegates and officials strongly condemned the traditional practice of fishing and hunting and destroying forest resources. The people were asked to change their outlook and consider this as a practice that could ruin the whole pleasant environment. It is a beautiful platform in which people from different communities can make contacts, interact, and exchange ideas to boost public harmony and collective unity.

17.2   LITERATURE REVIEW

In the past years, there has been an increase in research on event impacts, especially the economic impacts of tourism on host destinations. But more recently this emphasis has begun to move away from the assessment of only economic impacts more toward the investigation of social impacts of events and festivals. It is perceived from scholarly works that, although a return on investment is more adequately measured in financial terms, any real community gain is often through the more intangible impacts relating to community, society, and culture, but this should not lead to the exclusion of economic impact but the development of a more multidimensional approach. Sherwood (2005) considered a more holistic approach for the industry to evaluate impacts of events.

The current chapter will focus on the residents of the Miao region and measure their perceptions of the Namdapha Ecocultural Festival. The reason for studying residents and no other stakeholders in this study is rooted in the fact that residents are widely considered to play a vital role in overall tourism development in an area and, in particular, in acceptance or rejection of an event based on their perceptions and attitudes towards it (Delamere, 1992). The purpose of this study is to discover the main positive and negative dimensions of social impacts of the festival relevant to the residents of the city. In order to achieve it, the study will examine the relevant literature and previous research on festivals, events, and social impacts.

There are a number of problematic issues within sociocultural impact event evaluation research. To begin with, the analysis of the literature in the area of event research shows that measuring sociocultural impacts of events is recognized as a relatively new field of study. In addition, events/festivals produce various outcomes, and managers cannot concentrate only on event profitability as a measure of success. Instead, there is growing recognition that social and environmental aspects of running an event should be equally considered, articulated, measured, and understood. Considerable research on event management and event studies has been conducted in the tourism industry. Getz (2005, 2008) writes about event management as a field of professional practice devoted to production and management of events that focus on planned events with a social or economic purpose, whereas event studies focus on the importance of events in the economy in society and environment.

Research exploring the motivations of art and music festivals audiences has been conducted by authors such as example indicating that visitors exhibit different motives based on event type. Schofield and Thompson (2007) suggest that visitor motivations can be subdivided into "push" and "pull" studies. The increasing popularity of festivals and events, coupled with their positive and negative impacts on host communities, has led to a growing body of research on the impacts of festivals and events. As a substantial amount of this research has focused on assessing economic impacts, there is a growing demand for the measurement of sociocultural impacts of the festivals and events. Placing a value on festivals and other planned events has been obscured by an overemphasis on event tourism and other economic benefits. The social and cultural values of events have been given inadequate attention, so that until recently we have had trouble identifying, letting alone measuring them (Getz, 2009). Much of the literature studying festival and event impacts builds on the early work in the area of event tourism in which Getz (1997) is the most often cited author. However, these studies are not specifically designed to measure the impacts of cultural events, and their methods have mostly been applied to sporting events. Hede (2007) and Rogers and Ryan (2001) acknowledge the importance of the triple bottom line (TBL) approach in the area of special events assessment that combines economic, social, and environmental aspects into one framework. Hegde's research (2007) found that not all stakeholders in the events sector were interested in all the three elements in TPL approach.

Getz (2009) states that while volunteers and tourists are focused on the social aspects, most governments and residents are usually interested in the social, environmental, and economic issues concerning events; other stakeholders are mostly interested in profit and the financial bottom line. Much of the research on the impacts of festivals has been undertaken in urban contexts. However, in practice, rural economic policymakers struggling to encourage tourism have also joined the bandwagon: building festivals around local produce, art forms, and sports, and so forth. For many in this century, festivals have become elixir of rural economic regeneration. Jago et al. (2003) used a number of workshops to investigate current issues and practices around events and destination marketing. One of the findings suggests that a barrier to using events to promote and build destination image successful is a lack of cooperation between tourism policymakers and event managers but that such organizational cooperation was seen to be higher in small rural town. It should be noted, however, that even highly successful large-scale festivals may have a little impact on changing long-standing perceptions of a region.

The impact brought about by the interaction of hosts and tourists is a well-documented phenomenon and the findings of researchers. In the anthropology perspective of tourism, it is observed as a rapid and extended acceptance in consent with the academia. The categorization of tourists into typologies is now accepted as an orthodox tool in the study of sociocultural impacts. The social impacts as "the consequences to human populations of any public or private actions that alter the ways in which people live, work, play, relate to one another, organize to meet their needs, and generally cope as members of society. The term also includes cultural impacts involving changes to the norms, values, and beliefs that guide and rationalize their cognition of themselves and their society." Park (2007) terms social impacts as the changes in social and cultural conditions, which can be positive or negative, which directly or indirectly result from an activity, project or program. Moreover, Becker and Vanclay (2003, p. 77) suggest that social impacts are "impacts actually experienced by humans (at the individual and higher aggregation levels) in either a corporeal (physical) or cognitive (perceptual) sense." As the range of cultural festivals and major cultural events has grown over the years, their impacts have increasingly come under the scrutiny of funders, policy-makers, and planners. Various evaluations and more in-depth studies have found that large-scale events have a variety of potential impacts, including economic, social, cultural, political, physical, and environmental ones.

The impacts are not always necessarily positive, but can be negative as well, or have a positive effect on one dimension (e.g., economic) while having a negative effect on another (e.g., environmental or cultural). Much of the literature studying festival and event impacts builds on the early work in the area of event tourism in which Getz (1997), Ritchie (1984), and Hall (1992) are the most often cited authors. However, these studies are not specifically designed to measure the impacts of cultural events, and their methods have mostly been applied to sporting events. Some of the economic impact studies identified the need for additional research on social impacts. For instance, a report on Manchester's Pillar Events by Jura Consultants (2006) notes a major research gap in understanding the indirect impacts of major events upon host communities and point out that the intangible or less easily measured outcomes or outputs are often ignored or poorly dealt with. The authors argue for the use of focus groups to develop an understanding of cultural networks and impacts on industry and the effect on audiences, and so forth and furthermore suggest that such impacts are probably best studied through a longitudinal, multiyear approach. However, it has to be noted that some studies that claim to go beyond the assessment of local economic impacts, in fact, offer little more than some general observations based on a limited methodology.

For instance, the evaluation of the Ghent Festivities by the Centre for Tourism Policy Studies (2003) claims to assess the economic, physical, functional, social, and cultural effects of the event but in reality is mainly concerned with quantifiable economic benefits. Examples of impact assessments that do pay significant attention to noneconomic impacts are found in studies by Morris Hargreaves McIntyre and Arts About Manchester (2008), who evaluated the achievements of the Manchester International Festival against its set aims, objectives, and targets (which included certain social impacts), and Hamilton et al. (2007), who carried out an evaluation of the Highland Year of Culture, focusing on economic, social and cultural impacts before, during and after the festival year, using a range of qualitative and quantitative methods, including interviews, surveys, focus, and discussion groups and press impact analysis.

On the contrary, it is been argued that environmental, sociocultural, and political effects are probably more important than economic ones but have tended to be ignored because festival organizers and councils commission research to get economic data, sociocultural impacts are less easily quantifiable, and research concerned with sociocultural effects may find results that are less politically palatable particularly as negative consequences.

Festivals have occupied an important place in the event-related literature but have not previously been assessed separately. Prior to 1993, when the research journal *Festival Management and Event Tourism* was established (it was later renamed to event management), there was only sporadic research-based papers dealing with event tourism and festival/event management research. As confirmed by some seminal works, there were few articles related to event management or event tourism published in the 1970s—it was found a total of four in *Annals of Tourism Research* and *Journal of Travel Research*. Formica quantified the topics explored by the festival and special event research articles from 1970 through 1996, concluding that the main areas covered were (in decreasing order of frequency) economic and financial impacts, marketing, profiles of festival or events, sponsorship, management, trends, and forecasts. More recent reviews of event management and event tourism have been compiled by Getz (2000, 2008) and Sherwood (2007). Getz (2000) reviewed articles published in the journal *Event Management* from its inception in 1993 up to Vol. *6(2)* in 2000, concluding that the most frequent topics were economic development and impacts of events, followed by sponsorship and event marketing from the corporate perspective. Also in 2000, at the "Events Beyond 2000" Conference in Sydney, Harris et al. reviewed Australian events-related research. They determined that the most frequently examined topics were economic development impacts of events, other management topics, and community impacts (with resident attitudes and perceptions).

However, most of the research literature on impacts were related to sports events, not festivals. Some seminal work examines the satisfaction levels at a music festival comparing residents and tourists. Contemplating on the concurrent studies, it is explored that quantitative assessment too found a place in examining relationships between perceived festival service quality, perceived value, and behavioral intentions. What is not receiving much attention is an evaluation of the effectiveness or efficiency of event operations, or return on investment measures, evaluation of unanticipated outcomes, or learning systems.

17.3 METHODOLOGY

The current study will focus on the residents of the Miao region and measure their perceptions of the Namdapha Ecocultural Festival. The reason for studying residents and not other stakeholders in this study is rooted in the fact that residents are widely considered to play a vital role in overall sustainable tourism development in an area and, in particular, in acceptance or rejection of an event based on their perceptions and attitudes toward it (Delamere 1992).

The current chapter applies both primary and secondary tools of data collection. For the purpose of the study, the social impacts of Namdapha Ecocultural Festival will be assessed and analyzed. A structured questionnaire is being used for the study that is based on festival social impact attitude scale (FSIAS) developed by (Delamere, 2001) to evaluate the social impact of Way Out Festival. This scale is considered a comprehensive measure of the social impacts in the festival study area. This chapter raises certain specific objectives—primarily to study the relationship between sociocultural impact and festival tourism and to understand the dimensions of sociocultural impacts on the local residents. The role of festival tourism in developing tourism at a tourism destination is also examined so as to find out the positive and negative impacts of Namdapha Ecocultural Festival on the local residents of Miao. The chapter also analyzes the difference among various occupations on perception on tourism organizer in NEFC and examines whether any relationship between benefits and cost with net perceived with by income earned through tourism and nonincome through tourism This chapter also explores the impact of benefits variables on Net Perceived in NEFC.

17.4 FINDINGS

The analysis carried out among the general residents portray very positively in assessing both benefits and costs of the festival. Among the total sample of 100 respondents, maximum respondents were given by those in the age group of <30 years, constituting 39%. It was followed by the sample in the age span of 31–40 years, 36%. Then the least chunk of respondents was aged above 50, 5%. There is no statistically significant difference in net perception score and image on tourist organizer between men and women.

The residents <30 assesses more positive benefits than others showing that the younger respondents felt proud visiting the festival. There is a statistically linear relationship between perceived positive variables on net perception score of the residents of NEFC. Out of 100 respondents, 47% agrees to the fact that there is no source of income for the local residents from Namdapha Ecocultural Festival. Twenty-three percent of the respondents say that they receive little income with just 4% who get almost all income from this festival.

Pearson correlation is employed to find the association or relation between two variables namely benefits and net perception and cost with net perception. Totally three sets of correlation are used one for overall, a category of income from NEFC and category of nonincome from NEFC. In overall correlation, the relationship between benefits and net perception is .798 or 79% and cost with net perception is $-.553$ or 55.3% and also indicating a negative relation. Income group has got the higher correlation between benefits with net perception and, at the same, less score in cost with net perception in compared with nonincome group that is a likely expected outcome. Regression analysis was used to find the effect of perceived positive variables on net perception score of the residents of NEFC. The results of the analysis are shown in Table 4.6. It is seen from the table that the correlation coefficient value is (R) .809, which exhibits a fair amount of correlation between the independent variable (perceived positive) and dependent variable (net perception score), with the F-ratio being 44.98 and its associated significance level being small ($P < .01$).

The R-square value gives us the goodness of fit of the regression model. That is, the amount of variability explained by the whole of the selected predictor variables in the model for 65% ($R^2\% = .654 \times 100 = 65.4\%$) of variation in the dependent variable (net perception score).

The Tourism Department, Arunachal Pradesh should provide necessary inputs, support, and other facilities so as to boost tourism in Miao. Tourism in Miao should be developed in a sustainable manner keeping in account the latest trends in the tourism sector. Proper communication and media channels should be developed so that tourists, local residents, and service providers are able to be a part of this festival in a much better way. From the secondary data, that is, reviews, articles, books, we could see that festival study is in its infancy. Many festivals are part of important attractions in a destination, but there is neither visitor management nor proper assessment done on it. So, the researcher, policymakers, and others can look into this area in a much better way and contribute to the field of festival tourism.

17.5 CONCLUSION

Current chapter tries to bring forth the impact of tourism on a destination and also the ways in which the local residents or the community plays a major role in achieving sustainable development in that place. To fully assess the impacts of Namdapha Ecocultural Festival on the local residents of Miao, it is recommended to the management, organization, and stakeholders of the festival to apply a TBL approach research (economic, social, and environmental) framework. The main focus of the study was on the sociocultural impacts of the festival, but in order to embrace sustainable strategies, to maximize the benefits of this festival, to understand the big picture and interests of all stakeholders, it is important to use the TBL approach in the future. Furthermore, most social impact studies define social impact studies in terms of either positive or negative and by that implying negative connotations, and thus failing to recognize the existence of the diversity of opinions of those impacts and the "shades of gray." Maybe, the use of social consequences could be a more appropriate term for further studies (Reid, 2007).

Another opportunity for further research exists in an in-depth study of the social capital that festivals might generate for the city. The importance of social capital and networks is apparent in terms of individual and collective beneficiaries. There is a lack of research in festival tourism and also in understanding the positive as well as negative impacts on the local community or residents. Future studies could replicate this study in a different format, for a different festival and its relationship with the stakeholders and so forth. The festival organizers should take into account the residents perceptions and also the sustainability concerns of the destination. They should also promote and preserve the environment and other tourist attractions. Proper long-term planning should be done for better returns from tourism.

The chapter portrays the residents' perceptions on the social impacts of Namdapha Ecocultural festival at a single point in time. However, in order to deeper analyze the complexities of attitudes formation in regards to the festival, it is recommended to conduct a longitudinal study a repeated study of the same elements over a period of time which will enable researchers to obtain an accurate measure of the differences observed. A similar study can be done on other festivals across India. It is rightly said that the future tourism depends on the way the present generation preserves, protects, and maintains the environment and the resources around them. The concept of sustainable development encompasses the whole idea of achieving a sound tourism development at the destination. This is evident from the fact that local community and local resources are to be given the utmost importance, and their important role in this whole endeavor should be recognized and promoted by Govt., NGOs, planners, and policymakers. Tourism has moved on from being just an activity of sightseeing alone, and it is right now said to be a part of experiencing, volunteering, and also being responsible for the earth we live in.

KEYWORDS

- Namdapha ecocultural
- sociocultural
- local residents
- festival tourism
- measure perceptions

REFERENCES

Andriotis, K.; Vanghn, R. D. Urban Residents' Attitudes Toward Tourism Development: The Case of Crete. *J. Travel Res.* **2003,** *42*(2), 172–185.

Bhatia, A. K. *International Tourism—Fundamentals and Practices;* Sterling Publishers Pvt. Ltd.: New Delhi, 1997.

Delamere, T. A. Development of a Scale to Measure Local Resident Perceptions of the Social Impacts of Community Festivals. Paper presented at the Ninth Canadian Congress on Leisure Research. May, 1999; Acadia University: Wolfville, Nova Scotia. http://lin. ca/Uploads/cclr9/CCLR9_11.pdf.

Getz, D. *Festivals, Special Events, and Tourism;* Van Nostrand Reinhold: New York, NY, 1991.

Marsh, N. R.; Henshal, B. D. Planning Better Tourism: The Strategic Importance of Tourist-Resident Expectations and Interactions. *Tourism Recreation Res.* **1987,** *12,* 47–54.

Mathieson, A.; Wall, G. *Tourism, Economic, Physical and Social Impacts;* Longman: London, 1982.

Mowforth, M.; Munt, I. *Tourism and Sustainability—New Tourism in the Third World;* Routledge: New York, 1998.

Narasaiah, M. L. *Globalisation and Sustainable Tourism Development;* Discovery Publishing House: New Delhi, 2004.

Seth, P. N.; Bhatt, S. S. *An Introduction to Travel and Tourism;* Sterling Publishers Pvt. Ltd.: New Delhi, 2003.

Sherwood, P. A Triple Bottom Line Evaluation of the Impact of Special Events: The Development of Indicators. (Doctoral Dissertation, Victoria University, Centre for Hospitality and Tourism Research). Australian Digital Theses Program, 2007. http://wallaby.vu.edu. au/adt-VVUT/public/adt-VVUT20070917.123458/index.html.

PART III

Emerging Areas in Tourism

CHAPTER 18

THE INDIAN HYBRIDITY IN ITS CULTURAL EXPRESSION: BETTER UNDERSTANDING ONE'S CULTURAL HERITAGE

GITHA U. BADIKILLAYA

Destination Heritage, Bangalore, India

CONTENTS

ABSTRACT

Cultural assimilation and hybridity in art and architecture is an ongoing process occurring due to trade and missionary activities from ancient times. This cultural assimilation evolved into new artistic trends with heterogeneous elements bearing the traits of two or more cultures. This is known as hybridity. This synthesis led to the development of remarkable art and architectural forms. This process of interaction, assimilation, and transformation was diverse in different geographical and localized contexts. At times such influences improvised the domain of art with expressions of transcendence, immanence, and religious ecstasy. The various artistic persuasions have left an indelible impression on the Indian idiom that clearly shows cross-cultural assimilation and hybridity.

18.1 INTRODUCTION

Achaemenid, Greek, Roman, Scythian, Kushan, Turkish, and Mughal influences in ancient and medieval India were assimilated producing hybridized forms. But distinct Indian elements were discerned at all times. Throughout the assimilation process, the hybridism often produced variations that were in the language of local masterminds rather than just motivated borrowings. Though there were foreign influences in the Gandharan Art that flourished between 1 and 5th AD, a distinctive Indian Mathura Art developed simultaneously, the Buddha image of which was its singular contribution to the Buddhist traditions of Asia. The North West of India thus was an area of cultural confluence. Before the 5th BC, India had more Hellenic motifs. Sixth BC was the period when India, Greece, and Persia came into commercial and cultural contacts with West Asia (Assyria). In the process, each derived the same symbols but with different interpretations. Under Darius (522–486 BC) parts of India and Greece were the two ends of the Persian domain before Alexander.

The current chapter is an attempt to bring out this hybridism in art and architecture with a few examples as Indian cultural traditions developed through the ages with particular reference to ancient and medieval India. The scope is not wide enough to provide in its entirety, and only a few instances have been highlighted to drive home the point about better understanding the country's cultural heritage in relation to tourism.

18.2   NEED FOR THE STUDY

Heritage is inherited. It is much more than mere displaying, protecting, or restoring a collection of antique artifacts. As it is also intangible, ideas and memories also play a sizeable role in understanding a place. The tangible and intangible outlines specify who we are and how we identify ourselves. Indeed, the issues of cultural heritage that is precisely social identity and collective memory are serious elements to be taken cognizance by the tourism industry.

Today, travel is reduced to "been there, seen them" marker of visiting places. Research has shown that a majority of the present Indian tourists are the nouveau rich who would like to make a statement on social media. In addition, some youngsters think that traveling is a great fun for personal enjoyment (no questions on that) but are not mindful of the surrounding environs. How many of us are aware that Indian architecture is the only one in the world that brings out the music from the stone pillars?

Musical pillars are at Hampi Vitthala Temple, Suchindram Temple, Airavateswara Temple—Darasuram to name a few located in South India. Thus, a clear understanding of the importance of a place's heritage and its bygone stories will enable travel providers and professionals to iden- tify tourists accordingly and present the heritage in an interesting manner. Trained and professional guides will be able to give an impetus to the above.

18.3   OBJECTIVES OF THE STUDY

The basic objective of the study is to understand the many dynamics and influences of India's cultural heritage. Cultural heritage is an expression of the ways of life developed by a community and carried on for genera- tions. These ways of living include places, objects, customs, practices, artistic expressions, and values. What is worth saving? Can we, or should we forget? What memories can we enjoy, or learn from? Who owns "The Past" and who is entitled to speak for past generations? These aspects have to be addressed to better understand one's heritage without misrepresenta- tion as we are seeing a tendency of analyzing the past with present-day understanding and there are sections of people who are intent on painting everything with a "nationalistic" brush thinking that they are the sole torchbearers of history and heritage. One can be worthy leaders of thought if we learn to value our heritage in its right perspective and that history and past events can be pointers but cannot be changed however unpalatable. Science is curiosity about life, art is a wonder at life, philosophy is an attitude toward life, and religion is reverence for life. All together, they simply constitute what is known as CULTURAL HERITAGE.

18.4   THE BEGINNINGS

From Persepolis that was a combination of West Asian and Egyptian styles, the influence was felt in the polished Indian pillars and motifs of the Mauryan period. The earliest of the colossal square pillared hall of Kumrahar is a pointer to the Persepolis pillars, without any capitals as against their decorative capitals with a bell-shaped base (A. K. Coomaraswamy). The same is also characteristic of the Greece pillar ornamentation. The Persipolitan pillars stand on bases, either shaped like a bell or inverted lotus, or a plain rectangular or circular block (Singh, 2008) with a fluted surface. The bell-shaped corolla of petals does not bear resemblance to any known flower in nature. In its Indian variety, the corolla is crowned by a fillet-shaped sphere and later replaced by a bell that became a lotus.

In the decorative motifs of the honeysuckle, knops, and the acanthus, the Western influence is seen. The smooth Mauryan pillars at a later period as in the Sanchi torana pillars and architraves were admirably carved with scenes of the social life, the city structures, battles fought, and so forth. Ashoka transformed the pillars into epigraphic monuments, inscriptions of which carried messages on *dhamma*.

The elongated petals forming the fluting on the bell-shaped capital—the bell itself and the animals portrayed on the abacus are Achaemenid. As the structures were in the wood, they did not survive. Hence, it appeared as a dramatic innovation when the sophisticated stone pillars and the techniques made their appearance in the Mauryan period. A Megasthenes' report affirms the grandeur of Pataliputra that far exceeded that of Susa and Ecbatana in Persia. A discovery in an 1886 excavation of an elaborately carved capital with palmette motifs and a running row of abacus rosettes with four projecting volutes is a definite inspiration from the Hellenic and Achaemenid Ionic capitals and motifs. John Irwin suggested that the Mauryan/Ashokan pillars may be an indigenous practice dating to a pre-Buddhist tradition of cosmic pillars—the Axis Mundi. This aspect needs further research.

18.4.1 THE PILLARS/COLONNADES

The Colonnades of Rome and Greece are suggested in the Buddhist caves at Elephanta and Ajanta. But the bands on the walls surfaces, roof ledges, aedicules, and turrets are predominantly Indian. The proportion of the Greco-Roman columns was also felt at a later period in the pillared halls of Chola and the Vijayanagara temples. Pot and lotus-shaped capitals existed in the Cretan arch and the Egyptian pillars long before they did in India. But only the peculiar contour and the myrobalam (gooseberry) shaped capitals as seen in Ajanta pillars are Indian.

18.4.2 LION MOTIF AND ITS SYMBOLIZATION

The seated posture of the Mauryan lions with open mouths is suggestive of the Greek technicality and accompanying aggressiveness. But the Indian representation has warmth and softness as the mouth is slightly opened, at times with a slightly protruding tongue. Why was the representation of lion so popular in European architecture when it was not a native?

There was a time in history when the lion was known in the ancient world mostly through the Romans. It was due to their extensive hunting that the North African and Asiatic lions became extinct in Europe around 100 BC. Today, they are to be found only in Gujarat, South Africa, and Kenya. The lions were used in the gladiators' fight by starving them for a week. The term "feeding to the lions" became popular as these lions would devour the gladiators. From Biblical times, the lion was known as in the story of Daniel and the lion who removed the thorn from its paws. In gratitude, the lion recognized him and did not eat him in the gladiator's fight. In prehistoric times, there were the cave lions and in historic times the Barbary lions.

In Rome, the spear was the Senate emblem and the standard bearers would wear lion masks over their heads that would run up to the backsides with a bundle of sticks on either side with an axe in the center. During the Roman times, either the lion or the two-headed eagles was adopted as the symbol of many nations in Europe. In fact, Alexander was depicted as wearing the helmet having lion insignia that goes to show that the Macedonians were aware of the lion and this emblem was seen on their shields. The Macedonian lion was used in King Samuel's kingdom. He was crowned by the pope and the lion too got a crown. The Bible describes Jesus as the "lion of Judah." By the time the lion became a heraldic symbol it became extinct and held the same status as a griffon or a mythical animal in the minds of the people.

Thus in art and architectural representation, the symbol of the lion was a moniker of a conquering HERO. It is very much represented in Indian art, sculpture, and religion in the present times but Mauryan period highlighted it. The concept of simhasana or lion throne is mentioned in the scriptures. Subsequently, as a religious motif, it became popular especially in the form of KIRTIMUKHA, also used as a decoration.

18.4.3   OTHER MOTIFS

A Babylonian bas relief is with two intertwined serpents and flanked by guardian dragons on either side (Fig. 18.1(a)). This has a parallel with the Naga stones that are abundantly seen placed under trees and on platforms and worshiped. This is a feature very popular in the present times as women have them placed when their wish for progeny has been granted. Thus in India, the Naga or snake is associated with prosperity and fertility. In Babylon, was found a seated bull image on a pillared base (Fig. 18.1(b)). This resembles the Nandi or the bull vehicle of Shiva which is always in seated posture. The Greeks had their Bacchus with a bullhead/mask. If the Hindus have Garuda as the vehicle of Vishnu, The Egyptian God Ra or Horus is hawk-headed in a sort of anthropomorphic representation.

a   **b**

FIGURE 18.1a, b   Indian architecture.
Source: Ananthalwar and Alexander (1980).

18.5   CULTURAL ASSIMILATION—POST-MAURYAN PERIOD

In 1st BC, the Sakas or Scythians, who were the nomads of the Eurasian steppes inhabiting the Southern Russia and around the Altai Mountains invaded India followed by the Kushans in the 1st AD. The Sakas propagated the Greek ideas and started the syncretism of Iranian, Bactrian, and Indian ideas which reached its peak during the Kushan period. It can be said that they introduced image worship in India. The two major trends of the artistic activity of this period are the Gandhara and Mathura schools of Art. Gandhara located in the Afghan—Pakistan region provides evidence of a Western artistic activity.

18.6   GANDHARA ARCHITECTURE

The art was shaped by the Saka rulers around 1st AD after the decline of the Greek power when Roman power was at its zenith. Excavations of the second city Sirkap in the Gandhara region founded by the Bactrians and fortified by the Parthians revealed that the streets started from the North and laid throughout the length of the city. The smaller streets and lanes emerged at its right angle that had blocks of houses. Totally foreign in conception this was different from the grid road layout pattern of Indian cities. It was Greek in the urban planning of flat ground, Hippodamian street pattern and geographical location with natural defenses on all sides with round fortifications. After the original planning was implemented, the subsequent settlement was quintessentially Indian. "The Corinthian capitals of Gandhara have their nearest prototypes in Roman provincial examples in Syria and Palestine. The Calyx cups from which the spiraling fronds emerge in Classical Corinthians have disappeared while the acanthus leaves have lost their elongation and become stunted. Figures of Buddha and Bodhisattva have been introduced into the foliage. In the entablature on the pillar capitals, the beads of the astragalus molding are elliptical as in Roman tradition." (*Roman influence on Indian Architecture: A Reassessment*—D. R. Das). The so-called honeysuckle or naga pushpa motif on Indian pillar capitals is a symbolic connotation, unlike Greece and Persia. It is in India associated with geese and water that are fecundity symbols.

18.6.1 GANDHARA SCHOOL OF ART WITH REFERENCE TO BUDDHA IMAGE

Image worship was not in vogue and was introduced by the Sakas and Kushans, first on coins and then as imageries. The first of the image being Buddha, it was a unique combination of Hellenistic techniques and Indian theme. Yaksha statues were in existence in the Mathura belt and may have been worshiped. In early Gandhara, the Buddha had Hellenic features. But in no case does priority establish a claim of the Gandharan type as the origin of the Buddha image (Kramrisch, 1993). The Gandhara artist sculpted the Buddha as Apollo with muscular body robed in a thick Roman toga, wavy hair top-knotted, mustache, and a turban with expressions unknown to Indian norms. The earliest art though was the Bimran reliquary—a golden casket from Afghanistan. It has a series of figures adapted from 1 to 2nd AD Roman sarcophagi. A museum artifact can be mistaken as belonging to the European Middle Ages.

Further, the Gandhara Buddha sculpted from schist had a Persian halo, eyes in direct gaze, and legs covered while seated as the Padmasana posture of the leg was unknown to the sculptors. In the next phase, the drapery became diaphanous and top knot placed in the crown of the head. In the last phase of 1st AD, the figures were short with fluted drapery having schematic parallel folds. On the whole, the Buddha of this period was emotionless and lacked spiritual expression. Bodhisattva images were also carved, heavily ornamented, elaborate hairdos with or without turbans and wore sandals.

A popular Gandhara motif was the scenes of naked cupids with rich garlands, sometimes adorned with fruits that were an inspired Greek motif. But in the Bharhut and Sanchi panels, it was the stocky yakshas that replaced the cherubic Roman angels and shown with anklets. In the Amaravati art, the garlands became slimmer and resembled the lotus stalks. Without any real roots in India and with marked foreign features, the avenues of natural development seem to have been closed to this school, which finally disappeared. Nevertheless, it made vital contributions to the Buddha image of Central and eastern Asia, and several features, drastically transformed, was incorporated in Gupta art.

18.7   MATHURA SCHOOL OF ART

The Kushan Empire comprised Central Russia, Afghanistan, Pakistan, and North Western India. Mathura, the central Indian center of Kushans, probably a dynasty name who ruled for 200 years up to 3–4 AD became a prolific center of art production. This art was a continuation of older art prevalent in Bharhut, Sanchi, and Besnagar. The Mathura Buddha image in red sandstone was in round or high relief and was totally indigenous. The Buddha image was cross-legged, top knot properly positioned and coiled, with right hand raised. In seated images, the left hand often clenched rested on the thigh. In standing figures, the left hand held the folds of the transparent robe. Later the drapery ends fell sideways that later came to be treated as a separate entity not clinging to the body, unlike the Gandhara Buddha's Toga. Then it became invisible. The head was surrounded by a halo with lotus-shaped scallops. Initially, the open eyes and smiling countenance made no suggestion of spiritual introspection. Then the head was covered in tight curls. In the final stage, the calm face is one of the serene contemplations with the inward positioning of the eyes.

In the fifth century, the style with further refinement brought a series of magnificent life-size Buddha images (now scattered in museums throughout the world). The Mathura Buddha images established an iconography that became the norm for the Buddha image. Yakshinis appeared in erotic poses suggesting fertility reminiscent of the Greek dryads. It was during the Gupta period that the native Mathura and the classical Hellenic Gandharan style were merged to bring out the perfect expression of the ideals of Buddhism culminating in the well-known Buddha of the Gupta period in the Indian norm of depicting spirituality. A group of portrait sculptures of the Kushan rulers seen in Archaeological Museums gives an interesting glimpse of the foreign influences.

One of them, headless, is said to represent emperor Kaniska with heavy strapped boots, a tunic, and a coat, which are very simple. He is leaning on a mace. The posture is rigid. These Kushan portraits are the oldest in Indian sculptural art. Temples were built in the N.W. region with the images of the Kushan kings. Some scholars opine that the Kirtimukha depicted in art and sculpture of the post-Gupta period traces its roots from the Kushan headdress or the Indo-Scythian helmets on the heads of the Mathura and Gandhara regions figures.

18.7.1   OTHER ELEMENTS OF KUSHAN INFLUENCE

The concept of a savior god with human personality created a sort of revolution in Indian art. It gave a tremendous impetus to image worship among the Hindus that is its dominant feature. The worship of Sun in the form of icons installed in temples was another import. At Surkh Kotal, founded during the reign of the greatest Kushan ruler Kanishka, an entire hill resembled a giant fire altar with a temple to Ahura Mazda and cult images of the Kushan rulers. This was a throwback to the Kushan's contact with the Persian culture in Bactria in 1st BC. Considering the importance of fire and of the Mithraic ritual at Surkh Kotal, the depiction of a solar deity in the guise of a Kushan prince can hardly be doubted (Roy, 1986).

The image of Sun god depicted in coat, boots, and mustache have been shown in iconography in North-India till 1000 years after the Kushan kings exited. Interestingly, it is mentioned in a Puranic myth that the peculiar attire is due to the malpractice of the artificer of the gods Vishwakarma. Certain elements in the complex figure of Krishna, the ras-leela dance and the close connection with the pastoral tribe was also attributed to them. It was in the Kushan period that an affinity was developed between the two cultural centers of Gandhara in the North-West and Mathura in the Doab. The appearance of high-backed chair and both the legs hanging down (pralambapaadaasana as seen in the Buddha-deity of Ajanta) while seated was a foreign feature. It was a common feature to depict the bodhisattva and minor deities. There was never the concept of Portraiture in Indian Art through glimpses of the same could be seen in the Pallava period in the seventh century in the rock-cut reliefs of Mamallapuram. The Kushans did not come to India as the bearers of a new civilization similar to the Greco-Bactrian kings but similar to the Sakas adapted themselves to the culture of their subjects. The Kushana control of the silk route, the immense maritime trade with Romans and the spice lands of SE Asia brought in prosperity by way of gold into the country that accounted for the exuberance in art.

The third century was a period of turmoil in Central India in the fall of the Andhras and weakening of the Kushan power. But the Kushan Mathura Art survived leading to the Buddha icon in the Gupta period.

Mathura has a long and distinguished history spanning many centuries as an unparalleled center of artistic activity influenced by the Bactria Greeks, the Scythians, and Parthinians. Thus in Mathura, all coexisted at different times resulting in the Mathura school. It gave to Indian imagery the pantheon of Buddhist, Jaina and Hindu denominations. The schools of Mathura and Gandhara undoubtedly influenced each other, but essentially adhered to their own styles. The ancient Indian relief style found its fullest expression and development at neither Mathura nor Gandhara but in Andhradesha, notably at the great sites of Amaravati and Nagarjunikonda. Ultimately it was in the Gupta period that the native Mathura and Gandhara style merged to form the perfect expression of the ideals of Buddhism. This can be very much felt in the Buddhas of Ajanta. From the seventh century onwards, the Northern and Southern parts of India developed two different idioms of sculpture and architectural styles. Experimentation took place in Pattadakallu (Karnataka, India) and Mamallapuram (Tamilnadu, India) that culminated in the temple styles to be classified as Dravida, Nagara, and Vesara. In addition, local idioms also flourished resulting in a wide variety of schools by the tenth century.

18.8 ISLAMIC INFLUENCE

It was the Arab traders who brought Islam to India. The Sultanates with their Turkish origins conquered North India in the late 12th AD and the Deccan plateau in the 14th AD. They introduced new ideas and works of unusual refinement. This was epoch-making as it was diametrically opposite to the norms of Indian architecture. The contrast can be felt in the building conceptions of the mosque and the temple. The mosque minarets seem to have evolved from the low square towers of pre-Islamic Syrian temples. The beginning of the sixteenth century saw the vigor of an intellectual activity with the Bhakti movement giving an impetus to the Muslim and Hindu cultures. Many Hindu beliefs were accepted by the Mughal rulers. Arches and domes became prominent and the mosque came to form a part of the Indian landscape introducing a balanced technicality and gilt decorations. Thus in the 300 years of their rule, the Mughals became Indianized with their art and architecture culminating in the gem of Mughal Art in the miniature paintings and in such monumental buildings of Fatehpur Sikri, Humayun's tomb in red sandstone and marble and the marble Taj. Construction activity became more geared toward the demands of the elite with their sophisticated courtly manners.

The change in ethos was reflected mostly in urban landmarks of numerous prominent city gateways and in the design of royal mosques and tombs. But it would be incorrect to consider India's Islamic architecture as an entirely foreign implant as traditional Indian influences played an important role in shaping the most vibrant Mughal monuments. Although geometrical decoration is a common feature of all Islamic architecture, the use of patterned windows known as "Jaali" developed some original features. There was a combination of motifs considered auspicious in the Hindu tradition alongside arabesques and geometrical designs. The Pot motif appeared in a rainbow of colors. This may appear as a Persian transplant favored by Akbar. But the symbol of the pot in the form of Purnaghata was used in religious sculptures on the outer walls of temples.

Humayun built the old fort citadel in Delhi. On its Northern gate known as Talaqi Darwaza, two stylized lotus designs (Fig. 18.2) on either side of the arch is technically the ashta kamala or ashtaadala. This is the eight-petalled lotus with white marble inlay work on a sunken red stone panel. Above this is the framed shaardula facing each other. It is a stylized animal with lion's head and horse's body assertively standing on its hind legs. This is the second of composite animals in Indo-Muslim sculpture (1533–1534 AD). The shaardula is an Indian motif mostly used to break the monotony of repetitiveness as seen in Khajuraho panels (Fig. 18.3). It is believed to be an auspicious symbol to be placed at high levels. Keeping this in mind, Humayun depicted this on the most ambitious of his architectural projects. Similarly, the Western gateway the "Bara Darwaza" has a tantric representation of the shatkona—a hexagonal pattern just above the archway.

FIGURE 18.2 Hari smriti, studies on art, archaeology, and indology.

FIGURE 18.3   Hari smriti, studies in art, archeology, and indology.

Akbar's Hathipol gateway of Fatehpur Sikri is a majestic and imposing structure overlooking a precipice. As the name indicates, it is an elephant-framed gateway with two elephants on either side with their trunks intertwined at the apex. This resembles a beautiful "torana" or arch. Today only the torso remains. This gateway was represented in three miniature paintings from Akbarnamah (Albert and Victoria Museum London, namely—"Akbar's return to Fatehpur Sikri from Gujarat" (Fig. 18.4), "Akbar observing the construction of Fatehpur Sikri," and "the construction of Fatehpur Sikri" (Fig. 18.5). The elephant is auspicious for the Hindus, and for the Mughals it added a majestic dimension to their palaces and fort gateways as did the lions on palace gateways by the Babylonians and Assyrians. On the North-West side is the Mahal-i-ilahi that is a profusely ornamented and trabeated construction. The elephants on either side support a fringe of lotus buds (Fig. 18.6). Usually, one finds the crocodile motif but in Mughal architecture, the elephant is a popular motif. Inside in medium relief are swans and peacocks. These motifs sit comfortably with arabesque and geometrical motifs. Though the representation of human and animal forms is prohibited in Islam, they were represented in India. It was secular court art at its best combining the vitality of the indigenous Indian forms and the artistic temperament of the Indian sculptors with Mughal patronage.

FIGURE 18.4 Hari smriti, studies on art, archeology, and indology.

FIGURE 18.5   Hari smriti, studies on art, archeology, and indology.

FIGURE 18.6   Hari smriti, studies on art, archeology, and indology.

18.8.1 *PROVINCIAL ART AND ARCHITECTURE*

The provincial styles were developed incorporating the regional or local approaches. The Gujarat monuments used the symbolic Jain and Hindu motifs in their mosques or tombs. The Chakra, Padma, Purnakalasha, Kalpavriksha, Kalpalata, and the Jain "lamp of knowledge" became vital centerpieces in the Gujarat Sultanate monuments. The Hyderabad monuments stood out for their use of pineapple shaped domes. In fact, the provincial monuments are as appealing as the renowned Mughal monuments. When Moslem art and architecture went into rapid decline during the reign of Aurangzeb, a cultural renaissance of sorts occurred in the regional kingdoms of the North, Deccan, and the South.

18.9 HYBRID STYLES

A mention is made here of few exceptional hybrid styles that were seen in different parts of India that had no following but became a one of a kind architecture model. In Nakoddar (near Jullundhur in Punjab—Jehangir/ Shahjehan period) are two tombs that are unusual for a Moslem monument with brilliant polychrome decorations. The word Nakodar is said to be a corrupted form of "Neki dar"—meaning gate of virtue. Facing each other, there is an unusual tile-work. Interestingly, these were dedicated to a scholar and a court musician and not to royal personages as were the norm. One of the structures is known as "Baghdadi" as it was an imitation of a style popular in Baghdad. If one has geometric arabesques patterns in yellow, green, and blue tiles against a brick background, the other has incorporated the typical auspicious Indian motif of the Purnakalasa, the symbol of prosperity and fertility seen all across South Indian temples (Fig. 18.7).

FIGURE 18.7

In Gwalior, the 15th-century Man-Mandir palace has a magnificent outer facade done in polychrome tiles. A pleasant frieze of geese, palm, and other decorative motifs catch one's attention (Fig. 18.8). This has the nearest resemblance in the now ruined palace in the Raisen fort (near Bhopal) and the much later and elaborates Nayak palace in Madurai. Geese are rarely depicted on Indian walls.

FIGURE 18.8

The Mahabath Maqbara in Junagarh (Gujarat), a late nineteenth-century monument is a mixture of Islamic, Hindu, and European influences (Gothic). The fine arches, French-style windows, columns, and shining silver doorways with onion domes make for a perplexing mix of architectural styles (Fig. 18.9(a), (b)). But taken on the whole in the larger context of the complex history of the district of Junagadh itself this beacon of a monument does make sense.

FIGURE 18.9a The Mahabath Maqbara in Junagarh.

FIGURE 18.9b   The Mahabath Maqbara in Junagarh.

18.9.1 MUGHAL MINIATURES

This school of art was one of the greatest contributions by Akbar as the early miniatures were under the supervision of Persian master painters with about 24,000 illuminated manuscripts. The Akbari style was an admixture of Persian and Indian elements with the domination of space and action. In the seventeenth century, the Persian influence disappeared with single artist painting and no longer illustrating a text. Shah Jehan's use of semiprecious stones inlaid in marble and floral decorations is an influence from Italy (Fig. 18.10). When the Portuguese established trading posts in India, they gifted Akbar with illustrated Bibles that fascinated him to integrate European Realism and Christian subjects to the miniatures. These were the halos and angelic cherubs above the emperor's head, shading, landscapes, and the use of perspectives. Court scenes became frivolous and amorous encounters with courtesan and princesses depicted in an impersonal way as the painters had no access to the harem. By depicting people and fauna, Mughal portraiture swayed away from Persian and Ottoman traditions.

With the fall of the Mughals, the painters migrated to Rajasthan where the typical Indian themed Rajasthani painting flourished.

FIGURE 18.10 Mughal India.
Source: Berinstain (1997)

18.9.2 DECCANI MINIATURES

The Deccani miniatures with Hindu, Iranian, Turkish, and European influences were brought about by a flourishing sea trade rather than borrowing from the Northern Mughals. More than realism, there was an idealized imagery suggesting that the displaced artist after the fall of the Vijayanagar found patronage with the Deccani Kings. But by the time of the British, this was replaced by "Company Paintings" and Miniatures became a dead art. Major Handley mentioned in his *The Journal of Indian Art* (1886) that the most advanced artists have taken to clothing the gods in European clothing, with Shiva sitting in a hall with lighted candles and Krishna driving a phaeton. Later the Kalight paintings created at the Kali temple in Kolkata, adapted the watercolor techniques to bring in the illusion of rounded volumes. This was replaced by lithograph prints.

18.10 CONCLUSION

Similar to the pluralistic country's culture and religion, the art and architecture of India have seamlessly integrated and assimilated the best of foreign influences in its varied art styles. Thus, Achaemenid, Greek, Roman, Kushan, and Scythian influences were assimilated in the Gandharan Art but produced a distinctively Indian Mathura Art, the Buddha image of which is its singular contribution to the Buddhist traditions. The Greco-Roman influence was also reflected in the majestic pillared halls, the decorative motifs as honeysuckle, the acanthus, and the knops. The Achaemenid expressions were reflected in the four addorsed lions on the Sarnath capital of the Mauryan period. The rhythmic mind of the Hindu and the formality of the outside influences brought forth such architectural marvels that the best of Islamic architecture is to be found in India. Throughout the assimilation process, the hybridity often produced variations that were expressions of local mastermind rather than just motivated borrowings. Plasticity, naturalism, and dynamic coherence are reflected in the unity of life of man and nature in the art and architectural beauties of India, a level of tranquility little known to the modern Western mind. Egypt exhibited a crystalline purity, Greece the accuracy to anatomy toward perfection, and beauty of the human body whereas the Indian manifested the visual representation of the Sublime with his love for Nature and spiritual inclinations.

Thus, Indian art and architecture rendered in eloquent visuals the whole message of spirituality that India holds for humankind. Metal, stone, clay, or wood were treated in the same way as the gross matter had to be overcome that also had a life with the hands never separated from the mass and never losing touch with the material. In the Western world, the notion of sculpture was given form by detached movements to a hard and unyielding material. Portraiture belongs to civilizations that fear death. For this reason, portraiture in the current sense does not exist in India sculpture (Kramrisch, 2013). In light of the above, a tourist will appreciate the dynamic nuances of the assimilation and syncretization that had resulted in a hybridity. For this, the tourist guides will have to be trained from this angle. Cultural parity is not through the hypothesis of similarity but of dissimilarity. It will help if we could be little obsessed with the past as an understanding from the above perspective will make appreciation of our heritage better.

TIME HAS NO HOLIDAY AND LIFE HAS NO PAUSE BUTTON. Since a tourist will visit a place only once, a better understanding of the heritage of a place will make it a worthwhile trip.

"In this land of India, on the shore of vast humanity
We know not whence, and at whose call, these myriad
Streams of men have come rushing forth impetuously to lose
themselves in this sea.
Aryan and non-Aryan, Dravidian and Chinese, Scythian,
Hun, Pathan, and Moghul, all, have merged into one body.

—Rabindranath Tagore

KEYWORDS

- assimilation
- synthesis
- hybridity
- artistic trends
- cultural heritage

REFERENCES

Abram, H. N. *Art of India and South East Asia;* Hugo Munsterberg: New York, 1970.

Ananthalwar, M. A.; Alexander R.; *Indian Architecture—Styles of architecture;* Indian Book gallery: Delhi, 1980; Vol II.

Bachhofer, L. Early Indian sculpture, Paris 1929.

Berinstain, V. *Mughal India;* Thames and Hudson: London, 1997.

Chaturvedi, S. *Foreign Influx and Interaction with Indian Culture;* Agam Kala Prakashan: New Delhi, 1985.

Hari, S. *Studies on Art, Archaeology, and Indology.*

Havell, E. B. *Indian Sculpture and Painting;* London, 1928.

History of India: Indian Art, Architecture, Sculpture, Miniature Painting. www.jigyasa0. tripod.com.

Kramrisch, S. *Indian Sculpture—Ancient, Classical and Medieval;* Motilal Banarasidass Pvt Ltd: Delhi, 1933.

Kramrisch, S. *Indian Sculpture—Ancient, Classical and Mediaeval;* Motilal Banarasidass Publishers: Delhi, 2013.

Nath, R. *Mughal Sculpture;* A.P.H. Publishing Corporation: New Delhi, 1997.

Neville, P. *Marvels of Indian Painting: Rise and Demise of Company School;* Self-published: Gurgaon, 2007.

Pereira, J. *Elements of Indian Architecture;* Motilal Banarasidas Pvt Ltd: Delhi, 1987.

Rao, T. A. G. *Elements of Hindu Iconography;* Madras, 1914; vol II.

Roy, C. K. *Indian Art;* Thames and Hudson: London, 1986.

Singh, U. A *History of Ancient and Early Medieval India: From the Stone Age to the Early Medieval India;* Pearson Longman: New Delhi, 2008.

CHAPTER 19

CHALLENGES OF MEDICAL TOURISM: MANAGERIAL PARADIGM IN THE INDIAN FRAMEWORK

BINDI VARGHESE

Christ (Deemed to be University), Bangalore, India

CONTENTS

ABSTRACT

Medical tourism is multifaceted in nature as the versatility offers many variants to different segments that come from diverse backgrounds—India to mull over for value creation in a networked healthcare environment and also building professional competency through healthcare managers. There is an enormous potential for Indian healthcare system to reach out, with its services, beyond frontiers. The purpose of the study necessitates the role of the hospitality sector in promoting medical tourism in coordination with the hospital sector. Considering all these factors, there is an imperative need to undertake the present study of the various independent variables impacting the growth of medical tourism in south India. This is derived from the differing socioeconomic determinants, tourist arrival from different geopolitical regions; and demand generated. The general perception is that outbound medical tourism in the United States, the United Kingdom, Canada, and other Western countries is on a rise, and a lot of medical tourists are arriving in certain developing countries such as India, Thailand, Jordan, and Singapore for medical procedures that are cost effective. The dynamics of medical tourism, however, is much more intriguing beyond a naive representation. The research was undertaken keeping in mind the need for the study as mentioned below.

19.1   INTRODUCTION

Viewed from the threshold of the new millennium, Indian healthcare sector has never had it so good. Economic prosperity is at an all-time high with the healthcare system that is satisfying the expanding needs. The imperative growth resulting in reorganization of delivery systems becomes an immediate requirement. The reforms can contribute to improvements in the healthcare sector. The health-promoting hospital would respond to these types of hypothetical developments. The significant economic development would result from the inflow of structural funds and improved trade opportunities (Bagchi, 2009). Service providers in the past decades have invested the bulk of its scarce healthcare resources in developing its hospitals. Services provided are of a high standard but the huge investment involved is not producing noticeable improvements in the health of the population. The government accepts that investment in healthcare must be provided largely from its own resources as it is led by a competent vision which says that health is much broader than health care and that health care is much broader than hospital care.

Changing the emphasis from healthcare to population health suggests that fundamental change is required. Realistically health care is heavily reliant on the network of hospitals and in any new arrangements hospitals will play a central key role. Therefore, the hospitals have a key role to play in promoting health as well as in health care. Concepts such as social return on investment, health gain, and social gain have been devised to facilitate measurement of results on investments not amenable to measurement in financial return terms. In a more dispersed healthcare system, performance measurement will be important to ensure that the hospitals need to contain cost that does not displace quality of care as a priority.

Quality processes must be considered necessary to monitor, correct, and enhance their services. Increasingly external validation or accreditation is being seen as a necessary check to satisfy evolving accountability criteria. Occupational health is an area where hospitals should excel and, in doing so, demonstrate its potential, and the other employers should recognize the same in their places of work. Emphasis on quality through constant validation and improvement of protocols aimed at minimizing hospital risks to patients are necessary for every hospital (Knowledge@Wharton, 2011). It is sometimes necessary to recognize that quality improvement is not synonymous with or dependent upon investment in, or greater use of, high technology. The hospitals will achieve measurable quality improvements by developing protocols. Healthcare systems throughout are to be reformed or are in the process of being reformed. Challenges of medical tourism in the Indian travel market are because of the increasing concerns on quality norms and standardizing procedures followed in India. The concern could be indisputable as India is an upcoming medical destination.

19.1.1 MEDICAL TOURISM IN INDIAN SCENARIO

India possesses qualified and competent medical practitioners, high-grade medical facilities, upcoming brand image, and much more to its credit; there is a certain gap that can create concern in the minds of people in the developed countries when it comes to their medical travel to India. This gap is the haziness that can be a hurdle for India to progress as a medical destination. There are lots of exercises that need to be taken before India comes in proximity to global success. To simplify the ambiguity on the quality and standardization norms practiced in India, there could be some policies or innovative approaches that can help in benchmarking India's success as a medical hub (Nagaraj, 2009).

Clear and robust strategy formulation and strategic planning widely help one to syndicate the healthcare segment. It becomes the priority of the government to chart out a matrix to measure the performance. The public sector can propose a subcommittee or a steering committee for strengthening the leadership and effective practices for healthcare businesses. New corporate grants, increased number of new initiatives, public–private partnerships could be launched to enhance the quality norms of the healthcare sector. Developing a compelling value proposition for healthcare investors helps in delivering a comprehensive set of programs and services to medical travelers. This will be essential for the success in tapping health tourism market and thereby ensure a secure and sizeable return for the healthcare investors.

19.1.2   INDIAN MEDICAL TOURISM FRAMEWORK

To highlight India's healthcare and current tourism scenario, initiatives are taken up by both the government and the private sector to project India as an ideal healthcare destination. The major corporate hospitals of India have tie-ups with healthcare service providers, travel facilitators and other inter-mediaries for scientific collaboration and professional knowledge-sharing.

Some of the hospitals have tied up with government healthcare departments too. Conventionally, the dominated corporate hospitals provide impetus to quality improvement and accreditation process. Indian medical tourism framework also leverages the potential of spa and wellness centers. This unique combination is the provision of holistic wellness services to the patients (Bennur, 2009). Some hospitals these days are also pursuing the franchise model, wherein they collaborate with clinics and nursing homes to develop brand values and run the hospital on franchisee basis.

The strategies behind this model are sharing of technology and the medical expertise. Expertise and revenue model, on the other hand, shares the technology and expertise as a consultancy firm, with a one-off payment, without lending their brand. Expertise and revenue model is a low-capital-intensive expansion strategy wherein franchise model is a revenue-earning strategy. Many healthcare service providers have established a separate department to cater to the requirements of international travelers through "single window assistance."

The range of services provided start from the provision of prelimi-nary information on the travel-related arrangements to treatment, post-treatment, and follow-up. This assistance goes beyond medical care; along with coordinated services. There are certain generic practices adopted by these multispecialty hospitals such as technology advancement, research and development, continuous education and skill development. Specific practices or strategies adopted by these hospitals include achieving international accreditation and quality standards (Fig. 19.1).

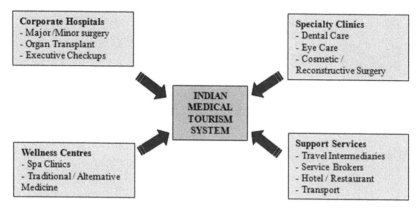

FIGURE 19.1   Indian medical tourism framework.

19.1.3   NEW PARADIGM ON INDIAN MEDICAL TOURISM SYSTEM

There is a twofold perspective associated with the new paradigm on the Indian medical tourism system. Value creation in a networked healthcare environment is one of the prime perspectives. Healthcare collaborative network (HCN) can be a new example of healthcare collaboration. The secondary perspectives cover building professional competency through healthcare managers. This can be ensured by proper hospital management, ascertaining the issues faced by the hospital managers, understanding the expectations of the patients, satisfying the internal clients, and quality-assurance parameters. Thereby patient satisfaction through prompt attention helps the hospitals in making profit (Sen Gupta, 2004).

In India, as in most countries, the communication between various entities in the healthcare ecosystem is extremely inefficient. It is judged by having a close look at the communication mess that was quite evident in the past. There is no coordination between the healthcare sector and the other allied parts of this industry. For an effective healthcare management, there is a need for proper coordination with pharmaceutical companies, insurance companies, and rural health centers, and others (CII, 2004). When there are no open standards ensured, the healthcare unit moves toward a thorough communication mess (Fig. 19.2).

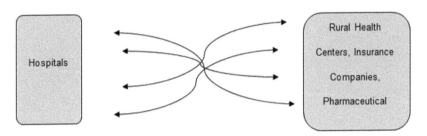

FIGURE 19.2   Communication mess in healthcare units.

To respond to the health challenges of the twenty-first century, the healthcare system must enhance its ability to gather, analyze, and disseminate critical health data, thereby suggesting a vision for tomorrow by having an interconnected network allowing open standards-based communication. Open standards-based collaboration can allow each part of the healthcare ecosystem to contribute to the system and receive benefits from the network.

Collaboration has benefits across healthcare ecosystem that support the needs of many stakeholders' relationships. When it comes to hospitals, collaboration foresees research and outcome analysis, adverse event detections, and others. Hospitals and insurance companies will project its concern with regard to coordination for case management, support for quality incentive programs, and others. Hospitals and pharmaceutical researchers will look at identification of candidates for clinical trials and observation for outcome analysis. Indian healthcare industry has an opportunity to adopt open standards-based information technology infrastructure early in its development that avoids costly integration down the road. This convinces the mass medical tourist in assuring what they desire in terms of quality enhancement and accessibility in connecting to the medical service with utmost reliance. To improve healthcare quality, clinical data must be integrated, shared and analyzed on a regular basis to enable proper decision-making. By acting early, Indian hospitals can establish themselves at the leading edge of healthcare globally and leapfrog competing countries. Integrated components in open standards are projected with various inter-related parts of this system.

A detailed matrix representation of the open standards in the healthcare sector is shown in Figure 19.3.

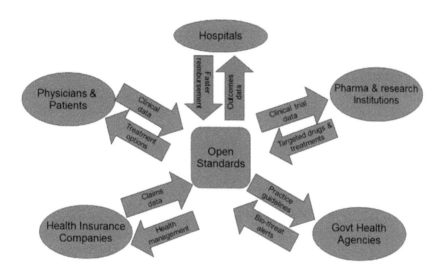

FIGURE 19.3   Open standards in healthcare sectors.

An open standard is an indication for a trouble-free networking with a variety of filaments attached, to the satisfaction of the medical traveler. For instance, a medical aspirant is at a lookout for faster service and settlement from the hospital; and the hospital indeed projects fast and processed outcomes. Pharmacy and research institutions relate to open standards in terms of effective clinical trial data and treatments. Open standards with regard to government agencies relate to effective practice guidelines and proper biothreat alerts. Health insurance companies will look for appropriate data for claims and in return, a medical traveler will look at health management. Physicians and patients relate open standards with efficacy in clinical data and varied treatment options.

All healthcare providers and stakeholders must practice healthcare ethics that respect the unique situation of a medical traveler. As the giving and receiving of health care go global, medical professionals should chart certain bill of rights for medical travelers that support good, safe, and appropriate medical outcomes. Vulnerable to misunderstandings and inappropriate care, or subject to the vagaries of foreign laws that offer less or no protection in certain situations than they expect, patients crossing borders are dependent on the foreign caregiver to offer appropriate care, observe high privacy standards, and guard against undue risks to safety and quality (MTQUA, n.d.). Thereby the concern could be in ascertaining appropriate international patient's rights, and those of the medical traveler. Equally important, the medical traveler must recognize that he or she is a major partner in this delivery of medical treatment and care across borders. Any medical service provider or medical travel partner, when accepting a medical traveler for care, makes both an explicit and implicit contract with the traveling patient. This treaty should recognize certain civil liberties. For instance, Premier Healthcare Germany takes the business of international management in medical tourism very seriously. Such visionaries will craft committed and highly ethical, legal, and professional standards when international patients are treated. India also should lay a concrete base to develop and enhance a qualitative approach to practice medical tourism. The partners and suppliers should share this commitment in order to develop a patient-focused collaboration. Patients are to be treated with compassion, respect, and dignity. Furthermore, to meet the terms there can be certain preset Bill of Rights for the medical travelers.

19.1.4   TRENDS IN MEDICAL TOURISM IN INDIA

Long before people stepped onto foreign soil for cardiac surgery, a tummy tuck or a dental job, medical travelers from around the globe have been searching far and wide to seek the best medical services (Ray, 2003). One can say that the concept of medical travel is as old as medicine itself. Medical tourism history, in fact, dates back to ancient times. The history of medical tourism indicates that if ever health care is in short supply wherever the location or whatever period of time it may be, sick and injured people will travel for healthcare. History is indeed full of medical travelers who made trips in various places across the globe to seek improvement for their health. India has enjoyed a rich history of providing yoga and Ayurveda for healing patients from around the world in the past. However, dental surgery, cosmetic surgery, and other more serious kinds of surgeries abroad is relatively a new phenomenon. It started in the late 1980s and 1990s when patients began looking for more affordable options other than what was offered in their homeland or country. For instance, in the late 1980s, Cuba started programs to attract foreigners from countries such as India, Latin America, and Europe for affordable eye surgeries, heart surgery, and cosmetic procedures, and there was tremendous growth during 1990 when Cuba had thousands of medical tourists across the globe (Understanding Medical Tourism, n.d.). Thailand also became a hot destination for cosmetic surgeries and other routine medical procedures in the late 1990s.

As medical tourism is already a global phenomenon, India has also joined the race in becoming a hot spot for promoting medical tourism. India is hastily becoming one of the world's leading medical travel destinations and the most diverse countries with a wide array of alternative treatment options. India offers travelers a wide range of experiences as one would imagine from a country that extends from the Indian Ocean in the south to the Himalayan mountain range in the north. India's healthcare infrastructure has been in place as the British colonial period. Until the early 1990s, India's health-care was primarily concentrated only in the public sector, however, with the development of the private healthcare sector the overall economic develop-ment that began in the 1990s rapidly expanded since 2000. Although there are advantages on one side, there are also risks or disadvantages perceived in medical travel as medical tourism is a trade-off (Ray, 2003).

19.1.4.1 MEDICAL TOURISM IN 1997–2001

The Asian economic crisis in 1997 and the collapse of Asian currencies prompted government officials to direct tourism efforts in marketing their countries as premiere destinations for international healthcare. It was in 1997 that the Joint Commission International was formed to check and investigate international healthcare facilities for conformance to inter-national standards due to the emergence of health providers around the world. An article found in September 2009 "Booming Medical Tourism in India—2009" states that medical tourism in India has emerged as the fastest growing segment of tourism industry despite the global economic downturn (Report Linker, 2009).

The high cost of treatments in the developed countries has been forcing patients to look for alternative and cost-effective destinations to get their treatments done. India represents the most potential medical tourism market in the world. Factors, such as low cost and range of treatments provided by India, differentiate it from other medical tourism destinations. Moreover, the growth in India's medical tourism market will be a boon for several associated industries, including hospital industry, medical equipment industry, and pharmaceutical industry.

19.1.4.2   MEDICAL TOURISM IN 2001–2006

After the events of 9/11 and the construction boom in Asia, medical tourism continued its massive growth with many citizens from the West and other countries who were traveling to destinations in Asia since 2006. During this time, the dentistry and cosmetic surgery industries reached new heights in these countries. Thailand, Singapore, and India became legitimate medical destinations due to JCI accreditation (Medical Tourism Guide, n.d.).

19.1.4.3   MEDICAL TOURISM IN 2007 AND BEYOND

A massive growth in the inflow of medical tourists is still going high as patients continue to look forward to offshore procedures such as face-lifts, bypass surgery, or fertility treatments (Storrow, 2005). Of late several healthcare and insurance companies in the developed nations had considered medical outsourcing. These offered the possibility to get nonemergency procedures and surgeries in other countries. Many are also considering foreign medical procedures as part of their health plan coverage. With the growth of medical tourism, healthcare travel regulations have become a foremost concern. Groups upholding global healthcare regulations are emphasizing the promotion of worldwide healthcare travel regulations.

International Association of Medical Regulatory Authorities (IAMRA) is looking forward to constructing a significant and effectual medical regulatory system to the fast transforming healthcare practices, technologies, and medical delivery procedures in the world. The IAMRA started in 2002, and it intends to uphold global medical regulatory authorities and safeguard public interest by advocating high standards for educating doctors, granting licenses, creating guidelines, and assisting in the ongoing sharing of information between medical regulatory establishments (IAMRA, n.d.).

The participants of the International Health Regulations (IHRs) of World Health Organization (WHO) recognize the IHRs as an entity providing an established code of conduct for community health crises of global concern. They focus on vital community health hazards and are capable of extending outside the borders of a country to other parts of the globe. Globally speaking there are many local healthcare regulators in countries such as India, Philippines, Malaysia, Thailand, and others. This is in addition to groups responsible for healthcare travel regulations. But as yet, there are no international regulations for medical tourism. There is also locally established healthcare travel regulations followed within the horizon. For instance, regulations regarding healthcare travel in India are governed by Quality Council of India that presents the standards for the Quality and Wellness Industry (Medical Tourism Guide, n.d.).

The Standards for Health and Wellness are a series of regulations that are relevant for accredited healthcare and wellness groups who provide medical tourism services in India. This launch is regarded as a very significant growth, as it will establish universal reliability for the health and wellness industry in India. This accreditation will now act as guarantor for quality services provided by a dependable, and a quality conscious worker to the contender who wants the best. The Standards for Health and Wellness accreditation considers a range of standard requirements for suppliers of wellness service regarding technology, skilled manpower, infrastructure, consumer protection, procedures, controls, and others.

Amongst several other statutory and regulatory conformities, these standards will set strict regulations for service contributors acquiring full accreditation for all the services they provide. For instance, healthcare travel regulations in Malaysia a governed by the Malaysian Society for Quality in Health an autonomous, a nonprofit group actively operating along with healthcare experts to assure safety and constant improvement in the quality of healthcare travel services offered by healthcare amenities in Malaysia (Medical Tourism Guide, n.d.). These standards are created and edited with assistance from professionals of public and private healthcare suppliers. Regulation for healthcare travel in Thailand is looked after by the Institute of Hospital Quality Improvement and Accreditation that appraises and sanctions every registered medical facility provided in the healthcare travel services.

19.2   NEW PARADIGMS IN HEALTHCARE BUSINESS

Another arena in the sphere is the fertility tourism or reproductive tourism that has drastically picked up in the process. Here the practice is off traveling to another country for fertility treatments and is a form of medical tourism. The main reasons for fertility tourism are legal regulation of the sought procedure in the home country or lower price. In-vitro fertilization and donor insemination are major procedures involved. It has been proposed to be termed reproductive exile to emphasize the difficulties and constraints faced by infertile patients, who are "forced" to travel globally for reproductive procedures. India is the main destination for surrogacy. Indian surrogates have been increasingly popular with fertile couples in industrialized nations because of the relatively low cost (Delhi IVF, n.d.). As commercial surrogacy in India is legal, there is a pulsating availability of medical infrastructure and potential surrogates, combined with the international demand that has fueled the growth of the industry. Surrogate mothers receive medical, nutritional, and overall health care through surrogacy agreements. Indian clinics are at the same time becoming more competitive, not just in the pricing, but in the hiring and retention of Indian females as surrogates. Clinics charge patients for the complete package, including fertilization, the surrogate's fee, and delivery of the baby at a hospital. Including the costs of flight tickets, medical procedures, and hotels, it comes to roughly quite less in comparison to the price in the developed countries. Surrogacy in India is low cost, and the laws are much flexible that has augmented the international confidence in going in for surrogacy in India. There is an upcoming assisted reproductive technology Bill, aiming to regulate the surrogacy business. However, it is expected to increase the confidence in clinics by sorting out dubious practitioners and in this way stimulates the practice.

Commercial surrogacy or "wombs for rent" is popular in India, but there are no reliable numbers that track such pregnancies nationwide and doctors work with surrogates in virtually every major city. Indian system acknowledges commercial surrogacy as a legal procedure since 2002, as it is in many other countries such as the United States, the United Kingdom, and others. India is the leader in making it a viable industry rather than a rare fertility treatment. Critics say the couples are exploiting poor women in India, a country with a distressingly high maternal death rate by hiring them at an economical cost to undergo the hardship, pain, and risks of labor (NY Daily News, 2007). The Indian Council for Medical Research has given guidelines in the year 2005 regulating assisted reproductive technology procedures. The Law Commission of India submitted the 228th report on assisted reproductive technology procedures discussing the importance and need for surrogacy, and also the steps are taken to control surrogacy arrangements (Law Commission of India, n.d.).

Foreign tourists visit India by the hundreds each year to hire surrogate mothers to carry their babies for them. Now, though, the booming rent-a-womb industry in India, which has become the international capital of outsourced pregnancies, will soon be subject to new restrictions that will make it harder for foreigners to hire a surrogate. Though India legalized commercial surrogacy, this system has certain complications, as citizenship is not conferred by India on kids who were conceived by foreigners and born to Indian surrogates. Eventually, Germany handed over the twins' travel visas, but it was a lengthy legal battle and pointed out the need for legislation to establish regulations for the surrogacy industry. Under consideration is a draft bill that would beef up surrogacy guidelines written by the Indian Council of Medical Research, which have often been ignored by the several hundred Indian fertility clinics that tend to write their own regulations. A new law would only permit a woman to be a surrogate up to five times and would set a 35-year age limit. The new law will stipulate that the foreign couple's home country would guarantee citizenship for the unborn infant (*NY Daily News*, 2010). India also witnessed cases were gay parents prefer India to get their babies delivered through surrogate mothers. Off late, a gay couple from Israel delivered twins through surrogacy in Powai's L H Hiranandani Hospital, Mumbai (Iyer, 2011).

19.2.1 CHALLENGES ENCOUNTERED WITH INDIA SURROGACY

Despite the prospects of surrogacy, there are some challenges one might encounter when opting for surrogacy in India. The location itself may be the hardest one to overcome. The monitoring of the surrogate and the baby's condition are addressed, however, by the surrogacy clinics' efforts in constantly updating the parents about their situation throughout the process. The parents are required to travel to India twice: during the start of the process and at the end to pick up the baby. Another challenge is the processing of documents in order to bring the baby home to their country. To help clients, the clinics also provide necessary papers and documents as proof that the baby belongs to the infertile medical traveler. However, clinics are not authorized to do so but they usually go an extra mile to provide all other assistance with this process. Looking for the right surrogate is the prime concern. First, the intended parents have to look for the right surrogate who can understand everything about this procedure, and someone who is happy in being serving as a surrogate. The intended parents should interact with the surrogates and feel the vibes before choosing her. This way the industry will not be named for "buying a baby" (Hari, n.d.). The legal and medical counseling attract great importance in the procedure of surrogacy. The intended parent must employ a suitable independent legal counselor who specializes in surrogacy, for making surrogate understand the legal aspects. Surrogacy agreements are sometimes a concern, especially in India. Surrogacy is purely a contractual understanding between the parties, which has been recently pronounced legal by the Supreme Court of India. Care has to be taken that the agreement does not violate any of the laws. There could be also tribulations with some cases when the surrogates breached the contract due to emotional attachment with the infant. Though the issue of surrogacy is more about human emotions, it can call for legal measures and cases can be held in court where all parties involved in the process get hooked. Thereby it has to be ensured that contractual relationships between the surrogates and intended parents are to be quite clear and authorized according to the state laws. Overall, India is a very effective destination for surrogacy. There have been cases in which the problem arises. But exceptions cannot be taken as examples. A careful cautious intended parent is likely to avoid all problems, making a wonderful surrogacy journey.

19.2.2 MYTHS ABOUT MEDICAL TOURISM—A GLOBAL PERSPECTIVE

Patients from developing countries are increasingly opting to travel abroad for high quality, affordable medical treatments. However, many people remain skeptical due to discrepancies regarding available medical tourism information. Inadequate information about medical tourism is the reason that some people avoid this option. Considering treatment abroad, one should make an informed decision based on research and discussion with medical tourists who have already been abroad for a treatment. There are many myths and preconceived notions regarding the medical tourism industry. One among the common myths that need to be set right is on medical tourism a new concept. The fact is that medical tourism is not new. Medical tourism dates back to ancient times. For decades, people have and continue to travel to foreign countries to receive treatments. Recently, medical tourism has experienced a huge boom. It is estimated that approximately 150,000 people received medical treatment abroad in 2007, and it is predicted that this figure will double by 2010 (Woodman, 2007). Another myth states that low-cost medical treatments take place in low-quality medical facilities but the fact reveals that people often assume that lower cost means lower quality. However, research on medical tourism indicates that the reason for medical treatments abroad is so low in terms of cost is due to cheap labor. The present popularity of medical tourism has encouraged many medical tourist hubs, such as Thailand, Costa Rica, India, Singapore, Argentina, and others, to improve their quality of service. Many private healthcare services abroad are using the most up-to-date healthcare methods and technologies.

Due to strong competition in this rapidly developing market, medical tourists can find medical facilities abroad that are better than, or on par with, the medical treatment facilities in the developed countries. It is perceived that clinics abroad provide sophisticated apparatus and qualified physicians who are educated in the Western countries. Many medical services abroad acquire proper certifications such as Joint Commission International (JCI, n.d.) and International Standards Organization (ISO). In addition, hospitals abroad provide an advanced level of healthcare services. One more factor stands to be a myth in which physicians abroad are not as good as physicians in the West. The fact states that the medical tourism information provided by National Center for Policy Analysis reveals that healthcare suppliers and medical travel mediators overseas also compete on quality by advertising their medical team's qualifications. These doctors are usually certified by U.S. boards, whereas others have educational certificates that are recognized worldwide. To find out the credentials of a physician overseas, one must verify that the doctor has the necessary accreditation and board certifications (Agarwal and Iyengar, 1999).

Hospitals and medical hubs abroad are technically substandard as compared with the West is also one of the myths in which the fact reveals that the economic and demographic expansion in Asia is the main reason for the rise of medical infrastructures in the recent past. Due to technological and medical development, the medical services are extremely advanced and refined. Most of the hospitals and medical hubs abroad are privately owned services that particularly look after medical tourists and the elite residents of these countries. In addition, they utilize the latest medical technology and produce an environment appropriate for global, multicultural patients. To ensure quality, one needs to look out for institutions authorized by the Joint Commission International or foreign hospitals that are affiliated with renowned healthcare providers. The ISO also recognizes hospitals that meet globally agreed standards. Liaisons with medical associations and certification bodies from other countries help medical tourism industry providers. The result is a mutual recognition of physician qualifications.

19.3 FUTURE OF MEDICAL TOURISM—CHALLENGES FACED: AN INDIAN PERSPECTIVE

Health and medical tourism are perceived as one of the fastest growing segments in marketing today. Although this area has so far been relatively unexplored, apparently not only the Ministry of Tourism, Government of India, but also the various state tourism boards and even the private sector consisting of travel agents, tour operators, hotel companies, and other accommodation providers are all eyeing health and medical tourism as a segment with tremendous potential for future growth (Knowledge@ Wharton, 2011). India is one of the most attractive medical tourism bargains for inhabitants in the West who look forward to high-end medical procedures or surgery overseas at a low cost. Private health care in India is comparable to much that is available at the best hospitals in the world and at a far lower cost. Even considering the cost of air travel and luxury hotel accommodation the cost savings comes out to be much lesser of what is offered in the developed nations. The experienced and talented pool of medical professionals seems to be another advantage as India offers a long history of subsidized medical education and high investments in medical research; it has one of the biggest pools of medical professionals and scientists across the globe. Due to increased exposure to varied ailments, the surgeons in India are more experienced.

Strong private hospital infrastructure adds on to the merit as India has one of the biggest private hospitals in the world. Many of them are affiliated with top world medical institutes such as Harvard Medical and John Hopkins. These medical centers have the infrastructure, experience, and high-end setup for quality-conscious medical tourist from the developed countries (Horowitz et al., 2007). Indian can boost on a government that is favorable to medical tourism. The Indian government has a special visa for medical tourists that allow them to stay for long periods in the country. Moreover, the government has a high investment in the pipeline for medical tourism. This is for setting up affordable hospitals in India and budget hotels for patients' relatives. Experience in medical tourism is also creating a large pool of medical aspirants particularly from South Asia and the Middle East, who have been coming for medical treatment to India for many years. The familiarity of Western patients with Indian doctors can be one of the reasons for increasing medical tourism in India.

The quality, affordability, and accessibility of medical procedures are the main pulses for people considering going overseas for surgery (McIntosh, 2004). Medical tourists have good cause to seek out care beyond their boundaries. The public healthcare system is so overburdened in many developed nations that it sometimes takes years to get the needed attention. Although this affordability makes medical tourism attractive to its prospective patients, risks such as lack of protection in cases of malpractice, possible lack of adequate preoperational assessment, or follow-up can also accompany it. In some countries, clinics are backed by sophisticated research infrastructures as well. India is among the world's leading countries for biotechnology research, and predominantly some healthcare centers assign patients a personal assistant for the posthospital recovery period and sometimes with a vacation incentive as well so the deal gets even more alluring. Medical tourism organizations work exclusively with leading and internationally accredited private hospitals to take care of patients from abroad. They make all arrangements including airfares, accommodation, airport to hotel transfers, and access to specialists and surgeons. Market trends guarantee that medical tourism in India will continue to expand in the years ahead. As in most tourist-oriented medical communities, the major attractions are cosmetic surgery and dental treatments. However, eye surgery, kidney dialysis, and organ transplantation also are among the other most common procedures sought by medical vacationers in India. India has top-notch centers for open-heart surgery, pediatric heart surgery, hip and knee replacement, cosmetic surgery, dentistry, bone marrow transplants, and cancer therapy. Virtually all of India's healthcare centers are equipped with the latest electronic and medical diagnostic equipment (Macguire, n.d.).

19.3.1 MEDICAL TOURISM BUILDING INDIAN ECONOMY

Analyzing the economic prospects of the current scenario, it is viewed that India, an emerging economy, has witnessed unprecedented levels of economic expansion. India, being a cost-effective and labor-intensive economy, has benefited immensely from outsourcing of work from developed countries, and a strong manufacturing and export-oriented industrial framework. As the economic pace is picking up, global commodity prices have staged a comeback and global trade has also seen reasonably healthy growth over the years (CII, 2014). As travel for medical purposes is one of the fastest growing niches, there is a high potential for medical tourism in developing countries. From a development economist outlook, everything that affects the growth of economy needs an intense research. Exploring more on population movements that include tourism, the temporary population movement for pleasure also demands an economic analysis. While researching the economic impact of tourism in developing countries, the study point toward that travel for medical purposes was one of the fastest growing niches. Over the years, it is examined that people who take up travel for pleasure toward developing countries will also think about medical attention for self and for their dependents on quality treatment options with the intense care provided, which is coupled with the low prices. Although most of the literature on medical tourism focuses on the medical and logistical aspects, it is the need of the hour to examine the economic impact of medical tourism and its effect on the healthcare infrastructure of developing countries.

The effect of medical tourism on the country's economy is scrutinized; it can be very well placed that medical tourism will have a serious impact, in the coming years. The attention is focused as the foreign currency that medical tourism brings to developing countries diffuses throughout the economy in the form of employment, income, savings, investment, tax revenue, and others. Under the right conditions, the growth potential could be huge. The new paradigm suggests that in the next decade, medical tourism will do for the Indian economy ten to twenty times what information technology did in the 1990s (Bookman and Bookman, 2007). Medical tourism might turn out to be the great healthcare equalizer; thereby, it can be professed for good because it offers options for health care that some countries might otherwise not have because of being expensive or unavailability of treatment options. However, if it continues to grow at its current phenomenal rate, there might be some negative consequences in the future for the medical traveler's home country. For example, if patient demand for some medical specialties and moves overseas, then the doctors in the generating country will need to adjust to that demand change. Moreover, if medical tourism in other countries takes off, some of the foreign-born doctors and nurses in the West might return home.

Medical tourism is not a universally feasible growth strategy and is successful only in countries with economic and political advantages that enable them to navigate around international and domestic obstacles to trade in medical services. For instance, when Malaysia has become a potential medical tourist industry, but Mali has not grown or when India attracts international patients at a large scale, a country such as Nepal does not generate. In response to these situations, it is identified that economic, social, legal, and political features that help medical tourism take off. These include a stable political system, reliable legal institutions, a market economy, a developed physical infrastructure, abundant human capital, and a domestic emphasis on research and development. Countries that have most of these features are better poised to deal with the international and national obstacles to the development of the medical tourism industry. The obstacles such as licensing and accreditation, visa requirements, and others could be a concern (Ginsburg and Moy, 1992). Researching on medical tourism, there are legal issues involved, which affect the development of medical tourism. These are to be taken with utmost concern as legal issues could undermine the potential of this budding industry. While observing and studying new developments in the medical tourism industry, it is explored that it has been rising not only among individual consumers but also among insurance companies and businesses.

One of the hovering concerns will also accentuate on the need for economic sustainability. The various actors of this service sector network and interact synergistically with each other, resulting in economic sustainability due to the multiplier effect or the exchange of money among the various players involved. The subsequent segment describes in detail the synergistic interactions of the various players of this network and the consequential economic sustainability. The various stakeholders in the network are The Traveler and Tour Operators, Indian hospitals, Insurance companies, Tourist destination, Local tour operator, Local guide, Local hotels, and Local market. Without proper synchronization, the entire system cannot function effectively and leads to a methodical communication mess (Lancaster, 2004). Acknowledging the opportunities that medical tourism can bring in the realm, there have to be appropriate initiatives taken by the various stakeholders to uplift this industry. The traveler and the tour operators is a vital stakeholder as the foreign traveler comes to India earning the countries valuable foreign exchange. Thus, the traveler and the tour operator are the initiators of the economic sustainability of the network. An Indian hospital also plays a pivotal role in the economic sustainability network. On arrival in India, the tourist heads toward the hospital where he is to be treated and will be put up with all the comforts and luxuries with complete attention of specialist doctors. The hospitals will charge the tourist for all the services that they offer to him, whereas the medical tourist is on their premises. The secondary employment generation also contributes to the economic sustainability at this stage of the network.

Insurance companies also come into the frame when it is required for the tourist to undergo a major medical intervention or a surgery, the Foreign or Indian medical insurance agencies come into the picture by ensuring the patient for the treatment that he is seeking. The insurance provided can either be a direct insurance cover or a third-party insurance cover. Moreover, a majority of the travelers from countries such as the United States and Europe are not covered by the insurance companies in their native place for medical treatment, due to the prohibitively high costs of medical insurance (Woodman, 2007). Healthcare facilitator's do play dynamic roles toward the patient, health system, and medical tourism industry. Facilitator roles toward the patient are typically described in terms of advocacy and the provision of information but limited by facilitators' legal liability. Facilitators also play an affirmative role in the lives of their patients. They also play a substantial and evolving role in the practice of medical tourism and are entering a period of professionalization. Because of the key role of facilitators in determining the effects of medical tourism on patients and public health, there is an intense requirement for planned conversation between medical tourism stakeholders to define and shape facilitators' roles. Facilitators have the potential to exacerbate or mitigate the ethical concerns associated with medical tourism, but their roles are sometimes poorly understood. This paves way for drafting a matrix in which the coordination between the medical travelers and a facilitator or health travel agent can be associated well (Figure 19.4).

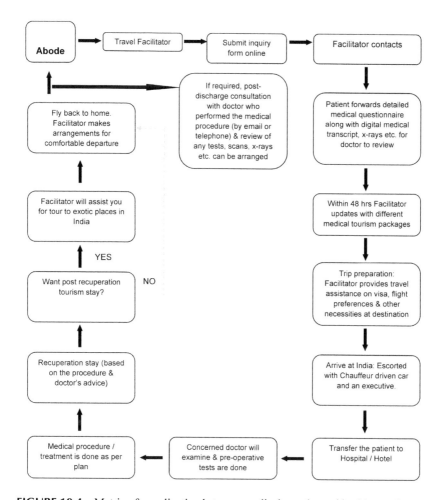

FIGURE 19.4 Matrix of coordination between medical traveler and health travel agent.

19.3.2   GLOBAL HEALTHCARE OPPORTUNITIES AND HEALTH TRAVEL AGENTS

Health travel agents are a growing industry to assist the global healthcare opportunities with a global marketing of healthcare opportunities internationally. Medical tourism facilitators act as intermediaries and perform subsequent services: Travel, Documentation, Healthcare, and Tourism (Woodman, 2007). The benefits to clients of using the medical tourism facilitators take account of coordination of services centralized, sharing of experience from other travelers, offering savings, having a representative, service of logistics of arrangements, aftercare, and providing cultural competence.

Health travel agents use common marketing strategies to improve business, such as word of mouth promotion, maximizing internet-based recruitment, collecting patient stories, and updating search engine optimization for medical tourism. Marketing for health travel agents could be improved by focusing on the integration of marketing strategies from medical facility operators and third-party administrators. For example, health travel agents are assisting medical facility operators in promoting their product, the actual health facility, and medical procedures performed. Health travel agents can use information from existing patient satisfaction surveys or patient testimonies from the availed facilities to obtain useful information regarding the desirability of a facility.

Health travel agents may also offer additional services such as immunization travel recommendations, travel visa assistance, or insurance products to coordinate with the desired location. The image of health travel agencies can be fairly improved. Currently, hospitality sector and medical travel facilitators are an unregulated business and a current method of marketing and verifying credibility of agencies is through communication through their websites and patient experiences.

19.3.3   THE OUTLOOK IN MEDICAL TOURISM

Medical tourism facts indicate a bright future for this industry. Bigger brands these days are considering on saving a major portion of medical costs by offering offshore medical treatments for their employees (Kaur et al., 2007). In a similar manner, insurance companies are also collaborating with global healthcare companies to provide overseas options to its members with maximum fixed benefits. Although medical tourism statistics show favorable figures, patients traveling abroad should research facts about the facilities and services in terms of quality assurance. Whether one is receiving surgery abroad are always bound to be covered with higher risks involved. Reviewing a doctor's credentials and being in conversation with previous patients going abroad is highly recommended when seeking quality healthcare.

19.4   BUILDING PROFESSIONAL COMPETENCY AND A BETTER HEALTHCARE MANAGEMENT

A new paradigm in healthcare segment gives a broader space for the government to play a role of healthcare facilitator with effective trade policies to ensure a seamless value chain. Indian healthcare businesses are receiving medical tourist from developing countries who travel for proficient medical procedures and cost and surgical competency being the prime focus. The policymakers need to focus on this segment and eye for a larger share of this market to reposition India as a premium upmarket medical hub. The stakeholders in India can provide medical services and auxiliary services with a larger scope for medical aspirants from Afro-nations and the Middle East who foresee a huge potential for high-end sophisticated medical treatments in India.

The stakeholders can also provide medical services and auxiliary services with a larger scope for medical aspirants from even the highly developed countries as there are two important niche markets that target India for shorter waiting time when compared with the Western nations, and there is a large segment of tourists who seek elective medical procedures that are generally not covered by medical insurance in developed world.

Homogeneity in medical aspirants and heterogeneity in medical services demanded would be challenging for South India from the healthcare provider's perspective. It also gives a bright prospect for better servicing when each hospital targets a segment with some Unique Selling Point. They must engage with source communities, healthcare systems, and governments over a longer period of time, thereby specializing in handling customers from specifically targeted regions and for specific products. Knowledge of markets, consumers, and channel partner over a period of time would allow competitive advantage.

The administrative authorities should undertake capacity building programs to train the subsidiary division in the medical tourism framework, that is, the paramedical and nonmedical staffs of the service providers who occasionally come across the barriers of cross-cultural sensitivities. There can be a stipulation for focused language training for select countries from where tourists are coming in larger numbers particularly in the corporate multispecialty hospitals. The policy-makers may consider placing hospitals with proficiency uplifting the infrastructure such as "hotels"; the benefits may be passed to customers making it more competitive.

The perception about the quality of medical treatment in South India is supreme not only assured due to cost but the prime cause of comparing quality is due to surgical competency as doctors were qualified and skillful and had rendered quality personal attention along with cost effectiveness and effectively coordinated services. South Indian healthcare segment can also focus on alternative forms of treatments such as Ayurveda, Unani, Siddha, and others to tap the potential global market and thereby creating a niche for itself. The private hospitals can network with the international embassies and government to attract the government-funded medical tourists, thereby globalizing its healthcare potential.

Thereby the Indian healthcare industry could imbibe the above-addressed recommendations to reduce their perplexities and to keep with a trend of quality assurance, quality service, and service proficiency. The arena of medical tourism can be transversely diagnosed to foster the prospects of medical tourism with the changing market expectations. The following areas can endow scope for further research in medical tourism:

- Determining the specialized areas of medical tourism from the demand and supply perspectives.
- The gap pertaining to the medical tourist's expectations and the relevance in the value chain of healthcare network.
- The complexity in rules and norms followed internationally and the influence on the medical tourists' decision in traveling abroad for medical treatments.
- Identifying the medical tourist skepticism on medical ethics or code of ethics and the prime concerns of medical tourists visiting India.
- To identify the bottlenecks in medical tourism industry thereby, addressing the lack of an open system approach to avoid a communication mess between the stakeholders in the industry.

- A comparative study on the prospects and facilities offered in the different parts of the country on the issues of cost, quality, and infrastructure.

19.5 CONCLUSION

The prospects of medical tourism have radically changed with the divergent role played by the stakeholders over the years. Among the healthcare providers, the most predominant stakeholder offering a kaleidoscope of services and amenities catering to the needs of the 'new medical tourist' is the healthcare managers. The increased competition and the growing scenario of medical tourism have pulled various other stakeholders into the trade. Predominantly, the policymakers, community and other private participants have contributed a significant role in globalizing the South Indian healthcare systems. Equally, challenging is the cultural and regulatory barriers that can affect significantly the healthcare globalization in Southern India. Giving a competitive edge for the South Indian market with its medical tourism prospects, all the stakeholders have contributed by effective policies and special initiatives to boost medical industry and to market South Indian destinations beyond the frontiers. Along with proficiency in delivering healthcare services and lesser perplexity in the healthcare network can enhance the capacity building process as South Indian market has been a cradle of offering divergent medical alternatives to its target market that itself has paved way to benchmark its medical competency.

Quality and standard assurance are some major parameters in benchmarking the healthcare medical hubs to prosper. The South Indian metros have largely outreached in the developed and developing countries and have benchmarked itself with increased goodwill and globally competitive brand image.

KEYWORDS

- **medical tourism**
- **stakeholder collaboration**
- **healthcare management**
- **surrogacy**
- **competitive advantage**

REFERENCES

Agarwal, D.; Iyengar, S. Attributes of a Service Programme that Reflect Adherence to Professional Standards, in a Congenial Service Environment and Satisfaction on the Part of the User. UNFPA technical report, 1999. Print.

Bagchi, S. Growth Generates Health Care Challenges in Booming India. *Canadian Medical Association Journal* 2009. Print.

Bennur, S. Health Tourism to Get a Boost. *The Hindu*, n.d. Web. 25 Aug. 2009. http://www.hindu.

Bookman, M. Z.; Bookman, K. R. *Medical Tourism in Developing Countries;* Palgrave Macmilan: United Kingdom, 2007; 66. (Print).

CII. It is Advantage India in Medical Tourism; Release CII [Press] 16 Aug. 2004. Print.

CII. Medical Tourism, the Next Big Wave. *Economic Times*, n.d. Web. 2014. http://www.economictimes.com.

Delhi IVF. Legal Aspect of Surrogacy in India. http://www.delhi-ivf.com, n.d. Web.

Ginsburg, P. B.; Moy, E. Physician Licensure and the Quality of Care: The Role of New Information Technologies. *Regulation* **1992,** *15,*(4) (Fall 1992). (Print).

Hari, G. R. How Safe Is Surrogacy in India? Indian Surrogacy Law Centre, n.d. Web. http://www.indiansurrogacylaw.com.

Horowitz, M. D.; Rosensweig, J. A.; Jones, C. A. Medical Tourism: Globalization of the Healthcare Marketplace. *Medscape General Medicine* 2007. (Print).

IAMRA. International Association of Medical Regulatory Authorities. http://www.iamra.com, n.d. Web.

Iyer, M. Twins Birth Showcases Indian Medical Skill. *The Times of India*, n.d. Web. 22 May 2011. http://www.timesofindia.com.

JCI. Joint Commission International. http://www.jointcommissioninternational.org, n.d. Web.

Kaur, J.; et al. Health Tourism in India Growth and Opportunities. International Conference on Marketing and Society (2007). (Print).

Knowledge@Wharton, India. Challenges of Medical Tourism in the Indian Travel Market. n.d. Web. June 2011. http://knowledge.wharton.upenn.edu.

Lancaster, J. Surgeries, Side Trips for Medical Tourists. Washington Post, 2004. (Print).

Law Commission of India. 228th Report of the Law Commission of India. http://www.lawcommissionofindia.nic.in, n.d. Web.

Macguire, S. Medical Tourism: The Future of Healthcare and Travel. Ezine, n.d. Web. http://Ezinearticles.com.

McIntosh, C. Medical Tourism: Need Surgery, Will Travel. CBC News Online, n.d. Web. 2004. http://www.cbc.ca.

Medical Tourism Guide. The History of Medical Tourism. http://www.health-tourism.com, n.d. (Print).

MTQUA. Medical Traveler's Bill of Rights. *The Financial Times*, n.d. Web. http://www.mtqua.org.

Nagaraj, N. Regulating Private Healthcare Hospitals, Clinics Must Register, Follow Standards. *The Times of India*, n.d. Web. 26 Oct. 2009. http://www.timesofindia.com.

NY Daily News. India's Surrogate Mother Business Raises Questions of Global Ethics. http://www.nydailynews.com, n.d. Web. 2007.

NY Daily News. Tourists Flocking to India to Hire Surrogate Moms to Carry Their Babies for a Fraction of the Price. http://www.nydailynews.com, n.d. Web. 2010.

Ray, M. India Fosters Growing 'Medical Tourism' Sector. *The Financial Times*, 2003. (Print).

Report Linker. Booming Medical Tourism in India 2009 Edition. http://www.reportlinker.com, n.d. Web. 2009.

Sen Gupta, A. Medical Tourism and Public Health. *People's Democracy* **2004**, *XXVIII*(19). (Print).

Storrow, R. The Handmaid's Tale of Fertility Tourism: Passports and Third Parties in the Religious Regulation of Assisted Conception. *Texas Wesleyan Law Rev.* **2005,** 189.

Woodman, J. Patients beyond Borders: Everybody's Guide to Affordable, World-Class Medical Tourism. *Healthy Travel Media* 2007. (Print).

CHAPTER 20

DEVELOPING A COMPETITIVE WINE TOURISM DESTINATION: A CASE STUDY OF VINEYARDS IN MAHARASHTRA, INDIA

DR. ANUPAMA S. KOTUR (KADDI)

Assistant professor, Department of Travel & Tourism, St. Joseph's College of Commerce, IGNOU, New Delhi, India

CONTENT

ABSTRACT

Special interest tourism is one of the most important phases in the evolution of tourism that has brought about a whole new dimension to the leisure perspective. Wine tourism, an offshoot of food and drink tourism, has caught the attention of tourists looking for experiential holidays—wine connoisseurs and wine amateurs alike. The state of Maharashtra may rightfully be considered as a pioneer in wine tourism or vineyard tourism in India. Although wine tourism in India is in a nascent stage as compared with its international counterparts, it is domestically growing as a form of special interest tourism. For a tourism destination to thrive and sustain in the long run, it must be competitive. In order to develop a competitive environment conducive to a sustainable wine tourism growth in Maharashtra, various aspects must be taken into account. The current chapter aims to examine and analyze all those elements that are necessary to develop a competitive and sustainable wine tourism destination in Maharashtra. The objective of this chapter is to describe the competitive environment of wine tourism in Maharashtra employing Porter's competitiveness model for the tourism destination. The research relies mainly on secondary data to assess and examine the competitiveness of Maharashtra as a wine tourism destination. The wider contribution of this chapter lies in illustrating and applying tested competitiveness model to Maharashtra's wine tourism in order to assess the destination's competitive environment. This is instrumental in identifying if the growth of the destination is in line with global trends. Further, the study is also aimed at contributing to research literature in wine tourism in India.

20.1   INTRODUCTION

Pioneer and frontrunner in India's wine tourism are the state of Maharashtra. The state being home to largest numbers of vineyards in India, offers a wide range of wine tourism products and services such as vineyard resorts, vineyard restaurants, wine festivals, vineyard-based events and wine tours clubbed with various vineyard-based activities for wine tourists. Although the growth of wine tourism in the state has not witnessed a similar phenomenal growth as in the case of its wine industry, wine tourism continues to make small but significant developments. Almost 16 years after organized wine tourism began in 2000 in Maharashtra; the quantum of growth has been rather slow. Although some larger wineries have successfully ventured and succeeded in turning wine tourism initiatives into profitable ones, many smaller vineyards are yet to venture into wine tourism fervently. At this juncture, it becomes important to reassess and study the developments in the light of its competitive environment in order to identify opportunities for a sustainable growth. Although globally there are many studies pertaining to destination competitiveness, very little or none exist with specific reference to wine tourism in Maharashtra. This lacuna presented an opportunity to the author in carrying out this study. This study is primarily aimed at assessing the competitive environment of wine tourism in Maharashtra. Through this study, an attempt has been made to describe the competitive environment of wine tourism in Maharashtra using Porter's Five Forces model. By assessing the competitiveness of Maharashtra's wine tourism destinations using Porter's model, an insight can be gained into how the destination is placed as against its global counterparts. Further, the study is also instrumental is highlighting how limited resources may be employed in a gainful manner to achieve sustainable destination growth. The wide-ranging contribution of this study lies in presenting general yet definitive attributes with specific reference to wine tourism in Maharashtra that is likely to influence its destination competitiveness. The findings of the study can be particularly useful to policy makers and strategic decision makers in decisions relating to wine tourism product development in Maharashtra.

20.2 LITERATURE REVIEW

20.2.1 TOURISM DESTINATION AND DESTINATION COMPETITIVENESS

A tourism destination has been defined by several authors highlighting its components and characteristics. Porter (1998) defined a tourism destination as "clusters or geographic of interconnected companies and institutions." Vanhove (2006) added that clusters could be understood as "a group of tourism attractions, enterprises, and institutions directly or indirectly related to tourism" (as cited in Mazurec, 2014). UNWTO (2002) defined a destination as "a physical space in which a visitor spends at least one overnight." It includes tourism products such as support services and attractions and tourism resources within one day's return travel time. It has physical and administrative boundaries defining its management, images, and perceptions defining its market competitiveness. Local tourism destinations incorporate various stakeholders often including a host community and can nest and network to form larger destinations. To summarize, a tourism destination can be understood as any defined geographic area that offers tourist attractions, resources, and other facilitating tourism products and services in which an organized effort has been made by destination management organizations to promote the same.

The concept of destination competitiveness essentially means the ability of a destination to offer tourism services and products to tourists that meet global standards and also provide sufficient and fair returns to the stakeholders who offer these services. "Tourism destination competitiveness can be defined as a general concept that encompasses price differentials coupled with exchange rate movements, productivity levels of various components of tourist industry and qualitative factors affecting the attractiveness or otherwise of a destination" (Dwyer et al., 2000; Matias et al., 2007, as cited in Mazurec, 2014). Further, Kim and Dwyer (2003) add that competitive advantage in tourism destination "would relate to climate, scenery, flora, fauna etc., while competitive advantage would relate to such items as the tourism infrastructure (hotels, events, attractions, transportation, networks), the quality management, skills of workers, government policy and so forth." Crouch and Ritchie (2010) stated that "what makes a tourism destination truly competitive is its ability to increase tourism expenditure, to increasingly attract visitors while providing them with satisfying, memorable experiences, and to do so in a profitable way, while enhancing the well-being of destination residents and preserving the natural capital of the destination for future generation." This definition comprises all elements that make up a competitive yet sustainable tourism destination.

20.2.2 TOURISM COMPETITIVENESS MODELS

The concept of destination competitiveness in tourism has been much researched by many academicians over the years. Some researchers focused on specific destination's competitiveness such as the United States (Ahmed and Krohn, 1990), South Korea and Australia (Kim et al., 2001; Kim and Dwyer, 2003), and Serbia (Dobrivojević, 2013), whereas some others focused on particular aspects of destination competitiveness "including destination positioning (Chacko, 1998), destination management systems (Baker et al., 1996), destination marketing (Buhalis, 2000), price competitiveness (Dwyer et al., 2000a, 2000b, 2000c, 2001, 2002; Stevens, 1992; Tourism Council Australia, 1998), quality management (Go and Govers, 2000), the environment (Hassan, 2000; Mihalic, 2000), nature-based tourism (Huybers and Bennett, 2003), strategic management (Jamal and Getz, 1996; Soteriou and Roberts, 1998), and package tours (Taylor, 1995)" (as cited in Crouch, 2007).

Yet another group of academicians focused on developing a general conceptual model of competitive destinations. One of the most important models was developed by Crouch and Ritchie, whose work began in 1992 and extended till 2007, and their model primarily focused on theories of destination's comparative advantage and competitive advantage. De Keyser and Vanhove (1994) introduced another model in which he argued that "competitive position should take five groups of competitiveness factors into account: tourism policy, macroeconomic, supply, transport and demand factors" (as cited in Gomezelja and Mihalic, 2008). "Porter (1998) developed in his book *The Competitive Advantage in Tourism* a model that is much more applicable to the tourism environment" (Mazurek, 2014). Porter's Five Forces model is widely used in analyzing the competitive environment, and it describes a competitive environment through five basic factors: entry of new competitors, the threat of substitutes, the bargaining power of buyers, the bargaining power of suppliers and the rivalry among the existing competitors. "Mihalic (2000) studied destination competitiveness from an environmental perspective. The environmental component was also taken into account in Hassan's model (2000)." The model defined a destination's commitment to the environment as one of the four determinants of tourism competitiveness and included also a comparative advantage, industry structure, and demand factors (as cited in Gomezelja and Mihalic, 2008). Dwyer and Kim (2003) and Dwyer et al. (2004) also undertook to contribute to the development of a general model of destination competitiveness. Their model also considers national and firm competitiveness theory as well as "the main elements of destination competitiveness as proposed by tourism researchers and many of the variables and category headings identified by Crouch and Ritchie" (as cited in Crouch, 2007).

The variously discussed models conceptualized on destination competitiveness highlight factors from both micro and macro environments that contribute to a competitive and sustainable tourism destination. Although no model is comprehensive and without drawbacks, each model, however, sheds light on importance and relevance of several elements that are critical for a competitive tourism destination.

20.2.3   WINE TOURISM IN MAHARASHTRA—A SNAPSHOT

Any study on wine tourism in Maharashtra cannot be undertaken in isolation, without understanding wine industry in the state. The state of Maharashtra saw the establishment of India's first international standard winery in the early 1980s in Narayangaon near Pune. Five more were established and functional by the year 2000. The decade that followed can be considered significant for Indian wine industry as over 60 wineries came into being in Maharashtra alone. As per a report by Hande (2013), in Maharashtra, the total area under grape cultivation is 7000 acres with annual production of 15 lakh metric tons of grapes. Nashik, Pune, Sangli, Solapur, and Osmanabad are important to wine regions in Maharashtra. As per current statistics for the year 2014 by All India Wine Producers' Association that indicates that there are as many as 75 wineries across the state. However, "as many as 50 wineries including 30 in Nashik are in financial trouble and have stopped production" (Times of India, 2014). Although some of the smaller wineries have been abandoning production, the larger and successful wineries in Maharashtra and Karnataka states, India continue to grow pushing up the production year after year. "The industry, which was barely 150,000–200,000 cases (of wines) strong at the turn of the millennium, was growing at the rate of 25–30% for the 5 years prior to the downfall in 2008; it reached a peak of 1.5 m cases, including about 250,000 cases of imported wines. The years 2008–2011 saw a slide in the domestic wine production and consumption, though the market flirted with a peak in April to March 2011–2012, and a growth of 20–25% is expected to continue over the next 5 years" (sic) (Arora, 2013). In 2014, "the country's wine production hit a record 17 million liters, with export sales rising 40% year-on-year to reach US $ 4.4 million in the first 7 months" (Tate, 2015). "Wine sales in India rose by 21% from 95 lakh liters in 2013–2014 to 1.15 crore liters in 2014–2015, according to the All India Wine Producers Association" (Thakur, 2015). Realizing the potential, the government has been slowly showing interest in the growth of wine industry with a "total investment on wineries in Maharashtra was Rs. 431.71 Cr in 2009 and rose to Rs. 452.10 Cr in 2012" Hande (2013).

Wine Tourism in Maharashtra is steadily moving into a growth stage in the product lifecycle, akin to its parent industry—the wine industry. Wineries in Maharashtra, slowly appreciating the benefits wine tourism inclusion brings to their core wine business, are now open to venturing into wine tourism. Nashik district in Maharashtra, which can rightfully be considered as the "wine bowl" of India, is but a natural location for all the wine tourism initiatives in the state. Although Nashik has emerged as the hub of wine tourism in the state with some of the most important vineyards located there such as Sula, York, Soma, Zampa-Grover, Vallonne, Reveilo, and Charosa; Pune and Sholapur too are competing with their wineries such as Four Seasons and Fratelli, respectively. Other important districts of Ahmednagar and Sangli hold a fair potential to be promoted as wine tourism regions.

20.3 METHODOLOGY OF RESEARCH

This research was undertaken with an objective to describe the competitive environment of wine tourism in Maharashtra employing Porter's Five Forces competitiveness model. The data used in supporting the study are secondary in nature. Books, research papers, and articles pertaining to tourism destination, destination competitiveness, and sustainability were reviewed in order to arrive at a suitable model that can be employed in this study. For the purpose of this study, Porter's Five Forces competitiveness model was employed as this model is most commonly used in understanding a destination's competitiveness. Although Crouch and Ritchie's model is more comprehensive, given the nascent stage of wine tourism in Maharashtra, this model may, perhaps, be less suitable for this study.

20.4 ANALYSIS AND FINDINGS

Michael E. Porter developed the five forces model for analysis and examination of the competitiveness of environment of an industry. This model is based on Industrial Organisation (IO) economics. In this model, Porter identified five competitive factors that shape an industry. "These forces determine the intensity of competition and hence the profitability and attractiveness of an industry. The objective of corporate strategy should be to modify these competitive forces in a way that improves the position" (Recklies, 2001). "Through Porter's five forces, the competitive environment is described by the intensity of rivalry among competitors in one branch of industry, entry barriers, bargaining power of buyers, bargaining power of suppliers, the threat of substitute products and services. Based on the analysis of these five factors, strategic decision makers can determine their opportunities and threats that exist in the competitive environment of a company" (Dobrivojević, 2013) or industry at large.

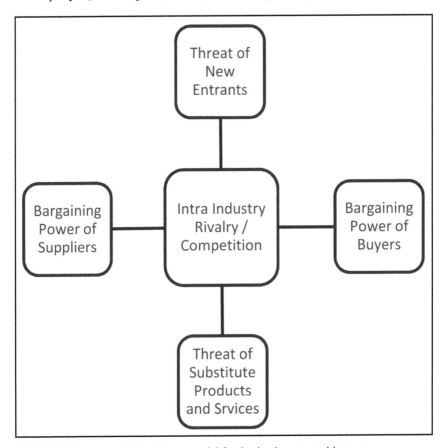

FIGURE 20.1   Porter's Five Forces model for destination competitiveness.

The illustration above (Fig. 20.1) depicts the positioning of these Porter's Five Forces. Competition or rivalry within the industry is marked by four other supporting factors. These forces determine the overall competitiveness, therefore, the attractiveness of the industry. Bruton and Ahlstrom (2008) explain that, for an industry, "Five Forces model are analyzed from the perspective of how they are able to limit industry profits." According to them, if all five forces are weak, then it is likely that the industry will be an attractive one with forms that are quite profitable. Moreover, if all of the forces are high, it is almost certain that the industry has low profit. They add that, even though an industry's forces all produce an unfavorable environment, it is still possible for individual firms in that industry to earn above-average profits. "Based on the analysis of these five factors, strategic decision makers can determine their opportunities and threats that exist in the competitive environment" (Dobrivojević, 2013) of an industry.

The following sections and table below describe all the five forces vis-à-vis wine tourism industry in Maharashtra.

The intensity of rivalry among competitors: "According to Porter, the level of rivalry among companies in the same industry is affected by seven circumstances.

a) When there are many equally balanced competitors
b) When demand for products of an industry declines and when the company, in order to continue to grow, has to win market share from competitors
c) When due to the elimination of the high fixed costs, companies use the full capacity, forcing competitors to cut prices, thus strengthening the rivalry between them
d) Due to the lack of product differentiation and replacement costs, which is why customer makes a decision based on price and service
e) When capacities are being increased on a larger scale, which inevitably leads to lower prices and tougher competition
f) Due to the differences, is hard to predict how the competitors will act in a certain situation, especially when they are ready to reduce their profitability in order to achieve goal for high strategic stakes
g) When there are high exit barriers, that is, when companies from certain economic, strategic, and emotional factors, are ready to do business with a small profit or even negative business" (Dobrivojević, 2013).

In the case of wine tourism service providers in Maharashtra—the wineries and vineyards—there is very moderate in terms of competition.

Industry being in a nascent stage, not more than a few wineries have realized their tourism potential in full. Nasik region, being in the forefront of wine production as well as wine tourism in the country, has Sula, York, Soma Grover-Zampa, Vallonne, Reveilo, Chateau D'Ori, and Charosa as important wine tourism service providers. Again, two of the above names Grover-Zampa and Vallonne operate in another subregion of Nashik known as Igatpuri. Sholapur—Akluj segment being the second most important wine-making region has Four Seasons and Fratelli competing for wine tourism market share. However, from a competition per se, there is moderately low competition. Further, in the state, however, competition at the local level is important to the industry's success. A small winery competes for customers through the winery tasting room, rather than on the external retail shelf. This means the winery competes against all other tourism destinations in the state offering similar entertainment, not just the other Indian wineries.

It is also worth noting that the scale at which vineyards operate wine tourism varies to a great extent with some offering a wide range of tourism services to choose from and others having the most basic wine tourism offerings. Sula, the largest and most recognized brand in both wines and wine tourism in the country, has a whole range of tourism services such as vineyard resort, vineyard restaurants, conferencing and social event facilities, annual wine events, and festivals besides the regular guided wine tours and wine tasting. The other vineyards in the region are slowly adding newer facilities and services to their existing repertoire in order to capture market share from Sula that enjoys a predominant position. These trends indicate that the competition within the industry exists albeit at a moderate level.

Entry barriers (threat of new entry): Entry barriers are obstacles to the entry of new companies into an industry. According to Porter, there are six basic sources of entry barriers:

h) The economy of scales—when with an increase in production, costs per a unit of product are decreased, which brings newcomers, in order to be competitive, before a choice to enter the market on a large scale, or work on a smaller scale with the high cost.

i) Product differentiation—when newcomers are faced with high costs, in order to cope with existing brands and their loyal customers.

j) Capital requirements—when newcomers need to invest substantial financial means in order to be competitive, especially if they do not have such resources at their disposal.

k) Cost disadvantages independent of size—which can derive from owning a technology for production of exclusive and propriety products, purchase of raw materials at an affordable price, state subventions or favorable state policy.

l) Access to distribution channels—when newcomers are denied access to distribution channels.

m) Government policy—when government imposes laws and regulations (Dobrivojević, 2013).

Wine tourism industry is entirely dependent on the growth and development of wine industry. Lower barriers to entry into the wine industry would mean lower barriers into the wine tourism industry. It takes a significant amount of expertise in wines and knowledge in winemaking processes. The entry barrier here is also in terms of large capital investment that goes into procuring specialized machinery required for winemaking. The threat of new entrants has a unique twist in the winery business. A winery is not an easy business to start because it is capital intensive and market entry can take multiple years due to licensing requirements and initial production time. The Maharashtra government, however, has rolled out several financial subsidies as well as other types of assistance to promote the industry. Due to all these factors, some wine brands in Maharashtra have created a sizeable share of the market for themselves owing to high-quality wines and extensive marketing. These wineries find it easier to capture the attention of wine tourists and tourists in general. It must be observed here that change of guard at the state government level has brought about change in the growth rate. The wine industry which saw a proliferation of wineries between 2000 and 2012–2013 is now showing signs of slowing down owing to lack of assistance thereafter.

Another important consideration is the economies of scale in wine production in which larger wineries, unlike the smaller wineries, are profitable due to larger production capacity, this translating into profits plowed back into wine tourism ventures. Smaller wineries unable to cope with a competition with larger wineries are, as a result, suspending production temporarily or, in many cases, abandoning production altogether. In Nashik region alone, 30 wineries had ceased to operate for the year

2014–2015 indicating a high-risk factor for new entrants into the wine industry. Consequently, wine tourism ventures also have become limited to that extent due to high-risk factor in the wine industry in Maharashtra.

Bargaining power of buyers (wine tourists): "The bargaining power of customers determines how much customers can impose pressure on margins and volumes. Customers bargaining power is likely to be high when

i)   There is a concentration of buyers
ii)   The supplying industry comprises a large number of small operators
iii) The supplying industry operates with high fixed costs
iv)   The product is undifferentiated and can be replaced by substitutes
v)   Switching to an alternative product is relatively simple and is not related to high costs
vi)   Customers have low margins and are price-sensitive" (Recklies, 2001)

Buyers here refer to wine tourists. Wine tourists visit vineyards for a day, weekend, or even a weeklong vacation. In this situation, competition for those buyers is actually any travel destination in the area competing for their leisure time. A winery can reduce the bargaining power of these customers by offering unique products and events that offer high value. The bargaining power of wine tourists in the state is rather low given the nascent stage of wine tourism in Maharashtra. There are not many vineyards that have ventured full scale into wine tourism. Most vineyards restrict themselves to the same day visits at present. With not more than a few vineyards—Sula, Soma, Vallonne, Fratelli, and Four Seasons— offering overnight accommodation facility, bargaining power of the wine tourists is curtailed to that extent.

Bargaining power of suppliers: The term "suppliers" comprises all sources for inputs that are needed in order to provide goods or services. Supplier bargaining power is likely to be high when

i)   The market is dominated by a few large suppliers
ii)   The supplier's customers are fragmented, so their bargaining power is low
iii) The switching costs from one supplier to another are high (Recklies, 2001)

iv) The bargaining power of suppliers is reduced by substitute products if they are present in that branch of industry (Dobrivojević, 2013)

With only a few vineyards in Maharashtra offering guided wine tours, wine tasting and overnight accommodation facilities for wine tourists, wine tourism service providers have a moderately greater bargaining power in the wine tourism industry. However, when wine tourism competes with other forms of tourism in the state, it may be said that wine tourism has a moderate bargaining power as tourists can easily choose another form of tourism for example heritage, nature based or beach tourism over wine tourism.

The substitute threat: Substitute threat refers to the risk of substitute products. Porter explains that it is necessary to see whether the other production branches have products that can perform the same function as the original products of a manufacturer. A threat from substitutes exists if there are alternative products with lower prices of better performance parameters for the same purpose. They could potentially attract a significant proportion of market volume and hence reduce the potential sales volume for existing players. This category also relates to complementary products. Similarly, to the threat of new entrants, the threat of substitutes is determined by factors like

i) Brand loyalty of customers
ii) Close customer relationships
iii) Switching costs for customers
iv) The relative price for performance of substitutes
v) Current trends

Many vineyards are slowly but surely realizing the potential of wine tourism in promoting their wine brands. It not only creates unique brand equity for the vineyard but also is a great marketing tool to connect with potential buyers. Given this advantage, many vineyards are adding overnight accommodation, in-house restaurants and wine events to attract tourists not only from the domestic market but also international tourist market. This growth trend is certain to create substitute threat for the existing players in the market such as Sula who enjoy greater dominance in wine tourism in Maharashtra. Further, there is also competition from other alternative forms of tourism in the state that may compete for tourists' attention such as heritage tourism, adventure tourism, beach tourism, and so on.

20.5   CONCLUSION

Studying and assessing the competitiveness of wine tourism in Maharashtra based on Porter's Five Forces model, being the primary aim of this chapter, allows the tourist destination to understand its position. By applying this model to analyze its competitive position, the industry can clearly see the opportunities and threat that face the industry. The findings of the study are instrumental in making a critical decision such as investment and expansion in wine tourism in Maharashtra. Table 20.1 enumerates the status of destination competitiveness of wine tourism in Maharashtra vis-à-vis *Porter's Five Forces:*

TABLE 20.1   Porter's Five Forces vis-à-vis Wine Tourism Industry in Maharashtra.

Porter's Five Forces	Competitiveness of wine tourism industry in Maharashtra
The intensity of rivalry among competitors	Low-to-moderate
Entry barriers (threat of new entry)	High
Bargaining power of buyers	Low
Bargaining power of suppliers	Moderate-to-high
The substitute threat	Moderate

From the analysis, following concluding observations emerge:

- Wine tourism industry in Maharashtra is dominated by a few players such as Sula, Fratelli, Vallonne, Ravioli, Soma, Zampa-Grover, and Charosa vineyards. Although profitability from venturing into wine tourism is less than attractive for smaller wineries with limited resources—financial, expertise and manpower, larger wineries continue to invest in wine tourism ventures. The wine market itself in Maharashtra is a growing one albeit slowly. Wine tourism being a form of special interest tourism attracts a niche segment of tourists. This segment is small and growing slowly. Therefore, more often than not vineyards find themselves fighting for a share from this small segment of wine tourists.
- Between the years 2000 and 2012 as many as 60 wineries were established under the aegis of Maharashtra's Grape Processing

Industrial Policy of 2001. However, in the year 2014–2015, as many as 50 out of the 75 wineries were on the verge of closure, 30 of which were located in Nashik region alone. This trend indicates the high risk involved for new entrants in the wine industry in Maharashtra. Although larger wineries with relatively stable market share and revenue have been able to survive through the turbulent market and unsteady demand phases. These larger wineries face little or no threat from new entrants in the industry.

- Nascent stage of wine tourism in Maharashtra is partly due to limited wine tourism products and services available to wine tourists. With limited offerings, prices normally tend to be dictated by the service provider leaving the buyers with no little bargaining power.

- On the other hand, wine tourism service providers gain from a market situation in which the wine tourism industry is presently monopolized by one or handful of service providers. This has resulted in a market condition in which wineries providing wine tourism products and services are better placed than wine tourists as far are pricing is concerned.

- Wine tourism being a special interest tourism attracting wine connoisseurs whose purchase decisions are made mostly based on their area of interest. Therefore, the threat of substitution is only moderate in the case of wine tourism.

KEYWORDS

- **wine tourism in Maharashtra**
- **destination competitiveness**
- **competitiveness and sustainability**

REFERENCES

Arora, S. *Beyond Making and Selling Wine*; 2011. www.indianwineacademy.com.
Bruton, G. D.; Ahlstrom, D. O. K. Entrepreneurship in Emerging Economies: Where are We Today and Where Should the Research Go in the Future. *Entrepreneurship: Theory and Practice* **2008**, *32*(1), 1–14.

Crouch, G. I. *Modeling Destination Competitiveness: A Survey and Analysis of the Impact of Competitiveness Attribute*. National Library of Australia Cataloguing in Publication Data. ISBN 9781920965389. 2007. http://www.sustainabletourismonline.com/awms/Upload/Resource/bookshop/Crouch_modelDestnComp-web.pdf.

Dobrivojević, G. Analysis of the Competitive Environment of Tourist Destinations Aiming at Attracting FDI by Applying Porter's Five Forces Model. 2013. https://zenodo.org/record/8651/files/1374391677-Dobrivojevic342013BJEMT4180.pdf.

Gomezelja, D. O. Mihalic, T. Destination Competitiveness—Applying Different Models, the Case of Slovenia. *Elsevier Tourism Management* **2008**, *29,* 294–307.

Hande, Dr. Ministry of Agriculture, Maharashtra, Personal Communication, 2013.

Kim, C.; Dwyer, L. Destination Competitiveness and Bilateral Tourism Flow Between Australia and Korea. *J. Tourism Stud.* **2003**, *14*(2), 55–67. https://www.jcu.edu.au/data/assets/pdf_file/0014/122180/jcudev_012874.pdf.

Mazurec, M. Competitiveness in Tourism—Models of Tourism Competitiveness and their Applicability: Case Study Austria and Switzerland. *Eur. J. Tourism, Hospitality Recreation;* **2014,** Special Issue, 73–94. http://www.ejthr.com/ficheiros/2014/SpecialIssue/EJTHR_Volume5_SE_Art4.pdf.

Porter, M. E. *Competitive Advantage: Creating and Sustaining Superior Performance: With a New Introduction;* Free Press: New York, 1998.

Recklies, D. Porter's Five Forces—A Model for Industry Analysis; 2001. related:vse.jires.org/sub_IZI212/get.php?subj=Eurotel&id=5_Porterovych_sil.doc Porter's five forces pdf.

Ritchie, J. R. B.; Crouch, G. I. *A Model of Destination Competitiveness/Sustainability: Brazilian Perspectives*. Revista De Administracoa Publica (RAP)—Rio de Janeiro **2010,** *44*(5), 1049–1066, Set./out. http://www.scielo.br/pdf/rap/v44n5/v44n5a03.pdf.

UNWTO. 2002. http://destination.unwto.org/content/conceptual-framework-0.

CHAPTER 21

AGRITOURISM IN INDIA: STRATEGIES FOR GROWTH

SURAJ NAIR

Cofounder, TravelSpends, Bangalore, India

CONTENTS

ABSTRACT

Travel is a journey about seeking and exploring and discovery of new destinations. Travel is about a discovery of seeking and exploring. Travel is evolving in the way it is conceptualized and consumed. Tourism in India is driven largely by three or four states—the "Incredible India" offering has largely been built around the tourist destinations of Rajasthan, Kerala,

Goa, and the diversity in culture, nature, and architectural wonders of India. In India, tourism is largely driven by the domestic tourists and to substantiate tourism growth, and in 2015, the Government of India being a protourism and firm growth-oriented governing body introduced the e-tourist visa facility to include new countries. The tourist arrival using the e-tourist visa has seen a quantum leap from the strategy-synergized overall tourist arrivals and has shown a phenomenal growth and is to be made available to over 180 countries in phases. The urbanization and rapid development of cities have kindled the desire amongst travelers to seek and explore new forms of tourism. Experiential travel is gaining ground across the world. The new age traveler is constantly seeking offbeat trails, the road less traveled, going back to roots. A large portion of the hinterland in India consists of villages where farming is the key occupation. India is an agrarian economy largely dependent on the vagaries of nature. The above text presents both opportunities and challenges in terms of the develop-ment of these theme-based tourist circuits based on agriculture and farms or farmlands. This chapter deals with strategies and measures to overcome challenges and evolve stratagems and actionable responses for the devel-opment of agritourism in the country. There is clearly a lack of primary research in the area of agritourism; this is an impediment; however, infer-ences can be drawn on the basis of the peripheral data and collaterals drawn based on the development in other geographies. This chapter also highlights various strategies that could contribute to the growth of agri-tourism in India. This greenfield opportunity can be curated and developed to realize the potential of agritourism.

21.1 INTRODUCTION

Agriculture is the backbone of Indian economy. The Indian economy and government are heavily reliant on the growth of agriculture in every budget as it contributes roughly 14% of the gross domestic product (GDP). Agriculture also employs over 60% of the population and feeds in excess of a 1.3 billion populations. It is essential to understand the importance of agriculture and its coverage in the Indian context to set the relevance for agritourism and its growth in the region. India consists of a union of states or a federation with strong central structure governed by a democratically elected institution. Agriculture and commerce are state subjects; however, the central government is permitted to make laws under state list for giving effect to international treaties. The center draws up the agriculture policy and agenda at the national level, and the states are responsible for execution. The center also monitors and legislates regarding the overall health of the agrofarming ecosystem and export and import of the produce. The land-holding pattern in the farmlands makes it impossible to undertake large-scale farming that is an ingredient of agritourism in some parts of the world. The lack of basic amenities like uninterrupted power, clean water, and hygiene standards are factors that affect community living and the experience of an agritourist. However, based on the spirit of entrepreneurship and local community initiatives, we have seen the growth of agricircuits. The grape vineyards of Nashik, the tea plantations of Assam, the coffee estates in Chikmagalur and Coorg, the mango orchards in Ratnagiri, and Krishnagiri district are all circuits that have been explored.

However, currently the theme is not the destination and the activity, rather the focus is on the property or a farmland and the activities surrounding it. The social fabric with deep roots of local customs, traditions, festivals, folk art, and delectable cuisines offer an unparalleled experience to the discerning tourists. Some of the key agricircuits that can be established are around cattle farms in Maharashtra, tea estates in Assam and West Bengal, apple orchards in Himachal, the evergreen fields in Punjab combined with rustic lifestyle.

21.2 AGRITOURISM DEFINITION AND BENEFITS

Agritourism or *agrotourism,* as it is defined most broadly, involves any agriculturally based operation or activity that brings visitors to a farm or ranch. Agritourism has different definitions in different parts of the world and sometimes refers specifically to farm stays, as in Italy.

Elsewhere, agritourism includes a wide variety of activities, including buying produce direct from a farm stand, navigating a corn maze, slopping hogs, picking fruit, feeding animals, or staying at a bed and breakfast on a farm. Agritourism is a form of niche tourism that is considered a growth industry in many parts of the world, including Australia, Canada, the United States, and the Philippines. Agritourism is seen as a fairly new practice that basically comes with the dual objective of promoting agriculture and encouraging urban tourism. So, it is the perfect amalgamation of the rural and the urban through the medium of tourism. It builds knowledge about the rural way of living and surviving (Ranganathan, 2012).

21.3 AGRITOURISM AND THE KEY ECONOMIC DRIVER

The potential agritourism holds in terms of social uplift in terms of economic prosperity it brings to the region has been established through various success stories. The research carried out at the University of Missouri serves as a good reference for understanding the positive impact of agritourism on farmers and local communities. Results from the Missouri Agritourism Survey in 2008 as published in 2010 by Carla Barbieri, Ph.D. and Christine Tew, M.S. indicates that nearly two-thirds (64.4%) of the 164 farm operators perceived that their farm profits increased after developing agritourism on their farms. Those perceptions of greater profitability after adding agritourism activities are especially interesting as responding farms vary in respect to their gross sales. The study also establishes a positive association for farms with greater acreage that perceive them as being more profitable businesses, on account of higher agricultural production and increased economies of scale.

"In simple terms, Agri-tourism is the crossroads of tourism and agriculture: when the public visits working farms, ranches or wineries to buy products, enjoy entertainment, participate in activities, shop in a country store, eat a meal or make overnight stays. Visiting a farm, ranch or winery offers wonderful, unique experiences. Picking your own peaches or apples in a beautiful orchard, roping a calf or stomping grapes are just a few of the fun and fabulous activities waiting for you." (Jane Eckert of Eckert Agri-Marketing).

21.4 COMPETITIVE STRENGTHS, WEAKNESS, OPPORTUNITY, AND THREATS ASSESSMENT MODEL

In order to identify the opportunity and understand the potential agritourism provides for India, we have attempted to assess the strengths, weakness, opportunity, and threats (SWOT). These can act as catalysts or inhibitors for the growth and evolution of agritourism. A SWOT analysis can be used effectively to build a strategy. Steps necessary to execute strategy-oriented analysis involve identification of internal and external factors (using popular 2×2 matrix), selection and evaluation of the most important factors, and identification of relations existing between internal and external features.

S		W	
Agriculture, Farms & Farming	Co-operative Movement - IRMA	Facilitators : Infrastructure & amenities	Industry Status : Policy & framework
Processed Foods : Tea, Coffee, Fruits & Vegetables	PPP Models : Economically Profitable	Facilities : Classification & standardization	Scale : Lack of integrated land Parcels

O		T	
Coverage : Area & spread Of farming	Markets : Domestic demand & consumption	Policy : Red Tape & Policy paralysis	Collaboration : Govt. bodies & farmers
Industry : Growth in greenfield tourism	Connect : Back to nature & roots	Sustainability : Methods & development	Politics : Geo-political stand-off's

We can classify the key drivers as below based on the graphical representation above. The interplay of these factors is present with the dynamic push and pull among the various drivers that can assist in the development of the agritourism model.

21.4.1 STRENGTHS

India a diverse and geographically vast expanse of land offers the abundance of multiple themes such as agriculture. It offers a multitude of crops and crop cycles, farming of grains, pulses, cattle, aquafarming, and diverse farming methods. There are various models of development that can be adopted. The most successful one being NABARD, and the most visible brand being marketed is AMUL. The processed food industry that includes jams, ketchup, syrups and juices, and canned foods has also mushroomed. This has resulted in an expansive supply chain, cold storages, and food-processing units that present an opportunity for agritourists to experience the entire chain and buy directly from the farms or affiliated processing units.

21.4.2   WEAKNESS

Scale plays a big role in farming and use of modern methods of farming. In the case of India, most of the land parcels are fragmented. Hence, there is a need for local community level structuring under a central nodal agency to integrate the offerings for the tourist. The key facilitators for good Infra-structure would mean access—good roads, good standards of hygiene and cleanliness, a minimum standard of accommodation standards and utilities.

The importance of creating a progressive policy framework to regulate and promote the agritourism industry is critical to attracting investments into this sector.

21.4.3   OPPORTUNITIES

The diversity in terms of cultivation in agriculture and a variety of crops and seasonality coupled with various types of farms presents a unique opportunity to develop a circuit or grid that can ride on different themes such as heritage, archeology, city tourism, wildlife, and pilgrim tourism.

The above themes also resonate the need for the urban traveler in terms of a strong emotional connect to go back to the rural way of life and share the experience with the family. The above hence presents a huge potential in terms of the opportunity. Globally greenfield and ecosensitive tourism has been growing as travelers look toward responsible tourism with a view to conservation. This again works as a growth driver for agritourism as it relies heavily on local resources for fulfillment.

The demand consumption for agritourism will be largely driven by an increasingly mobile Indian traveler for which the growth is 11.9% in 2014 (source—Ministry of Tourism, Indian tourism statistics—2014). This segment will continue to grow as the economic indicators, and the dispos-able income levels continue to rise in India. The incoming global travelers will further fuel this demand. This segment is growing exponentially on the back of Tourist Visa on Arrival facility launched by the Government of India.

21.4.4   THREATS

The key challenge in the execution of the above initiatives can be on account of continuing inaction in policy and decisions. Red tape and political nonalignment can be inhibitors and can derail the attempt to grow agritourism. The relationship between states is highly volatile on the issue of water resources, and this has a direct bearing on agriculture. Agriculture is a core industry for agritourism, the impact on rousing passions and disintegration of people and community connect is real. The lack of collaboration amongst the various local, district, state, and national bodies is another factor that can reduce the development of agritourism. Finally, the need for channeling the growth in a sustainable manner will require a well-constructed policy document, strong compliance, and penalties for noncompliance, investments, training and coordination, and collaboration. A sustainable model can only be built on the basis of discipline and strong connect with the key stakeholders including the local communities who will be the hosts. The theme of "Athithi Devo Bhava" is an apt theme and needs to be lived in letter and spirit for the concept to succeed.

21.5 A STRATEGIC APPROACH TOWARD AGRITOURISM IN INDIA

The key drivers for the growth and development of agritourism in India are listed below. India ranked 11th among 184 countries in terms of travel and tourism's total contribution to GDP in 2015, and the travel and tourism sector in India estimated to contribute 9% of total employment, generating 37.4 million jobs in 2015. To introspect on the ongoing agritourism initiatives and existing schemes to promote agrotourism in the country, special measure is to be initiated. Credentials and certifications of existing business models in agrotourism are highly imperative. This chapter details out the strategic role of extension and advisory services in the sustenance of agrotourism, and we will attempt to study them in detail to understand how they can facilitate the growth of agritourism in India.

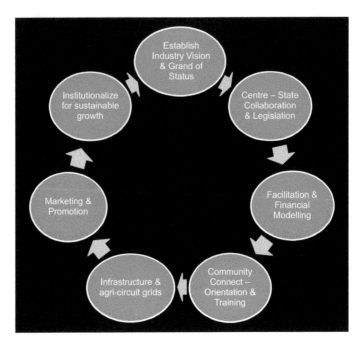

Let us review the above key strategies for the development of agri-tourism. We will attempt to study these in detail to understand the scope and opportunities these strategies could present to the sector.

21.5.1   ESTABLISH VISION AND GRANT OF INDUSTRY STATUS

The establishment of a cohesive vision and establishing of convergent goals by the key stakeholders is critical to progress this initiative. The various bodies need to congregate under a single platform and discuss the opportunities and conflicts whether policy and legislation convergence or conflicts in political or commerce ideology to establish the agenda for the growth of agri-tourism. The identification of pilot states and mapping of circuits within these states could be a good beginning to start piloting the growth of agritourism. There are already some established circuits such as the one in Gujarat where the milk cooperatives have collaborated and established a "white revolution" in the absence of a large-scale dairy farm model has evolved a sustainable model that can promote agritourism. The success, in this case, lies in the fact that most of the dairy farms are small to midsized farms working under the Gujarat Cooperative Milk Marketing Federation that markets the product under the brand AMUL. Currently, visits by school children are popular in the diary. The creation of a nodal body is of primary importance. The various stakeholders such as Ministry of Agriculture, and respective central and state nodal bodies for agriculture, commodities trade, and development, the Tourism Promotion Council, National Association of Tour Operators need to collaborate to ensure that agritourism initiatives are evolved and implemented. The key challenge in India is the lack of coordination or in plain words the lack of a *collaborative* effort among the industry bodies.

The job functions of the nodal agency will be to establish guidelines and also work on the development of integrated agritourism circuits, single window permits or clearances and affiliations and financial aid to facilitate participation. Further, this nodal body will work closely with the local bodies and cooperatives to enhance participation for the model to gain mass acceptance. Currently, the nodal body that provides indirect support for agritourism is the Ministry of Agriculture, Food, and Fisheries. The key activities it is engaged in include assistance and subsidies for drip irrigation, seeds, food-processing machinery and equipment, and financing for fish and aqua farming.

There are various state agricultural colleges and universities that give training and orientation to farmers, and these institutions could be used as the nodal centers for the promotion of agritourism initiatives. Once the participation and connect is established at the ground level the central and state bodies can facilitate common platforms for communications and collaboration. The grant of an industry status can be accorded by the inclusion of agritourism as a derivative to agriculture. This will allow the central monitoring and support for the initiative and act as a catalyst for the rapid development of the sector. It is recommended that the Prime Minister's Office should create a council under the aegis of the Ministry of Agriculture with a separate charter to identify and develop 20 circuits in the pilot phase in collaboration with the states. The learning from this pilot phase could be instrumental in designing the secondary initiatives for growth.

21.5.2   CENTER–STATE COLLABORATION AND LEGISLATIVE CONVERGENCE

There is an urgent need to create legislation and avoid conflict within legislations between the center and the state. The need for convergence of the legislation and progressive gains as the farmers and other trade bodies engage in this sector is very important for the health and sustainable development of agritourism. The need to engage and involve individual farmers or establish a cooperative of farmers who can pool their land or make their farms accessible through participation is essential to create the requisite infrastructure and facilities for the agritourist are a very important milestone. This is critical in a country where the land parcels are irregular, and the nature of landholding is largely ancestral and based on family tree subdivisions. This does not provide economy of scale for setting up the infrastructure. All the government agencies should act in a homogenous and progressive manner to act as a catalyst by establishing by providing a policy framework and promotional financial aid to encourage enrolment and participation. The policies need to be crafted keeping in view the local land under cultivation and the pattern of crop cultivation and the farmer's interest in mind.

21.5.3   FACILITATION AND FINANCIAL MODELING

It is extremely important that any social model is ably supported by a commercial model for it to be sustainable. The local community participation is critical to creating a model that aids development and growth of agritourism, and this should be facilitated.

In the Indian context, Agritourism Development Company was founded by Pandurang Taware at Pune in 2005, also known as the father of agritourism in India. Its vision is to introduce agriculture tourism to Indian villagers in order to help them earn better and live better. Its activities are largely centered around Maharashtra; however, its charter includes expansion into other states. A robust financial model to curate the engagement and involvement of the local community will ensure long-term viability of this model. Government bodies can provide financial aid and assistance that can aid facilitators. Agritourism can facilitate financial gains for the communities. It can further provide the following key benefits to the community in terms of the below.

1. Rural employment
2. Income certainty
3. Promotion of cottage industry
4. Local handicrafts and garment industry

A successful strategy should blend and adopt, adapt to the needs of the consumers and be commercially viable. The growth of agritourism will largely be influenced by the ability to institutionalize the framework including the model of public–private participation. This model ensures that local-level participation ensures sustainability and financial viability. The various stakeholders such as farmers, village communities, the infrastructure providers, and governing bodies at the local level need to see a commercial benefit from this model for it to be sustainable.

The growth of greenfield tourism has immense benefits to rural communities and is sustainable as it promotes responsible tourism. The USP of the model is that it nurtures the resources and the socio and natural eco-system for longevity.

A strong domestic market within the country can supplement the international tourist arrivals and the cyclical tourism syndrome (a syndrome when foreign tourists visit a place in a particular period of the year) can be overcome.

Goa is a prime example of domestic market fueling the demand. The summer period of April–June is dominated by the domestic tourism, and the winter November–January occupancy is largely driven by "Inbound tourists."

21.5.4 COMMUNITY CONNECT—ORIENTATION AND TRAINING

The blending of harvest festivals, the local communities, and the fabric of village life alongside the promotion of agritourism needs to be nurtured. The promotional activities have to be synchronized with the other state tourism bodies to influence traveler choice of destinations and themes.

The key challenges in the context of India to promote agritourism can be broadly classified as below:

1. Infrastructure—good bedding and sanitation
2. Hygiene and cleanliness
3. Standardization of facilities

The concept of a community living, the local customs, traditions, and cultural festivities are the binding themes. The emotional connect of going back to the roots blends well with the communities who live a harmonious life. The success of any orientation for the community will have to take into considerations the local customs and practices. The development and maintenance of sanitation and general health standards are challenging in most parts of the country. The idea of "Swachh Bharat" is an idea the high time of which has come. In order to achieve this, a concentrated effort at the village, local municipality, and town level will be required to bring about a paradigm shift. This is a critical factor for the success of the circuit and acceptance of the product by both local and global tourists. The circuits should be able to weave the local festivals, the local way of life, sports, and games into the experience along with a culinary experience that dishes out the local fares. The key challenge in training the local community in communication, hospitality orientation should be relatively easier considering that these do exist though in an unstructured manner.

21.5.5 CREATION OF INFRASTRUCTURE AND AGRICIRCUITS BASED ON GRIDS

The creation of infrastructure and identification of the agricircuits are instrumental for the development and growth of agrigrids. The Kaapi Trails was one such product conceived and conceptualized by Bangalore Airport. However, this experiment for inclusive tourism has not progressed on the basis of its true potential. We will attempt to study this in detail as it has all the ingredients and the recipe for the creation of an agricircuit. The Kaapi Trails was a beautiful idea that the Kempegowda Bangalore International Airport conceptualized to promote the Coffee Trails on the lines of the French Wine Trails. The circuit includes landing at the Bangalore airport and then winding upward to Chikmagalur and Coorg that are the coffee-growing regions in Karnataka, India.

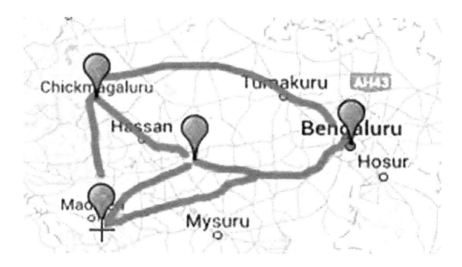

The tourism initiative had multiple stakeholders who signed up for the project. These included the Bangalore Airport, Coffee Board of India, a leading Indian inbound tour operator Travel Corporation of India, owned by Thomas Cook India Ltd. The product was christened to include three themes:

1. Heritage Kaapi Trails
2. Wild Kaapi Trails
3. Leisure Kaapi Trails

"Kaapi Trail, as wine is for France, Coffee is for South India, and there is a beautiful story of this aromatic drink. In the journey of the bean is the journey to understand South India. Culture, Heritage, Experience, Life."— a promotional message from BIAL to promote Kaapi Trail, source—Kaapi Trails brochure. The concept was to create an experience for the tourist through the coffee country; the different varieties of coffee and take them on an educational and coffee tasting experience. The coffee regions in Coorg also known as the Scotland of the South and Chikmangaluru which is the birthplace of the Coffee Day.

The varieties of coffee grown here are the Arabica and the Robusta. A unique experience of the process of coffee pulping (the coffee puri-fication method), early evening visits the coffee museum, this museum gives an insight of Indian coffee history and its preservation and stay at a coffee estate. The "Bean to Coffee Powder tours" as they are christened by

Café Coffee Day and marketed using their flagship hospitality brand christened the "Serai." Ministry of Tourism, Indian tourism statistics—2014e garments can provide an interesting journey. The silk journey can also be integrated to heritage, and wildlife as the Nagarhole and the Bandipur national Parks is in close proximity.

The mantra of going back to roots and tracing the way rural India lives, experiencing a bullock cart ride, sugarcane fields, silkworms, and silk weaving "From the Cocoon to Six Yards of Grace—The Saree."

21.5.6   MARKETING AND PROMOTION

There are several success stories of marketing campaigns that have been successful—Kerala Tourism promoted Ayurveda along with houseboats and beaches and the tea estates in Munnar to attract a global traveler. There are other success stories around the "Incredible India" campaign and the various state tourism bodies such as the Karnataka tourism, India that promote the concept of "One State, Many Worlds". However, the collaborative effort between Karnataka, Kerala, and Goa Tourism can create incremental benefits for each of these bodies.

The key challenge for any promotional campaign is the imagery and the popularity of the circuit to create the magnetic pull. The case study of "Marketing the Gallo Rosso" in Italy provides many meaningful insights and learning's for the evolution of agritourism in India.

The concept commenced in 1999 in a small town in Italy, due to big problems with occupancy in the area, an abundance of agritourism but not selling. The farmer's union started the brand "Red Rooster" with over 22,000 members, over 2500 accommodation providers, and 40 farms. It created the brand to promote the region and increase the sales for the agritourism produce; a coordinated marketing approach through regional branding was established. The key theme was established and the Red Rooster branding was the distinguishing feature.

We put in touch people of the world with South Tyrol.

The Red Rooster branding symbolized the offering and became the brand.

1.   The "Red Rooster" trademark stands for quality and transparency, guaranteed via strict quality criteria and controls.

2.   Evolved from offering Farm Holidays in South Tyrol to including Farm Inns and Bars and Quality Farm Products in South Tyrol.

In a digital age when mobile internet and the internet of things (IoT) are evolving the need for promotion, and coordinated efforts in marketing especially digital marketing are important to spread awareness of the circuits. The need to do push marketing of the social and cultural themes and linkages to the local traditions and festivals are important to capture the essence of rural tourism that has a magnetic pull on tourists across the world.

An integrated marketing campaign for the promotion of agritourism can be modeled as follows:

i)   The blending of agritourism circuits and airport gateways will create a seamless traveler experience. The creation of an agritourism circuit in collaboration with the state and central state tourism bodies and aviation—both airports and airlines will result in an experiential product.

ii)   The ability to offer multiple experience and cuisines and culinary delights based on the agricircuits including the processing of food and pulses and target key inbound tourist generation hubs.

iii) The ability to tap the discerning Indian tourist based on an appeal of the emotional quotient and connects of "a journey back to the roots" in which agriculture and a village experience are at the center of this campaign.

iv) The digital marketing campaign needs to further convert the leads and digital footprints into conversions. This needs to be ably supported by both language support and e-mail engagement to convert the potential tourist into an agritourist.

A collaborative approach will result in the growth of agritourism along with more established circuits offering a varied experience for a traveler's itinerary.

21.5.7   INSTITUTIONALIZE FOR SUSTAINABLE GROWTH

It is important to institutionalize the framework and the charter for sustained growth of the sector. The key sustainability benefits of agritourism are listed below:

a) Agritourism helps maintain the natural landscape and demographic balance of the community. It helps in creating an ecosystem including processed food-processing industry to procure and store unprocessed natural agriproduce.

b) It blends the local culture and creates income opportunities through direct and indirect channels. The direct benefits include selling direct to consumers or agritourists and indirect ancillary revenues could be from branding collectibles, sale of an ancillary farming kits, soil, saplings, and other agriproduce.

c) Ancillary income generation by local communities is possible by a marketplace for selling of handicrafts, local cottage industry.

21.6   EXTENDING OUTREACH FOR WIDER MARKETPLACE

Sustenance for the image of Indian farm experiences, publicizing supplies could be established for better synthesis and connectivity. These supplies should include regional brochures that provide visitors with specific information on farm experiences along with the Product Guides for better engagements with farm-based leisure activities. Furthering marketing initiatives of this kind serves to effectively promote the agritourism industry. There are media opportunities that individual farmer and agritourism associations can use to reach a wider marketplace. For instance; the central and state tourism avenues, website, or toll-free number or call center that can be used by the general consumer to obtain travel information and to book a farm-based holiday, the product guide that is placed at all visitor information centers; regional tourism association brochures, and others. Similarly, communication channels can be established between agritourism operators and potential travel markets with ingeniously placed websites.

21.7   CONCLUSION

The key focus of this study was to look at an approach for the growth and development of agritourism based on a SWOT analysis within the ecosystem. By using the SWOT analysis, we attempt to analyze the interplay of key variables to identify the opportunities and threats that face the industry. The primary goal of this presentation was to establish the key drivers and drive executive decisions that are essential to facilitate the growth of the agricircuits.

The key conclusions drawn based on the SWOT analysis and strategies recommended can be structured as below.

i)   Agritourism will have to be established as an industry or affiliate industry status for the financial investments and entry of larger hospitality brands. They will bring in the desired expertise and manpower for building the infrastructure and scale, which is essential for demand management. The participation of the private sector alongside the government is critical to the development of agritourism

ii) The current circuits are packaged around the hospitality provider or the conventional themes and have no support in terms of branding. On the lines of the Red Rooster, there could be various branding campaigns based on the agricircuit and the offerings. An integrated approach will result in higher tourist acceptance of this agritourism product and higher conversions.

iii) Agritourism holds the promise of sustainability as the use of natural resources with minimal ecological imbalance. The integration of local communities and their traditions and customs, improvements in infrastructure, social, and financial uplift are other benefits that can enhance the potential of this sector.

The recommendations and approach suggested by this study can assist in building the framework, establishing the industry status and linked legislations to control, regulate, and facilitate the growth of this sector.

KEYWORDS

- agritourism
- agricircuit
- industry status
- Kaapi trails
- incredible India

REFERENCES

AgriTourism. Indian Agritourism Industry—Challenges and Strategies. http://www.agri-tourism.in/tourism-in-india.html.

Baggett, A. Agritourism Success. https://www.ext.vt.edu/topics/agriculture/agritourism/files/presentations/agritourism-success.pdf.

Central Silk Board. Introduction to Sericulture. http://csb.gov.in/silk-sericulture/sericulture/.

India Ministry of Tourism. Statistics of India Tourism. http://www.tourism.nic.in/writereaddata/CMSPagePicture/file/marketresearch/statisticalsurveys/India%20Tourism%20Statistics%20at%20a%20Glance%202014New.pdf.

NDTV Express News Service. "Kaapi Trail" at Bangalore International Airport. http://www.ndtv.com/karnataka-news/kaapi-trail-at-bangalore-international-airport-570410, n.d. Web. 2011.

Porcaro, P. The Italian Agritourism Model. http://www.tourismfutures.com.au/Publications/2009Presentations/Porcaro%20Pauline%20PP.pdf.

Ranganathan, D. Agri-Tourism Helping Bridge Metros to Farms. http://www.thealternative.in/lifestyle/agro-tourism-helping-bridge-metros-to-farms/. Web. 2012.

Red Rooster. Farm Holidays in South Tyrol. http://www.redrooster.it/en/holidays-in-south-tyrol/destination-south-tyrol/.

Rural Bounty. Promoting AgriTourism. http://www.ruralbounty.com.

CHAPTER 22

COMMERCIALIZATION OF ART FORMS: A KERALA TOURISM PERSPECTIVE, INDIA

ANU AJAYAGOSH

Academic Consultant in Toronto, Canada

CONTENTS

ABSTRACT

Culture does not survive in any boundaries and it spreads in different ways in human beings' life. Culture helps to combine different people together. It does not make any changes in the way of caste, creed, status, and so on. Culture is also considered as an important form of social life and it brings different human beings together. Different scholars have defined cultural tourism differently in view of cultural attraction emerging as a major motivational factor for tourists to visit destinations. In India, Kerala is famous for various arts, poets, and musicians, traditional dances, cultural art forms, and so on. The cultural heritage is considered as a real treasure of Kerala. Kerala has its own classical art form that shows life and outlook of the people. The temples of Kerala have always acted as a center for arts and a breeding ground for the artists and this continues even today. Kathakali is considered as one of the famous art forms of Kerala. It is a combination of drama, music, and dance. Theyyam, Koodiyattom, Kalaripayattu, Mohniyattom, Krishnanattom, Kolkali, Thriuvathirakali, Thullal, and so on are the famous art forms of Kerala. The various festivals and art forms are the unique beauties of Kerala. Nowadays, these art forms have been seen only occasionally. But in the present scenario, most of the art forms and other cultural programs are performed for tourism purpose. Therefore, the current study aims to identify whether the art forms are commercialized through tourism and identify the contributions of government and other stakeholders for maintaining these art forms for future generation. Less concern and low remunerations are the reasons behind the declining art forms in Kerala. Both primary and secondary data were used in this research study. Primary data were collected through two different sets of a questionnaire that was validated with reliability test. The data were collected by two different sets of the sample group, which consisted of 150 tourists who were spectators of the art form performance in Kerala and 30 artists who perform various art forms.

22.1 INTRODUCTION

Tourism helps in preservation, conservation, and revitalization of culture and tradition in its authentic manner. Tourism sustains its rich culture and tradition for the present generations as well as for the future generations. In the recent years, although there is an uncontrollable increase in commercialization of art, some countries like India are still aggressively encouraging their artisans to slash their traditional forms. One such form receiving increasing attention and international accolades these days is Kerala's art forms. They remain covered within the sanctum sanctorum of some of the oldest temples and royal palaces in Kerala for centuries. Due to unique features, Kerala is known by the tagline "God's Own Country." Nowadays, there is a large increase in the number of cultural centers in Kerala. Most of the cultural centers specialize in Kerala art forms and cultural programs are customized. Both international and domestic tourists are attracted to these cultural centers for the exciting experience of the art forms without knowing the authenticity level of their performance.

22.2 REVIEW OF LITERATURE

Hennessey et al. (2008) is a case study conducted on cultural tourism at Prince Edward Island in Canada. The main objective of the study was to examine the meaning and significance of cultural tourism in this destination. The authors attempt to analyze the difference between the cultural tourists and noncultural tourists in this specified place. The study demonstrates that cultural tourists are important in terms of their economic contribution as they stay longer, use more information sources, recall the communities they visited, and spend more money at each destination. The study suggests that tour operators should focus more on forming packages and special services for attracting cultural tourists. Ravenshaw University organized the Society for Promotion of Indian Classical Music and Culture among Youth for the revival of Indian art forms. An article reviewed from Times of India on "Dying art forms find revival among youth" (2011) gives more importance to the classical dance forms and to revitalize the various dying art forms. Through these performances, many got to know about various art forms, handicrafts, paintings, and so on. It helps to identify the inborn talents of many people while participating in the event. In other words, it also gives importance to the revitalization of various dying art forms of India by providing various awareness classes to the youth.

"Foreigners charmed by Kerala art forms" is an article from Times of India (2013), which talks about the traditional art forms of Kerala like Kathakali and Mohniyattom. These art forms are highly demanded by foreigners and they are ready to leave their family and homeland for years together for studying these art forms from Kerala. The article also highlights the mental status of an average younger generation of Kerala who is not much excited or interested in learning these art forms. An article reviewed from The Hindu (2016), on "Cultural burns bright," emphasizes the rich cultural art forms of India and the importance of sustaining these cultural art forms for the future generation. The article also highlights the various possibilities and aspects of performing art forms—classical, folk, and ritual in various temples.

From the evaluation of literature, it was instituted that only generic studies were conducted upon the art forms, and these studies, however, don't deal with the commercialization of art forms in Kerala. Hence, this chapter aims to find out whether tourist destinations are exploring the art forms of Kerala and are ascertaining to popularize the local and ethnic art forms of the locale. In the present situation, the importance of art forms of Kerala is degrading. There is a speculation that the younger generation of Kerala is not interested in watching the art form performances. A review on article published in Times of India (2013) on "Foreigners charmed by Kerala art forms" talks about the traditional art forms of Kerala such as Kathakali and Mohniyattom that are still demanded by foreigners and they are ready to leave their family and homeland for years together for studying these art forms from Kerala. The article also highlights the mental status of an average younger generation of Kerala who is not much excited or interested in learning these art forms. The perseverance of this chapter reconnoiters whether the art forms (i.e., Kathakali, Kalaripayattu, and Mohiniyattam), which are performed in Kerala at various tourism destinations, are adequately explored or not. Hence, the study helps to understand the reality of the present stage of art forms of Kerala. This chapter objectifies the role of Kerala tourism in sustaining the art forms and analyzes whether the art forms are commercialized because of tourism promotion. It is also pertinent to examine the importance of sustaining the art forms for the future generation. The scientific examination portrays certain suppositions to substantiate the arguments outstretched in this chapter.

22.3   SPECIFIC RESEARCH PROPOSITIONS

This chapter dealt with certain fragmented areas and directed the efforts toward few specific research paradigms and propositions. The primary hypothetical understanding is laid on tourism which does not play any role in sustaining the art forms of Kerala. The second proposition emphasized that the art forms are not commercializing because of tourism promotion. Introspecting into the domain of art forms, it was ascertained that quality of art form performance is not a reason for the tourist's visit to Kerala. Contemplating through the literature, another hypothetical stand substantiates that the art forms do not lose their originality when those are customized.

22.4 RESEARCH METHODOLOGY

The sample of the survey consists of various artists who perform art forms of Kerala and tourists who were an audience of the art form performances. Convenient sampling method was used for data collection. Sample size embraces a sample group consisting of 150 tourists, which contains both international and domestic tourists. These tourists are the audience of the art form performance and 30 art form-performing artists. The study conducted in various resorts, tourist destinations, cultural centers, and cultural training centers where the art forms are performed. Both primary and secondary data were used in the research study. Primary data were collected through the help of two sets of structured questionnaires. The questionnaires were run through reliability test and 0.6 was the Cronbach's alpha score. Secondary data were collected from various research articles, books, journals, newspaper articles, and so on. The statistical tools used for the study are percentages, cross tabulation chi-square, binomial, one-sample Kolmogorov–Smirnov, and one-sample t-test.

22.5 RESULTS AND DISCUSSION

Hypothesis-based results and discussion on the predominant role of tourism in sustaining the art forms are quantitatively assessed with the statistical exploration.

One-Sample **Kolmogorov–Smirnov Test.**

		Sustain the art form
N		30
Normal parametersa	Mean	4.73
	Std. deviation	0.450
Most extreme differences	Absolute	0.457
	Positive	0.277
	Negative	−0.457
Kolmogorov–Smirnov Z		2.501
Asymp. Sig. (two-tailed)		0.000

Binomial Test.

		Category	N	Observed Prop.	Test Prop.	Asymp. Sig. (two-tailed)
Sustain the art form	Group 1	≤3	0	0.00	0.50	0.000[a]
	Group 2	>3	30	1.00		
	Total		30	1.00		

From the given table, the two-tailed P value is less than .05, therefore null hypothesis H_0 was rejected.

22.5.1 TOURISM AND COMMERCIALIZATION OF ART FORMS

One-Sample Statistics.

	N	Mean	Std. deviation	Std. error mean
Commercializing the art forms	30	3.70	0.466	0.085

One-Sample Test.

	Test Value=2.5					
	T	Df	Sig. (two-tailed)	Mean difference	95% confidence interval of the difference	
					Lower	Upper
Commercializing the art forms	14.102	29	0.000	1.200	1.03	1.37

From the above table, the calculated t-value is greater than the critical t value, thus null hypothesis H_0 was rejected.

22.5.2 QUALITY OF PERFORMANCES AND TENDENCY TO REVISIT KERALA

Quality * **Tendency Cross Tabulation.**

			Tendency			
			Occasionally	Very Frequently	Always	Total
Quality	Extremely poor	Count	1	0	0	1
		% within quality	100.0%	0.0%	0.0%	100.0%
	Below average	Count	0	1	0	1
		% within quality	0.0%	100.0%	0.0%	100.0%
	Average	Count	5	12	0	17
		% within quality	29.4%	70.6%	0.0%	100.0%
	Above average	Count	23	46	12	81
		% within quality	28.4%	56.8%	14.8%	100.0%
	Excellent	Count	3	23	24	50
		% within quality	6.0%	46.0%	48.0%	100.0%
Total		Count	32	82	36	150
		% within quality	21.3%	54.7%	24.0%	100.0%

Chi-Square Tests.

	Value	Df	Asymp. Sig. (two-sided)
Pearson chi-square	32.910[a]	8	0.000
Likelihood ratio	36.444	8	0.000
Linear-by-linear association	23.429	1	0.000
No. of valid cases	150		

From the above analysis, the calculated value is greater than a critical value; therefore, the null hypothesis H_0 was rejected.

22.5.3   CUSTOMIZATION AND ORIGINALITY OF ART FORMS

T-Test.

One-Sample Statistics.

	N	Mean	Std. Deviation	Std. Error Mean
Losing originality	30	3.70	0.466	0.085

One-Sample Test.

	Test Value=2.5					
	T	Df	Sig. (two-tailed)	Mean Difference	95% Confidence Interval of the Difference	
					Lower	Upper
Losing originality	14.102	29	0.000	1.200	1.03	1.37

From the above table, the calculated *t*-value (14.102) is greater than the critical *t*-value (2.045), so the null hypothesis H_0 was rejected. From the above hypothesis-based findings, some of the other important findings are as follows: It was found that Kathakali, Kalaripayattu, and Mohini-yattom are the most demanded art forms among the tourists. It was clearly proved that tourism plays an important role in sustaining the rich culture of Kerala. For increasing the goodwill and reducing the competition are two major reasons for conducting these art forms in various cultural centers. It was also instituted that some of the resorts conduct these art form performances according to the demand of tourist. They also customize the performances according to the tourist requirements without compromising the authenticity of the art forms. It was also determined that the inflow of international tourists into the cultural centers is increasing day by day. Tourism contributes immensely to the revitalization of various dying art forms and also plays an important role in the promotion of art forms of Kerala and the tourism promotion of the state.

22.6 CONCLUSION

In the present scenario, most of the art forms can be seen only in the tourist destination. The cultural values and various art forms are the major reasons for the development of tourism in Kerala. The main intention of conducting this study on "commercialization of art forms with special references to Kerala" is to find out whether the tourism plays any role in the promotion of art forms of Kerala. This also facilitates in identifying whether these art forms are losing their authenticity while customizing and commercializing in the name of tourism. From the data analysis and interpretation, it was clearly proved that various art forms and cultural performances are happening in tourism destination but it is not losing its authenticity. Tourism plays an important role in sustaining the dying art forms of Kerala. There are some suggestive implications that can revitalize the essence of art forms as the public sector could encourage and can promote with equal importance to all art forms of Kerala.

Thereby, domination of single art form can be reduced. They should also create an awareness and interest in the minds of the public and the tourists for sustaining these art forms for the future generation. The key stakeholders should take an initiative for providing proper financial assistances to the artist. Thereby, reducing the number of art form artists can be managed. Updating and uploading the proper information and unique cultural values of art forms, in various websites and social networking media, will help to attract and create an interest in the young generation of Kerala. Evolving diverse policies pertaining to conservation, preservation, and immersing the art forms will help to sustain for the upcoming generation. The introduction of norms, rules, and policies concerning the analogous registration fee and other tourist formalities for both domestic and international tourists can boot better morale among the inbound travelers. The authenticity of performance, reducing the customization, and low deterioration in culture-service delivery will uphold the cultural sanctity at the culturally stimulated destinations and will help to attract more international tourist. The legacy of cultural costumes and traditional ethnic apparels of performers are also key determinants in preserving the cultural authenticity and postulates the cultural eminence at the destinations.

KEYWORDS

- art forms
- culture
- cultural tourism
- commercialization

REFERENCES

Chawla, R. *Cultural Tourism and Development,* 1 ed.; Sonali publications: New Delhi, 2004; pp 5–40.

Gupta, I. D. *Trends and Resources of Cultural Tourism,* 1 ed.; Adhyayan publishers and Distributors: New Delhi, 2008; pp. 1–20.

Hennessey, S.; Yun, D.; Macdonald, R.; MacEacher, M. A Study of Cultural Tourism: The Case of Visitors to Prince Edward Island, 2008.

Ramacharya. *Tourism and Culture Heritage of India,* 2 ed.; RBSA Publishers: Jaipur, 2007; pp 131–146.

Stover, W. J. Cultural Interaction and International Change. *Int. J. World Peace* **1990,** 7(4), 53–63.

The Hindu. Reviving a Dying Art Form. 2011, January 11.

The Hindu. Cultural Burns Bright. 2016, January 13.

Tillotson, S. Cultural Tourism or Cultural Destruction. *Econ. Polit. Week.* **1988,** *23*(38), 140–143.

Times of India. Dying Art Forms Find Revival Among Youth. 2011, May 25.

CHAPTER 23

HINDU PILGRIMAGE: ISSUES AND CHALLENGES IN KERALA, INDIA

NIKHIL RAJ

Department of Tourism Management Jyothi Nivas College, Bangalore, India

CONTENTS

ABSTRACT

Pilgrimage is a voyage or pursuit of ethical or spiritual significance. Several religions attach spiritual status to places—the place of birth or death of saints or founders, the home of their spiritual awakening or of their connection with the celestial, places where phenomena were witnessed and completed, locations where a goddess is said to be "alive" or to be "stored" and places seen to have distinct godly controls. These sites may be honored with shrines or temples that devotees are encouraged to visit for their own divine benefit or to attain some other divine value. An individual who makes such a journey is called a pilgrim. The chapter investigates the problems faced by Hindu Pilgrim centers in Kerala and the crisis management initiative undertaken by the authorities. Examine whether the interest of the pilgrims and the locals are safeguarded. The environmental threats faced by Hindu pilgrim centers in Kerala are also detrimental and at par with the increasing population of pilgrims. The chapter investigates on various issues and challenges with each of these destinations in relation to crowd management, infrastructure and provision of basic amenities, traffic movement, hygiene and other related issues. These issues have to be tackled to safeguard the needs of pilgrims and local residents and provide a better environment for the sustainable development of the destination. Moreover, much more can be done by the governing authorities concerned in developing the scope of this form of tourism in future.

23.1   INTRODUCTION

Over the last 30 years, there has been sustained growth in Tourism, both as an activity and as an economic factor. In 2011, the World Travel and Tourism Council demonstrated the tremendous scale of growth achieved by the Tourism Sector Worldwide. "Tourism directly and indirectly generates and supports about 195 million employments globally. This is equivalent to 7.6% of the world's workforce and the forecast indicates an increase to over 250 million jobs by 2015." Holiday business and leisure are perhaps the two nicest things in contemporary society, which promote peaceful coexistence, the happiness of an individual and well-being of the society. Tourism is traveling to and staying in places outside one's usual environment for the purpose of enjoying leisure, recreation, or novelty. It is not remunerative and can take place either from within the tourism destination or from elsewhere. Tourism is the most popular global leisure activity. There are different kinds of tourism, for example, leisure tourism, winter tourism, pilgrim tourism, medical tourism, and others, which can be further subdivided into many types.

Pilgrimage is one of the major tourism activities followed by the believers of any religion. In the early 21st century, the number of individuals belonging to multiple religions going on a pilgrimage has witnessed a steady rise, with 39 of the most popular sites alone receiving an estimated

200 million visitors every year. Pilgrimage is a voyage or pursuit of ethical or mystical significance. Naturally, it is a voyage to a temple or a sacred place of importance according to a person's faith, although occasionally it can be a symbolic journey into someone's individual self-discovery. Most religions attach a spiritual status to particular places, for example, the place of birth and death of a saint, or to a place of spiritual awakening, or of their connection with celestial beings, or places where a phenomenon is witnessed, locations where a goddess is said to be alive, and places seen to have distinct godly controls. These places may be honored with shrines or temples that devotees are encouraged to visit for their own divine benefit, to be healed or have questions answered or to attain some other divine value.

An individual who makes such a journey is called a pilgrim. Conferring to some of the earliest folklore, by going on a pilgrimage, an individual can wash away all his sins and be free of them. The world is a place of varied religions that are followed by their own respective believers. The three foremost religions followed all over the world are Christianity, Hinduism, and Islam. The oldest religion in the world is Hinduism, which is followed by millions of people all over the world. Sanatana Dharma, another name for Hinduism in Sanskrit, means the everlasting trail. Hinduism is rated as the third major religion in the world after Christianity and Islam. Hinduism comes from a spiritual tradition, which was formed in India. There are numerous holy Hindu destinations which attract people from faraway places. The pilgrimage undertaken by the Hindus are not easy as they require a lot of devout and strength of mind. Hinduism originated in India and has various pilgrimage destinations within the country. Char Dham is the main pilgrimage tour for Hindus, which is rendered as part of the rituals. The tour includes Kanchipuram in the South Dwarkapuri in the West, Badrinath in the North, and Jagannath Puri in the East.

23.1.1 PILGRIMAGE TOURISM—INDIA

India is a land of pilgrimage. Tourism due to holy determinations has been prevalent from the olden eras. Pilgrimage has always been the main motivation for most of the domestic tourists in India. All major temples, shrines, and sacred locations are located near water bodies or in the hills. Churches and Mosques are also visited by people. Almost all religions have their main pilgrimage locations in the various destination of India.

The act of pilgrims traveling to holy shrines is termed as "Theerth" which means "to cross." This is a clear indication that pilgrimage is an extended journey. In the holy locations, human beings obtain the coincidental to transcend themselves when they come face to face with religion. From ancient time, rivers have been the symbol of the transformation of humans. Rivers also play a decisive role in the religious life of an average Indian. The meeting place of the holy rivers is named "Sangam" and is a fascination among millions of tourists every year. Travelers gather here to swim in these holy rivers. Among the holy rivers, the Ganges is believed to be the holiest for all Hindus. Numerous holy shrines such as Gangasagar, Gaumukh, Gangotri, Haridwar, Kannauj, Garmukteshwar, Allahabad, Rishikesh, Varanasi, Patna, and Devprayag have developed along the banks of the river Ganges over time. River Yamuna is reflected to be the most prominent to carry out Gayatri Jap, worship of Keshav. Moreover, the month of "Kartik" is auspicious to take a dip in the Yamuna. Pilgrimage tourism is a combination of modern and ancient cultures. Holy memorials have been visited extensively by domestic travelers all through the years. Divine shrines fascinate millions of domestic pilgrims every year. Societies believe that the Godavari, before dividing itself into seven branches and joining the sea, is the greatest sacred river for a dip. It is also referred to as "Sapta Sagar Yatra."

The 12 Jyotirlingas, five Bhutalingas and many other shrines of the "Lingas" in their sanctum are ideal destinations for domestic tourists. They are sub-divided into Kalahastishwar (Vayulinga) at Kalahasti, Jambukeshwar (Appulinga) at Trichy, Arunachaleshwar (Bhatalinga) at Thriuvannamalai, Ekambareshwar (Prithvilinga) at Kanchipuram, and Chidambareshwar (Akaslinga) at Chidambaram. In a struggle to unify the country, Adi Shankaracharya established 14 centers in all four corners of the country. Some of them are Kashi Vishwanath (Uttar Pradesh), Baijnath (Karnataka), Jyotirlingas (Kedarnath), Somnath (Gujarat), Ghushneshwar (Maharashtra), Rameshwaram (Tamil Nadu), Bhimashankar (Maharashtra), Mallikarjuna (Andhra Pradesh), Mahakaleshwar (Madhya Pradesh), Omkareshwar (Madhya Pradesh), Nageshwar (Gujarat) Tryambakeshwar (Maharashtra) and others. Sringeri Mutt in the state of Karnataka, India is also claimed to be a sacred Peeth. In addition to holy waterways and sacred temples situated on the banks of these rivers, "Shakti" is also worshiped as the Heavenly mother of creative power, both as an enforcing discipline and for securing morality. There are approximately 51 Shakti Peethas around the country. These Peethas are visited by tourists throughout the year.

23.1.2   KERALA—AN OVERVIEW

Kerala was formed on November 1, 1956 by the States Reorganization Act through a merger of many Malayalam speaking regions present in Southern India. Kerala is a state located on the Malabar Coast of South-West India. The state covers an area of 38,863 km^2, and its population is 3.33 crore. It is surrounded by Karnataka in the north and north-east, India, the Arabian Sea in the west and Tamil Nadu in the east and south. Thiruvananthapuram is the capital of the state of Kerala, and the other major towns are Kochi (Cochin) and Kozhikode (Calicut). In comparison with the rest of the country, Kerala experiences comparatively little sectarianism. Conferring to the figures of the 2011 Census of India, 56.2% of Kerala's residents are Hindus, 19% are Christians, 24.7% are Muslims, and the remaining 1.1% belong to other religions. Kerala's main religions are therefore Hinduism, Christianity, and Islam. The major castes among Hindus are Nairs, Ezhavas, Dalits, and Nambudiris. The rest of the Hindu castes, included in the list of other backward classes, are smaller societies. Kerala comprises of 3.44% of India's population; at 819 people per km^2, the land is nearly three times as densely populated as the rest of India, which has a density of 325 per km^2. Kerala's coastal regions are the most densely settled, leaving the eastern hills and mountains comparatively sparsely populated. Kerala's society is less patriarchal than the rest of the third world countries.

23.1.3   KERALA TOURISM

Admiringly known as God's Own Country, Kerala undeniably deserves its place in the list of "Top 10 Paradises of the World" and "50 Must See Destinations of a Lifetime" compiled by National Geographic Traveller Magazine. Every tour program that extends to South India includes a trip to the sandy sun-kissed beaches and the backwaters amidst verdant green surroundings in Kerala. These trips always steal the hearts of every visitor in a moment. Increasing annually at 13.31%, the holiday business is the main donor to the Kerala's economy. Till the early 1980s, the state of Kerala was a comparatively unidentified location. Most of the tourism circuits were focused on North India. In the periods that followed, Kerala Tourism transformed itself into one of the major holiday destinations in India. Kerala is regarded as one of the terminuses with the highest product recall. In 2010, Kerala is reported to have fascinated 0.66 million foreign visitors. Aggressive advertising operations thrown in by the Kerala Tourism Development Corporation, the government organization that manages tourism forecasts for the state, had placed the groundwork for the development of tourism as a business in Kerala.

Heritage sites, such as Hill Palace, Mattancherry Palace, Padmanabhapuram Palace are also going to by tourists. Kerala's tourism programs encourage environmentally sustained tourism that focuses on wilderness adventures, native culture, volunteering between local residents and personal development. Kerala Tourism also promotes the Grand Kerala Shopping Festival every year during the December–January period. Kerala is also known for her backwaters, wildlife sanctuaries, beaches, and mountain ranges. Kochi ranks number one in the entire amount of domestic and international tourists visiting Kerala. The famous attractions of Kerala are Varkala, Cherai, and Kovalam, lake resorts around Vembanad Lake, backwater tourism areas, wildlife sanctuaries, and national parks such as Eravikulam National Park, Kumarakom–Periyar sites, and hill stations and resorts at Munnar, Nelliampathi, Vagamon, Wayanad, and Ponmudi. The wide network of interlocking rivers, canals, and lakes in Kumarakom, Alappuzha also attract substantial tourists.

23.1.4   THE CULTURE OF KERALA

The culture of the south Indian state is mostly derived from the greater region of Tamil tradition known as Tamilakam. Kerala's culture was developed and formed due to centuries of contact with external cultures. Kerala's performing arts include Kathakali, Koodiyattom, Mohiniyattam, Thullal, Theyyam, and Padayani. Kerala has many traditional fine arts, of both modern and ancient origin. Old-style paintings are found in ancient churches, temples, and forts. Images of these typically date back to 9–12th centuries AD, displaying a unique style, and a color code mainly including orange and green. Kerala is prominent for religious diversity; major religious beliefs are Christianity, Islam, and Hinduism. Jainism, Sikhism, Buddhism, and Judaism have few followers. Kerala has well-known churches, temples, and mosques. Knowing the possibility of tourism among various spiritual faiths, related festivals, and constructions, the tourism department has launched numerous pilgrimage tourism development initiatives. Foremost among the pilgrim tourism fascinations comprises of Sabarimala, Guruvayur, Chettikulangara Bharani, and the Attukal Pongala, which finds a place in the Guinness Book of World Records for organizing the biggest ceremony with women in the world.

23.1.5   PILGRIMAGE TOURISM IN KERALA

Kerala has been labeled through thinkers and historians as "God's Own Country." This one appears factual when one appearance at the amount of places of devotion and pilgrimage located in the state. One can observe ethnic and religious varieties in the state, which is a fascination in India. The south Indian state hosts a number of festivals through the year. Nearly all the mosque or temple in Kerala has a huge inflow of devotees annually. Kerala is filled with holy shrines of deities, the water of holy rivers or the company of sacred men. People cross any extent to reach these centers of devotion. The south Indian temples fascinate groups of followers all over the world and are famous for the faith and belief of the devotees. The focal point of pilgrimage in Kerala is to deliver a perfect setting for devotees to pause in between their hectic schedule and delve into the meaning of their life. A pilgrimage tour in Kerala is a stimulating journey to some of the significant and holy temples and the tour includes a trip to the world-renowned pilgrim centers such as Attukal, Guruvayoor, Aluva, Kodungalloor, Padmanabha Swami temple, Sabarimala, and so forth.

Pilgrim destinations in Kerala have a vivid projection of secular co-existence and religious synchronization. These spiritual residences in Kerala can also be termed as pilgrim centers since a maximum of them have developed as significant journey sites over the period. The rich custom and culture of Kerala have attracted many tourists. Annual festivals are significant occasions in several temples. The feasts are mainly based on the Malayalam calendar. Most of these temples are managed by the Devaswom Board, a trust which is under the Kerala government, and there are different boards like Malabar Devaswom Board, Devaswom Board of Cochin, Travancore Devaswom Board, and Guruvayur Devaswom.

Hindu temples in the state of Kerala are devoted to different gods. The statue of the god is made out of wood or stone. Temple structures are magnificent and have wooden or stone details that are attractively engraved. Most of the shrines have separate topographies which symbolizes divine powers. Folks from all over the world visit these temples to pray, perform ceremonies and poojas, daily. Some of the Hindu pilgrim centers of the state are Ambalapuzha Sree Krishna, Padmanabha Swamy, Chettikulangara Bhagavathy, Vadakkumnatha temple, Sabarimala, Attukal Bhagavathi, Aranmula Parthasarathy, Chottanikkara Devi, Kadampuzha Devi, Guruvayur Sree Krishna temple, Ettumanoor Siva temple and so forth. Temples are also visited by the public to conduct weddings. Guruvayoor is very famous for conducting marriages. In a single day, temples such as Guruvayur conduct more than 100 marriages. During the marriage rituals, poojas are performed by the priests in the temple, and distinct galleries are also provided within the temple compound for wedding feasts. Certain other rituals conducted in the temples in Kerala include Choroonu (feeding child rice, for the first time), "Vidyarambham," and others.

23.1.6   THE MAJOR HINDU PILGRIMAGE DESTINATIONS IN KERALA

The state temples have great architecture, exceptional and harmonized with the natural and climatic condition of Kerala. A multicolored calendar festival is yearly happening in this God's own country. Elephants are an integral part of these celebrations. Shri Dharma Sastha temple dedicated to Lord Ayyappa, at Sabarimala in the State of Kerala, is located on a hilltop at a height at 467 m above sea level and deep in the dense forest in the southernmost part of the Periyar Wild Life Sanctuary in the Western Ghats. The holy place is situated in a space of over 200 km from Cochin. It is situated amidst the reserved forest of Pathanamthitta district of Kerala.

The temple is accessed by a footpath starting from the foothills of Pampa, which gets its name from the river flowing around it. The remoteness between the foothill and the temple located at the top of a steep hill is around 5 km, which is covered by foot by the pilgrims. Guruvayoor is located 29 km northwest of Thrissur District in Kerala; Guruvayoor is one of the major pilgrimage centers of India. Guruvayur is also known as Bhoolokavaikunta, or the heaven on Earth. The four-sided figure inside the Sreekovil in the sacred sanctum belongs to Lord Krishna, a personification of Lord Maha Vishnu. Sree Padmanabha Temple at Thiruvananthapuram is a modern sacred temple, situated in the heart of the city. It is one of the richest temples in India, and the city of Thiruvananthapuram gets its name from the temple. It is one of the 108 great Vishnu temples in India. The God, Sree Padmanabha, a unique form of Lord Vishnu, is seen here in a rare sleeping position. The temple belongs to the Travancore Royal family. The Royal Crown of Travancore is also preserved inside this temple, and it cannot be viewed by the public. Non-Hindus are strictly not allowed inside the temple. The pilgrims from all over the country, who visit Sree Padmanabha Swamy temple, do not consider their visits complete without visiting the holy place of the supreme Mother Attukalamma. The Attukal temple, in Thiruvananthapuram, is commonly referred to as the Sabarimala for women, and it attracts millions of women every year. Attukal temple attracts the biggest host of women devotees for the annual Attukal Pongala celebration. This temple and its main festival have also found a place in the Guinness Book of World Records. It has been recorded that 1.5 million women offered Pongala February 23, 1997. The number of women devotees visiting the place has also been found to increase every year. It is estimated that around three million women will offer Pongala in the coming year.

23.2 NEED FOR THE STUDY

Among the noteworthy Hindu pilgrim centers in India, Kerala occupies a prominent position and hosts a large number of religious festivals throughout of the year. Devotees from all over India visit these centers, especially during the festival seasons. Review of available information and findings on the various researches undertaken on different aspects of the subject under the study have helped frame the course of work. The review of the literature reveals that there has not been any constructive effort made for an in-depth study to understand the various problems faced by Hindu pilgrimage destinations in Kerala that are caused due to the increased inflow of pilgrims, particularly with four major Hindu pilgrim destinations. Explicitly, Sabarimala, Guruvayur, Padmanabha Swamy temple, and Attukal Bhagavathi temple are highly affected with the high inflow of pilgrims. These issues have been tackled to safeguard the demands of the pilgrims and local residents and provide a better environment for the sustainable development of the destination.

Thus, the need for the study is a thorough investigation into the issues and challenges associated with pilgrimage tourism, because the increase in the number of devotee's year after year has created various issues and challenges at each pilgrim destination. This chapter focuses on four major Hindu pilgrimage centers in Kerala, namely, Sabarimala, Guruvayur, Padmanabha Swamy temple, and Attukal Bhagavathi temple. This seminal chapter identifies different issues and challenges with regard to infrastructure, deforestation, hygiene, provision of basic facilities, traffic movement, and related issues and explores if there are any common problems in these pilgrims centers which could be addressed with necessary recommend measures to reduce the issues. Hindu pilgrimage centers indicate certain issues and challenges in Kerala; this chapter accentuates to investigate the problems faced by Hindu Pilgrim centers in Kerala and the crisis management initiative undertaken by the authorities. It is also imperative to examine whether the interest of the pilgrims and the host populations are safeguarded with regard to basic facilities, pollution control, crowd management and so forth. There are also certain environmental threats faced by Hindu pilgrim centers in Kerala which drive critical interest for pertinent stakeholders to address them with utmost care. It is highly significant to recommend measures which are to be taken by the authorities to bring down the various problems of Hindu pilgrimage tourism in Kerala while addressing the basic needs of the ever increasing population of pilgrims.

23.3   REVIEW OF LITERATURE

Pertinently, the research gap identification was decisive as the review of literature substantiated the need for executing a study on the issues and virtues. Some of the major literature reviews portray on challenges of pilgrimage tourist (Tomer and Arora, 2012). This chapter attempts to highlight the opinion of pilgrim visiting Golden Temple and few problems expressed by them during a survey so that people managing the Gurudwara are able to know about them. Some of these problems can be attended to by them, whereas others government can be persuaded to do the needful (Yamin, 2007). Hajj is a unique gathering of its kind, and it is a well-managed activity. The Hajj management by the Saudi authorities is done in a satisfactory manner. Sensor devices can be used to track movements of individuals during the Hajj period. Various types of scanners such as palm, fingers, and eye-lid, retina, and face scanners can also be used to correctly identify individuals who are lost or dead in some unfortunate circumstances (Shinde, 2009). Large scale movement of visitors during pilgrimages has a high potential to influence the environment in sacred sites. In traditional pilgrimage, environmental effects are governed by seasonality and are limited time and space. This chapter argues that significant changes in scale, frequency, and character of such visitation over the past few decades reflect new pressures on the environment of sacred sites (Libison and Muraleedharan, 2009). Pilgrimages to these destinations bring enormous economic gains to local residents.

The number of pilgrims visiting famous Sabarimala temple in Pathanamthitta district of Kerala is almost equal to the population of Kerala state (Karar and Raj, 2010). Tourism becomes an engine for economic development and plays a great role toward socioeconomic changes. According to Indian sentiment, the pilgrim centers or Tirthasthan used to visit by a number of tourists to earn virtue. Haridwar—"The Gateway to the abode of Gods" is one of such holy city situated at the base of Shivalik ranges of high Himalayas, as well as on the flow path of the river Ganga (Kreiner, 2010). The aim of this research is to examine key issues, arguments, and conceptualizations regarding the research of pilgrimage. This is to indicate the shifts that the study of pilgrimage has undergone (Shinde, 2011). This article examines discourses about environmental change and their impact on the environmental behavior of different social groups at the Hindu pilgrimage site of Vrindavan in India, which receives more than 6 million visitors annually (Rathod and Rathod, 2009). As it is associated with "Sevabhaya" and "Jagdambadevi" Temple, it worshiped by the millions of people from all over the state and outside the state as well. During the last decade, Poharadevi has witnessed remarkable changes in population number occupational structure, business structure and so forth. Geography is mainly related to the study of cause–effect relationship of various phenomena in the context of space and time (Babu, 2012).

The flow of people to places of religious importance in India has increased in the last couples of decades tremendously with the availability of modern means of travel, such as the road transport, railways and air travel, increase in accommodation facilities, the growth of Information and Communication Technology that provides vast information about the places. Pilgrims concerns were found over security, crowd management, and so forth (Hormage, 2010). This research deals with the phenomenon of pilgrimage to the graves of saintly Jews in Israel. Its aim is to analyze the characteristics of Jewish pilgrims to holy grave sites in Israel at the present time and to assess the phenomenon of pilgrimage. This includes the motives for pilgrimage, activities during the pilgrimage, and the influence of tourism on it (Kremer et al., 2008).

We estimate the impact on pilgrims of performing the Hajj pilgrimage to Mecca. Our method compares successful with unsuccessful applicants in a lottery used by Pakistan to allocate Hajj visas (Chauhan, 2011). This research examines the rural residents' attitudes toward the impacts of the pilgrimage tourism. The results of the research point out that the sustainable development is important for responding to the current problems as caused by tourism development, as well as to address the needs of future generations (Wong, 2011). This chapter encompasses details of pilgrimage and religious tourism in a Chinese Buddhist context, with a focus on both the host monastic community and visitors. The attitudes of the Pu-Tuo Buddhist monks and nuns toward receiving visitors and tourism are found to be mostly welcoming and supportive (Vázquez et al., 2012). This chapter compares the characteristics, behavior, motivation, and satisfaction of participants in Saint James Way versus participants in El Rocío pilgrimage, the two most important pilgrimages in Spain (Janardhan and Mhaske, 2011). The study presented in the chapter has been useful for critical assessment of the nature of pilgrim tourism with respect to the tourist profile the technique used to analyze data generated in the field for understand the pilgrim tourist profile with help of aspects such as education, age group, purpose, state-wise visitors, profession, use of vehicles, accommodations, and planning of journey, helping essential for planning designing strategy in tourist place. While contemplating the literature, it was perceived that the researchers were concentrated on specific aspects of environmental issues, behavioral patterns, economic impact, problems related to the pilgrims, local residents, and so forth. So the determined that there was dearth about a destination to be versioned in a comprehensive manner.

23.4 DELIBERATIONS ON THE ISSUES AND CHALLENGES

The southern state of Kerala has a lot to offer to the ancient temple traditions. The temples of Kerala remain the greatest legacy of glory for ancient Keralite. Many of the traditional art forms in Kerala are connected with the temple festivals of Kerala. Strict worship practices are followed by every temple in Kerala. A pilgrimage through the temples in Kerala elevates ones spiritually and at the similar period offers a glimpse of the architectural style as well. Amidst the noteworthy Hindu pilgrim centers in India, Kerala has a remarkable position, and it hosts a number of festivals all over the year. The increasing number of devotees year after year has created various problems and challenges to each destination. These problems have to be tackled to protect the needs of pilgrims and local residents and provide a better environment for the sustainable development of the destination. With this in mind, the study has helped identify any problems existing within the Hindu pilgrimage tourism in Kerala. The major findings are as follows. Most of the pilgrims approached by the scholar belonged to Kerala; data were also collected from pilgrims of the neighboring states of Tamil Nadu and Karnataka, India. The study showed that the pilgrims have a good opinion about the accommodation facilities offered. The heavy influx of pilgrims to the centers has led to accommodation problems. Most of the hotels and guest houses are booked well in advance, forcing pilgrims to search for dwelling places elsewhere. To address the crisis, many landlords in areas near pilgrim centers are providing rented accommodation at nominal rates. This has served as a source of income to vendors and small hotels in these areas as they offer meals. The pilgrims too are pleased as they are able to get food and lodging at nominal rates. This chapter indicates an officious need for crowd management, as most of the pilgrim's projected an unexceptional evaluation toward the intense flow of patrons toward there pilgrim centers.

The pilgrims are of the opinion that these centers lack proper queue systems. A near-stampede situation continuously prevails in the Sabarimala Sannidhanam, as the crowd turns uncontrollable during the festive seasons. Failure to divert pilgrims returning from Sabarimala through a Bailey bridge also contributes to the overcrowding of pilgrims along the Forest Office—Valiyanadappanthal stretch. This study explored upon the security system in the pilgrim centers as an ordinary phenomenon. Most of the pilgrims were of the opinion that the waste-disposal management is a crucial factor toward hygiene and sanitation. It was assessed that building a modern sewage treatment plant for safe disposal of the waste generated at Sabarimala would be supreme and a substantial aspect. The outcome of this chapter indicates that most of the pilgrims are concerned with the poor quality of water and its distribution. A proper water distribution system is not available in any of the destinations and because of the poor water quality, devotees are forced to depend on plastic package drinking water, and littering of plastic bottles has been creating environmental problems.

The study also brought out the opinion of pilgrims on the sanitation facilities offered. They are not at all pleased with the hygiene facility. Most of the pilgrims remarked and rate the services offered as below average. It is imperative for better schemes and policies which are to be introduced to ensure that the manufacturing of "Appam and Aravanna" (sweet delicacies offered as Prasadams) be carried out in more hygienic surroundings. The research findings also indicated that the pilgrim centers are expensive. The promised facilities have not been effectively set up, whereas available facilities are not being properly used by the pilgrims. Hotels and eateries should be instructed to display the price list of all food items, and small eateries should be directed to charge only nominal rates. The officials should also ensure that pilgrims from other states are aware of the facilities being offered; otherwise, they would not be able to make effective use of them. According to the study, most of the development activities are occurring in an unplanned manner. The findings showed that the parking facilities offered in pilgrim centers were only average.

The lack of adequate parking facilities at temple premises is causing trouble for pilgrims, and many of them are unaware of the alternate parking spots available. Although pilgrims from within the state do not face much hardship, pilgrims from other states feel the need for more clean toilets to be urgently set up at major centers. They are also of the opinion that the limited number of toilets present at the temple premises were not enough for a large number of pilgrims visiting the shrines. Most of the local residents were of the opinion that the waste-disposal management was not good. New strategies have to be implemented for successful execution of waste-disposal management. The pilgrim centers are facing acute problems with regard to lack of equipment for waste collection and transportation, increased quantity of waste, lack of capacity in waste disposal, nonorganized recycling system, and low level of public awareness about waste management. The findings indicated that the medical facilities provided could also be improved. Lack of well-equipped medical stores at the pilgrim center are creating problems during times of epidemic outbreaks for millions of pilgrims who visit the holy place and also to thousands of workers and contract laborers who have settled there. Devotees and contract laborers who live in the dense forest for more than three months during the season are in dire need for essential medicines. Most of the local residents were also of the opinion that the waste-management initiatives undertaken could be improved.

The exploration highlighted the comments of the local residents about the distribution of basic facilities for managing waste. Most of the local residents responded that the measurements to avoid environmental hazards were important for the tourist centers. The local residents' outlook on the guest behavior is critical toward cleanliness as, the pilgrim centers face more problems related to waste management, crowd management, queue system, water quality, security system, and environmental problems. Compared with other temples, Sabarimala is facing major issues related to pilgrimage tourism. Therefore, the government has to take immediate measures to bring down these problems in Sabarimala.

23.5 APPLICATIONS

Several suggestions and recommendations that could be made for further development of pilgrimage tourism in Kerala were extracted from the in-depth study through the distributed questionnaires and also from discussions and observations made in the course of the study. This research was conducted in the four major Hindu pilgrimage centers in Kerala, Sabarimala, Guruvayur, Padmanabha Swamy temple, Attukal Bhagavathi temple.

Different issues and challenges faced by the pilgrims and the local residents were identified, and efforts were made to find out if there were any common problems being faced by the pilgrim centers in Kerala. With the collection of data from pilgrims and local residents, a set of suggestions, that could help reduce the issues in the shrines, were extracted. According to the study, the government and temple authorities have to take a lot of measures to overcome the issues in the pilgrim centers in Kerala. Constant evaluation of basic facilities and controlling the crowd are some of the very integral steps in temple management in Kerala. Here, each aspect of the study has been evaluated, and suggestions have been provided. According to the pilgrims, the accommodation area is good enough to satisfy their needs as they are not expecting luxury accommodation facilities in the area. The authorities have to create basic accommodation facilities. Pilgrims commented that the parking facilities were below average. This is one of the major issues in all pilgrimage centers, and clearing of forest areas to increase parking facilities is also taking place. Authorities need to keep heavy vehicles away from the pilgrim centers and offer them parking space a little away from the main center. Authorities need to provide a proper water distribution system, and they also need to monitor the careless wastage of water taking place in the area. They need to build a sufficient number of centers to obtain clean drinking water on the way and in the premises of the pilgrim centers. Constant checks on the purity and quality of water have to be carried out.

Pilgrims have a good opinion about the medical facilities offered, but it is suggested that the authorities provide more assistance and number of medical equipment and facilities such as oxygen cafes especially in Sabarimala. The authorities need to devise a good queue system through a virtual queue system that should be implemented appropriately. The system is already implemented in Sabarimala, but it is still in the stage of infancy. Authorities need to have a good security system in place to tackle any threats or terrorism activities. CCTV cameras, security personnel, and watchdogs should be deployed especially during the rush times. They may also introduce entry through biometrics or face or eye detection systems. Authorities need to ban the use of plastic in the pilgrim centers, and proper monitoring should be carried out to identify people illegally littering the place. Garbage removal has to take place from time to time. Awareness drives, warning boards, and hoardings should be displayed and moni-tored. To avoid unprecedented crowds, the temple can introduce the quota system which has already been introduced in Mecca, Saudi Arabia, and in the Vaishno Devi Shrine in Jammu and Kashmir.

Authorities need to also provide better sanitation facilities and main-tain good cleanliness of the restrooms, with an appropriate fee to be levied for the pilgrims. Pilgrims commented that the police and volunteering services at the centers are good, but more multilinguistic volunteers and guide facilities need to be deployed. The government can coordinate with other states and demand for more police force. The government needs to monitor the demand and supply at the destination, and they need to monitor the price distribution of all commodities in these destinations. Efforts need to be enforced to ensure that the pilgrims are not cheated by the suppliers. From the feedback of the locals, garbage disposal is a major issue. Therefore, proper awareness and timely removal of garbage are required. The temple and government authorities should undertake conservative measures to avoid natural hazards related to deforestation, unplanned building constructions, and so forth. The government and the authorities should provide and monitor the distribution of basic facilities and commodities. Due to the crowd, scarcity and inflation is constantly faced by local residents. Hence, a proper government monitoring and distribution system needs to work simultaneously. Awareness should be provided to pilgrims on behavior with regard to sanitation and cleanliness. The authorities need to monitor the activities of the pilgrims so that it does not affect the normal living conditions of the local residents. According to the pilgrims and the local residents, though development is taking place, it is not sustainable. For example, roads, buildings, and structures should not be built by cutting down many trees and encroaching on forest land. The government needs to monitor and control such issues.

The government needs to ensure that good road facilities to the shrines are built at least before the start of the season and good transportation services such as interstate bus services are provided from the neighboring states and from different parts of Kerala. Kerala is placed with rich historic Hindu pilgrim centers and has always attracted pilgrims from different parts of India and from around the world. The pilgrim centers have been fascinated by the devotees, and they are an asset to our nation. But these pilgrim centers face numerous problems which have never been assessed or studied. Pilgrim tourism is a major asset of Kerala, and the Kerala economy is regulated by the income generated from pilgrim tourists; it also supports the multiplayer effect. Therefore, safeguarding the areas with necessary steps is a collaborated duty of the authorities, the pilgrims, and the residents.

23.6 CONCLUSION

Tourism is one of the biggest industries in the world. India has got a lot of tourist attractions and should make use of its natural resources and other resources to expand its tourism potential and secure maximum gain in the field. The successful history of tourism in many countries has set an example for India to motivate the industry within her boundaries. The state of Kerala proudly bears the caption of "Gods own country" and can be a beloved tourist destination for foreigners and domestic tourists, if wide publicity is provided by highlighting the attractive packages for pilgrimage tourism. The state cannot ignore the negative aspects that come along with it, which tourists view seriously; for example, poor road conditions, poor accommodation facilities, poor drainage and sewage system, presence of slums, lack of cleanliness, poor transport facilities, frequent strikes, infectious diseases, commercialized begging, and stray animals on the streets are to be addressed before welcoming foreign and domestic tourists to "God's own country." There is an immediate need to improve the physical and social environment in the pilgrim centers of Kerala. The physical environment includes the improvement in basic infrastructure, the standard of cleanliness, and so forth. Basic amenities, such as toilets, should be more user-friendly and well-maintained. Good standards at lesser costs will make the state more attractive to pilgrimage tourism and a value-for-money destination. For this, there is an urgent need to progress the connectivity and physical infrastructure. "The pilgrim centers are highlighting our heritage and tradition to tourists; the shrines are the assets of our country, and it is our duty and our responsibility to protect them."

KEYWORDS

- **Hindu pilgrimage**
- **sustainable development**
- **basic amenities**

REFERENCES

Babu, J. Pilgrimage Tourism to Tirumala—An Empirical Study. 2012.

Chauhan, V. Sustainable Development of Pilgrimage Tourism in Jammu Region: An Investigation of Rural Residents' Attitude. *Int. J. Soc. Ecol. Sustainable Dev.* **2011**, *2*(2), 54–65.

Greathouse, L. M. Religious Tourism in Mexico: The Journey to Tepeyac. 2010.

Hormage, D. Graves as Attractions: Pilgrimage-Tourism to Jewish Holy Graves in Israel. 2010.

Janardhan, G. D.; Mhaske, P. H. Pilgrims Assessment in Shirdi Religious Tourist Center of Ahmednagar District (M.H). *Int. Referred Reseach J.* **2011**, 1(17).

Kar, J. Religious Tourism: A Case Study of the Greatest Religious and Tourism Industry of Eastern India: Puri in Orissa. 2009.

Karar, A. The Impact of Pilgrim Tourism at Haridwar. *Anthropological Surv. India* **2010**, *12*(2), 99–105

Karar, A.; Raj, K. Impact of Pilgrim Tourism at Haridwar. **2010**, *12*(2), 99–105.

Kreiner, N. C. Geographers and Pilgrimages: Changing Concepts in Pilgrimage Tourism Research. *R. Dutch Geogr. soc.* **2010**. DOI: 10.1111/j.1467-9663.2009.00561.x.

Kremer, M.; Khwaja, A. I.; Clingingsmith, D. *Estimating the Impact of the Hajj: Religion and Tolerance in Islam's Global Gathering*: National Bureau of Economic Research. 2008.

Libison, K. B.; Muraleedharan K. P. Economic Benefits of Pilgrimage Tourism: A Case Study of Sabarimala Pilgrimage with Special Reference to Pandalam Rural Locality in Kerala (India). *South Asian J. Tourism Heritage* **2009**, *1*(1), 57–64.

Phukan, H.; Rahman, Z.; Devdutt, P. The emergence of Spiritual Tourism in India. 2012.

Shinde, K. Pilgrimage and the Environment: Challenges in a Pilgrimage Centre. *Monash Tourism Res. J.* 2009.

Shinde, K. This Is Religious Environment Sacred Space, Environmental Discourses, and Environmental Behaviour at a Hindu Pilgrimage Site in India. *J. Space Cult.* **2011**, *14*(4).

Singh, S. Managing the Impacts of Tourist and Pilgrim Mobility in the Indian Himalayas. 2002, 25–36. DOI: 10.3406/rga.2002.3070.

Tomer, P.; Arora, R. S. Pilgrimage at Golden Temple (Amritsar): Problems and Remedies. *Int. J. Asian Res.* **2012**, *5*(2).

Vázquez, G. M.; Naranjo, L. M. P.; Carranza, R. C. Analysis of the Pilgrim Profile in Spain: Two Case Studies. *Int. J. Appl. Sci. Technol.* **2012**, *2*(4).

Wong, U. Buddhism and Tourism at Pu-Tuo-Shan, China. *University of Waikato*. 2011.

Yamin, M. A Framework for Improved Hajj Management and Future Research. 2007.

CHAPTER 24

SUSTAINABLE TOURISM INDICATORS: A LITERATURE REVIEW ON CONCEPTS, FRAMEWORKS, AND APPLICATIONS

SHAMIMA AKHTAR

TriCounty OIC, Harrisburg, Pennsylvania, Pennsylvania, USA

CONTENTS

ABSTRACT

Tourism industry requires reliable and correct information to support its sustainability. Feedback and evaluation systems can become the main source of this information. Therefore, a need for monitoring devices arises at the outset and these monitoring devices give rise to the formation of sustainable tourism indicators. To audit the process of tourism development to achieve "triple bottom line," there is a need to have these indicators that help to evaluate and coordinate sustainable development. Developed more than a decade ago, these indicators provide critical information to those in planning and management so that they can anticipate and prevent unacceptable and unsustainable outcomes. Precise and specific data about tourism interfaces with sustainability issues through indicators contributes to the ability to assess the risks to key assets, to communities, to the values most important to the communities and tourists, and the extent of alertness of a destination in case of problems, and as a method of anticipation and prevention. This article describes the logic behind the use of creation of these assessment tools with an overview of sustainable tourism development. By using concepts and theories, expert opinion, subject knowledge, researched work, and past experiences, this article looks at the fundamentals of indicators, their significance, procedural development, selection, and types, and their implications for the decision makers. This article is a review of the development of the concept of sustainability, affirming the concept of sustainable tourism indicators through the window of sustainable development in tourism destinations. The paper concludes with a discussion of the future direction of sustainable tourism indicators and the likelihood of development of the same, specific for different destinations.

24.1 INTRODUCTION

The tourism industry is a crucial engine of any economy. As is already proclaimed, tourism and travel industry is one of the world's largest industries with a global economic contribution (direct, indirect, and induced) of almost 7.6 trillion U.S. dollars in 2014 (Statista, 2015). There has been a steady growth in the industry, worldwide, over past few decades. In the recent past, international tourist arrivals have seen an increase in numbers from 528 million in 2005 to 1.13 billion in 2014 (United Nations World

Tourism Organization (UNWTO), 2015). Countries like France and the United States are famous tourism destinations and leave no stone unturned to take the giant share of the tourism market. Similarly, other less well-known destinations are also learning quickly to emerge as competing tourism locations to reap the economic benefits of the industry. India, being one such example, is the second largest tourism market in Asia after China. Ranked amongst the 20 fastest growing tourism destinations worldwide by the World Travel and Tourism Council, tourism industry contributed a total of 113.2 billion U.S. dollars to gross domestic product (GDP) in India in 2013, and this accounted for 5.35% of India's total GDP (Statista, 2015). The above facts and predictions suggest that this industry is burgeoning at a constant pace. Along with different elements of this industry, the element of nature-based tourism and ecotourism have seen a substantial increase in its growth. The concepts of sustainable tourism, responsible tourism, and the like have gained momentum, although this sector is still, comparatively, small and compartmentalized as "special interest." However, growth in tourism industry indicates a surge in people traveling to different places, irrespective of their choice in nature-based focus or otherwise, and therefore, bringing upon the inevitable impacts on the host destination.

Some of these impacts can be positive like income generation into the local economy, cultural promotion, peace and understanding, and conservation and preservation initiatives. Others could be negative like environmental degradation, cultural commoditization, and social disintegration. These two aspects of this lively industry have sometimes completely negated the benefits of tourism phenomenon and therefore, the concept of sustainability comes to the fore. This concept is a push factor within the industry which, in its very essence, focuses to stop negative impacts and improvise positive effects of the tourism industry. In short, as more regions and countries develop their tourism industry, it produces significant impacts on natural resources, consumption patterns, pollution, and social systems. Therefore, the need for responsible planning and management is imperative for the industry to survive as a whole.

24.2   ADDRESSING THE LACUNAE

Even after securing a place amongst the topmost industries of the world, the tourism industry is still very underdeveloped when it comes to issues related to sustainability. There is plenty of work left to improve this aspect of tourism phenomenon. The main issue with sustainability is that the concept in itself is not properly understood by many which include the decision makers and interest groups. Moreover, the evaluating tools required to resolve the issues related to the accomplishment of sustainability have hardly been heard of by many stakeholders. Therefore, there is an immediate need for understanding the abstract related to sustainable development of tourism. Moreover, in the light of theories related to sustainable tourism development (STD), the path that leads to the attainment of sustainability of the industry has to be thoroughly examined. Further, importance, development, and procedures related to monitoring devices, which are called as indicators, are required to be methodically investigated and interpreted for easy understanding and implementation by interest groups.

24.3   PURPOSE STATEMENT

Sustainable practices in the tourism industry can influence stakeholders to act more responsibly with a better understanding of the concept itself. For the past few decades, there have been many initiatives by tourism industry worldwide to promote and integrate the values of sustainability. Over the years, the efforts have seen some commendable success rates. This article attempts to embark on such an endeavor of achieving STD with a thorough understanding of sustainability tourism indicators (STIs). This work reflects interpretations of what STIs are and how they could be used as monitoring devices to achieve sustainability in the tourism industry, thereby ensuring the full potential of tourism phenomenon. Furthermore, this article, apart from introducing to the topic of STIs, also narrows down on the spectrum of sustainability tools that monitor the effectiveness of specific elements of STD.

24.4   RESEARCH METHODOLOGY

The basic approach to this article is a systematic review of existing literature on STD and sustainable tourism indicators. The method included identifying, critically evaluating, and integrating the findings of all relevant, high-quality studies taken up by individual researchers and research organizations like UNWTO to formulate general statements and identify relationships. The data analyzed for this study were retrieved mostly from literature, UNWTO case studies, research journals, and theoretical and conceptual paradigms of tourism systems. Overall, this systematic review was taken up in order for it to have the potential to provide the most practical implication for sustainability of tourism destinations.

24.5 SUSTAINABLE TOURISM DEVELOPMENT—AN OVERVIEW

Before delving into theories and practices of STD, it becomes an imperative to understand the concept of "sustainable development." The term, sustainable development, became famous in *Our Common Future*, a report published by the World Commission on Environment and Development in 1987. This report was also known as the Brundtland report, and it included the "classic" definition of sustainable development: "development which meets the needs of the present without compromising the ability of future generations to meet their own needs" (Hunter, 1997). It is a well-known fact that sustainable development proclaims a convergence of the three pillars, namely, economic development, social equity, and environmental protection. According to a report Sustainable development (2010), "Sustainability is a visionary development paradigm; and over the past 20 years' governments, businesses, and civil society have accepted sustainable development as a guiding principle, made progress on sustainable development metrics, and improved business and nongovernmental organization (NGO) participation in the sustainable development process." The businesses involved in tourism industry equally pledge to follow philosophies and practices of sustainable development.

However, during early movements of sustainability, tourism was not considered a part. In fact, when tourism began to develop on a global level, it had a very little impact on nature protection (Theories, 2010). During the 1960s and 1970s, tourism was commonly referred to as 'Green Industry' and therefore, was not discussed as an environmental issue in any conference or convention. Largely, the industry was considered a positive phenomenon, with only advantages to benefit from. It wasn't until the end of the 1990s that tourism was lured into the debate on biodiversity (Hunter, 2002). For the first time in an international conference in 2001, rules were established for biological diversity and sustainable tourism (Convention on Biological Diversity in 2001). Following that, the United Nations declared 2002 as the Year of Ecotourism. In addition, with this landmark, the concept of sustainable development in tourism started playing an important role at the very grassroots level. Many stakeholders, volunteer action groups, NGOs, and environmental associations took a special interest in the development of sustainable tourism, while international discussion of sustainability shed new light on the issues in support of regional and national initiatives.

Sustainability is a holistic approach emphasizing with a perception of visiting a place as a tourist and trying to make only a positive impact on the environment, society, and economy. This definition is an attempt at simplification of an otherwise complex phenomenon that many find difficult to interpret. Some others define sustainable tourism as that tourism which respects both local people and the traveler, cultural heritage and the environment, and seeks to provide people with an exciting and educational holiday that is also of benefit to the people of the host country (TLSF, 2010). In other words, sustainable tourism is the concept of visiting a place as a tourist and trying to make only a positive impact on the environment, society, and economy. However, the most widely accepted definition of sustainable tourism comes from UNWTO (2005), which is, "Tourism that takes full account of its current and future economic, social and environmental impacts, addressing the needs of visitors, the industry, the environment and host communities." The concept of sustainable tourism is sometimes confused with ecotourism, which is only one aspect of sustainable tourism. Therefore, it becomes important to mention that STD guidelines and management practices are applicable to all types and forms of tourism in all types of destinations, including mass tourism and niche tourism segments. The three of these basic significant principles are given below: (*Source:* United Nations Environment Programme, 2004).

STD should make optimal use of environmental resources that constitute a key element in tourism development, maintaining essential ecological processes and helping to conserve natural heritage and biodiversity. Respect the sociocultural authenticity of host communities, conserve their built and living cultural heritage and traditional values, and contribute to intercultural understanding and tolerance. Ensure viable, long-term economic operations, providing socioeconomic benefits to all stakeholders that are fairly distributed, including stable employment and income-earning opportunities and social services to host communities, and contributing to poverty alleviation.

Achieving STD at any destination is not an easy task. It requires an active and informed participation of stakeholders involved and positive leadership of decision and policy makers to ensure participation of all and strong consensus building. The process of sustainable tourism is a continuous process and therefore needs an evaluation of impacts along with the introduction of necessary preventive and/or corrective measures. This feedback and monitoring system is the backbone of STD and is called STI. The next section of this article opens up this discussion.

24.6 SUSTAINABLE TOURISM INDICATORS

24.6.1 LET US REVIEW

When a well-planned and well-managed tourism system, which uses sustainable criteria, is developed, substantial benefits occur for local communities, society, and the natural and cultural environments (Vereczi, 2006). Moreover, sustainability concerns are increasingly being addressed in national, regional, and local tourism policies, strategies, and plans. According to Rajaonson and Tanguay (2011), "Policy implementation usually entails the use of follow-up and assessment tools such as indicators." Indicators are part of the main recognized evaluation tools used to support sustainable tourism policy implementation (Choi and Sirakaya, 2006). They form a group of facts that help to analyze critical changes that can occur during development and management of tourism phenomenon. In other words, these tools are considered essential means of accounting for unexpected outcomes and measuring the consequences of action or inaction (Bell and Morse, 2008). Measuring the performance of entire tourism sector, at the local, national, or global level, or even that of a particular tourism enterprise has traditionally concentrated on its economic and financial dimensions (Vereczi, 2006). However, sustainable tourism indicators have been developed to guarantee that such developments will be sustainable socially, culturally, economically, and environmentally in the long run.

For all the stakeholders, indicators correspond to a diagnosis of internal and external factors that affect the structure of tourism industry (Tanguay et al., 2013). They help to identify priority actions by reflecting on the benefits and impacts of tourism phenomenon on their regions (World Tourism Organization (WTO), 2004). For this purpose, all tourism operators and/or those who take decisions, accurate information is needed for the process of defining of effective indicators. This denotes that the indicators act as catalysts, which support the planning process of any tourism development (Mascarenhas et al., 2010). In other words, indicators act as monitoring devices that help in measuring the accomplishment of aims and objectives. To consider an indicator in determining whether a plan meets the initially set objectives, it needs to promote precision along with an illustration of inconsistencies in some of the cases (Bell and Morse, 2008). Prediction and/or mention of inconsistencies beforehand make it possible for evaluators to check for the reliability degree of such tools, which not only provides an accurate picture of sustainability but also promotes transparency amongst stakeholders.

24.6.2   REFINING THE CONCEPT

According to Vereczi (2006), "In the context of sustainable tourism development, sustainability indicators are information sets that are formally selected for regular use to measure changes in assets and issues that are key to the development and management of a given destination." Sustainable tourism indicators can be considered as fundamental building blocks for tourism planning, management, and monitoring process. The main goal of sustainable tourism indicators in STD is to offer a global assessment of the link between nature and society to help decision-makers evaluate actions to undertake or not and thus orient tourism and related activities toward sustainable development (Hunter, 1997).

Indicators are measures that are expressed in single numbers, percentages or ratios, qualitative descriptions, or the existence/nonexistence of certain elements concerning environmental, social, and economic issues (Twining-Ward, 2005). According to McGrath (2006), "indicators are signals of current issues, emerging situations or problems, the need or otherwise for action and the results of such actions." Rajaonson and Tanguay (2013) quoted, "Sustainable tourism indicators are generally used in two distinct contexts I) comparisons between destinations using a series of common indicators, II) the scorecard or the use of a series of indicators specific to a destination according to specific objectives." In the first context, comparisons on the basis of performance in sustainable tourism develop a critical attitude toward a destination's own initiatives and this minimizes passive attitude through competition from comparing destinations (European Environment Agency, 2007).

In the second context, destinations tend to develop their own indicators according to their particular needs (Holman, 2009). In other words, destination-specific indicator series is compiled to make a scorecard that helps in identification of sustainability-related tourism issues. These indicators can be adjusted according to the sustainable development concerns and characteristics specific to each destination, therefore is a preferred method for a lot of stakeholders (Bell and Morse, 2008).

24.6.3   DEVELOPING THE TOOLS

To develop sustainable tourism indicators for a destination, an integration of scientific expertise and local experience is needed. As is a well-known fact, developing a set of sustainable indicators is a difficult task to undertake. There is a good chance of inevitable subjectivity to get introduced at each step in the process of selecting of indicators till their interpretation (Wong, 2006). Many researchers have put forth different conceptual frameworks to build a concrete paradigm based on which sustainable tourism indicators could be constituted. The area of environmental management, in particular, has been guided well through various proposed approaches by many authors in the process of formulating indicators (Bell and Morse, 2008). To consider any sustainability indicators good, it should be easy to understand and economically and technically feasible to measure (Vereczi, 2006). However, according to WTO 2004 Guidebook, projects certain predominant criteria for selecting sustainable indicators in tourism.

It portrays Relevance as an important indicator of the selected issue. Feasibility of obtaining and analyzing the needed information is also a critical aspect. The credibility of the information and reliability for the users of the data are also of immense significance. Clarity and understandability to the users along with comparability over time or between destinations or tourism operations are also of imperative nature. Many times, however, the set criteria for choosing sustainable tourism indicators might not be appropriate to use in a particular situation. For example, sometimes factors like cost or lack of technical know-how might cause a hindrance in using a particular indicator. According to Mascarenhas (2010), "While providing the necessary technical capacities and funds for the use of an indicator can be a development objective itself, it is important to use alternative or approximate measures in the meantime, to obtain at least some indications of the importance of the issue, even if it means limited accuracy."

It is a thoroughly understood fact that the road of reaching appropriate and feasible sustainable tourism indicator is a tough process, however, the perks and overall advantages of good indicators take over all the hardships and difficulties experienced during the process of indicator development. In the year 2004, UNWTO provided subsequent and leading benefits of good indicators. Primarily, better decision-making and lowering risks or costs are of high significance. Identification of emerging issues and consenting prevention is most pivotal in the context. Identification of impacts with countenancing corrective action when needed could be an ideal pedagogy. Performance measurement of the implementation of plans and management activities with evaluating progress in the sustainable development of tourism can corroborate critical standpoints. Reduced risk of planning mistakes, while identifying limitations and opportunities, can facilitate greater accountability with credible information for the public and other stakeholders of tourism. Fostering accountability for prudent use in decision-making and constant monitoring can lead to continuous improvement with building solutions into management.

24.7   TOOLS FOR THE POLICY PLANNERS

STIs can undoubtedly clarify issues, improve communication with stake-holders, and provide greater public accountability. Decision makers can apply indicators at various levels of tourism planning and management and at international to national levels ranging from local destinations like specific attractions or individual tourism businesses. The overall monitoring of the data of tourism industry at different levels is closely networked and the indicator information becomes interrelated, making it easy for policy planning and development. Different indicators have different uses for decision makers.

However, the basic aim is the prediction of problematic zones. Based on this, different types of indicators are devised by the UNWTO in

2004. Early warning indicators like decline in numbers of tourists who intend to return with indicators of stresses on the system can illuminate overbearing concerns. Measures of the current state of the industry, for example, occupancy rate and tourist satisfaction are of precarious nature. Measures of the impact of tourism development on the biophysical and socioeconomic environments resembling indices of the level of deforestation, changes in consumption patterns, and income levels in local communities, and so on are of premier premonition. Measures of management effort with mounting issues like cleanup cost for coastal contamination and measures of management results or performance are of an inordinate parameter. Depending on various circumstances, factors like methods of data collection, information gathering, methods of calculation, policy requisites, technical capacities of staff handling the issues in question as well as the level of user's understanding, indicators are portrayed in different ways (Vereczi, 2006). Moreover, therefore, indicator types can also be expressed in the way they utilize measurements, namely, quantitative (ratios, percentages, etc.) or qualitative (category indices, nominal indicators, etc.). The detailed account and explanation of these categories can be well understood from WTO 2004 Guidebook.

24.8 SUGGESTED PROCEDURE FOR INDICATOR DEVELOPMENT

If the relevance of certain data and information to sustainability issues, which already exists at a destination, is well understood, then this can serve as an automatic indicator. According to various researchers (Mascarenhas, 2010; Vereczi, 2006; Tanguay et al., 2013), the most widely used and well-understood indicators are—economic factors like tourism revenues and expenditures or baseline data and statistics like tourist arrivals and accommodation capacities. Conventionally, this type of data is used to measure the success rate of the tourism industry. These data can, however, be used in essential information to a number of different sustainability issues and hence, mostly assimilated into effective indicators. Since the early 1990s, WTO has been in a continuous process of promoting the application of sustainability indicators. The past three decades have seen discourses and dialogues related to approaching sustainable tourism indicator development for tourism destinations (Fennell and Dowling, 2003).

Some of these discussions and debates have led to fruitful results with many success stories of sustainable destinations. Hence, one can factually point out that the suggested procedure for indicator development for any tourism destination goes through a systematic process of research and development, which is given below in a step-wise manner (Adopted-WTO Guidebook, 2004). Gazing through the indicative framework set by the research and organizational aspects, a systemic preview advocates tactical strategies with chronological theory phases.

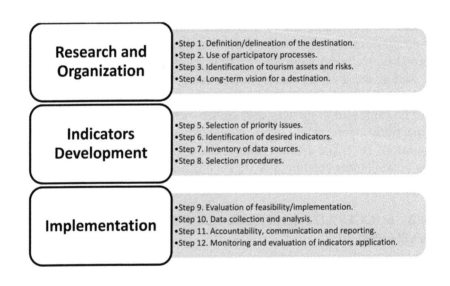

Research and Organization
- Step 1. Definition/delineation of the destination.
- Step 2. Use of participatory processes.
- Step 3. Identification of tourism assets and risks.
- Step 4. Long-term vision for a destination.

Indicators Development
- Step 5. Selection of priority issues.
- Step 6. Identification of desired indicators.
- Step 7. Inventory of data sources.
- Step 8. Selection procedures.

Implementation
- Step 9. Evaluation of feasibility/implementation.
- Step 10. Data collection and analysis.
- Step 11. Accountability, communication and reporting.
- Step 12. Monitoring and evaluation of indicators application.

The first WTO indicator guidebook appeared in 1996 after years of rigorous efforts put in by experts. Since then, varied activities were undertaken, which included pilot studies and comprehensive review of international experiences and involvement of 60 experts working actively in the improvisation of the already existing philosophies, principles, and practices of sustainability phenomenon. Thus, in the year 2004, WTO published a revised *Guidebook on Indicators of Sustainable Development for Tourism Destinations*. This guidebook explains about more than 40 main sustainability issues. Covering the "triple bottom line" approach, this guidebook describes issues ranging from natural resources to policy control, tourist feedback, and the local population, heritage management, financial status of communities, and environmental well-being. For all these issues and others too, indicators and subindicators are suggested and measuring techniques are provided. A well comprehensible procedure is revealed to develop destination specific indicators like indicators for a coastal destination or urban small communities, and so on. Various examples along with 25 case studies have been provided in this guidebook, which covers all continents at the organization, destination, national and regional levels.

24.9   MEASURING SUSTAINABILITY THROUGH INDICATORS

Arriving at the center of "triple bottom line" has become somewhat simple through STIs. Indicators have cut through the complexity of clutter created around the concept of STD. The most relevant indicators of any type of tourism destination or concern focus on measures that link to its basic principles (Wong, 2006). In general, following two indicator subdivisions, given below, cover up all three Ps of the "triple bottom line" approach, namely, People (social), Planet (environment), and Profit (finance), though destination specific changes need to be made accordingly.

24.9.1   CONSERVATION OF NATURAL ENVIRONMENT AT A DESTINATION

From the pool of indicators available in WTO 2004 Guidebook, specially selected indicators can be used as a monitoring and evaluating tools for all natural areas. Some of the specific elements that would be relevant for indicator implementation are portrayed in Figure 24.1.

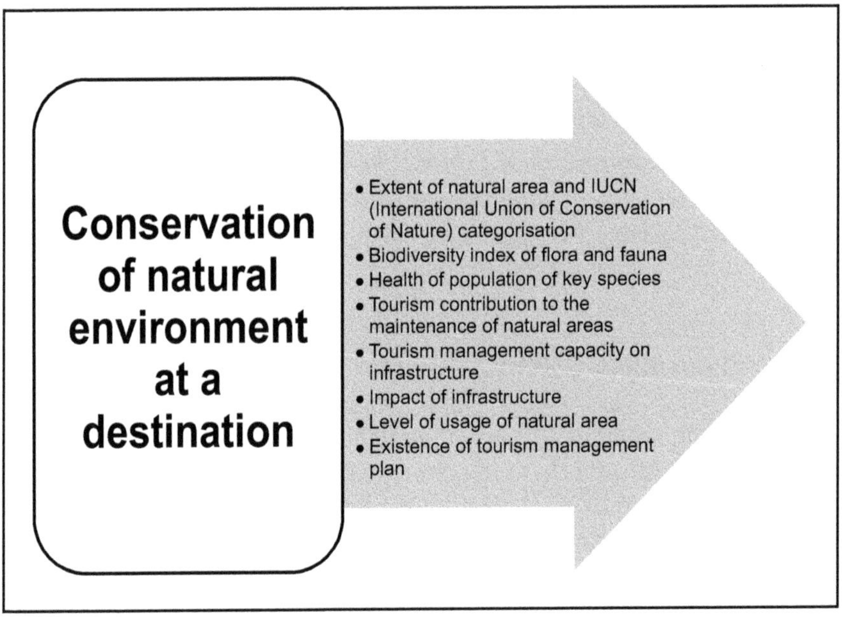

Figure 24.1

24.9.2 ECONOMIC AND SOCIOCULTURAL BENEFITS ALONG WITH LOCAL COMMUNITY RELATIONS

While evaluating, environment effects are easier to measure and appear more tangible than sociocultural and economic impacts. Most of the destinations are highly sensitive to sociocultural effects and both economic and sociocultural components of any destination tend to be relatively subjective. However, some examples that might be considered are portrayed in Figure 24.2.

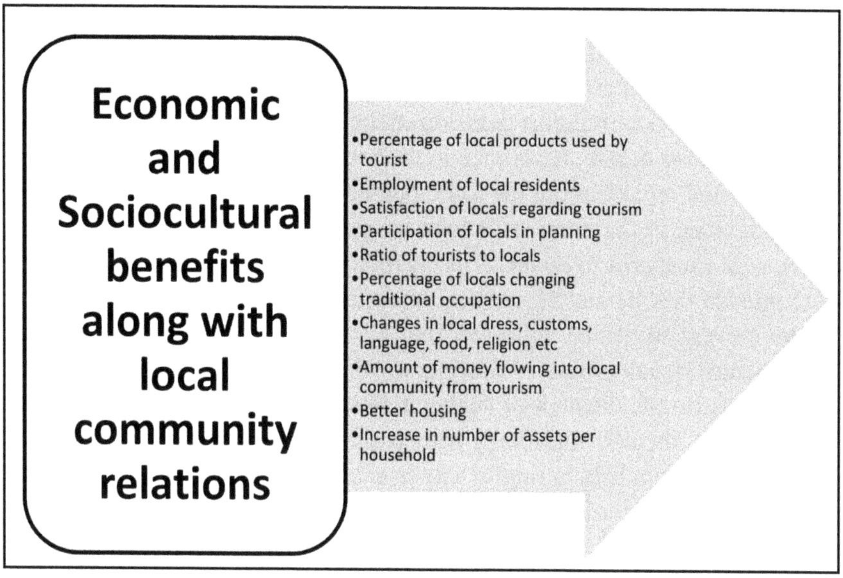

Figure 24.2

The above list is just a basic minimum to start the process of STD through indicator application. It should, though, be noted that each tourist destination, site, and operation has its own specific environment, socio-cultural, and economic characteristics and therefore, require those specific STIs to monitor impacts properly.

24.10 IMPLICATIONS

Over the time, due to its reliance on the quality of the sociocultural, economic, and natural environment, STD has been considered the leading force behind achieving cutting-edge techniques and mechanisms, develop-ment of research-based theories and concepts, and comprehensive under-standing of the same to attain sustainability. This chapter is one amongst the pool of such endeavors in understanding the rationale behind STD. It has been seen that the current understanding of the concept of sustainable tourism indicators is still relatively weak and there are as yet very few examples of successful long-term sustainable tourism monitoring programs in practice. A detailed discussion about sustainable tourism indicators as the backbone of sustainability has been put forth by all stakeholders to practically use them. The importance of monitoring tourism systems using indicators has been evaluated as being central to sustainable development policy, which not only helps decision-makers to approve sustainable plans but also ensures quality assurance in the tourism industry.

A detailed review about the logic behind the use of indicators as monitoring devices in the context of tourism phenomenon assists in feedback along with measures to be taken as corrective actions is one of the biggest outcomes of this article. Moreover, the article has taken up the assessment of the current indicator approach that has led to a suggested procedure for indicator development of tourism destinations. To sum up, this article emphasizes on the concept of sustainable tourism indicators with a backdrop of STD, thereby ultimately trying to maintain a high level of tourist satisfaction through meaningful experience to the tourists, ensuring the sociocultural and economic benefits to the community involved, raising their awareness about sustainability issues, and promoting sustainable tourism practices amongst tourists, locals, and every stakeholder involved.

24.11 CONCLUSION

For the past few decades now, it is a well-understood fact that to ensure the long-term sustainability of any tourism destination, there is a need for effective policies and plans at all levels. This requirement is especially felt more at the local destination level, where tourism activities occur, tourists interact with service providers and local communities, and where the positive and negative effects of tourism phenomenon are most felt. Given the fact that the nature of tourism systems is complex, tourism destinations represent complex situations with a broad span of attractions and activities being offered to a tourist. This indicates that a wide variety of local tourism stakeholders get involved from the public, private, and civil sectors, affecting the environmental, sociocultural, and economic resource base of the tourism sector.

Therefore, for the sustainable development of tourism destinations, there has to be a collaborated effort amongst all concerned groups, through methodically developed and implemented programs and plans, along with a strong auditing system for control and preventive measures. Hence, a comprehensive knowledge of the STD paradigms is required at the outset. More importantly, much broader awareness and a thorough insight of sustainable tourism indicators have to be interpreted, mastered, and exploited in whichever applicable. UNWTO's 2004 Guidebook about sustainable development of tourism destinations puts across a range of technical guidelines about sustainable tourism policies, with practical tools for destinations. Among these are the sustainability indicators that form the important mechanisms in tourism planning, management, and monitoring processes, providing accurate information for decision-makers. This article has taken an effort to experience the use of practical approaches of indicators for the context of tourism destination with sustainable development in the background. The importance, development, and application of indicators in the sustainable development of tourism destinations have been the very essence of this article. However, this chapter does not focus on the selection of a series of sustainable tourism indicators that can be adopted by any specific tourist destination. This article gives a general view of sustainable tourism indicators, providing a framework within which destination specific indicators can be developed. Therefore, the formulation of specific indicators that are destination-specific can be worked on in future research projects.

KEYWORDS

- sustainable tourism indicators
- sustainable tourism development
- tourism industry
- monitoring

REFERENCES

Bell, S.; Morse, S. *Sustainability Indicators: Measuring the Immeasurable?* 2nd ed.; Earthscan: London, 2008; p 228.

Choi, H. S.; Sirakaya, E. Sustainability Indicators for Managing Community Tourism. *Tourism Manage.* **2006,** *27*(6), 1274–1289.

Fennell, D.; Dowling, K.; Eds. *Ecotourism Policy and Planning;* CABI Publishing: Wallingford, UK, 2003.

Holman, N. Incorporating Local Sustainability Indicators into Structures of Local Governance: A Review of the Literature. *Local Environ.* **2009,** *14*(4), 365–375.

Hunter, C. Sustainable Tourism as an Adaptive Paradigm. *Ann. Tourism Res.* **1997,** *24*(4), 850–867.

Hunter, C. *Aspects of Sustainable Tourism Debate from a Natural Resources Perspective, Sustainable Tourism: A Global Perspective;* Butterworth, and Heinemann: MA, USA, 2002.

Mascarenhas, A.; Coelho, P.; Vaz, P.; Dores, A.; Ramos, T. B. A Framework for Regional Sustainability Assessment: Developing Indicators for a Portuguese Region. *Sustainable Develop.* **2011,** *18*(4), 211–219.

McGrath, G. Tour Guides as Interpreters of Cultural Heritage. In *Quality Assurance and Certification in Ecotourism;* Black, R., Crabtree, A., Ed.; CABI: Oxfordshire, UK, 2006, pp 364–391.

Statista. Global Tourism Industry; Statistics and Facts. The Statistics Portal, March 20, 2015. http://www.statista.com/topics/962/global-tourism/.

Sustainable Development: From Brundtland to Rio 2012. International Institute of Sustainable Development, Sept 19, 2010. http://www.un.org/wcm/webdav/site/climatechange/shared/gsp/docs/GSP1-6_Background%20on%20Sustainable%20Devt.pdf.

Tanguay, A. G.; Rajaonson. J. Selection Strategy for Regional Indicators of Sustainable Tourism. *Teoros* **2011,** (Special Issue), 77–84.

Tanguay, A. G.; Rajaonson. J.; Therrien, M. C. Sustainable Tourism Indicators: Selection Criteria for Policy Implementation and Scientific Recognition. *Cirano Report Res.* **2013,** *4*(3), 18–27.

Theories. Background of Sustainable Tourism. Tourism Theories. April 6, 2010. http://www.tourismtheories.org/?p=958.

TLSF. Sustainable Tourism: An Introduction. Teaching and Learning for Sustainable Future. Feb 12, 2010. http://www.unesco.org/education/tlsf/mods/theme_c/mod16.html.

Twining-Ward, L. Adapting the Indicator Approach. In *Quality Assurance and Certification in Ecotourism;* Black, R., Crabtree, A., Ed.; CABI: Oxfordshire, UK, 2005; pp 116–132.

UNWTO. United Nations World Making Tourism More Sustainable—A Guide for Policy Makers, UNEP and UNWTO, 2005, p 11–12.

Vereczi, G. Sustainability Indicators for Destinations and Operations. In *Quality Assurance and Certification in Ecotourism;* Black, R., Crabtree, A., Ed.; CABI: Oxfordshire, UK, 2006; pp 101–115.

Wong, C. *Indicators for Urban and Regional Planning;* Routledge: New York, 2006; p 217.

WTO. Sustainable Development of Tourism. World Tourism Organization Network. Sept 15, 2015. http://sdt.unwto.org/.

CHAPTER 25

SOCIAL MEDIA IN TOURISM: CHALLENGES AND CORRECTIVE MEASURES

SNEHA N.[1] and B. GEORGE[2]

[1]*Mount Carmel College, Bangalore, India*

[2]*Madurai Kamaraj University, Tallakulam, Madurai, India*

CONTENTS

ABSTRACT

The growing popularity of social media has been a trending research topic in the recent years. Social media has revolutionized the marketing industry. This is true in the case of tourism and hospitality industry as well. Social media services are used for travel information search, tourism promotion, creating brand awareness, and understanding buying behaviors, sharing real-time visitor experiences through posts, comments, photos, and videos. Social media is thus one of the most important platforms for marketing in tourism, but it is developing into a double-edged knife. A slight mishap anywhere snowballs into a national-level problem and even onto law and order problem. However, social media cannot be banned. It needs appropriate ethics and reality for the clean usage. This chapter focuses on finding out the challenges of social media in tourism through comprehensive literature review and primary data so as to identify the problems and to offer the possible panacea. The social media landscape has evolved so fast that many feel ignorant or fear being left in the cold with all these changes. Lack of consistency, the absence of measurable strategy and return on investment, intellectual property, fraudulent practices and online security, data quality control for the development of social media are some of the major concerns in social media. Other risks include the negative word-of-mouth received from dissatisfied customers, which can create irreparable damage to tourism business. Therefore, social media, if not managed properly, may result in negative consequences. This chapter thus provides an overall picture of researching the possibility of addressing the challenges faced by social media in tourism and hospitality industry.

25.1   INTRODUCTION

The quest to venture into the unknown, mainly for the purpose of leisure or pleasure, mainly saw the emergence of tourism as a result of curiosity of mankind. The humble beginnings from a wanderer, explorer, settler, trader, conqueror to the period of Renaissance and Industrial Revolution has transitioned the movement of mankind into the present day modern tourist and into an interesting transformation of tourism practices. The shift from unintended pleasure out of travel to traveling exclusively for pleasure constitutes the history of tourism, which is closely related to man's economic growth and cultural and political development. In particular, it was the Industrial Revolution that paved the way to win potential customers through effective services. This led tourism turning into a business proposition and thus providing personalized and customized services to tourists.

In today's digital era, tourism businesses have moved a step further from offering their products and services online onto mass-interaction methods through social media to engage with customers. India, an upcoming super-power, is well-endowed with the use of information technology services in social media for tourism. However, the digitalizing process in India and its prospective usages have not matched with the international standards yet. In such a situation of lopsided development, social media services for the development of tourism industry can face certain challenges. This research chapter explores those challenges through the types of problems faced by the customers of tourism industry through social media. It also suggests corrective measures to mitigate the same.

25.2   REVIEW OF THE LITERATURE

Marianna Sigala, Evangelos Christou, and Ulrike Gretzel in their book *Social Media in Travel, Tourism and Hospitality: Theory, Practice, and Cases* (2012: Ashgate) talk about the fundamental changes that the social media is bringing about the way travelers and tourists search, find, read, and trust, as well as collaboratively produce information about tourism suppliers and tourism destinations. It also examines the ways in which tourism organizations reengineer and implement their business models and operations, such as new service development, marketing, networking, and knowledge management.

Dave Evans in his book *Social Media Marketing: The Next Generation of Business Engagement* (2012: Wiley) explains how to successfully implement a variety tools, how to ensure higher levels of customer engagement, and how to build on the lessons learned and information gained from first-generation social media marketing efforts and to carry this across one's organization.

Xiang and Gretzel in the article "Role of Social Media in Online Travel Information Search," *Journal of Tourism Management* opine that social media is playing an increasingly important role as a source of information for travelers. Their main study investigated the extent to which social media flashes in search engine results in the context of travel-related searches. The study employed a research design that simulates a traveler's use of a search engine for travel planning by using a set of predefined keywords in combination with nine U.S. tourist destination names. The findings clearly showed that social media constitutes a substantial part of the search results, indicating that the results of searches more often direct travelers to social media sites. This study confirms the growing importance of social media in the online tourism domain. It also provides evidence for challenges faced by traditional service providers. The authors also imply online marketing strategies for tourism marketers.

Hvass and Munar in their article "The takeoff of social media in tourism," in the *Journal of Vacation Marketing*, believe that online marketing has grown in importance in the tourism industry. The authors highlight that social media platform offers companies a number of marketing tools and one of the most recent being social media. Social media allows companies to interact directly with customers via various internet platforms and monitor and interact with customer opinions and evaluations of services. Their study explores the travel portion of the tourism experience through airlines' use of social media on two social media platforms for a six-month period. The social media content posted by airlines is analyzed and categorized according to the promotional marketing mix. In addition, the authors propose four categories to describe the overall communicative behavior. Among the results, it is shown that there is a lack of strategic perspective on airlines' utilization of social media as it is being used with limited uniformity. These findings may aid marketing departments in their marketing and social media communication strategies while complementing current marketing research.

25.3   RESEARCH GAP

The literature reviews listed elaborate on theoretical concepts and services of social media in tourism and its scope in the tourism industry. However, there is a dearth of literature material on challenges and corrective measures for social media in the tourism industry in Bangalore. Hence, the researchers have decided upon this topic with the aim of researching the following objectives. The chapter captivates certain objectives in the course of study and examines the extent of popularity of social media as a marketing tool in tourism in Bangalore. To identify the challenges of social media in tourism, the chapter highlights the nuances. This chapter suggests corrective measures for the challenges faced by tourism industry through social media.

25.4   SOCIAL MEDIA—MEANING

Social media are websites and applications that enable users to create and share content or to participate in social networking. Social media, unlike traditional media, is aggregated and produced by the general public. The impact of social media on the public is so heavy that, in the recent, many organizations offering medical, educational, political, and social counseling, and many more services have developed exclusive social media sites for themselves so as to reach out to potential customers on a mass-customization.

25.4.1   DEFINITIONS OF SOCIAL MEDIA

Social media are "a group of Internet-based applications that build on the ideological and technological foundations of Web 2.0, and that allow the creation and exchange of user-generated content." This content is distributed to the masses on the internet free of charge. A social networking media is any website or application that focuses on connecting its users. These connections are often based on shared interests, activities, or real-life relationships. Users are typically single individuals, though businesses organizations and public figures are often represented on social networks.

Kaplan and Haenlein (2010) stress the importance of acknowledging that social media marketing is essentially about participation, sharing, and collaboration rather than straightforward advertising and selling. Social networks are limited to a registered population; anyone who is over the age of thirteen can join the community. Social networking enables travel businesses to target groups of customers by means of advertising. Some of the major types of social media are listed in the following, with their number growing in geometric progression.

25.4.2   TYPES OF SOCIAL MEDIA SERVICES

There are various types of social media outlets, which include blogs, content sharing portals, social networks, professional networks, microblogging, social bookmarking, and preference sharing. The types of services offered by these social networking sites are varied such as the following:

25.5   REVIEW AND EXPERIENCE SHARING

Blogs have become the new source for consumer information. Citizen and professional journalists utilize blogs to target a niche audience whom traditional media neglects. Blogging is an influential tool used to help the public to form an opinion about vacation packages, airlines, cruise ships, hotels, and other forms of entertainment. In addition to traditional blogs, travelers post location-specific messages on Twitter, Facebook, and Myspace. These online posts often contain the name of a restaurant, hotel, or an attraction and any destination-specific reviews and personal travel experiences of the bloggers.

25.5.1   PHOTO SHARING AND VIDEO SHARING

The general public is the best marketing tool that the tourism industry has to offer. When people are on vacation, they capture their moments on camera and film. With the invention of digital formats, consumers post their videos and photos for the world to see. Videos and pictures are taken at sites of general interest such as in famous restaurants, at city landmarks, and in other venues. Each time a user posts new material, they are creating exposure for that destination and the travel service providers.

25.5.2   TRIP PLANNING AND REFERRAL SHARING

Consumers are voicing their opinions across the internet with the help of websites such as TripAdvisor, Facebook, and Yelp. These sites provide special attention to focus on small boutiques, restaurants, shops, and attractions that you may not normally notice. Both locals and tourists use these services to look for something new to do. In addition, the more a company is referenced, their search engine rankings improve. The trends in the market sense the high potential of referrals through social media.

25.6   IMPORTANCE OF SOCIAL MEDIA IN TOURISM

1. Social media provides a direct contact between the service providers and the users.

2. The audio-video posting options provide the users an option of awareness of the products.

3. Pull factor of tourism destinations and services are created for every sector of tourism.

4. Niche tourism products are focused on customers and service providers.

5. Region-specific and season-specific tourism products are marketed to make tourism a synchronized product round the year.

6. Exclusive marketing strategies are used to attract customers with deals and offers.

7. Even tailor-made itineraries and group tours are advertised on social media.

8. Updates on a travel and trade fair and exhibitions and major tourism events are posted.

9. Loyal customers promote tourism organizations through referral marketing.

10. Online contests are organized for customers.

11. Testimonials of tourist experiences are also available on social media pages of most state tourism boards.

12. Social media pages are integrated with the tourism organization's official website, making it very transparent.

All these highlight the significance of social media in the tourism industry. This importance faces challenges too. Some of the challenges are listed in the following section.

25.7 SURVEY ON PROBLEMS OF SOCIAL MEDIA

A survey was conducted with the help of a questionnaire to identify the challenges for social media through the problems faced by the customers and some observations for problems faced by service providers like Indian Railway Catering and Tourism Corporation (IRCTC), SOTC Travel Ltd., and Thomas Cook. Questionnaires were mailed to customers varying different demographics in Bangalore. The sample consists of 50 customers who were considered for the study in Bangalore.

25.7.1   PROBLEMS FOR USERS

1. Based on the survey findings, it is observed that users are not comfortable with using social media as a booking platform for tour packages.
2. Lack of clarity for service provider selection on social media.
3. Social media as a tool is not used by users above the age group of 40 for travel-related information.
4. Social media page is not considered as a reliable tool to check travel offers and deals.
5. Social media pages of the tour companies are not constantly updated.
6. Unethical content pops up on social media, which creates a negative influence on youth.
7. Psychological influence on the society due to peer pressure created through social media.
8. Lack of trust in making online financial transactions on social media.
9. A certain degree of lack of trust on the authenticity of data posted on social media.
10. The absence of safety using social media for tourism.
11. Difficulty in tackling misleading reviews.

25.7.2   FINDINGS OF THE SURVEY

Some of the main findings of the survey are as follows:

1. 90% of the respondents are not comfortable using social media for tour packages. This could be either because they are really uncomfortable or not aware of this possibility.
2. 68% of the respondents opine that the social media pages are not updated constantly. There is a high chance of also seeing many duplicate pages of such companies, which are not updated.
3. 48% of the respondents feel that the data posted on social media pages are not authentic. This may be because the users perceive the offers on social media as a marketing gimmick.

4. 60% of the respondents do not believe in making online payments through social media. This may be primarily due to the security issues faced at social media websites.
5. 70% of the respondents are not clear about how to select a service provider on social media.
6. Only 5% of the respondents belonging to above the age group of 40 years use social media, of whom, 4% do not use social media as a tool to follow travel-related information posted by friends.
7. 95% of the respondents do not refer to a social media page for travel offers and deals.
8. 80% of the respondents do check for reviews and experiences on social media before they make buying decisions.
9. Some of the organizations like IRCTC and SOTC claim to be active on social media and use social media for brand awareness. SOTC and Thomas Cook constantly update their blog every week. They use Facebook as the most preferred social media page. Thomas Cook faces issues of many duplicate pages created on Facebook.
10. 95% of the respondents feel insecure using social media for travel.
11. 95% of the respondents use social media as their most preferred social media page for tourism followed by TripAdvisor (Tables 25.1–25.4).

TABLE 25.1 Comfort Levels of Respondents using Social Media for Tour Packages. (*Source:* Primary Data.)

S. no.	Level of comfort	Number	Percentage
1	Totally uncomfortable	45	90
2	Slightly uncomfortable	4	8
3	Regularly comfortable	0	0
4	Slightly comfortable	1	2
5	Very comfortable	0	0

TABLE 25.2   Social Media Activeness of Tour Companies. (*Source:* Primary Data.)

S. no.	Level of activeness	Number	Percentage
1	Not at all active	34	68
2	Slightly active	5	10
3	Regularly active	4	8
4	Always active	1	2
5	Don't know	6	12

TABLE 25.3   Authenticity of Tourism Information on Social Media. (*Source:* Primary Data.)

S. no.	Levels of authenticity	Number	Percentage
1	Yes	4	08
2	Sometimes	05	10
3	Maybe	11	22
4	No	24	48
5	Don't know	06	12

TABLE 25.4   Comfort Levels to Make Online Payments in Social Media. (*Source:* Primary Data.)

S. no.	Level of comfort	Number	Percentage
1	Totally uncomfortable	30	60
2	Slightly uncomfortable	14	28
3	Regularly comfortable	3	6
4	Slightly comfortable	2	4
5	Very comfortable	1	2

25.8   CORRECTIVE MEASURES SUGGESTED

Some of the corrective measures suggested by the respondents were as follows:

1.   A common framework for social media has to be designed.

2. Laws to govern the online social media operations for tourism.
3. Ensuring that the marketing teams constantly update their social media pages and post authentic offers for users.
4. Integrate the official company website and their respective social media pages.
5. Make financial transaction online by minimizing fraudulent practices by integrating with the official website of the company.
6. A mechanism should be developed to check the authenticity of the reviews posted by users.
7. Service providers can introduce training sessions for using social media sites as done by State Bank of India for its online banking facilities.
8. Introduce validity time for the online content of the social media so as to confirm the status of content.
9. Let the regional government make the availability of tourism information as a prerequisite for online business in that region.
10. It is important for the service provider to open a special tie-up with exclusive bankers to make the transactions safe.

25.8.1   USEFULNESS OF CORRECTIVE MEASURES IN TOURISM

Some of the suggestions received from the survey are feasible. It is important to have a common regulatory framework to check the operations of social media in tourism. There must be adequate laws to cater to the problems arising out of social media. A social media policy must be created for the nation to streamline its functioning and provide positive results for the tourism industry. A well-integrated social media page with the official website gives a better account for authenticity. Marketing strategies of all tourism business must be active and develop their social media presence. This should also lead to the measurement of return on investment due to usage social media for tourism businesses.

25.9   CONCLUSION

Social media, a recent development of internet-based technologies, has opened up the marketing venture into new heights. Marketing from being a mass approach has moved to pinpoint marketing that is customer-specific through social media. In such a development, it is important for the organizers and individuals to avail these developments in a way that creates exclusive customized products and services so that the aspect of leisure is both delightful and personalized for the potential customer. As every development is bound to open up certain difficulties, the stakeholders should be ready to clear the bottlenecks then and there so that the technological advancements are used not only for awareness creation but also used to achieve trouble-free and fool-proof customization. In the light of the identified problems and the suggested corrective measures, it is felt that the creation of a social media policy at the national level will mitigate most of the issues faced by social media in the tourism industry.

KEYWORDS

- social media
- challenges
- tourism

REFERENCES

Anand, M. *Tourism and Hotel Industry in India*. Prentice-Hall of India: New Delhi, 1976.

Evans, D. Social Media Marketing. Wiley: Indianapolis, Ind., 2008.

Horwitz, J. Semiocast: Pinterest now Has 70 million Users and is Steadily Gaining Momentum Outside the US. The Next Web. Retrieved Feb 10, 2016. http://thenextweb.com/socialmedia/2013/07/10/semiocast-pinterest-now-has-70-million-users-and-is-steadily-gaining-momentum-outside-the-us/, Josh Horwitz (accessed July, 2013).

Hvass, K.; Munar, A. The Takeoff of Social Media in Tourism. *J. Vacation Marketing.* **2012,** *18*(2), 93–103. http://dx.doi.org/10.1177/1356766711435978, http://en.wikipedia.org/wiki/YouTube.

Kaplan, A.; Haenlein, M. Users of the World, Unite! The Challenges and Opportunities of Social Media. *Bus. Horiz.* **2010,** *53*(1), 59–68. http://dx.doi.org/10.1016/j.bushor.2009.09.003.

Sigala, M.; Christou, E.; Gretzel, U. *Social Media in Travel, Tourism, and Hospitality;* Ashgate: Farnham, Surrey, Burlington, VT, 2012.

Xiang, Z.; Gretzel, U. The Role of Social Media in Online Travel Information Search. *Tourism Manage.* **2010,** *31*(2), 179–188. http://dx.doi.org/10.1016/j.tourman.2009.02.016.

INDEX

O

P